A CIRCUIT OF THE GLOBE

A CIRCUIT OF THE GLOBE

A.MCLEAN
J.H. GARRISON

GYAN

Published by

GYAN

Gyan Publishing House
5, Ansari Road
Daryaganj, New Delhi-110002
Phone: 011-47034999, 9811692060
E-mail: books@gyanbooks.com

Distribution Network
gyanbooks.com
India, USA, Canada, UK, Australia

ISBN: 978-93-7447-323-8 (PB)

First Published, 1897

2nd Impression 2026

Printed at: Gyan Press, Delhi.

A CIRCUIT OF THE GLOBE

Authors: A.MCLEAN, J.H. GARRISON

A. McLEAN.

A Circuit of the Globe

A SERIES OF LETTERS OF TRAVEL ACROSS THE AMERICAN CONTINENT, THROUGH THE HAWAIIAN REPUBLIC, JAPAN, CHINA, THE STRAITS SETTLEMENTS, BURMA, INDIA, CEYLON, AUSTRALIA, EGYPT, PALESTINE, SYRIA, TURKEY, GREECE, ITALY, SWITZERLAND, GERMANY, SCANDINAVIA, FRANCE AND ENGLAND.

BY A. McLEAN,
Corresponding Secretary of the Foreign Christian Missionary Society.

WITH AN INTRODUCTION

BY J. H. GARRISON,
Editor of the Christian - Evangelist.

ILLUSTRATED.

ST. LOUIS:
CHRISTIAN PUBLISHING COMPANY.
1897.

LIST OF ILLUSTRATIONS.

LIST OF ILLUSTRATIONS

TABLE OF CONTENTS.

INTRODUCTION.

He who goes abroad to visit strange lands and peoples, and comes in contact with strange scenes, customs, laws and languages, if he but have eyes to see and a mind to understand, can tell many things to interest and instruct those who are denied the privileges of such a journey. When the traveler who is to tell us the story of his travels is a man of cultivated mind, enriched by wide reading, and with a consecrated heart and life, who undertakes "A Circuit of the Globe," not from idle curiosity, but on a high and holy embassy, connected with the extension of Christ's kingdom in the world, and as the official representative of a great missionary society, his report of what he saw and heard, and his reflections thereon, possess a special and peculiar value. There are many globe-trotters in these days who go around the world without seeing or hearing anything that is of any great value to anybody. But this volume is the record of one who had been sent by his brethren to investigate the problem of missions in other lands, and especially to note the condition, progress and needs of our own missions in the Old World.

It was at the national convention at Richmond, in 1894, that Prof. B. C. Deweese, at a proper place in the proceedings, presented a preamble and resolutions setting forth Mr. McLean's long and faithful service to the society, his unstinted labors and sacrifices to further its interests, his need of a rest, the encouragement that a visit from him would impart to our missionaries in foreign lands, and resolving that the society send him on a visit to our foreign mission stations, the details respecting time of departure, duration of tour, etc., to be left to his discretion after conference with the executive committee.

This preamble and resolution were received by the Convention with a spontaneous applause that left no doubt as to the sentiment of the delegates on the subject. It was unanimously adopted and in a few moments a large sum was raised to cover the expense of his journey. The journey was begun in the following August and occupied over a year.

During the absence of Secretary McLean, the financial secretary, F. M. Rains, who had heartily forwarded the movement to send his associate around the world, cheerfully assumed the extra work which this arrangement involved, and carried it on with such energy and ability as to increase the receipts of the society in spite of the hard times.

The readers of our various papers which published these letters, not only read them as they appeared, with the deepest interest, but they have demanded their publication in permanent form. This demand was anticipated by the publishers, however, who requested the Secretary to arm himself with a kodak and bring back some permanent impressions of places and persons he might see in his travels. Many of these, with other pictures, appear as illustrations in the following pages, and form an interesting feature of the book. The faces of the faithful missionaries and the buildings in which they live and carry on their work will serve to strengthen the links that bind these brave workers abroad to the churches at home in an indissoluble fellowship of sacrifice, of joy and of triumph.

It can scarcely be doubted that the publication of this volume of Missionary Letters, written from the field while the author was in living contact with the work and its needs, and pulsing, as they do, with the mission spirit, will deepen the interest in the cause of missions among the churches, and thus help to hasten the subjugation of the world to the reign of Jesus Christ our Lord. That it may accomplish this beneficent mission, while serving as a memorial to our faithful and beloved Secretary, when he has finished his useful labors on earth, will be the hope and the prayer of all who have followed him in his "Circuit of the Globe."

J. H. GARRISON.

Rose Hill, St. Louis.

A CIRCUIT OF THE GLOBE

I.

ACROSS THE CONTINENT.

At the Annual Convention of the Foreign Christian Missionary Society, held in Richmond, Va., in October, 1894, it was decided that I should make a circuit of the globe in the interest of world-wide missions. It was thought that I would learn much about the nature and needs of the work that I could never learn by correspondence; that I would cheer the hearts of the workers on the fields, and that I would return built up in mind and in body, and prepared for more efficient service. A handsome sum was raised to defray expenses.

The tour mapped out is as follows: From Cincinnati to San Francisco; thence to Japan, by way of Honolulu; from Japan to China, and from China to India; from India to Australia; thence through the Indian Ocean and the Red Sea to Egypt; thence to Jaffa, Jerusalem and Beirut; thence to Cyprus, Smyrna, Constantinople, and other points in Turkey; thence to Athens, Corinth and Rome; thence across Europe to Copenhagen and several cities in Norway; thence to Hamburg, Cologne, Paris, London, Liverpool, New York, and home. I go to Australia because some of the churches there are co-operating with us in India. They support Miss Mary Thompson and two native helpers. This tour will occupy about a year, and will cost about $2,000.

Before starting on this long journey good friends arranged several receptions. The first was in the Mt. Healthy Church, on the evening of July 21, 1895. This is the church I served for ten years. The house was tastefully decorated. Brief and eloquent addresses were made, appropriate songs were sung, and earnest prayers were offered. The memories of that hour will go with me around the world; they will abide with me forever. Mt. Healthy is noted as the home of Alice and Phœbe Cary. Here they were born and educated, and here they did much of their best work.

The trees they planted, the well from which they drank, the house in which they lived, are objects of interest to their innumerable admirers. At the edge of the village David S. Burnet had once a famous school for girls. There he and Benjamin Franklin lived and published *The Reformer* and *The Christian Age*. The Mt. Healthy Church is first and last and always a missionary church. The good people of this place have found by actual experience that there is that which scattereth and yet increaseth. The name of this church is known in every field and by every missionary. In the corner-stone of the building there is one thing, and only one, namely, a Bible. This church stands for Biblical Christianity. On the next Sunday evening the churches in and about Cincinnati abandoned their regular services. A thousand people assembled. Some came from quite a distance. The exercises throughout, the songs, the Scripture lesson, the prayers and the talks were pre-eminently missionary. The great commission was emphasized, the workers were tenderly and lovingly remembered, some of the difficulties and needs of the work set forth. No one went away without a better knowledge of missions and a deeper interest in the missionaries. Cincinnati has been intimately connected with our missionary work from the beginning. Here the American Christian Missionary Society was organized. The Foreign Society was located here because Isaac Errett, W. T. Moore, W. S. Dickinson, Jacob Burnet, James Leslie and Dr. E. Williams lived here. Here, too, was the home of the *Christian Standard*. Its editor had been Corresponding Secretary of the American Society for four years. Nearly every number contained some missionary information. The editor made his appeals to the hearts and consciences of his readers, and his appeals were not in vain. On Monday H. M. Hickok gave a farewell banquet. He invited the leading spirits in our missionary societies and in our journalism and some personal friends to meet him at the Grand Hotel. Twenty guests sat down with him. After partaking of the good things provided, some admirable speeches were made. It was a delightful occasion. The spirit of the Lord was present. The cause of missions was helped by this banquet.

On Wednesday morning a group of personal friends came down to the station to see me off. E. E. Faris, the bright young Texan, who goes to Africa as our pioneer, was my traveling companion that day. On reaching St. Louis we found a number of friends on the platform waiting for us. That night the churches gave up their prayer-meetings and came together to manifest their interest in world-wide missions. After an hour's service in the auditorium, we adjourned to the parlors for social intercourse and for refreshments. Nothing was left undone to make the stranger feel at home. To the Disciples of Christ St. Louis is an interesting city. Here the *Christian-Evangelist* is published. Here W. W. Dowling edits *Our Young Folks* and the Sunday-school supplies sent out by the Christian Publishing Company. Here is the Christian Orphans' Home. Here Mrs. J. C. Black, the superintendent of Children's Work in connection with the Woman's Board, lives. Here O. A. Bartholomew carries on his work. In seven years he has built seven churches in St. Louis, and many others in different parts of the country. From this city, Dr. A. W. Hitt and Miss Sue A. Robinson went to India.

The next morning I left St. Louis for Kansas City. E. S. and G. W. Muckley and Judge Clarke came down to the depot to meet me. They refreshed my spirit. I was hungry and they fed me. While talking about the work in that city and other places the time passed rapidly. Kansas City is the seat of the Missouri Board of Missions. Here, too, the Board of Church Extension has its principal place of business. Here G. W. Muckley has his home. From this city he goes out to inform the churches about the work and to bring back their contributions to its support. The next stop was made at Denver, the Queen City of the Plains. At its gates W. S. Priest was waiting to extend a cordial welcome. That night the churches, with their ministers, met in the South Broadway Temple to speak words of good cheer and to listen to a brief account of the progress of the work. J. W. Ingram, W. S. Priest, Judge Barnum and Melville Putnam spoke for the churches and spoke hopefully and impressively. Denver has suffered greatly from the panic. Thousands are out of employment. Many of those who had saved something in other years have had to live on their earnings, and now have nothing. The churches are making heroic struggles to meet their obligations and to help in the regions beyond. With the return of better times the debts will be paid, new churches will be established, and thousands will be given to help the work in other fields. The hard times are not without their advantages. They consolidate the membership and drive them closer to God. Let the good men in Denver take heart and hope and hold on until the day dawns and the mists and shadows flee away. The night is far spent, the day is at hand.

From Denver to Salt Lake City is a distance of seven hundred and sixteen miles. The Denver and Rio Grande Railway is the scenic line of the world. For several hours Pike's Peak is clearly seen in the distance. This giant lifts his snowy head over fourteen thousand feet above the level of the sea. There is no more magnificent scenery in the Alps or the Himalayas than in the Rocky Mountains. Denver is a mile above the sea. The highest point on the road is nearly a mile above Denver. The train is scheduled to make the distance between Denver and Salt Lake City in twenty-nine hours. B. F. Clay was on the platform waiting for me, and drove me to the parsonage, where Mrs. Clay and Master Sam repeated the welcome. That night I spoke to a large audience in the Endeavor Church. The building is convenient and beautiful. A ride of eight hundred and seventy-one miles through Utah, Nevada and California, brings the traveler to the city beside the Golden Gate. Galen Wood preaches in Ogden. J. E. Denton preaches in Sacramento. I understand that there is no church between these two cities on the Central Pacific Railway. In San Francisco I spent some time in the hospitable home of H. H. Luse. No missionary passes through San Francisco without being entertained by this family. E. W. Mathews, editor of the *Pacific Christian*, went with me to Santa Cruz to attend the State meeting. No Secretary ever had a more royal welcome. Nothing was lacking to make my visit pleasant and effective. The large audience listened intently for an hour. At the close of the service they gave me the right hand of fellowship and sent me away with their prayers and good wishes. Nor was that all. At the suggestion of A. C. Smither, they made a generous offering toward the expenses of my long journey. This was the culmination of a series of ovations, beginning in Boston and extending across the continent. This afternoon I go aboard the City of Peking and sail out through the Golden Gate toward Honolulu. Now, our Lord Jesus Christ himself and God our Father, who loved us and gave us eternal comfort and good hope through grace, comfort our hearts and establish us in every good word and work.

II.

A PLEA FOR MISSIONS IN AMERICA.

YEARS ago, so the story runs, a band of skeptics crossed the Mississippi near where St. Louis now stands; they sang unclean songs; they drank wine and beer, and vowed that Jesus Christ should never cross that river. If one will start from St. Louis and go west till he reaches the Golden Gate, he will see and know that Jesus Christ has crossed the Mississippi. Or if he will go south through Arkansas and Texas and Arizona and New Mexico, or north through Iowa, Minnesota, Dakota, Montana, Washington, he will see indubitable evidences all the way that our Lord is trusted and served in all this western country. On the crest of the Rockies and the Sierras, and in the fertile valleys between, wherever two or three are gathered together, there He is in the midst. Christian people are going everywhere; churches, schools, and Christian institutions of all kinds follow. No power can exclude Christ and the Gospel. Japan and China and India tried to do that, and failed. As well try to keep out the sunshine and the dew; as well try to keep out the sweet influences of spring and summer. Skeptics may join hearts and hands in such an attempt; He that sits in the heaven shall laugh. The West no less than the East belongs to Christ, and he shall have it.

Let no one think that everything has been done. The fact is, there remaineth much land yet to be possessed. Here and there forts have been established, but the victory is far from being complete. The saloon is omnipresent. Beer cars are seen in every train. Gambling runs riot. Many who were active in the churches at home have lost their faith, and are in haste to get rich. What then? Those who have the truth must carry it everywhere, and fill all hearts and homes and institutions with its spirit. Everything opposed to Christ must give place, as the wolf and the bear give place to civilization. In order to do this, the churches must arouse themselves and put forth such efforts as have never been witnessed. For be it known that the powers of darkness are mustering and marshaling themselves for the conflict; they are entrenching themselves in the great West. The strong man armed keeps his house and his goods; one stronger than he must come and bind the strong man and take away the armor wherein he trusted, and spoil his goods. This is a critical period in the history of the West, for it is a formative period.

Great populations are pouring in. The nation gains more from immigration than from all her mines of gold and silver. Capable, energetic and ambitious men come here to better their condition. In 1835 there were not 5,000 white inhabitants in all the vast region between Lake Michigan and the Pacific. Now there are in this territory Chicago, Milwaukee, St. Paul and Minneapolis. In 1840 Chicago had a population of 4,500; now it has 1,438,000. In 1834 there were two log houses where Milwaukee now stands; the present population numbers 204,000. In 1842 a trading house was built on the site of St. Paul. A small community of whites and half-breeds engaged in barter with the Indians and trappers. In 1850 St. Paul was in the wilderness; wild animals and Indians haunted the grounds about it. St. Paul has now 133,000 people within her borders, and Minneapolis has 164,000. In 1870 Duluth was laid out on speculation in the woods. Duluth is now "the zenith city of the unsalted seas," and has a population of 33,000. San Francisco in 1844 had a population of fifty souls; now she has 300,000. Kansas City, Denver, Seattle, Tacoma and Portland have grown in the same way. The time to reach these immigrants is on their arrival. They are then free to listen to the plea we make. In ten years it will be tenfold more difficult to reach and win them.

We hear of "the wild and woolly West." In a ride of two thousand miles I did not see one prairie dog, or one jackrabbit, or one coyote, and only a score or two of Indians. The West is neither wild nor woolly. The people are as intelligent and enterprising as in the East. Some one said to Knowles Shaw that the people of the West were "the scum." He said they are like the scum that rises on milk. The papers of San Francisco, Salt Lake and Denver contain all the news found in the great dailies of Chicago and New York. San Francisco in many respects reminds one of Boston. The streets are wider, and are not suffering from curvature of the spine. But the schools, and churches, and shops, and homes, and sidewalks, and street cars are not much, if any, behind those of "the Hub of the Universe." There is poverty and there is vice on the Pacific Coast, but these things are found on the Atlantic Seaboard as well. Preachers say it is harder to build up churches in the West than in the East. The spirit of the men who crossed the plains in 1849 is still here. The people want wealth, and they want it at once. Solomon said, "If the axe is dull, one must put forth more strength." So if it is harder to make converts and build up self-supporting churches, we must work the harder. At Reno, Nevada, we saw a few Indians. They were dressed and acted like white folks. Some were smoking cigars or cigarettes, thus showing that they are bone of our bone and flesh of our flesh. Of the 300,000 Indians of the West, 66,000 pay taxes. The noble savage, so-called, is cultivating the arts of peace. He has been created anew in Christ Jesus.

One who has not traveled over this country has only a faint conception of its extent and resources. Texas alone is considerably larger than the German Empire, California is larger than Turkey, Oregon is larger than England and Scotland and Wales. I have traveled from ocean to ocean, and from the lakes to the gulf. The more I travel the vaster the country appears. There is room in this magnificent domain for a thousand millions of people. Then our population will not be as dense as that of Britain. The Gospel must be carried into every city and hamlet of this broad land. Wherever the beer keg can go the Bible must go. If the Bible could go in advance and keep out the accursed thing forever it would be better. Wherever men go to mine gold or silver or copper, or to raise corn or wheat or fruit, or to engage in any form of work, there the ministers of the Gospel must go and preach the unsearchable riches of Christ. It will avail nothing that we have three-fourths of all the coal in the world within our borders, that we have wide and fertile fields, that we raise more hogs and cattle than any other nation, that in manufactures and mechanical appliances we lead the world, that we are the richest of nations, if we are not a righteous people, and if our God is not the Lord. Let us know and remember that it is righteousness that exalteth a nation.

We are well able to do the work which the Lord requires of us. We must plan and work on a larger scale than in former years. We must spend hundreds of thousands of dollars where we have been spending tens and fifties. There are mines in the Rocky Mountains with machinery that cost a million dollars. See what vast sums have been invested in railroads! Capitalists pour out money like water. They spend any amount in the sure and certain hope of profits in the years to come. We must go at this work as men go into great business ventures. We must capture the great cities. What has been done in Kansas City, in Des Moines, in St. Louis, can be done anywhere. It can be done in Chicago, in New York, in New Orleans, in Boston, in Cincinnati, in Indianapolis.

Greater triumphs can be won if we will do our whole duty. God says of each of these great centers of population, as he did of Corinth, "I have much people in this city." We cannot do the Lord's work without a very much larger expenditure of money and a much larger evangelistic staff than we have thus far dared to even dream about. In Salt Lake City our people were offered a lot in a most desirable section if they would erect a building upon it. They could not accept the offer. There are hundreds of such opportunities in the new and growing West. We ought to be ready to seize every one. We are playing at this work; we are trifling with a great trust. We need to hear the voice of God like a fire-bell at midnight, "Awake, thou that sleepest, and arise from the dead, and Christ shall give thee light."

There is not only room for the Disciples of Christ, but there is urgent need of them. Our growth in Missouri shows this. The fact that we have increased in fifty years from almost nothing to 130,000 amounts to a demonstration. The great churches in Mexico, Columbia, Sedalia, Warrensburg, Holden, Harrisonville, St. Joseph, Liberty, Lexington, Springfield, Kansas City, Topeka, Salina, Denver, Salt Lake City, Sacramento, Oakland, Los Angeles and San Francisco, could not have been called into existence if we had no vital truths for this generation. While recognizing all the good there is in other communions, we must hold to our conviction that in some important matters they are at sea in a fog. It is for us to publish the truth which God has revealed to us till all shall see it. It is high time for us to understand what God would have us do. We must make the spread of the Gospel of the glory of Christ our first and supreme concern. This is a time for heroic giving. It is a time for men to go out without purse or scrip or two coats, assured that God will supply their need according to his riches of glory. If we do this we shall have such a measure of prosperity at home as shall cause the scoffer to say, "God is in these people of a truth." The churches thus planted and watered will be missionary from the first, and will do their utmost to send the Gospel into all the ends of the earth. The Lord help us to see our duty and to perform it.

III.

FROM SAN FRANCISCO TO HONOLULU.

On the third of August, at three P. M., the City of Peking left her dock for Hong-Kong. She is to touch at Honolulu, Yokohama, and Nagasaki, on the way. Honolulu is 2,100 miles from San Francisco; Yokohama is 3,478 from Honolulu. As we steamed down the Bay and saw the enormous docks and the number of ships going in all directions, and saw the crowded city stretching away for miles, it seemed incredible that half a century ago San Francisco was a village of fifty people living in log huts and bartering food and clothing for tallow, hides and horns. San Francisco is now one of the great cities of the world. What New York is to the East, that San Francisco is bound to be to the West. She must always be the chief port of entry to the commerce of the Pacific. In an hour and a half we were beyond the Golden Gate and the Seal Rocks. Here the pilot left us, and we felt that our voyage was fairly begun. Gradually the land faded from our sight. There was a tinge of sadness in this thought. It was like leaving home for the first time. America now leads all nations. What she is now is nothing compared with what she shall be. Her welfare means the welfare of the world. "Blessings brighten as they take their flight." So our country seems more and dearer as we leave it for a season.

> "Great God, we thank thee for this land,
> This bounteous birthland of the free;
> Where peoples from afar may come
> And breathe the air of liberty.
>
> "Still may her flowers untrampled spring,
> Her harvests wave, her cities rise;
> And yet, till Time shall fold his wing,
> Remain earth's loveliest paradise."

Before we left the dock a group of people sang "All Hail the Power of Jesus' Name" and "God be With You Till We Meet Again." It was plain that there were missionaries on board. Probably no ship leaves this port for the Orient without having some missionaries among her passengers. God is thrusting out young men and women of culture and consecration into his harvest.

As the spiritual life of the churches is deepened, workers will go out in ever-increasing numbers. H. H. Luse and Jeu Hawk came down to bid me farewell. The first represented the Occident; the second, the Orient. The first was born in Pennsylvania; came West and settled in Oregon, and afterwards removed to San Francisco. Jeu Hawk was won to Christ by Miss Sue A. Robinson, one of our missionaries to India. He was educated in Drake, and now is in charge of the Chinese Mission in Portland. The San Francisco workers were at Santa Cruz, else a large number would have been on the dock. I thought then of the great host of Disciples of Christ who are interested in this trip, and who assured me that they would pray for me, and I was comforted. May their prayers bring down blessings upon their own heads, like rain upon the mown grass and like the showers that water the earth.

Our ship was built in 1874. She was a fast boat in her time. She makes three hundred and thirty-five miles a day, burning seventy tons of coal. The greyhounds of the Atlantic consume over four hundred tons and cover five hundred miles. The officers are Americans; the crew is made up of Chinese and Japanese. The officers are gentlemanly fellows. They give civil answers to proper questions. They take an interest in the passengers, and try to make them feel at ease. The chief steward, Mr. W. S. Chandler, was especially kind. I crossed the Atlantic twice, and found the bearing of the officers there very different. Civility adds much to one's comfort. On the train as we passed through Nevada, I asked a Pullman official how many large places there were between Ogden and Sacramento. He drew himself up and said with crushing force, "If I were to enumerate all the large places between Ogden and Sacramento, I would not have time for much else to-day." As there is not one large place between the points named, something I discovered after, it would not have taken his lordship long to give me the information I sought. As it was, I wilted and said no more. Not only this ship, but the entire fleet is manned with Orientals. One of the officers spoke of the crew in high praise. They are polite, sober, willing and efficient.

We have few passengers, less than twenty in the cabin, and not over fifty in the steerage. This is more enjoyable to the passengers than profitable to the company. Our ship will carry a hundred cabin passengers and a thousand steerage. With a small list every one can have a state-room. At table one receives more attention. On deck there is ample space to walk and sit. The passengers are pleasant people. One is an officer in the German Army. One lives in Honolulu, and is full of information respecting the islands. Several represent large business houses. The missionaries interest me most. Three of these four are women. It is a significant fact that more women are offering than men. Robert Cust says we shall soon have to change Wellington's famous order and say, "Up ladies, and at them." Mrs. Nevius goes to Chefoo. She has been in China forty years. Her illustrious husband died recently. She is going back home. A medical missionary is going out for the first time. She goes to Chinkiang. One of the group has been in Japan six years. She and her parents had been traveling extensively in the East. She became interested in missions and remained in Japan. She is now on her way back after a year's furlough. An ordained minister is going to Amoy. They are the happiest people on board. Their faces shine. They have heard the joyful sound, "Jesus saves." They are going out to publish glad tidings. Their faces illustrate their message, and commend it to the sad-hearted peoples of the East. There is no suggestion of the ascetic or the Pharisee about them. They are as full of mirth and as ready for any innocent games as any on board. The ladies wear no jewelry, dress very simply, and look remarkably attractive. Dr. Goodell, of the Turkish mission, was one of the happiest of men. His associate rebuked him for his mirth, and asked him if he expected to enter heaven laughing. He said he would rather enter heaven laughing than crying. He was incorrigible. There was no more to be said. Missionaries have obeyed the Lord's command, and they have entered into his joy.—There are some Chinese passengers in the cabin. The women wear bloomers and smoke cigarettes. Are these the harbingers of the coming woman? Their dress may be more comfortable, but to the eye of an amateur is less comely than the present style. There is one thing lacking in our list. *There is not a bride on board.* The captain states that he has had twenty-one in a single voyage. The raw material is here, but not the sweet, finished article. This is quite a loss. A bridal party on a train or on a boat is as good as a play. The fact that there should be a superabundance of brides on one voyage, and none on the next, constrains one to believe with John Calvin in total depravity.

The Chinese passengers in the steerage are not without interest. They play cards and dice early and late. The Chinese are a race of gamblers. They stake their money as long as it lasts. When it is gone they stake themselves or their children. Rice is their principal article of food. The way they shovel the rice into their mouths with their chopsticks is a marvel to the uninitiated. In addition to rice they eat dried fish, fresh and salt meat, and vegetables. They have a common bowl containing some liquid resembling vinegar. Into this they dip their meat or vegetables, as the disciples did at the last supper. This is to make their food palatable. Their diet does not seem very inviting, but it makes great, brawny and athletic fellows. There is no cabin passenger, notwithstanding all the savory food and all the delicacies served to him, that can compare with some of these Chinese in muscular development. So life has its compensations. The rich have more than heart can wish for, and dyspepsia besides. The poor have little, but they have good appetites and superb digestion. In point of comfort, the upper class has not much advantage over the lower.

On board ship we have every comfort and every convenience that we could have on shore. The state-rooms are spacious, and are supplied with everything needed. They are lighted with electricity. Every day you can have a bath in salt water. Pow Sing will call you at any hour you may wish. The table is excellent. The bill of fare must have been designed for epicures. Meats and vegetables and fruits and milk are kept in huge ice-chests. Fowls and sheep are kept on deck waiting their doom. No one need go hungry. The first evening the chief steward explained the arrangement for meals. You can have coffee in your room when you wish it. Breakfast is served at half-past eight; tiffin at one; dinner at seven. If you should feel famished between breakfast and tiffin, or between tiffin and dinner, or before turning in for the night, you can have tea and cake and fruit. The cooks are artists. They would do credit to any hotel. The service cannot be excelled. The "boy," Ah Hee by name, is intelligent and obliging. In his soft slippers he moves as noiselessly and as swiftly as a cat. He anticipates your wish and hastens to supply it. He does not address you as "Sir" or as "Boss." He offers you the bill of fare, and inclines his ear.

When the voyage began I thought I would get out of it all I could. I proposed to play high jinks at sea. The first morning I touched an electric button with my toe, and Ah Sam, a bright-faced Celestial, with a queue reaching down to his heels, appeared. I ordered coffee. In the twinkling of an eye it was before me. Having partaken, I turned over like a door on its hinges, and fell asleep. An hour later another Celestial appeared and announced that the bath was ready. I felt conscience-smitten at first, but soon became reconciled to it. The "boy" was paid for this service. Besides, he was so affable and acted as if he were receiving a favor rather than conferring one, that conscience soon ceased to smite.

After three or four days, however, I found that this arrangement was not satisfactory. Heretofore, when urged to eat more than three times a day I have pleaded the statute of limitations. I found it expedient to return to the old order. Capacity for eating is like capacity for singing or speaking. It is a gift; it cannot be acquired. Coming down the Sierras a girl of some thirty summers sat opposite me at the table. She began with a drink that to an innocent prohibitionist looked suspiciously like a cocktail. Then she had a bottle of Apollinaris water, then a pot of tea, meanwhile drinking several glasses of ice-water. She ordered and inclosed a breakfast such as would have satisfied Samson or Goliath, or both. She read while eating, to improve her mind. When she was done she wiped her tapering fingers and her rosy lips, and looked as if she had been sipping nectar and tasting ambrosia. An omnivorous girl amuses me. Such an appetite here would be a treasure.

Life on a ship is a lazy life. There is nothing to do, and all day and all night in which to do it. Carlyle said that every man is as lazy as he dare be. Who has not found it so? The first few days one chafes a good deal. The demon of work still possesses him. When Charles Lamb was retired on a pension he did not know what to do with himself. His desk and his soul had grown together. He wanted to be back again. So one feels for a time. I work eight hours a day, and am getting a reputation for industry. But eight hours compared with the hours I worked for twelve years are child's play. Sometimes I long to be back in the Mission Rooms, sharing in the work and in the joy. But my prophetic soul tells me that I shall soon feel like joining the society spoken of by Ian MacLaren, "The Amalgamated Sons of Rest—a society with conscientious objections to work between meals." We get no letters and no papers, we know nothing and care little about what is going on in the great world. This is a season for rest and for storing energy. After it is over one will feel like a race horse. He will enter upon his work rejoicing in it, as a strong man to run a race.

Birds have followed us all the way. Where do they build their nests? How do they live? They sow not, neither do they reap, nor gather into barns; God feedeth them. He will care for us. We are as safe on sea as on shore. There are watchful eyes in every part of the ship day and night. If a fire should break out it can be extinguished. Twice a week there is fire practice. In case of a storm the ship would ride the waves like a duck. In case of a wreck there are boats enough to carry all on board. We lie down at night and sleep feeling as secure as if we were at home.

In 1888 I crossed the Atlantic twice. The days and nights were cold. Passengers sat on deck wrapped in heavy rugs. They wore their winter clothing. We have had warm weather from the first. There has been no need of an overcoat or of a rug. One can sit on deck for hours and watch the play of the waves and listen to their music. Their glory and beauty remind one of the words, "The sea is his, and he made it." On the Atlantic you see ships every day. We have seen one only since we left. What does that mean? This, that the bulk of the commerce of the world belongs to Christian nations. As China and Japan receive the Gospel, the Pacific will be covered with ships as is the Atlantic.

On Friday night we dropped anchor before Honolulu, and waited for the day. We have had a delightful passage. There has been no fog, no storm, and no sickness. On Monday the screw lost one of its blades. This accident broke up the monotony and was a positive refreshment. The captain and engineer decided to go on. By using all the sails we have made as good progress with three blades as otherwise we would have made with four. One passenger, evidently a son of Belial, insists that the accident was because of the psalm-singing before leaving the dock. Whatever the cause, we have lost no time and are nearing port with thankful hearts. God is good. He has given us a prosperous voyage. He has answered the prayer we offered when starting, "Keep us, Lord, for the ocean is so wide, and our boat is so small." Blessed be his glorious name forever, and let the whole earth be filled with his glory!

IV.

THE EVANGELIZATION OF THE HAWAIIAN ISLANDS.

In 1809 a native of these Islands sat on the doorsteps of Yale College and wept. His name was Henry Obookiah. In a civil war his father and mother had been slain; he had been taken prisoner. Escaping, he made his way to New Haven. He thirsted for knowledge, and went to the college buildings hoping that his thirst might be slaked. Hope failing, he sat down and wept. A resident graduate found him and took him as a pupil. That autumn Samuel J. Mills visited New Haven to awaken an interest in missions. Obookiah told him his story. "The people are very bad; they pray to gods made of wood." He longed to be able to read the Bible that he might go back and teach them to pray to God up in heaven. Mills wrote Gordon Hall, "What does this mean? Bro. Hall, do you understand it? Shall he be sent unsupported to reclaim his countrymen? Shall we not rather consider these Southern Islands a proper place for the establishment of a mission?" Other Hawaiian lads came to America, and after their conversion wished to go back and preach Christ to their own people. Obookiah did not live to publish the glad tidings in his own land. He died before completing his college course. A sketch of his life was published. It created a profound and widespread interest. It called forth legacies from the dying, tears, prayers and donations from the living. Two years later the American Board sent a band of missionaries to evangelize these Islands. In the band there were three Hawaiians and seven Americans and their wives. They sailed in the brig "Thaddeus." *

The ten Islands of this group have an area of a little less than Massachusetts. The people were in the lowest depths of barbarism. They were a race of thieves, gamblers and drunkards. Children wore no clothing; men and women almost none. The king visited the missionaries on board ship. He wore a narrow scarf about his waist, a silk scarf thrown over his shoulders, a string of beads around his neck, and a wreath of feathers around

* See "The Hawaiian Islands," by Anderson; "The Hawaiian Mission," by Bartlett and Hyde, for further information.

his head. Polygamy and polyandry were prevalent. A man could marry as many wives as he could feed; he could turn them adrift at pleasure. A woman could have as many husbands as she chose: she could turn them off and take others. The king had five wives. Each one had her day of service, when she followed her lord with a spit-dish and a fly-brush. Parents prostituted their daughters, and husbands their wives for gain. Two-thirds of the children were either strangled or buried alive. Aged parents were buried alive, or left to die of neglect. Maniacs were stoned. Captives were tortured and slain. Government and religion were oppressive. There was no law but the will of the chief. The people were ruled with a rod of iron. They had no rights that the chiefs were bound to respect. The land and all its products and the people belonged to the rulers. It was a crime punished with death for a common man to let his shadow fall on a chief, or for a woman to eat with her husband, or to eat fowl, pork, cocoanut, or banana. When a chief died the people knocked out their front teeth, shaved their heads, burned themselves, broke through all restraints, and practiced all manner of crime, as if it were a virtue. All ages and both sexes gave scope to the vilest passions, of self-torture, robbery, licentiousness and murder. Whatever the priest wanted for the god—food, a house, land, or human sacrifice—must be forthcoming. When the people built a temple, some of them were offered in sacrifice at its dedication. It was among such people that the missionaries were to live and work. So dark was the prospect that a clergyman said to them before sailing, "Probably none of you will live to see the downfall of idolatry." But God is better than our fears, better than our hopes even.

After a voyage of five months the missionaries caught a glimpse of Hawaii. In a few hours a boat put off and soon returned. One of the native workers was seen swinging his hat in the air and heard shouting, "The idols are no more." He learned that the old king was dead, and that his son succeeded him; that the images of the gods were all burned; that the men ate with the women; that but one chief was killed in settling the affairs of the government, and he for refusing to destroy his gods. The missionaries wrote, "Sing, O heavens, for the Lord hath done it." What was predicted they should not live to see was done before their arrival. Surely God had anticipated them with the blessing of goodness. A council of chiefs was called to decide whether they should be allowed to remain. The king, seeing that the strangers had one wife each, objected that if he received them he would have to content himself with one. Some foreigners did not want them to stay. They said: "They have come to conquer the Islands." The chiefs replied: "In that case they would not have brought their women." The decision was favorable. Not only the king, but the high priest threw his weight into the scale. The missionaries began work at once. The king and the chiefs were the first pupils. In three months the king could read English; in six months several chiefs could both read and write. The first convert was the king's mother. She was the daughter of a race of kings, the wife of a king, and mother of two kings. Her person was sacred. There were times when no one might see her. When she walked abroad at the close of day, whoever saw her fell prostrate to the earth. Several of the high chiefs followed her example. Within five years after the missionaries landed it was decided to recognize the Lord's day, and to adopt the Ten Commandments as the basis of government. It was made unlawful for women to visit ships for immoral purposes. In eight years the converts numbered fifty, and the Sunday-school scholars 26,000. The workers made repeated tours of the Islands, and pressed homo the claims of the Gospel. The effect was wonderful. The natives came in companies to inquire what they should do to be saved. Ten or twenty would be in the mission house conferring with the missionary, and as many more would be outside waiting their turn. The inquirers numbered 2,500. They were kept waiting for a year, and then admitted to the church only on the strictest examination. So inviting was this field that the American Board sent out thirty-two new workers, male and female, making a total staff of sixty-four. Scarcely had they reached the field when one of the most remarkable awakenings in tho history of the Church began. The congregations were immense. They numbered from four to six thousand. Men preached from seven to thirty times a week. There were conversions at almost every service. From 1838 to 1843 there were 27,000 admitted to the churches. The next twenty years there were over 20,000, making the whole number added about 50,000. In a little book entitled *Eshcol*, the story is told of the work of Titus Coan. He labored at Hilo. His parish was from one to three miles wide, and a hundred miles long. He had 15,000 people in his charge. They were vicious, sensual, and shameless, living like wild animals. Under his preaching nearly the whole population turned out to hear the Word. The sick and lame were brought on litters, or on the backs of men; the infirm crawled to the trail where the man of God was to pass, that they might catch some word of life. The interest deepened. It was found that the missionary could not go to the people; so they came to him. Two-thirds of the entire population left their homes and built their cabins near the mission house. The village of Hilo saw its population of one thousand increase to ten thousand. For two years this camp-meeting lasted. There were meetings daily for prayer and preaching. Mr. Coan once preached three times before breakfast. Often he had no leisure; no, not so much as to eat. In twelve months he admitted 5,000 to the church. Among these were men and women who had been idolaters, unclean, robbers, sorcerers, thieves and drunkards. In his ministry he had 12,000 conversions. As many people can read in that district in proportion to the whole population as in Illinois, and the Lord's day is better observed than in New England. The institutions of civilization have taken the place of the old savage life. These people were not content with having the Gospel; they wanted to send it to those who had it not. They have sent workers to the Marquesan, to the Marshall, and to the Gilbert Islands. In 1870, when the American Board withdrew from this field and left the churches to maintain and to manage the work, it was reported that the natives gave $30,000 that year for Christian objects; thirty per cent of their ministers were foreign missionaries; twenty-two per cent of their contributions were for the foreign field. Their church buildings are worth $250,000. Such is an outline of what forty ordained workers, their wives, and their lay helpers, under the blessing of God, accomplished in fifty years. Had Obookiah been alive he would have said, "Behold, what hath God wrought!" He would have seen Honolulu, once a village of grass huts, a substantial city; a race of once naked savages clothed and in their right mind; a nation of readers, whereas he left them without an alphabet; Christian marriage instead of polygamy and polyandry; property secure everywhere, whereas once it was safe nowhere; hundreds of churches and common schools; two female seminaries; a normal and a high school; a theological seminary; twenty-nine native preachers, beside eighteen male and female missionaries; some 20,000 living church members, and a government with a settled constitution, a legislature, and courts of justice.

Are no deductions to be made? Yes. The converts are not all just men made perfect. They do not rank as high as do the people in the United States. It would not be reasonable to expect that people removed only one generation from barbarism would show the stability, the culture, the moral excellence of those who have had the Gospel for a thousand years. It would be fairer to compare them with the churches in the apostolic age. Here as there the tares grew among the wheat. In Corinth a crime was committed that was unknown among the heathen. Yet this very church was enriched in all utterance and knowledge so that it came behind in no gift. In Hawaii there were those who were living epistles known and read of all men. They were the joy and crown of the workers. If some were babes when they ought to be full grown men, and if some apostatized, we need not marvel. Such things have happened before and will again. Besides, it should be borne in mind that these people have been exposed to peculiar temptations. During the whaling season the foreign population equals one-half the population of Honolulu. Their influences are not good. Before the Gospel came women swam out to the ships. When the missionaries interfered, they imperiled their own lives. The house of Mr. Richards was twice assailed by men from English and American ships. They threatened to destroy the property and to take the lives of the missionaries if the laws interfering with their lustful indulgence were not abrogated. Had it not been for the natives they would have executed their threats. The population of the Islands is declining. Before the missionaries came, war, infanticide and licentiousness cut down the people as the reaper cuts down grass. Since then drink, measles, small-pox, leprosy, and vile diseases introduced by seamen, have increased the mortality. The use of clothing has had its disadvantages. The natives dressed heavily and then undressed and sat in the draft and took cold. Cold developed into rheumatism and consumption. When they drank they drank to excess. A savage people know nothing of moderation. At one time the king and the people formed a great temperance society; what was drunk on the Islands was for the most part by foreigners. There is cause for sadness in the thought that the Hawaiian people are dying out. But the work done among them was not in vain. Thousands were born into the kingdom. A whole race was uplifted and ennobled. The missionaries established free schools in every district. They gave the people a literature in their own tongue. Children were taught to read, write, sing by note; they were taught arithmetic, grammar and geography. They were given the open Bible, the *Magna Charta* of all our liberties, the source of all our blessings. If the nation should cease to exist, the work done has been worth many times what it cost. From first to last, about a million dollars was spent on this mission. That would not pay for one-fourth of an iron-clad. It would not defray its current expenses for a year. It is a paltry sum when eternal issues are at stake. The Indians near Boston and near Philadelphia perished; but the labors of John Eliot and David Brainerd were not in vain. The churches that Paul planted on his missionary tours have disappeared, but he did not live and die to no purpose. God has been honored and obeyed. The power of the Gospel was demonstrated when demonstration was needed. A good work was done. One competent witness said: "The deeper I pushed my inquiries, the stronger became my conviction that what had been on your part necessarily an experimental work in modern missions, had, under God, proved an eminent success. Every sunrise brought me new reasons for admiring the power of divine grace, which can lift the poor out of the dust and set him among princes." He found the Bible in almost every hut; prayer a popular habit, and the Lord's day more strictly observed than in New York. Richard Henry Dana states that in no place in the world were the rules which control vice and regulate amusement so strict. They are reasonably and fairly enforced. He found no hut without its Bible and hymn book in the native tongue; and the practice of family prayer and grace before meat, though it be no more than a calabash of poi and a few dried fish, and, whether at home or on a journey, as common as in New England a century ago. Dr. A. P. Peabody said: "Fifty years ago the half-reasoning elephant or the tractable and troth-keeping dog might have seemed the peer or more of the unreasoning and conscienceless Hawaiian. From that very race, from that very generation with which the nobler brutes might have scorned to claim kindred, have been developed the peers of saints and angels." This is the Lord's doing, and it is marvelous in our eyes.

V.

THE HAWAIIAN ISLANDS.

OUR ship reached her moorings in Honolulu on Saturday morning, August 10th. We remained there three days for repairs. T. D. Garvin came on board and invited me to his home. W. C. Weedon was on the pier to repeat the welcome already extended. Mrs. Garvin had a hot breakfast waiting. She knows the direct route to the heart. Miss Wirick had arrived on the Belgic the night before, and was domiciled with the Garvins. She was on her way from Tokyo to Des Moines. Miss Harrison and Miss Beard and the gentlemen who are members of the preacher's family showed me much kindness. This brief stay enabled me to see the place and the people, and to learn some things that otherwise I should never know.

The Hawaiian Islands lie between the Tropic of Cancer and the Equator. They extend from northwest to southeast a distance of three hundred and eighty miles. They are in the track of commerce between the United States and Australasia, and Panama and China. They are now, and must continue to be, an important commercial center. They are not a group, it has been said, but a string of islands, or rather a string of pearls in the sapphire center of the great American seas. They are of volcanic origin. They contain many extinct craters, while on one island there are two craters still active. On the Island of Maui there is the largest extinct crater in the world. The mountain is ten thousand and thirty feet above the sea. The crater is twenty miles in circumference and two thousand seven hundred feet deep. London and New York could both be placed in it. The Island of Hawaii has the two largest active volcanoes on the globe. One is as high as Pike's Peak. Oahu is the most important Island, since it contains the capital, Honolulu, and possesses the best harbor. Hawaii is much the largest, and gives its name to the group. Though the Islands are within the tropics, the weather is mild. The average temperature for the year is 74°. The average of the coldest months is 69°, the average of the warmest is 78°. The trade winds and ocean currents moderate the heat. The weather consists of sunshine and breezes.

Captain Cook discovered and brought these Islands into connection with the rest of the world in 1778. He called them the Sandwich Islands, after his patron, the Earl of Sandwich, but the official name is the Hawaiian Islands. Cook left goats and pigs and seeds of melons, pumpkins and onions with the natives. He left, too, diseases unknown before, which spread and caused misery and death. For a time Cook was worshiped as a god. Pigs were offered and prayers were recited to him. He was installed as an incarnation of the god Lono. He moved among them as an earthly deity, observed, feared and worshiped. His men were looked upon as supernatural beings. The messengers sent to the other islands said: "The men are white; their skin is loose and folding; their heads are angular; fire and smoke issue out of their mouths; they have openings in the sides of their bodies into which they thrust their hands, and draw out iron, beads, nails and other treasures; and their speech is unintelligible." On his second visit Cook was killed. The natives grew weary of the conduct of his crews. Quarrels arose and several perished. George Vancouver, a captain of the British navy, visited the Islands three times, in 1792, in 1793, and in 1794. He introduced orange trees and grape vines and cows and sheep. He refused to sell firearms or ammunition. He was a friend of the natives, and his name is held by them in grateful and loving remembrance. Horses were introduced by Captain Cleveland in 1803. Some of the men that visited the Islands were kind and courteous and did what they could to uplift and ennoble the natives. The most were not so. They debased and debauched them; they outraged and robbed and shot them without cause. The king that was on the throne in Cook's time and Vancouver's time put an end to petty wars and feudal anarchy and consolidated the Islands under one government, and thus prepared them in part for Christianity and civilization.

The first missionaries landed in 1820. Some Botany Bay convicts had preceded them and circulated all sorts of evil reports about them. It was a question whether they would be allowed to remain. God decided the issue in their favor. It was not long till the term missionary became one of honor. If a man was decent and paid his debts quarterly he was set down as a missionary, though he might have no more to do with the spread of the Gospel than Claus Spreckles has to-day. The missionaries found the idols abolished. But although idolatry was formally and legally done away, its superstitions were destined to survive for generations to come, and to blend with and color their conceptions of Christianity. In the first group of missionaries there were two clergymen, five laymen and their wives, and three natives that had been educated in America. The names of the clergymen were Hiram Bingham and Asa Thurston. To some the whole enterprise seemed the very acme of folly. A ship owner said: "These women are fools. They cannot live there, and will, everyone of them, be back within a year, and I have given my captains orders to give them their passages whenever they apply." He had more of the milk of human kindness in him than faith. These women were neither fools nor cowards. They did live there, and many of them died there. The first sermon was preached April 25, 1820, by Mr. Bingham, from the text: "Fear not, for behold I bring you good tidings of great joy." The first church was built the next year. It was a thatched house. In course of time a second was built on the same site. It was of thatch and seated 2,000. Some years later a large stone building was erected. The stones were carried for about a mile on the shoulders of the men. Trees were cut on the mountains and dragged to the sea and floated around to Honolulu. This house still stands. A slab of marble in memory of Mr. Bingham states that he preached there for twenty years, taught confiding kings and queens and chiefs, faced dangers, bore calumny from abroad, aided in reducing the language to writing, translated the most of the Bible, composed books, hymns and tunes, baptized a thousand converts, planned this edifice, and with his loving people, on June 8, 1839, laid the adjoining corner-stone, beneath which was placed a Hawaiian Bible, which was first published May 10, 1839. From here, amid loud wailings of many of his flock, he sailed on August 3, 1840, to visit his native land; but never returning was not with them when on July 12, 1842, with joyful acclamations they thus dedicated this church to Jehovah our God for ever and ever. More than once his life was in peril. A drunken sailor brandishing his knife said, "You are the man every day." Another aimed a blow at him with an ugly club. His pupils interfered and saved his life. He had interfered with their passions and lusts; that was the head and front of his offending. The first printing was done in 1822. The first marriage was solemnized the same year. The relations between the sexes had been very loose in the dark days. Almost everything connected with the lives of the people had to do with religion, except marriage. The missionaries introduced a new order of things. The original workers were strongly reinforced from time to time. The good work spread all over the Islands. The whole people were gathered into churches and schools and Christian homes.

They were clothed and in their right mind. Missionaries were sent to the Gilbert, to the Marshall, and to Marquesas Islands. When the Jubilee was observed the motto seen everywhere was this: "The life of the land is perpetuated by righteousness." Back of the old stone church is the graveyard where the missionaries and their families are buried. Under royal palms and firs they rest from their labors. This is holy ground; it is God's acre. I saw the mausoleum where the ashes of kings and queens repose, but no place in Honolulu stirred my soul so deeply as this.

Next to the churches the most interesting place in Honolulu is the Bishop Museum of Polynesian Ethnology and Natural History. This museum is the most extensive and the most complete of its kind in existence. It contains between fifty and sixty thousand curiosities. Every group in the Pacific is represented. In this museum we can see how the natives lived. Here are models of their houses, and specimens of their furniture and clothing and ornaments. We can see how they prepared and served their food. Here are their canoes and fishing tackle and surf boards and weapons of war. Here are the tools they used and the gods they worshiped. Here are specimens of the animal life of the Pacific,—birds, fish, snakes, kangaroos, insects and shellfish. The Curator, W. T. Brigham, A. M., is a very intelligent and interesting gentleman. He took us through and explained everything. It was a rare treat. The houses of the people were of frame and thatched with straw. The king's palace looked like a haystack. The building of a house was a religious act. The priest must select the timber and decide the time for cutting it. He must select the site. A man must be sacrificed and placed under the main post. After the building was thatched the priest must locate the door. A raised portion of the floor served for a bed. There was no chimney; the smoke got out as best it could or stayed within. The thatch soon got full of vermin, and the house, being poorly ventilated, became musty and unwholesome. The furniture was simple. It consisted of a few calabashes to hold food and clothing, some dishes for pig, dog or fish, some water bottles, a few rolls of mats and bundles of cloth. The mat could be used for a bed, or for a coat, or for a sail. The chiefs used no spoon or fork. The greasy nature of roast pig or dog or the sticky nature of poi made finger-bowls a necessity. Slop basins were used to receive the refuse of the food, such as fish bones and banana skins. These were often inlaid with the teeth or bones of slain enemies. We saw one that must have had two hundred teeth in it. A chief when dying would strictly charge his

T. D. Garvin. Lieut. Stileman.

friends to see that his bones were buried where no enemy could find them to make of them arrows to shoot mice, or fish-hooks, or to adorn his slop basin. Clothing was made from the bark of a tree. It was beaten out thin on a wooden anvil. They had a method of coloring it. Some patterns are quite pretty. The principal source of food was the taro plant. This was beaten in a wooden dish with a stone pestle. When it fermented it was called poi. It is palatable and nourishing. It was man's work to prepare food; it was woman's work to prepare clothing. Their ornaments consisted of bracelets, fans, anklets, bangles, necklaces, ear-rings and combs, made of beautiful shells. Their canoes were well made. Their weapons of war are poor things compared with Krupp guns, but they answered their purpose. The stone adze was their chief cutting tool. With it they felled trees and made canoes and paddles and spears and idols. They had gouges and chisels which were made of sharks' teeth and drills made from shells or lava splinters. They used lava and corals of various surfaces to polish with. With these simple instruments they accomplished surprising results. They made bowls as round as if they had been turned in a lathe. Among the thousands of things seen were pillows of quaint designs, sandals, scratchees, stone lamps, loving cups, spittoons, bone needles, large tureens in which human flesh was served at cannibal feasts, coats of armor, cloth shields, swords, fish-nets, mirrors, pipes. One curious thing was a chief's belt with one hundred and twenty human teeth fastened to it. The teeth indicated that he had killed and eaten that number. The teeth were trophies and were worn as an Indian savage wore his scalps. The idols do not resemble any thing in heaven above or on earth beneath. No doubt these gods are still worshiped by a few. We saw in one case an offering that was made in June of the current year. It consisted of two bottles of whisky. Each had a corkscrew for the convenience of the spirits, who have no teeth.

In one room are portraits of all the kings and queens, beginning with Kamehameha the Great (1737–1819) down to the present time. Not only so, but there are portraits of many distinguished people who were connected with the Islands in some way. The Curator pointed out Princess Ruth. She weighed about four hundred pounds. It took five men to help her into the saddle when she went out for a ride. She measured around the waist sixty inches. Once she proposed to compress her waist as foreigners do. She got a corset and got a number of court flunkies to assist. She emptied her lungs and asked them to haul in the slack. She repeated this process two or three times, but when she began to breathe everything broke, and she was as large as before. She despaired of a wasp waist. Once the Curator tried to waltz with her. He might as well have tried to get his arm around a hogshead. He wished he had been able to take Sydney Smith's advice and dance with her by sections or read the riot act and disperse her. There are books of all kinds in this room relating to the Islands. The one that interested me most was a copy of the Hawaiian Bible published in 1839. It contains 2,331 pages. In addition there are Bibles in the following tongues: Tahitian, Malagasy, Rarotongan, Tongan, Maori, Gilbert Island, Marshall Island. The Curator pointed out a cannon ball that was fired at Mr. Richards' house to compel him to permit the women to visit the ships as they did while in their heathen blindness. "Mr. Richards did not scare a bit," was the only comment. One of the blackest chapters in human history is that which records the deeds of some British and American seamen in their dealings with the natives. It would have been better for them if a millstone turned by an ass had been hung about their necks and they cast into the sea.

We visited the Palace and saw several members of the Cabinet. As we drove up ex-Queen Liliuokalani came out on her balcony. She is a state prisoner, and is not allowed to receive visitors. We found the Legislature in session. The question before both houses was that of a subsidy toward a cable between the Islands and the United States. In the lower house an interpreter repeated every speech; the Senate needed none. The government is a Republic in name. In some important respects it differs from our American notion of a Republic. For example, the Constitution was "promulgated;" it was not adopted by the people. The Constitutional Convention elected a President to serve six years. His successor will be elected by the Legislature. But in his election there must be a majority of all the Senators. The aim seems to be to keep all the power in the Senate. No man can be a Representative unless he owns property in the Republic worth not less than one thousand dollars over and above all incumbrances, or has received a money income of not less than six hundred dollars during the year preceding the election. To be a Senator one must own property worth three thousand dollars, or have been in receipt of twelve hundred dollars during the year just before the election. And no one can vote for a Senator who has not real property worth fifteen hundred dollars over and above all incumbrances, or personal property worth three thousand dollars over and above all incumbrances, or has actually received a money income of not less than six hundred dollars the year before the date of the election. The franchise is in the hands of the property-holders very largely. There is no such thing as manhood suffrage. All agree that the government is wisely and honestly and economically administered. It is by far the best government the Islands have ever had.

The commerce of the Islands is constantly increasing. In 1893 the imports and exports amounted to $16,089,467.08. In ten years (1884–1893) they aggregated $157,815,052.77. There are eighty-one corporations registered with an actual paid-up capital of $21,937,160. The gross income for the year ending July 1, 1893, was $10,004,187. The cultivation of sugar-cane is the chief industry. In 1893 the crop was 150,000 tons. This at seventy dollars a ton represents $10,500,000. The rice crop is estimated at 30,000,000 pounds. The raising of cattle comes third. The coffee industry is yet in its infancy, but 5,000 acres being planted. The people claim that it is the best coffee in the world. The real and personal property is assessed for taxation purposes at nearly $40,000,000. It is said that all the tropical trees and fruits will flourish on the Islands. At the present time one can see the orange, lemon, citron, bread-fruit, mango, persimmon, almond, cocoanut, pineapple, banana, fig, lime, tamarind, plum, algeroba, grape, pear, banyan, and almost every variety of palm. Beside these the soil produces yams, potatoes, beets, carrots, onions, peas, beans, corn, melons, cabbage, cauliflower, squash and tomatoes. Taro is largely grown and used. The revenue from all sources amounts to $1,625,000. The public debt is $3,400,000. The government pays for free schools $240,000 a year. Practically every man and woman and child on the Islands can read and write. The government pays $170,000 for the support of the lepers. They are segregated on the Island of Molokai. They have 5,000 acres set apart for their use. On three sides they are surrounded by the sea, and on the fourth there is a precipice over 2,000 feet high. It was there that Father Damien did his work and won immortal fame.

The natives are dying out. Captain Cook estimated that there were 400,000 people on these Islands. This estimate was too high. In 1832 there were 130,313. Between 1850 and 1884 there was a decrease of 62,385. The population in 1894 was 100,044. Of this number 41,736 are Hawaiians; 15,000 are Chinese; 21,600 are Japanese, and 21,708 are Americans or Europeans. The property is now for the most part in the hands of the whites. The industrial development of the Islands has changed the character of the population. On the street one sees people from all parts of the world. Honolulu is cosmopolitan. There are on the streets Portuguese, Chinese, Japanese, South Sea Islanders, Scotch, English, Germans, Canadians, Americans, and Hawaiians. The population being changed, there is now a new religious problem. The American Board felt that it could withdraw from the field thirty years ago. But new peoples are coming in. As this industrial development continues, more and more will come. A walk with W. C. Weedon through the Chinese and Japanese quarters near midnight shows that there is room for all who wish to work. The Hawaiian Evangelical Association is doing a great work; still there are thousands whom the Gospel has not touched. The Roman Catholics entered the Islands in 1827. Their claims were backed with French cannon. They have now a strong staff and many adherents. The Church of England sent some workers here in 1862. They have not made much headway, so far as I could learn.

For several years there have been a number of Disciples in Honolulu. Their homes and their business interests are here. They are incurable Disciples. They want their children to grow up in the faith. Nearly two years ago they invited T. D. Garvin to settle among them and to organize a church. One year ago a congregation of eleven members was organized. They number now thirty-five. Nine others were added, but these were organized into another church on board the British ship of war, *The Hyacinth*. Lieutenant Stileman is their minister. A Sunday-school was organized last December. There was then one scholar; now there are fifty. A chapel is in course of erection, and will soon be ready for use. It will not be as fine as the Union Central Church, which cost $137,000, but it will answer all purposes just as well. Last year six men assumed all the expenses of this enterprise. It was a brave thing to do, but they did it. Miss Harrison is at work among the Japanese. The day I was there one was baptized in a pool that once was used only by the great chiefs for bathing purposes. Dr. Garvin has baptized a hundred Japanese since he came to Honolulu. Many of these are scattered far and wide. Some of them will carry the good seed into their new homes, and God only can foresee the results. On Sunday I spoke twice in Harmony Hall, and once to the Japanese through Miss Harrison. The audiences were good and attentive. Among them were Hon. A. S. Willis, American Minister, and his wife and son. They invited us to break bread with them on Monday. Under their hospitable roof we forgot time and space, and fancied we were back in an old Kentucky home. There was some feeling at first against our people organizing a church in Honolulu. But that feeling is giving way. Dr. McArthur told the pastors that if the Disciples had not begun a work, he would urge the Baptists to send a man there at once. As it is, there is no need.

In 1820 Honolulu had a population of 4,000, living in grass huts; a few cocoanut trees, no flowers, no greensward, no water, no horses or carriages. All around was a barren waste. Now it is a well-built town, with beautiful groves and flowers of every kind, carriages and horses without number, electric light, water-works, a kindergarten, schools for boys and girls, a college and seminary, a public reading room, a Young Men's Christian Association, eighteen papers and magazines, the Queen's Hospital, with its magnificent grounds, the Lunalilo Home for the aged poor, elegant mansions occupied by men who have made colossal fortunes, the Palace and the Temple of Justice, the telephone, and all the appointments of modern civilization. W. M. Hopper took me to the Punchbowl, an extinct volcano back of the city. One might go over the world and not see a finer view. At the foot of the mountain is the beautiful city; far away in one direction is Pearl Harbor; in another direction is Diamond Head; back of you are the mountains; before you is the wide ocean. It was a glorious sight. While there the thought was suggested, suppose Captain Cook could revisit this place, what would he think? He would think he had lost his bearings, and was borne by wind and wave to the "Paradise of the Pacific."

My visit in Honolulu was exceedingly pleasant. The friends there did everything in their power for my comfort and for my profit. Miss Beard and Mrs. Hopper placed their carriages at my service. Dr. Garvin went with me everywhere. I saw more than I could have seen in a month had I been alone. The native women wear their Mother Hubbard dress on the street and to church, but I soon forgot that. Even the mosquitoes were better than their reputation. Only one thing disturbed my equanimity. W. C. Weedon gave my shoes to his Japanese servant to clean. He looked at them in dismay, and said, "Big! Me could live in them." Aside from this unfeeling remark of the diminutive Asiatic, all my memories of Honolulu are delightful.

VI.

"THE ISLES SHALL WAIT FOR HIS LAW."

As WE steam out from Honolulu towards Japan, we cannot but think of the islands lying to the south of us. A glance at the map of the Pacific will show how numerous these are. "The whole ocean is studded with ocean gems, as if the mirror of the starry sky above it." Three hundred of these islands have been evangelized, and are centers of light and life.

The Hawaiians felt at an early day that they ought to carry the Gospel to those sitting in darkness and in the shadow of death. They rightly felt that only thus could they retain the truth which they had received, and become strengthened and established in the faith. In 1853 two native pastors and their wives, in answer to a call from the Marquesas Islands, volunteered for that field. Rev. P. W. Parker, an American, accompanied them that he might counsel and encourage them. A Roman Catholic priest demanded that these missionaries should be sent away, on the ground that these Islands belonged to the French. One of the chiefs said: "No; the land is not yours. It belongs to this people. There never was a Frenchman born here. These teachers must not be sent back." Some years afterward a native was invited to dine on board a whale-ship. He would not eat anything until he had asked a blessing. In his broken English he said: "O Great Fader! Got no fader; got no moder; got no broder; got no sister! Make first the sea; make first the dry land; make first the moon and stars; make first the trees; then he make man. And now Great Fader, give man his belly full. Amen." This might have been couched in smoother language, but it would be difficult to make it more expressive or more appropriate. Once an American whale-ship touched at these Islands for supplies. The mate, on going ashore, was seized and dragged away to be killed. Some young men had been stolen by another ship to be sold as slaves. The day of vengeance had now come. The mate was in their power. Through the interposition of a Christian girl and one of the missionaries the mate was saved and sent back to his ship. President Lincoln, hearing of this, sent two gold watches and two silver medals, and other gifts, costing five hundred dollars in all, to be distributed among the deliverers. The missionary wrote to the President, "When I saw one of your countrymen ill-treated, and about to be baked and eaten, as a pig is eaten, I ran to deliver him, full of pity and grief at the evil deed of those benighted people. As to this friendly deed of mine, its seed came from your great land, and was brought by certain of your countrymen who had received the love of God. It was planted in Hawaii, and I brought it to plant in this land and in these dark regions, that they might receive the root of all that is good and true, which is *love*." When this letter reached Washington, the President was dead and the nation in mourning.

Other workers were sent to the Marshall Islands and to the Gilbert Islands. In the last named group there are nine Hawaiian missionaries and their wives. One of the most precious incidents of my stay in Honolulu was a visit to Dr. Hiram Bingham and his family. He is a son of the pioneer missionary of the same name. His wife is a born linguist and a born missionary. She is a descendant of the Brewster of the Mayflower. His sister is the wife of the sainted Titus Coan. His son, the third Hiram Bingham, is a student in Yale, and expects to go to China as a medical missionary. Dr. Bingham now lives in Honolulu, but he has given his life to the Gilbert Islands. He and his wife were left alone with God among a savage people. Those who think that the natives without the Gospel are innocent and happy, would do well to interview Dr. Bingham. They began the study of the language at once. As none understood English, this was slow work. They picked up one word after another till in six months they were able to address the people on Gospel themes. They visited the Islands and preached Christ wherever they found an open door. They took their own food and cooking utensils and bedding with them. They heard from the great world beyond only once a year. They undertook to reduce the language to a written form. There are only thirteen letters in this language. In 1859 Dr. Bingham began the translation of the New Testament. In fourteen years it was completed. In 1883 he began the Old Testament. This was completed in seven years. Mrs. Bingham greatly assisted him. Two natives aided him on the Old Testament. When they came to the last verse a photographer took a picture of the translators and their tools. Dr. Bingham gave me a copy. No other gift could be so highly prized. Mrs. Bingham has written a book of Bible stories. They have also prepared a hymn-book.

The London Missionary Society, the Wesleyan Missionary Society, the Church Missionary Society, and the United Presbyterian Society of Scotland, have sent workers to these islands. It was in Fiji that John Hunt and James Calvert did their work. John Williams and his associates labored in the Hervey and Samoan groups and won them to Christ. Norfolk Island was the scene of the labors of Patteson. Marsden and Selwyn did their work farther south among the Maoris. The New Hebrides were evangelized by Geddie, Gordon and Paton. Several efforts were made to drive Paton away; he would not go. He would stay at any cost. They sought to kill him; he would not be killed. He lived to see fourteen thousand converts. He still lives, and may see as many more. He tells of his effort to print the Bible. He was not a printer, but by persistence he got the types in their proper place. When the first page was printed, he went out and threw up his hat and shouted and danced for joy. It was long after midnight; the natives were sound asleep; and he was a missionary. But his dance was like David's when he brought back the ark; it was an act of worship. When water failed, he proposed to dig a well. The people thought he was insane. They had seen the water come down from the clouds, and never heard of it coming up from the heart of the earth. When they did strike water, they changed their minds and regarded him as a god. He describes the dress of a bride. Over her grass skirts she wore a man's overcoat, buttoned from her chin to her toes. Over that she wore a man's vest. To each shoulder she fastened a man's shirt; one was red and the other was striped. When she walked these moved like wings. Then she took a pair of man's pantaloons and placed the body of them over her head and allowed the legs to hang down her back. Her head dress was made of a red shirt, and one sleeve hung over one ear, and the other sleeve over the other ear. In this apparel she came to the altar in a July day. The humorous is blended with the heroic.

On Savage Island all captives and strangers were sacrificed for their inhuman feasts. A number of Society Island converts determined to make an effort to introduce the Gospel among them. The effort cost the participants their lives. Some three years later a native convert, named Luke, sought permission to make another trial. He was taken in a ship as near the island as was thought prudent for it to go. Luke took a bundle of clothes and a New Testament, and fastening them on his head leaped into the sea and swam ashore. He was seized and was about to be sacrificed. He made himself understood and was allowed to deliver his message. The people were interested and spared him till the next day. Having gained their ears he soon gained their hearts. Two or three years later the missionary ship ventured near these shores. They found, to their astonishment and delight, the whole island revolutionized. Savagery had been renounced, and the whole people wanted to be taught the Christian way. In course of time some workers from this island went to New Guinea. They were all massacred. The question was asked, Who will take their place? Twenty arose and offered themselves for this desperate service. So the work spreads from island to island. The Gospel must propagate itself. Those who have it cannot keep the good news to themselves. The natives of the Friendly Islands were so ignorant they did not know of fire. They ate everything raw. They did not know that water would boil. One missionary says: "When I kindled a fire and boiled some water, I could scarce restrain them from worshiping me as a god. You can imagine how they marveled when myself and wife reduced their language to writing, and printed the word of God on our little printing press." This man lived to see thirty thousand converts on this group. Montgomery wrote:

> "The immense Pacific smiles
> Round ten thousand little isles,
> Haunts of violence and wiles;
> But the powers of darkness yield,
> For the Cross is in the field,
> And the Light of life revealed."

It is even so. War and waste are giving place to fruitful strifes and rivalries of peace. These islands that once produced nothing now produce figs, limes, oranges, bananas, bread-fruit, guavas, melons, pineapples, yams, sweet potatoes, peanuts, tea, coffee, hemp, leather, silk, wax, timber, copper, tin, gold. And people who once were as stupid as death, and as indifferent as the grave, are now intensely interested in the Word and work of life.

The Lord, speaking through the prophet, said: "The isles shall wait for his law;" "The isles shall wait for me, and on mine arm shall they trust;" "Surely the isles shall wait for me." These prophecies have been largely fulfilled. The Gospel has reached Madagascar, Formosa, Java, Sumatra, Celebes, Borneo, New Guinea, New Zealand. Over the door of the postoffice in Hong Kong are the words: "As cold water is to a thirsty soul, so is good news from a far country." In Ceylon a Brahman was asked if he worshiped the gods. He said, "The gods worship me." A traveler saw some trees marked "X." He asked what this mark indicated. He was told that every X tree was devoted to the Lord. He saw a woman throw a handful of rice into the pot for every member of the family, and then two handfuls into a pot near the fire. She said, "This is the Lord's rice pot, and I remember him when cooking each meal." So on every continent and every island of the sea the Gospel is having free course and is being glorified. So it must continue, for the promise confirmed with an oath is this, "As I live, saith the Lord, all the earth shall be filled with my glory."

VII.

FROM HONOLULU TO YOKOHAMA.

The Hawaiians are passionately fond of music and flowers. The Royal Band plays when ships arrive and when they depart. Friends cover those about to leave with wreaths and garlands. The ship and officers and passengers are decorated. Mr. and Mrs. W. M. Hopper, W. L. Templeton and W. C. Weedon, drove me to the ship and arrayed me in becoming style, and stood on the pier waving good wishes and farewells as long as they could distinguish one passenger from another. Their wreath made my room fragrant for a week; their kindness will be precious for all time.

There is another Hawaiian custom that is not so beautiful. When a ship comes in or goes out, scores of boys swim out and call on the passengers to throw a nickel or a dime into the sea that they may show how they can dive and get it. These lads are "tolerably amphibious." They swim like fish. When a coin is thrown they dive instantly and some one catches it before it reaches the bottom. It would be better if passengers did not encourage this somewhat demoralizing practice. The boys earn a precarious living. The strong and swift succeed fairly well; the weak and slow get little or nothing. It would be better for these stout lads to earn a living in some other way.

When our ship was across the bar we looked about a little. It was plain that our passenger list was greatly increased. We took on four hundred Japanese in Honolulu. The Government imports Japanese and Chinese and Portuguese, and leases them to the planters. They come on a three years' contract. When the contract expires they can remain on the Islands or return home. The Government sees that the rights of these people are conserved. Truant officers see that all children of a certain age are in school. A portion of their wages is deposited in the Savings Bank every month to their credit. This is paid over to them in bulk when the contract has been fulfilled. With this amount of capital they can start in business in a small way on the Islands, or they can return home and buy a small property or go into business there. Those that took passage on the City of Peking had finished a term of three years. As times are dull on the Islands, and as the fare was reduced to ten dollars or less, this large number decided to return to Japan. The Japanese are warmly attached to the land of their birth, but not so much so as the Chinese. The Japanese take their wives with them; the Chinese do not. If a Chinese dies on board ship or in a foreign land his body is embalmed and sent to the Flowery Kingdom. Should the annexation of the Hawaiian Islands ever become a live question in the United States this system of contract labor would have to be dealt with. The planters say they would be ruined if they had to pay American prices for labor.

The list of cabin passengers has been more than doubled. As usual, we have people of all kinds. Some are going on business and are sensible people. Some are making the grand tour just because it is the thing to do. They have struck oil or pay dirt or something else, and can afford to go. They are well-dressed, have as many diamonds as they can display, and look as if they did not need to offer the Scotchman's prayer for a "good conceit of themselves." When they open their mouths and expose their minds, and set forth their plans and purposes, the disenchantment is complete. Coleridge met a handsome man at a dinner party. His head was covered with great knobs as if the brain was too large for the skull. He seemed to be Solon and Solomon and Aristotle and Bacon in one. "I wish he would speak," thought Coleridge. "In his capacious mind are treasures of knowledge and wisdom by which we all might profit." Toward the close of the banquet he did speak, and this is what he said: "Pass me them dumplings; them's the jockies for me." It was enough. The poet and philosopher was satisfied. There are people who cross the Atlantic and the Pacific every year ostensibly to improve their minds. The real reason is, it is the thing to do. It requires more than a letter of credit and a vulgar display of diamonds and an extensive wardrobe to make such a trip with profit. A ride from Sleepy Hollow to Frogtown and return would do them as much good. The steamship and railroad companies, the hotels and dealers in bric-a-brac make something out of them. The rustics among whom they dwell will regard their trip as a nine days' wonder, but that is all. If they were willing to deny themselves and use this money to give some boy or girl an education, or to aid some worthy enterprise, they would make far better use of their time and their means. How is the world advantaged by any number of people carrying their low aims and vulgar conceptions of life and their bad grammar around it simply because they have more money than they can use at home? There are men and women who travel, and every day is a feast to them, and when they return they make good use of what they have learned, but they are not, as a rule, the people who make a display of their wealth.

When we started from San Francisco I thought we were on a temperance ship. No one would think so now. It is astonishing how many respectable people drink, and the amount they drink. Women drink as much as men. A man orders a quart of champagne for dinner. He and his wife drink every drop of it. He has a quart of beer or claret for lunch, and as much Apollinaris for breakfast, and a bottle or two during the day. Christian men and women drink on board ship on the plea that the water is bad. The water is not bad, but even if it were it would still be more wholesome than the villainous stuff with which they saturate themselves. On this ship, years ago, a European clergyman was accustomed to take a class of wine before going to bed. One good woman saw him and took the glass from his hand and threw it overboard and gave him a piece of her mind besides. I wish she were with us now. The human appetite is a curious thing. It got our first parents into trouble in Eden, and it has been getting their offspring into trouble ever since. Now, as in Paul's day, there are those whose stomach is their god.

Four days out from Honolulu we crossed the one hundred and eightieth meridian and dropped a day. Had we been going the other way we would have added a day. We woke one morning and called it Friday; we woke the next morning and called it Sunday. We lost one whole day and can never find it unless we retrace our path. The Captain told us that he crossed the meridian once on his birthday. He had no birthday and did not count that year. The ladies exclaimed, "Wasn't that lovely! I would like to cross on my birthday." In going east he once had two Easter Sundays together. Some cannot understand this yet. It is a great mystery. We have had all sorts of diagrams and explanations. To most it will remain an insoluble problem.

Captain Ward asked me to conduct service on Sunday. On British ships the captains, I believe, read the Episcopal service, unless there is an Episcopal clergyman on board. When I crossed the Atlantic in 1888, there were on board Dr. Noble, Dr. Gladden, Dr. Ellinwood, and many others, but the captain read the service. He was not a religious man. On the way back there were several ministers among the passengers, but no one was asked to lead. The captain, a profane man, took the service. Our ship is under the American flag, and every captain is at liberty in such matters. We met for worship under some disadvantages. The social hall had been swept away by a typhoon a year ago. The books and seats went with it. We met on deck in the open air. Some books were found. The passengers brought their chairs together. The ship rolled and tossed not a little. But we got along very well. The text was: "Ye know that the rulers of the Gentiles lord it over them, and their great ones exercise authority over them. Not so shall it be among you: but whosoever would become great among you shall be your minister; and whosoever would be first among you shall be your servant: even as the Son of man came not to be ministered unto, but to minister, and give his life a ransom for many." The pagan thought that the great man was the man that was served, and the larger his retinue of servants, the greater the man. Christ taught that the great man is the man who does most to serve and save. The world has called Cyrus, and Alexander, and Pompey, and Frederick, and Constantine, and Napoleon great. This appellation was given by court flunkies and flatterers. The men whose names shall be held in everlasting honor and love are the men who have done most to help and bless their kind. It is not by self-assertion, but by service and self-sacrifice, that greatness and eternal life are won. The audience was most respectful. A reference was made to George the Fourth. At that point one auditor bobbed up and strutted off in high dudgeon. Perhaps he was related to George and resented any allusion that was not complimentary. In the afternoon a service was conducted in Japanese by S. R. Sasaki. He spoke from the thirteenth chapter of First Corinthians. In the evening Rev. A. D. D. Fraser conducted a service of song. This service closed appropriately with the hymn, "Jesus, Saviour, Pilot Me." It was a good day. It was the most pleasant day of the voyage. Several were thankful for the services, which they spoke of as helpful.

The conversation at the table and on the deck is of the most trivial character. I have not heard a bright remark, or a noble sentiment, or an anecdote worth remembering since I came on board. The talk is about the run, or about the food, or about the prospect of reaching land. Passengers are giving their mind a rest. They must be. They think with their teeth. What is lacking in thought is made up in strong language. The soup is "perfectly lovely;" the hash is "perfectly beautiful;" the baked beans are "perfectly delicious;" mangoes are "horrid;" and onions are "dreadful."

One man sleeps "magnificently." I have listened to tittle-tattle and extravagant expressions till my soul is sick. There is some advantage in being deaf and dumb. I wish we had some savage chief here to pronounce these misused words *tabu* for the next ninety days. Some things have been said that would be important if they were new or true. "Prohibition does not prohibit;" "Prohibition is a stupendous failure in Kansas and Iowa;" "Prohibitionists are fools and fanatics;" "Missionaries are on the wrong track; if they would teach the natives to sewer their cities and observe sanitary laws they would do them good; but to send them the Gospel is casting pearls before swine." Some "chestnuts" have a tough life. The nine lives of a cat are not a circumstance in comparison. Men and women who know no more about these questions than a mule knows about metaphysics talk as dogmatically as if they were omniscient. One passenger maintains that there are no gentlemen in America. There are none who came over with the Conqueror and fought at Hastings; there may be none that came from the castles on the Rhine or on the Danube. But there are men who have done things far nobler, and things that fairly entitle them to be called gentlemen.

> "Kind hearts are more than coronets,
> And simple faith than Norman blood."

The way American girls are being changed into Countesses and Duchesses and Marchionesses and Princesses shows that the nobility of the Old World does not consider itself essentially superior to the people of America.

The books read are novels and guide-books. The novels as a rule are poor stuff. They indicate the caliber and culture of their readers. I have read "Beside the Bonnie Brier Bush" twice. I gave it to a Scotch missionary. He devoured it at a sitting. This is a noble book. No one can read it without being made better. I have read Froude's "Oceana," and some other solid works. I can understand how Stanley threw away book after book till his Bible only was left. The more one reads, the more this Divine Book becomes to him, and the more evident its immeasurable superiority becomes. It is at once the newest and the oldest of books. It is the most fascinating book to read on train or ship, in the wilderness or in the city. We are supposed to be on a vacation, "There is nothing but space and color and breath of the sea; no soil, no mail, no rail, nothing but rest and God." We drink in ozone from every wave and every breeze. The mind is being fertilized and invigorated. Let us hope that because of this season of inaction it will give expression to thoughts that will shine and sparkle, to truths that will wake to perish never.

A daily walk about the ship is not without interest. The sheep and chickens and turkeys have nearly all disappeared. They have found their way into the pot, and then into the human stomach, the final receptacle of so many things. Man claims to be "lord of the fowl and the brute." It would be interesting to know what the fowl and the brute think of this omnivorous being. The Japanese sleep on the upper deck. There are berths below, but they are stifling hot. They spread their blankets and pillows on the deck and lie down by the hundred. An awning keeps off the sun and rain. Their clothing is very simple. An average outfit does not cost over seventy-five cents. They wear no hat. Their sandals are worth about five cents a pair. They eat rice and vegetables and meat, and drink tea. They smoke cigarettes or pipes. Women and men smoke. They gamble as continuously as the Chinese. No one would think from these that cleanliness was a national trait. One is reminded rather of the man who said he made it a rule to wash once a year, whether he needed it or not. Their babies are like babies elsewhere. They would look sweeter if their parents would wash them instead of shaving their heads. These coolies are bone of our bone and flesh of our flesh. It would be interesting to look into their minds and learn their hopes, fears, yearnings. The barrier of language keeps a stranger afar off. It is interesting to watch the machinery that never sleeps and never tires, the officers taking the log and observation, and the Chinese scouring the deck and polishing the brass and iron, so that the ship is clean and bright throughout. A cat and dog below are great pets of the seamen and of the passengers. Two men are in irons. They are partially insane, and are tied to keep them from doing mischief. The cabin passengers sit on their easy chairs, and read or flirt as they feel inclined. The married women do more flirting than the widows or the maidens. Only one man has been seriously sick, and he made no end of fun for the others. He was a fool to go to sea. If he gets ashore alive, he will not venture again. He berates the company for tossing him about, and then charging him for it. That is adding insult to injury. The purser told him as long as he could smoke he was not very sick. That was the straw that broke the camel's back. That made him appear a pretender. He got angry and got well. For two days the ship rolled a good deal. The passengers went tobogganing about the deck. But no one was hurt. We are as safe as if we were on shore. Our ship is practically unsinkable. We are in God's care and keeping. He is the confidence of all the ends of the earth and of them that are afar off upon the sea. No sparrow falls to the ground without his permission. Day after day we sail on, seeing no ship and no land. We are impressed with the vastness of this wide ocean. "It is," as Byron said, "boundless, endless, and sublime, the image of eternity." As we watch and think we are reminded of Faber's sweet lines:

"There is a wideness in God's mercy,
Like the wideness of the sea;
There is a kindness in his justice,
That is more than charity."

As we approach Japan letters are written. Trunks are packed. The passengers are in commotion. Everybody is alive and alert. Those who leave the ship in Yokohama and those who do not are alike in earnest. The long voyage is over. We are safe in port. We have heard nothing from the great world since the 3d of August. We shall soon know what has happened in the meantime. Some will hear good news, and some doleful tidings. But God is good and makes all things work according to the counsel of his own will.

VIII.

JAPAN.

We cast anchor in the Bay of Tokyo, August 24. This is the bay into which Commodore Perry steamed in 1853. Then there were a few junks to be seen; now the Bay is covered with ships from all parts of the globe. It was not long before a hundred boats came out to take the passengers ashore. Most of the men in these boats wore only a loin-cloth. It was a strange sight. We felt that we were in a different world from the one we had left. In one of the boats I saw H. H. Guy and two Japanese Christians. They had been waiting for us for three days. A familiar face in a strange land is a pleasant sight. It is like rivers of water in a dry place; like the shadow of a great rock in a weary land. They took charge of me and my baggage, and in a few minutes we were on the pier in Yokohama. We were not detained long in the Custom House. The officers did not ask me to open anything. They took my word that I had no dutiable goods in my possession. Some did not fare so well. Some wealthy people had to open their trunks and display all their finery.

Yokohama is the chief commercial port of Japan. Ships passing between Australia and China and Japan and America call here. Yokohama is the port of Tokyo. Both cities are situated on the same Bay. Seventy-five years ago Yokohama was a village of eighty-seven houses; now it has a population of 110,000. The foreign part resembles an English city. The streets are narrow; the buildings are solid and unattractive; the business for the most part is conducted by Englishmen. The merchants are not there for their health or for any benevolent purpose. They are there for the money they can make. They charge much more for their goods than men do at home. Some of them are warm friends of missions and illustrate in their own lives the truths of the Gospel, but not all. If all who come here from Christian lands were Christians in deed and in truth, the work of evangelizing Japan would be much easier than it is. At the same time it is admitted that these men have made a substantial contribution to the advancement of Japan. They have introduced new methods and new appliances,and have insisted on the rights and the worth of the individual as the Japanese did not. Yokohama has its temples and churches and art stores and other places of interest. In one temple an idol sits on a rock amid flames of fire, having a two-edged sword in the right hand and a rope in the left. The meaning is said to be this: It cuts asunder vile thoughts with the sword, purifies the mind with the fire, ties up passions with the rope and keeps them completely under the sway of reason. How many worshipers understand this is not stated.

A ride of two miles in a jinricksha brought us to the railroad depot. A jinricksha is a little wagon hauled by a man. The two wheels are about four feet high. It has a cover for rainy weather. The jinricksha was invented by a missionary who had a sick wife. This is now the chief means of going about in Japan. A man will run along at the rate of six miles an hour. The passenger is expected to get out and walk up steep hills. The fare is three and a half cents an hour. The jinricksha men form a guild. This is their life work. For a young man this seems well enough, but when a man gets past sixty or seventy it does seem that he ought to have a lighter task. These little carriages fill the streets. There are thousands of them in every city. They have the right of way. The Japanese seldom drive horses. You see a few hauling carts or serving as pack-horses. But they are slow, sad brutes. They do not look as if they had a spark of ambition in them. Their harness is cumbersome and uncouth. It is enough to make a self-respecting animal wish he could hide or kill himself. The weight comes on the collar and on the saddle. The horses used by the police and in the army are fine animals. Oxen are used in the same way. They draw by a rope fastened about their necks. If the load was heavy it would choke them. Horses and oxen are sometimes shod with straw shoes. Most of the hauling is done by human beings. You can see them hauling timber, stones, rice and charcoal in bulk, iron castings, and supplies of every kind. The jinricksha makes good time, but it is not a comfortable carriage, and a passenger is glad when he reaches his destination. A stranger cannot help but think of and pity the coolie who bears him along.

A ride of eighteen miles on a railroad brought us to Tokyo. The railroad is of the English pattern. The cars are divided into compartments. One can go first, or second, or third class. The fare is very reasonable. One can travel third-class for half a cent a mile; second-class for less than one cent; or first-class for less than two cents. We passed through rice, millet, sugar-cane and cotton fields; along pear orchards and lotus beds; past temples and picturesque villages of Old Japan. Reaching Tokyo, we took a jinricksha for our home, a distance of four miles. There is a street railway in this city, but it did not go our way. We were glad when we reached the mission premises. We were most cordially welcomed by Mrs. Guy. Tokyo is a city of over a million souls. It covers one hundred square miles. Since the Revolution of 1868 it has been the capital.

Japan is called the Land of the Rising Sun. The Empire consists of four large islands and three thousand small ones. It has an area of 147,000 square miles. It is about as large as California. The greater part of Japan is covered with mountains. Only about twelve per cent of the land is cultivated, or can be cultivated. These islands are of volcanic formation. The earthquake shocks number about five hundred a year. Rice and cotton are raised in great abundance on the main island. Tea and silk are also raised. One-half the value of all the exports comes from raw silk; and the larger part of the remainder comes from tea. In the southern islands cotton, rice, tobacco, sugar, sweet potatoes, oranges, yams and other fruits of a warm latitude flourish. In the Shinto temples in early times prayers were offered for the growth of rice, millet, barley, beans and sorghum. Millet, barley and beans are the principal articles of food among the country people; with the city people rice is the great staple. The land is always made to bear two crops a year.

Little is known about the origin of the Japanese people. The authorities are not agreed. One man thinks they are the descendants of the Ten Tribes. Another thinks they are of the same stock as our North American Indians. The more probable view is that they are Mongols. It is likely that they are a mixed race. The Ainu were the aborigines of Japan. They live now in the northern part of the Empire. They are a hairy people. Their food and clothing and houses are of the most primitive character. They seldom wash themselves or their clothes. They worship rocks, rivers, and mountains. They are afraid of the spirits. The Mongolians reached Japan, so it is thought, by way of Korea. They drove out or exterminated most of the aborigines. In some cases they intermarried. The Japanese in the main have "yellowish skin, the straight hair, the scanty beard, the broadish skull, the more or less oblique eyes, and the high cheek bones, which characterize all well-established branches of the Mongol race." But some have full and long beards. Some are as fair as if they were Caucasians. It is with some difficulty that they can be distinguished from them. The average height of the Japanese men is 5.02 feet; of the women, 4.66 feet. It will be seen that they are a small race. Yet some of them are fine, large fellows. The population of the Empire is nearly 41,000,000. Most of the people live in cities and villages.

For more than a thousand years the government was an absolute monarchy. The Mikado was a descendant of the Sun-Goddess, and held in his hand the supreme authority. He selected some one of his own sons or some prince of the imperial family to succeed him. It was customary for Mikados to abdicate and go into retirement. Thus one began to reign when he was nine and abdicated when he was twenty-six. Another began to reign at eight and abdicated at twenty-three. Another began to reign at five and abdicated at twenty. Another still began to reign at two and abdicated at four. There were as many as four or five Mikados living at the same time. The Mikado that resigned was said to *ascend to the rank of an abdicated Mikado*. It often happened that the Mikado had no choice in the matter. The men who had the power wanted to keep it in their own hands. If a Mikado began to assert his independence, he was forced to give way to some one who would be more obedient to his masters. Nominally, the Mikado was supreme; really, he was a puppet in the hands of his ministers. One family monopolized all the important offices of the government for four hundred years. The wives and concubines of the emperors were taken from that family. Other families were jealous of this one. As a result, there were plots and counterplots, and wars and rumors of wars. Furthermore, it was customary for men who had reached middle life to retire. It was not deemed becoming for a man to engage in the tug for wealth and power till old age. The abdicated Mikados sometimes had their wives and court, and exercised far more influence than while they were on the throne.

For seven hundred years the government of Japan was dual. There were two Emperors, one a spiritual and one a temporal. The Mikado lived in seclusion and was seen by no one but his wives and ministers. He was taught that it was unfitting that a descendant of the gods should mingle in ordinary earthly affairs. The administration of the government was left to the Shogun. In theory the Mikado was still the source of all authority, but the Shogun wielded all power. The Mikado lived in Kyoto; the Shogun lived in Yedo. Sometimes the Shogun was dealt with as was the Mikado. All power was taken from him and was exercised by his chief retainers. At such times the government was a triple one. But the Shogun was not a son of the gods, and could be displaced by a successful general of another clan. This happened several times. There grew up around the Shogunate a feudal system. The land was divided by the Shogun among his followers. By so doing he bound them to his house. The feudal barons governed their own provinces. They assessed and collected taxes, made roads and bridges, promoted education, punished crime, enforced contracts. In Japan there was no such thing as law emanating from the capital. Below these feudal barons were the *Samurai*. They were the fighting class. Below these again were the farmers, artisans and merchants.

Japan was "the land of the gods." Other peoples were barbarians, and the sacred soil must not be polluted with their presence. This could not continue. China and California being opened to trade, Japan, lying between, must be opened also. There must be ports into which ships could go in a storm, and into which they could go for coal and provisions in time of need. The shipwrecked must be cared for. The opening of Japan became a necessity. Commodore Perry visited Japan in 1853. He bore a letter from President Fillmore to the Emperor. He had four ships in his squadron. Such a force had never been seen in Japanese waters. The officials wanted him to leave, but he would not till he had executed his commission. He was determined to exhaust every peaceful resource before resorting to coercive measures. A Japanese writer says that it was fortunate that Japan was not brought into contact with the world earlier than it was. Had it been, it might have fared as did Mexico and Peru. He regards Perry as one of the greatest friends of humanity the earth has seen. Unlike Cortes and Pizarro and Clive, he woke up a hermit nation without wounding its pride. The next year Perry returned for an answer to the President's letter. The upshot of this expedition was that a treaty of peace and amity between the two nations was formed. Two ports were opened for trade; coal and provisions were to be furnished American ships when they needed them; the shipwrecked were to be cared for, and Consuls or agents of the United States were to be allowed to settle in Japan. The Empire being opened to our nation, it must open its gates to all. In dealing with the foreigners the right of the Shogun to make treaties was called in question. The conservatives gathered about the Mikado in Kyoto. The blame of admitting the hated foreigners and making treaties with them was laid at the Shogun's door. Japan was awakening from the slumber of ages. A dual government was felt to be an anachronism. Feudalism was felt to be a thing of the past. Embassies were sent to Europe and America. They reported what they saw and heard. The Shogun was urged to resign. He did so, and the office was abolished. The feudal barons surrendered powers which they had held for centuries. The Mikado emerged from the seclusion in which he had lived, and took part in the affairs of the nation. To emphasize the change that had taken place, he removed his capital from Kyoto to Yedo, and changed the name of the city to Tokyo.

The change could not stop with the termination of the Shogunate and the feudal system. If Japan was to preserve its independence, it must have a modern army and navy; it must have schools of all grades; it must have a postal system, the telegraph, railways; it must disestablish Buddhism and cease to persecute Christianity. All this has been done, and much more. Once all ships over fifty tons were burned. Only the junks remained. Japan has now as fine ships of war as any other nation. Her postal system is unexcelled. Nor is this all. Absolutism has granted a constitution. The Emperor has sworn to forego many of the powers claimed by his predecessors. This ruler, desiring to promote the welfare of, and to give development to, the moral and intellectual faculties of his subjects, and hoping to maintain the prosperity of the state, gave the constitution. In this document it is said that no Japanese shall be arrested, detained, tried or punished, unless according to law. The right of property of every Japanese subject shall remain inviolate. Except in special cases no house shall be entered or searched without the consent of the owner. The constitution is not perfect, but it is a great stride in advance. The Emperor exercises the legislative power with the consent of the Imperial Diet. He declares war, makes peace, and concludes treaties. He and his successors shall rule in an unbroken line for eternal ages. The suffrage is based on property and not on manhood. This disfranchises the bulk of the nation. But making all deductions and abatements, it must be conceded that a new day has dawned on Japan. And as revolutions never go backward we may feel sure that what has been accomplished is only an earnest of what is to come.

IX.

MY FIRST SUNDAY IN JAPAN.

THE morning was cool and bright. After breakfast and worship Mr. and Mrs. Guy took me to see the first Sunday-school. The hour of meeting was eight o'clock. The school met in one of the buildings used for the charity schools. The first piece sung was Knowles Shaw's noble hymn, "Bringing in the Sheaves." Imagine my feelings on listening to a hymn written by one of our own illustrious men! It was like meeting an old friend in a strange land. In his youth, Knowles Shaw was wild and wayward. He went to balls, and played the fiddle while the others danced. This wild lad gave his heart to God. His was a thorough and genuine conversion. He preached and won thousands to the faith. His sweet songs have been naturalized in every land, and are sung round the globe. He died in the prime of life, but his work abides. The Scripture was read and prayer offered. Kodaira San, Mrs. Guy's Bible woman, taught the children. The lesson was "Christ Sending Out the Twelve." The children responded to the questions as promptly and as heartily as at home. This was my introduction to the work in Japan. Here, in a non-Christian land, children were being taught of God. My soul was deeply stirred. One little girl was pointed out by Mrs. Guy. Her father was a soldier and was killed in the war. Her mother was left with several children. Because of her poverty she feels that she must sell this child. God only knows all that that means. If she is sold, she will be doomed to a life of shame and sorrow. Such things are not uncommon in this land. But when a child that we have known and loved is thus sold, we feel differently. Mrs. Guy hopes to be able to take this girl into her own home, and bring her up in the nurture and admonition of the Lord.

At nine o'clock we went to another school. The singing and the responses were as hearty here as at the other. The lesson was "The Transfiguration of Christ." Some of the children had faces as bright and as full of interest as one can see in the schools of America. They sang "Jesus Loves Me," and "When He Cometh," as if they understood and believed them. Others were there

1. Dr. Nina Stevens. 3. Mr. and Mrs. M. B. Madden. 2. Miss Wirick.
5. Dr. Verbeck. 4. C. E. Garst. 6. E. S. Stevens.

TOKYO, JAPAN.

for the first time. Their faces were blank and dull. They did not know what to expect. A few were suffering from some disease. Their heads were covered with blotches and knobs. Evidently the sins of the fathers are being visited upon their children to the third and fourth generations. One of the workers testifies that he is surprised in finding how much Bible truth has been sown by the children taught in the Sunday-schools. They carry the essence and the aroma of the Gospel into homes that are closed to the Bible women. Parents say that their children tell every night what they have learned in the Bible. The mother of one of the smallest and most uninteresting girls told the missionary that she had heard about Christ from her little girl, and wanted to hear more. So the Scripture is fulfilled—"A little child shall lead them."

At half past ten there was a preaching service; Nishioka San spoke. He urged his hearers to bring forth fruits meet for repentance. He set forth what the Lord required of them as his redeemed children. After the sermon we had the communion. We sat together in heavenly places in Christ, and partook of the emblems of his broken body and shed blood. I trust we drank deeply into his spirit at the same time. The service was orderly and impressive. The audience gave earnest heed to the words that were spoken. Though I did not understand what was said, I felt, "Surely God is in this place. This is none other than the house of God, and this is the gate of heaven." We were separated by race and by language, and by habits of thought and life, but we were one in Christ. For in one Spirit were we all baptized into one body, whether Japanese or American, and were all made to drink of one Spirit. I was asked to say a few words. Emai San interpreted for me. After the benediction I was introduced to all present. I was assured over and over again that I was a welcome visitor. The people of Japan do not shake hands. The women do not kiss each other. They salute by bowing low and bowing repeatedly. Each strives to go lower than the other.

In the evening we had a sermon from Emai San from the text, "Blessed are they that mourn: for they shall be comforted." At this service a young man made the good confession and was baptized. The audience came forward to congratulate him. They did this by bowing low and speaking a few appropriate words. So the Gospel runs and is glorified. The good seed is sown at all hours, according to the Divine command: "In the morning sow thy seed, and in the evening withhold not thine hand; for thou canst not tell which will prosper, either this or that, or whether both will be alike good." Some may fall on rocky ground, or among thorns, or by the wayside, but some will surely fall on good ground and bring forth fruit a hundred or a thousand fold. God's word shall not return to him void, but shall accomplish that which he pleases, and prosper in the thing whereunto he has sent it. There is in the grounds of one of the temples in Japan a young tree growing out of a mammoth stump. One is alive and vigorous; the other is dead, and must give place and feed the new life that has grown out of its heart. One must increase; the other must decrease. So it is with the Gospel in Japan. It must prosper and prevail, for it is alive and has in it the power of an endless life. At the close of each service the audience sat down and engaged in silent prayer for a few moments. This was better than if they had slapped each other on the back, or proceeded to light their cigars, or to talk about the baseball score, or any other irrelevent topic. There was no flirting or writing of notes. The young men did not take the young ladies to church or escort them home. There is no courtship in Japan. Marriage is arranged for by middlemen, and not by the parties most deeply concerned. The young people get married, but they miss a deal of fun.

The audience was a study. It was evident that some were without Christ. Their faces were hopelessly sad. How could these people be happy? Life with them is an incessant struggle after food and raiment. The catechism which they repeat every morning is this: "What shall I eat? What shall I drink? And wherewithal shall I be clothed?" There is nothing in their experience or in their horizon to fill them with hope and joy. Their worship in the temples does not elevate and spiritualize them. The priests are no better. There is as much animation in the face of a mummy as there is in theirs. They have blank, leathery faces. The faces of the Christians are very different. The face of Mrs. Guy's teacher shines as the face of Moses did when he came down from the mountain. She has seen the glory of the Lord. She is busily engaged in his service and she has entered into his joy. The Gospel makes beautiful faces. So it is said, "But we all, with unveiled face reflecting as a mirror the glory of the Lord, are transformed into the same image from glory to glory, even as from the Lord the Spirit." The first convert in Japan has a handsome face. It is intelligent and spiritual. The same thing is seen at home. People come into the church, and their faces have no expression and no illumination. They look as if they were carved out of a turnip. After they are in harness for a season they are transfigured. Their faces look like porcelain that has a light within. In the church and on the street I have watched the faces of the people. The young are pretty. This is especially true of the girls. They marry young and they age young. It is said that there is no word in Japanese for "old maid." All of a marriageable age are married. Mothers do not wean their children till they are six or seven years old. Sometimes a woman nurses three children at the same time. Their vitality is sucked out of them. Small wonder that they fade early in life. As they grow older they lose the beauty of youth, and there is no other to take its place. One sees few handsome faces among the old in Japan. In Christian lands this is not the case. Nor is it the case here among the believers. As Christians advance in years they grow more handsome and more attractive. The hoary head when found in the way of righteousness has a glory and a beauty far surpassing anything that youth can show. As the outward man perishes, the inward man is renewed day by day.

The oldest man I met in the Tokyo church has a fine face. He has been ennobled and glorified by the Gospel. Some of the women in the audience had black teeth. That signifies that they are married, and that they are not believers. It is not known how this abominable custom originated. Perhaps some jealous husbands compelled their wives to black their teeth, as in other lands they cut off their wives' noses so that their neighbors would not fall in love with them. The present Empress and the missionaries use their influence against this practice. It is doomed to disappear. There were some Buddhist women present. The workers hope that they will yet be won to the faith. They are kept back by the ties that bind them to the graves of their kindred and by their associations with the temples. They are a part of a great system, and it is not easy to prevail upon them to come out and take the consequences. Many have done this already, and many more will certainly do so.

As we went to church and as we returned we saw that there is no Sunday in Japan. That is an infallible proof that we are in a non-Christian land. The schools, banks, government offices, and some stores in the Foreign Concession are closed, but the people as a whole work away as usual. There is no difference on the streets or in the workshops and stores. In the temples one day is like another. The only difference is in the feast days. The people feel that they cannot afford to rest one day in seven. They think they would starve if they did. One of the serious problems the missionaries have to deal with grows out of the non-observance of the Lord's day. If a convert is employed by an unbeliever, his employer may, and often does, insist on having his service every day in the week. Should the servant lose his place he may lose his good name at the same time. The Japanese work not only every day in the week, but early and late as well. They think they could not live if they worked only ten hours a day. Merchants are at their place of business at three or four in the morning and remain there till nine or ten in the evening, or even later. The same is true, to a great extent, of mechanics. True, they do not work under our high pressure. Flesh and blood could not stand that. They are poor and they keep working constantly, hoping thereby to keep the wolf from the door. With all her industry Japan is a poor nation. She cannot compare with the nations that observe the Lord's day, and that labor ten hours or less a day. "It is vain to rise up early and sit up late, and to eat the bread of sorrows, for so he giveth his beloved sleep." On Sunday night the streets were unusually full of people, and the merchants were selling more goods than in the day. The explanation given was that women of the middle class, not having servants, were ashamed to be seen buying and carrying home their purchases by day. They wait till it is dark, and then go out and buy what they need and carry it home.

The cholera officers swarm everywhere. Already 17,000 have fallen victims of this disease this year. In Tokyo one hundred die a day. The people are poor and half starved. They have no strength to withstand the plague. If they had robust constitutions and superabounding vitality, the rate of mortality would be very much lower. The lack of proper sanitary conditions has contributed to the ravages of the cholera. In some respects the Japanese are the cleanest people in the world; in other respects they are far from this. They bathe themselves several times a day. They wash and scour their houses continually. They think Americans and Europeans extremely filthy. But an American city is far cleaner and far more wholesome than a Japanese. A city with few or no sewers can not be clean. The stenches in certain parts of Japanese hotels and homes are insufferable. Where all the filth and offal are kept rotting under the same roof as that which covers the family and the guests, the place can not be healthy. It is not strange that the Japanese fall beneath this pestilence as grass before the reaper. It would be strange indeed if they did not.

That night several thoughts were suggested by the experiences of the day. As in the first Christian century, so now the wise and noble and great, as a class, stand aloof. They were not in the Sunday-school nor in the church. They glory in their wisdom and power and station. They feel that they are rich and need nothing. A few of the highest class have been won to the faith. Among these are the Chief Justice of the Supreme Court, several judges of the Court of Appeals, a Cabinet Minister, the Vice-President of the Lower House and several members of the same. But now, as then, God chooses the things that are not to bring to naught the things that are, that no flesh should glory in his presence. The things that are hid from the wise and prudent are revealed unto babes. "Even so, Father, for so it seemed good in thy sight." It is easy to see why our Lord likened the kingdom of God to a child. It is the humble and teachable spirit that enters therein.

Man and beast need one day in seven for rest. They do more and live longer in consequence. Man needs bread, but he does not live by bread alone. He has a stomach to feed and a back to clothe, but he is a soul. We need time for thought and memory and hope. We cannot be profitably engaged from youth to old age in "the tug for wealth and power, the vain low strife that makes men mad and wastes their little hour." We are made in the image of God and capable of entertaining thoughts that wander through eternity. Who can tell how much the Lord's day has been worth to Scotland, to England and to America? Who can tell how much it has been worth to himself? We need to be admonished frequently, for we forget so soon. "This is the day the Lord has made; we will rejoice and be glad in it."

> "Thou art a port protected
> From storms that round us rise;
> A garden intersected
> With streams of Paradise."

Japan has taken long strides in the right direction, but Japan is yet very far from being a Christian nation. Some thought at one time that by the close of the present century the work of the missionaries would be done. Some expected that Christianity would be adopted as the national religion. This expectation is not likely to be realized. Government offices and banks and schools may be closed on Sunday by an imperial edict or by an Act of Parliament, but not thus can the heart of the nation be touched and renewed. The presence and services of the missionaries will long be needed. While Japan is not yet Christian, there are forces at work that are destined to effect this great change. In the Roman Empire there were numerous groups of believers. The statesmen of that day did not think them worthy of notice. If a historian spoke of them it was with a sneer. Christianity was to the wise of that time "a detestable superstition." But from these little groups of believers influences went forth that changed customs, literature, laws, worship, life and everything. So shall it be in Japan. As we bowed that night around the family altar we thought of our Lord's words, "I beheld Satan as lightning fall from heaven." The victory was prospective, but it was as certain as if it had been an accomplished fact.

"Jesus shall reign where'er the sun
Does his successive journeys run,
His kingdom spread from shore to shore
Till moons shall wax and wane no more."

X.

A TRIP TO THE NORTH OF JAPAN.

In order that I might see Japan to the greatest advantage and in the shortest time practicable, it was thought by the missionaries that it would be well for me to visit the churches in the north of the Empire first; after that, see the work in Tokyo and Yokohama; and after that again, see the leading cities of the South, namely, Kobe, Osaka, Kyoto and Nagasaki. The first thing to do was to secure a passport. This can now be had for the asking. No one can travel in Japan or live outside the Foreign Concessions without a passport. There is a reason for this. If a foreigner should commit any crime, he cannot be tried in a Japanese court. If a native has a claim against a foreigner the same is true. He can be tried only before the Consul of the nation to which he belongs. The Japanese Government can not try him in its own courts for violating its laws, but it can recall his passport, and thereby compel him to live in the Foreign Concession or leave the country. Every foreigner in Japan is located. He is constantly under police surveillance. Before you are in a hotel five minutes a policeman calls and asks to see your passport. The proprietor of the hotel records your name and number. So before you can buy a railroad ticket you must produce your passport and thus convince the agent that you have the Emperor's consent to travel within his domain. A child in arms, no less than his parents, must have a passport in order to go anywhere. When the new treaties go into effect in 1899, this nuisance will be abated. Then foreigners can go and come at will. Then, too, Consular courts will be abolished, and foreigners and natives must appear before the same tribunals and answer for any charges preferred against them. Ten years ago it was a difficult matter to get a passport. It took weeks and months and no small amount of pressure to secure this document from reluctant officials. Now it can be had in a few minutes and without any charge or any condition.

It was arranged that Mr. and Mrs. Guy should act as my escorts part of the way. They are most agreeable traveling companions. The baby went along and added immensely to our joy. A little child makes the whole world kin. Dignified judges and lawmakers unbent and noticed us because of the pretty boy. When you are in a strange land and do not understand a word of the language, and the people do not understand a word of what you say, you are in a helpless and pitiable condition. At such a time you find it hard to entertain a very high opinion of those men whose misconduct in building the Tower of Babel caused the confusion of tongues. I have not been left for an instant without an interpreter, and so have gotten along smoothly enough. Had I been left without a guardian I should have fared differently. Our first stop was at Nikko. Here I had my first experience in a Japanese hotel. The proprietor and his wife and chief clerk and all the servants in sight bowed their heads to the earth as we approached. They assured us that we did well in coming. After removing our shoes we were shown to our rooms. There was neither chair nor table in sight. The only furniture in the room was a recess with a scroll hanging in it. Some mats were brought in and we were asked to sit down. I tried to sit on my feet, but it was not a brilliant success. Either my feet are too large, or my backbone is too long, or my joints are not constructed properly. Perhaps if my ancestors had been accustomed to sit on their feet for "ages eternal," to borrow a Japanese phrase, I could do it as easily and as gracefully as the natives, but with all my efforts and good intentions, I must confess that I can not. My guardian apologizes for me when guests are in the room. The first thing brought in is a tray containing a little fire and a spittoon. Smoking is universal in Japan. The priests in the temple and the teachers in the schools and the people in the theaters smoke. The pipe holds only a pinch of tobacco. Four or five puffs exhaust it. The cost of smoking on this scale is not more than two cents a week. They could not smoke as Americans do on their incomes. The next thing brought in is another tray containing tea and sweets. The cups hold a tablespoonful. The tea is served without cream or sugar. In a Japanese hotel there is no dining-room where all the guests eat. You eat in your own room. The bill of fare is different from that served in American hotels. It has no bread, no butter, no cheese, no potatoes, seldom any meat, no tea or coffee, no pepper or salt. Rice is the main dish, and is cooked and served without seasoning. Besides rice, you have fish, soup, eggs in some form, and vegetables, either fresh or pickled. These last are intended to be relishes. Each guest has his own food on a lacquered tray. This tray is placed before you on the floor. You find no knife or fork or spoon; chopsticks answer all

MRS. GARST AND SCHOOL, TOKYO, JAPAN.

purposes. It is astonishing to see how deftly a native can dispose of any dish with chopsticks. I tried mine. I got them by the wrong end, and could not make them lift anything. When I got a piece of food so that I could move it I could not find my mouth. The little maid, with all her inborn and inbred politeness, could not help laughing outright. In her own mind she set me down as a full-fledged barbarian. The food is clean and palatable and digestible. You look about for a washstand and find none. You are expected to carry your own soap and towel and to go to the public wash-room whenever it suits your convenience. Travelers carry their own pillows, sheets, mosquito bar, and insect powder. The hotel supplies the floor and some rugs. The mats and thatched roofs of Japanese houses afford fleas a superb refuge. If you wish to sleep in peace you must protect yourself. With all this protection a bed on the floor is not quite to the taste of a pampered American who has been accustomed to a mattress with springs under it. The bath is a curiosity. The water is kept at a point near boiling. One water lasts the whole day. The family and the guests are expected to use it. Some fastidious persons object to this feature of a Japanese bath. Knowing that we were likely to have some scruples on this point, the clerk came to us and told us that the bath was ready. We asked him if it had been used since it was filled. He said that it had not. He added that a Korean had been in it, but a little thing like that did not count with him. Before lying down to sleep you try to lock your room. You can not lock it. Three sides are screens and can be lifted out bodily. The screens are made of paper. There is no door with hinges that you can lock. A burglar or a rat could walk in any hour of the day or night. You put your valuables inside your fly-net and sleep the sleep of the weary. The people about the hotel are all politeness. They bow when we go out, and assure us that we shall be welcome when we return. We come back, and they bow again and thank us for our kindness. Fancy an American hotel clerk bumping the floor with the top of his head whenever a guest went out or came in! When we left, each one received a present and a letter of recommendation to other hotels. For our food and lodging we paid sixty cents a day. In other hotels in the interior we paid twenty-five cents. Aside from this difference in price, one hotel is like another hotel. All have the same bill of fare.

The Japanese have a proverb to the effect that no one ought to use the word "magnificent" till he has seen Nikko. Chamberlain says of this place that it has a double glory—a glory of nature and a glory of art. "Mountains, cascades, and monumental forest trees, had always stood there." Japanese artists have produced there the most perfect assemblage of shrines in the whole land. One of the greatest of the Shoguns, the founder of a dynasty that swayed the destinies of Japan for two hundred and fifty years, lies buried above the temples. His grandson, a man almost equally renowned in Japanese history, is also buried there. Their family and friends spared neither pains nor money to make the grounds and buildings near their tombs as magnificent as possible. The temples are square wooden buildings. Externally there is nothing striking or beautiful about them. They do not compare in either size or grandeur with the cathedrals of Europe. They were not built to accommodate great audiences. Men and women go to Nikko to worship, but not in our sense or according to our method. They pray for a few seconds in one place, and then hasten on to another place, and so continue till they have made the rounds of every temple and pagoda and shrine within the inclosure. People do not visit this place to hear words of instruction or admonition from the lips of some eloquent preacher. For this reason no vast auditorium is needed. The glory and the beauty of these buildings are seen within. In the Buddhist temples there are numerous idols. You may see the Buddha in pure gold, and the Goddess of Mercy, and Fudo, and many others. On the walls and on the ceilings are the works of the most famous Japanese artists. They have carved lions, tigers, dragons, cats, flowers and trees of almost every kind, birds and sages. In one group there are three monkeys. One has his hands on his eyes, another on his ears, another on his mouth. The lesson is that a good man should have neither eyes nor ears nor mouth for evil things. In one shrine we saw the sacred horse. One of the gods of the place rides on him when he goes out. We inquired as to his pedigree and age and record and value, but could get no answers. He is selected because he has four white feet. More magnificent than the temples and the grounds are the trees in and about Nikko. There is an avenue of white cedars which extends for twenty miles toward Tokyo. Along this avenue the mighty Shoguns were borne by their retainers when they went to Nikko to worship the gods and to make offerings to the spirits of their ancestors. There are tens of thousands of those noble trees about the grounds. They lift their massive trunks a hundred feet or more into the air. It is a most glorious vision. We stayed there a day longer than we expected because we heard that some friends were on their way to Nikko to see us.

Our next stop was at Hanobuchi. The Garst family were spending a few weeks there. Miss Alice Miller and W. K. Azbill were visiting them. We had a warm welcome. The house in which we ate and slept and talked cost only sixty dollars, but we were as comfortable and as joyful as if we had been in a palace. Several missionaries from Sendai and the region round about were spending their vacation at this place. They asked me to speak to them on Sunday afternoon. After the service we walked over to a Shinto temple and some shrines in a grove about a mile distant. This temple is said to be two hundred and fifty years old. In one small shrine there is a wooden horse. His worshipers have thrown in beside him about fifty pairs of straw shoes. The rice placed in his manger supplies the mice and rats with food. On the way home we walked through the village. The people are fishermen and farmers. The children ran about the streets naked. The men and women wore scant clothing. The dogs barked at us as if we were intruders. On our return we canvassed the situation. It was agreed that Mr. and Mrs. Garst should go with me to Akita and the adjacent towns. They had lived in the North, and knew the people and the roads.

Monday morning we were off. That night we reached the point where we were to leave the railroad. On reaching our hotel a policeman called to inspect our passports. He had hardly gone when the hotel clerk came in and asked permission to record the same. He spent twenty minutes examining the outside of the envelopes. Not finding what he wanted, he touched the floor with the top of his head, and asked if he might examine the contents of the envelopes. He asked our ages and caste. He was told that we belonged to the heavenly caste. After an hour or so he took his leave. About midnight he was back again. He begged to see our passports once more. The names of the Garst children were on both passports, and the children were not present. That fact must be reported to the authorities in Tokyo.

The next morning we were in our jinrickshas at six. We reached our destination a little after midnight. We made fifty miles that day. We had two men each, and changed men eight times. Most of the day we were climbing the mountains. The scenery is as fine as can be found in West Virginia. The roads are well made. The bridges are narrow and slight. No heavy loads pass over them. At one town on the way we met two believers, and had a service with them in the hotel. One is a traveling merchant. They were urged to be ready for every good work.

Opportunities are constantly presenting themselves; they were taught to be prepared to make the most of them. The day was the Shinto "All Saints' Day." It was the day for making offerings at the graves of their ancestors and for feasting and for attending the temples. Such a day usually ends with a general spree. For this reason we found it difficult toward evening to get men. By patient and persistent effort we succeeded. We reached our hotel a little weary, but thankful that no evil had befallen us, and that this was the point for which we started. On Wednesday we left Yuzawa for Innai, a town twenty miles distant. We visited the public school of this place. One of the Akita Christians teaches here. When she was studying the claims of Christianity, she sat up late on winter nights without any fire. Her father asked her why she did so. She said she would go to sleep if she was warm. As long as she was cold she would keep awake. There are seven teachers and four hundred pupils in this school. As long as we were in sight the children yelled with all their might. Probably we were the first Caucasians they had seen. Our visit was an event in their lives. We were introduced to the principal and to several of his assistants. He smoked his pipe and drank his tea, and paid very little attention to us. He bowed very slightly when we entered and when we left. He feels as large as the Mikado. Perhaps he is. Innai is a mining town. Kudo San is the evangelist. Besides preaching, he has a school of seventy scholars. The audience at this point was made up mostly of young men. They were really fine-looking fellows. The address was based on the words, "I have written unto you, young men, because ye are strong, and the word of God abideth in you; and ye have overcome the evil one." In the midst of a rough population these young men live so that their lives commend the Gospel to the people. As one result, the community is becoming more favorable to Christianity. As another result, believers are being added to the Lord. We are told that the church is made up of young men, because the young are more easily won than the old. It is made up mostly of men, because no Bible woman has been here to work among the women. After the service we returned to Yuzawa and had a second service there. The teacher whom we saw in the morning came back with us. She traveled forty miles that she might join in the service. There are two or three believers in this place. They meet to break bread. Yuzawa is a dark place. The believers were exhorted to let their light shine. The next morning we were on the road before sunrise. We wanted to make fifty miles, but fell short five. It was election day, and the politicians were about. Many of the men were still drunk, and we could not go as far as we wished.

On Friday we went to Arakawa. The church in this place has quite a history. A Christian from Akita went there to work in the mines. By his zeal and devotion he led another to Christ. These two won others. They built a little chapel. The owner of the mine is a zealous idolater. He is a plutocrat and owns the place. They were obliged to build outside the gate. The most zealous of these men was dismissed on account of his preaching. He was gone a year, but is now back again. We had a service here. The address was based on the words, "Be thou faithful unto death, and I will give thee a crown of life." That evening we left for Akita, reaching it about nine o'clock.

On Saturday morning we visited the school and spoke a few words to them. In the afternoon we went down to the seaport of Akita and spoke in the chapel. The audience was large. Noto San is the evangelist. He is a baker and lives near by. On the way home we visited the cemetery where Mrs. Josephine W. Smith is buried, and scattered some flowers on her grave. This saintly woman was born in Nova Scotia, and died here. In her life of purity and devotion we see the best imitation of the Christ. In her case

> "Love took up the harp of life
> And smote the cords with might;
> Smote the cord of self that, trembling,
> Passed in music out of sight."

At night the church gave us a reception.

The next morning we went to Sunday-school. Afterwards we had a preaching service. The sermon was suggested by the text, "Be perfected; be comforted; be of the same mind; live in peace: and the God of love and peace shall be with you." There was a meeting for women in the afternoon, led by Mrs. Garst. In the evening Mr. Garst preached. At both services I spoke briefly. We had a good day. Akita is the place in which our work in Japan began. Here the first church was organized. Here the children built the Josephine W. Smith Memorial Chapel. From this point the work branched out into other centers.

Monday morning we took our leave of Akita and started for Honjo. Our road was between the mountains and the Sea of Japan. The country is poor; the people are chiefly fishermen. Part of the day we rode in an omnibus. The horse was emaciated. A boy went along to hold his head steady and to help him up hill. We walked most of the way. This outfit is inspected and approved by the government every month. We were over four hours making twelve miles. We saw this horse fed. His dinner consisted of dirty water tinctured with meal. The owner does not know that a horse cannot thrive on a cold bath and on such thin gruel. If this company could see a horse at his best estate, and know what he is in strength, in speed, and in beauty, they would not send out such animals as they now have to distress their patrons. In Honjo, Tashiro San is in charge of the work. He is a man of good repute, and deservedly so. The church here has had some trouble. An evil-minded man sought to get possession of the property. He was defeated in the courts, but the fact that a suit was brought damaged the work. The believers were urged to hold fast the beginning of their confidence unto the end. We were assured that a better day is dawning. It took us a day and a half to reach Shonai. Here we had a service in the chapel. Here the Garst family spent four happy years. Their former friends were delighted to see them. The work at this point received a great impetus from the conversion of a drunkard. The people said that a religion that could work such a change must be true. It took us two days more to reach Sendai, and one day more to reach Tokyo.

On this long trip into the country we got a better knowledge of Japanese life than we could have gotten had we stayed in the large cities. In the cities the people are adopting foreign ways. They dress and live in many respects as Americans and Europeans. Where we were they live very much as they did before the advent of Commodore Perry and the entrance of foreign ideas. We were able to get a more accurate view of mission work as a whole than we could have gotten otherwise. We saw many proofs of the fact that the leaven of the Gospel is at work. Ten years ago the hotels would not entertain a missionary. They pretended that they were full. Now they are anxious for his patronage. A priest in a remote village told one of our men that his temple and its services were a part of the Jehovah worship. An old man in the same place was asked if there was any prospect that the people would soon give up the worship of the Fox-god. He said: "If you will come and preach a few sermons, I think they will." The Bible is read in all parts of the Empire. The people are glad to get a copy. At nearly every place we visited we heard of some who are inquiring about Christianity. We met and talked with several of this class. We learned of some baptisms at different points. The Japanese move from place to place a great deal. Many of them exemplify the Gospel in their own lives and press its claims upon their associates. Beyond question the truth is spreading. The picture is not all bright. We heard of some who have gone back. Iniquity abounds, and it is not strange that the love of some grows cold. Nothing saddens the heart of a missionary like the apostasy of his own children in the faith. This trial is not peculiar to Japan.

In the farming districts the people do not live on their farms, but are grouped in villages. They go out to their work in the morning, and return to their homes in the evening. As rice is the main crop, and as rice grows in water, perhaps this arrangement is a necessary one. One of the hindrances to the spread of the Gospel among the farmers grows out of this fact. The village is a unit. There is almost no individuality among the people. If a man does not join in the worship in the temple and in the graveyard, and participate in the feasts, he is in danger of being boycotted. If each man lived on his own farm, he would be more independent. This is one reason why so few farmers have been won to the faith. In the cities it is different. There one's circle of acquaintances is small. There even neighbors know very little and care almost nothing about each other. Nevertheless, among the farmers there are some who have heard and believed and have been baptized. One of our evangelists is at work among this class. He is a man of uncommon earnestness. Once he was dissipated. After his conversion he resolved that he would serve the Lord with as much zeal and fidelity as he had served the devil. He is a burning and shining light. His field is a large one. His reports are encouraging. Under the preaching of the Gospel these farming communities will be reached as a whole. Then they will abandon idolatry, and accept Christianity in a body.

We saw and heard something of the poverty of the people. Miners earn not more than fifty dollars a year. This is not a large sum if one has a family to support. Thousands of skilled laborers earn no more than this. Rice is cheap, to be sure, and many have little else. The money used shows the same thing. There are coins representing a tenth of a cent. In the hotels and temples and elsewhere we saw great quantities of copper. It would seem as if most of the business was done with this kind of currency. In California at one time the smallest coin in use was a quarter of a dollar. Money was abundant. The community was prosperous. The houses, as a rule, are small and cheap. They did not cost more than two hundred dollars on an average. Many of them did not cost a third of that sum. In some large towns most of the shingles on the roofs are held in place by cobble-stones. The roofs are paved and resemble streets. One man said to us that in time of flood these stones held the house on its foundation; but in an earthquake they were a source of peril to the family. We called to see one family. We found three old people living in a shed five feet wide and eight feet long. How they live at all is a mystery. Thousands must lie down hungry every night.

In Akita we saw a class of people that interested us exceedingly. They were once called *Eta*. The word signifies *non-human*. They were supposed to be below the level of humanity. They were said to be the descendants of Korean prisoners. They made their living by digging the graves of criminals, and by killing and skinning cattle. In 1871 there were nearly 300,000 Eta in the Empire. Then they were raised to the rank of human beings by an imperial edict. Their political disabilities were removed, but they are still socially ostracised. Men are not restored to their original position in this way. At the time of the Revolution there were about a million outcasts in Japan. For these Christ died, and to them the Gospel of his grace comes with its offer of peace and joy and eternal life.

The land is full of idols and superstition. In the treaty ports the people have lost faith in the old religions, and have not yet accepted the Gospel. This is true especially of the student class. But in the interior this is not the case. The present condition of Japan reminds one of the times in Israel, when on every high place and under every green tree there were idols of some kind. We saw temples and shrines and images of the Buddha, and sacred tablets everywhere. The Fox-god seems to be exceedingly popular. We met some women going to a distant temple. We learned that they felt that they would not be human beings at all if they did not make a pilgrimage to this place. We met a man carrying a shrine on his back. The people could make offerings without leaving their homes or their work. He would recite a prayer for a money consideration. One man carried about a lion's head to eat up the cholera germs. He would save any family if they would pay his price. In the temple we found some eating rice and drinking sake and gossiping. Others were beating drums and repeating prayers. There is much yet to be done. Those who have no faith and those whose faith is erroneous must be guided into all truth.

The Japanese eat little animal food; in former days they ate almost none. This abstinence is one of the fruits of Buddhism. The founder of this system used to sweep the ground before he sat down lest he should kill or injure some living creature. He taught his followers that it was wrong to take life to supply man's need. Fish was allowed for the hardness of man's heart only. In the tour through the country, extending over ten days, we saw many horses, only two or three cows, a few chickens, but no pig and no sheep. In one place we inquired for beef, and were told that we could not have any for two days. That was in a town of ten thousand people. In another place we tried to get a chicken, but failed. Until recently, chickens were kept as time-keepers. Their crowing announced the dawn. The only sheep and pigs I have seen in Japan are in the zoological gardens in Tokyo.

Living apart so long the Japanese know nothing of the progress made by other nations. They do not use animals and wind and water and steam and electricity to bear their burdens and to do their work. They have horses now, but they are not used extensively. Away from the railways the mail is carried in a hand-cart or on a man's shoulder. Charcoal, rice, sand, stone, timber, and almost everything else is transported in the same way. It is not an uncommon thing to see two men or a man and his wife hauling a load of some kind. We met a man and a woman hauling stone. The woman pulled with a breast-strap and carried her infant on her back. We saw men and women carrying fire-wood, and hay and vegetables. We traveled three hundred and fifty miles in wagons propelled by human strength. The men sweat as if they were in a furnace. All the while one feels disposed to get out and walk. This is a painful method of travel. Cheap as coolie labor is, one can ride on the best railway in the world for a third of what it costs to ride in these little wagons. The worry is considerable. You reach a place and are told that there are no men. You are asked if you are in a hurry, and if you wish one man or two. If you are in a hurry, you will be told that if you are willing to pay for two men you can get one. If men are present they must have time to think whether they will go on to-day or wait till to-morrow. One would think that they would be glad to go at once. But these men are never in a hurry. Haste is undignified. At every turn you must pay extra. The foreigner is rich and can be "squeezed." Give one man a tip and you must give every man a tip. The news will be passed all along the line. It would seem that these men would be ambitious to make a reputation for promptness and efficiency. What do they care for reputation! They have lived from hand to mouth all their days. Years of oppression have taken all heart and all hope out of them. Several times Mr. Garst told them that a traveler from across the seas was present, and that they owed it to Japan to contribute to his progress and comfort, so that he might get a favorable impression of the country. Strange to say, this appeal to their pride succeeded when everything else failed. Sometimes we had to resort to the police. They wear the chrysanthemum, the badge of the Emperor, and their word is law. We felt relieved when we reached the railroad, and realized that the "squeezing" was over.

There were many pleasant things about this trip. The believers came out to meet us, and to see us off. They were glad we came, and assured us that our visit would do good, and that their prayers and good wishes would follow us all our days. My companions left nothing undone that could add to my comfort. C. E. Garst, by his knowledge of the people and their language, by his unfailing good humor and patience, helped me much. On a long journey like this one, a woman that can speak and pray and sing and interpret and cook and make the best of everything, is a treasure indeed. One thing tried me. I have sat on my feet and looked happy when suffering torture; I have eaten soup with chopsticks; I have parboiled myself in hot baths; I have touched the ground with the top of my head a hundred times in a day; but nothing has tried me so much as speaking while sitting on the floor, and through an interpreter. It is as natural for a man to stand up when he has anything to say, as it is for him to sit down when he is through. The human organism is a galvanic battery, and the mind works best when it has two ground connections. The audiences were so attentive that speaking in any posture was not so difficult as otherwise it would have been. We reached Tokyo late Saturday night in good health and in good spirits, and thankful that we had been permitted to make this trip.

XI.

A WEEK IN TOKYO.

On the Sunday after returning to Tokyo from the trip in the north, I worshiped in three places. In the early morning I visited the chapel in which J. M. McCaleb preaches, and spoke briefly. He has a neat and convenient place of worship, and is doing a good work. There was a feast in that part of the city at the time. Lanterns and banners were hung out in front of almost every house. The streets were full of people. The boys were as noisy as at home on a national holiday. The people within were reverent and attentive. Each had a Bible and followed the leader when he read or referred to passages. After an hour spent there we went to the chapel in charge of H. H. Guy. This is the building that Miss Wirick erected with money saved out of a modest salary. Here I spoke on the new life in Christ. One of the evangelists interpreted for me. In the evening I went to the chapel in charge of E. S. Stevens. In nearly every ward of this great city the Gospel is preached every week. The buildings, as a rule, are neither large nor costly. They do not begin to compare in these respects with the temples. But in them the message of salvation is proclaimed, and therefore they are worth more to the Japanese than all their Buddhist temples and Shinto shrines. One is a savor of life unto life; the other is a savor of death unto death. Strange feelings come over one while sitting in one of these chapels in this great city. Outside the people are engaged in their secular occupations. The majority do not know and do not care to inquire concerning the new faith. But Jesus Christ is destined to reign over Tokyo, and over Japan. The institutions of this Empire shall be filled with his spirit, and the people shall serve him.

The next day we called to see Miss Rioch's work. She has charge of the Girls' Home. There are nine girls under her care. They are being educated to serve as Bible women. Should they not devote their lives to this work, they will become Christian wives and mothers. Some of these girls are from Christian homes, and some are not. They themselves are all Christians, most of them having turned to the Lord since they entered the Home. For their secular education they go to the government schools. In the Home they are under Christian influence and receive Biblical instruction. At present they are studying the Life of Christ. They do all their own work, the matron overseeing and giving instruction when necessary. They learn to cook, sew, wash, nurse the sick, and many other things. In this way they are prepared to become good housekeepers, and while serving as Bible women they will be prepared to turn their hands to almost anything. They dress and live in Japanese style. No attempt is made to denationalize them. They are Christians, but not American Christians. Their field of work is here, and it is for it they are prepared. In her work Miss Rioch is aided by Mrs. Garst, Miss Johnson, and Messrs. Guy and Stevens. Each one teaches an hour a week. The course of study at present is the Old Testament in Outline, the Life of Christ, Geography, Church History, and Methods of Work. Under the last head the girls are taught how to approach the people, and how to answer their objections to the Christian religion. All the more advanced girls teach classes in the Sunday-schools. Thus every day in their school life they are influencing those around them for good, and when they can they tell them of the Savior who died for them. When the new building is completed, this work will be enlarged.

On Tuesday morning we visited, by request of W. K. Azbill, one of the famous schools for girls in Japan. At his suggestion the President and Faculty invited me to deliver an address before the whole school. President Iwamoto is a man of ability, culture, position and moral worth. He is justly regarded as one of the foremost teachers in the Empire. He is not only a teacher, but a preacher, and an editor as well. His school is one of the best of its kind in Japan. It is a Christian school of high grade. The President is an earnest advocate of self-support in all such institutions. He could easily get foreign aid in case he was willing to place the school under foreign control. This he is not willing to do. The teachers work for very small pay. If any can donate their services they cheerfully do so. W. K. Azbill, Miss Alice Miller and K. Ishikawa are on the staff of teachers. We had a very pleasant visit with the President and his accomplished wife. She has translated some of the works of Charles Dickens into Japanese, and has done much other literary work. She conducts a department in the *Japanese Evangelist.* Professor Azbill took us through the buildings and over the grounds. He showed us the rooms in which he lives, and the chapel in which he and his associate preach every

Sunday. He took us to the lot which he has purchased, and upon which he hopes to build a chapel in the near future.

On the way back we called to see Dr. D. C. Green of the American Board. He has been in Japan since 1869. He was here three years before the first Protestant church was organized in Yokohama, and four years before the edicts prohibiting Christianity were taken down. He has a great story to tell, and the heart beats faster while listening to him. He spoke of some of the changes that had taken place since his arrival. Those who visit Japan now can have no adequate conception of the greatness of these changes. The nation and its institutions are essentially different from what they were at that time. He spoke of the triumph of the Gospel in Japan. He confessed that the enthusiasm of a few years ago has abated. The outlook for the immediate Christianization of Japan is not as bright as it was then. But this, in his opinion, is only a temporary lull. The great movement has slackened; it has not ceased. Dr. Green accounted for the present condition by saying that it is owing partly, if not mainly, to the readjustments which have followed the general acceptance of the theory of evolution. Many men who would otherwise be leaders of evangelistic effort, are giving themselves to the solution of the new problems in theology. Some are at sea in respect to doctrine. They are in doubt, and a doubtful mood is not a victorious mood. He referred also to the intense nationalistic spirit as hindering the progress of the Gospel. This spirit manifests itself in Russia, in Germany, in Australia, and Japan. It is different in different countries, but in every case it emphasizes the national as against the universal. Christianity being a foreign religion has suffered in common with everything else that is foreign. As to the future, Dr. Green has no doubt. Year by year substantial gains are being made. There are many indubitable proofs that the worst is past, and that a better day is dawning.

In the afternoon we visited the Imperial University. Dr. Yoshida volunteered to be our guide. He is one of the teachers in the Nobles' School, and does some work in the University. In 1856 a place was opened for the Examination of the Barbarian Writings. This was the germ of the present University, with its Colleges of Law, Medicine, Engineering, Literature, Science and Agriculture. The staff of professors is quite large. The lectures are in various languages. The Medical College is manned by Germans. Several of the professors are men of world-wide renown. Gradually the foreigners are giving place to Japanese. The Government sends a number of the most promising young men to America and Europe, and supports them while prosecuting their studies under the ablest specialists. There are in all departments 1,300 students. This is now the greatest school in the East. The Japanese are determined that it shall not be surpassed by any school in the world. One of the interesting pieces of apparatus shown us was that for registering earthquakes. As there are about five hundred earthquakes a year in Japan, it will be seen that this instrument has much to do. It records the motions of the earth in all directions, and the duration of the same. Dr. Yoshida showed us a piece of wire bent so as to represent the movements of the earth in a severe shock. It was bent in all directions. Seeing this, one can readily believe the reports of the destruction caused by earthquakes. The scientific men are making experiments from which they expect good results. For example, they are building houses that will best withstand the shock of earthquakes. They are sinking a well 3,000 feet deep. They hope to learn something from this. In the evening the Japanese Christians gave me a reception. Several addresses of welcome were made. They charged me to assure the churches in America of their gratitude for what they have done for them. One man came three hundred miles to the reception. He is a country evangelist. He is not a great scholar, but he has apostolic faith and zeal, and is doing a good work.

The next day we visited the Presbyterian College, and saw the President and several of the professors and some of the work. The buildings are spacious and suitable. In the Theological Department there are fifty students; in the Literary Department about the same number. There is no lack of schools in Tokyo. Nearly every society has felt that it must train its own workers and must educate the young people connected with the churches. There are schools representing every variety of doctrine. In one of these, so it is said, there are no text-books, only lectures and essays; the faculty is composed of Christians, Buddhists, Shintoists and Confucianists. All have the same object in view—search for truth wherever it may be found. The men connected with this school do not build churches, impose creeds, nor pay salaries to preachers, nor import foreign organizations, nor reproduce foreign cults. They wait for and help along native effort, which is honestly directed toward gaining the highest truth and securing the best life in religion and morals. It is a poor way to search for truth to overlook Him who said, "I am the way, the truth, and the life."

Most of Thursday was devoted to a conference with the missionaries. We had accounts from all as to the present condition of the work and the outlook. The work in the schools and the meetings for women and the work in the several chapels were reported. Plans for enlarging the work were discussed. The need of a school in which evangelists shall be trained was emphasized. The general feeling is that no college for literary or scientific training is needed, because the Japanese schools are excellent, and this work can be done in them more economically. In answer to a petition from the believers in Akita for a missionary family Mr. and Dr. Stevens volunteered to go to the North. They will be more than three hundred miles from Tokyo, and far removed from any Americans, but they go joyfully because they feel that the Lord's work there requires their presence and service. That day we visited the Imperial Museum near by and saw many things relating to Japanese antiquities, art, manufactures, mineral and agricultural resources. We had a bird's-eye view of Japan. In the park we saw the tree General Grant planted and some of the camels captured at Port Arthur.

The following day was devoted to a conference in the home of Miss Scott and Miss Hostetter. All the workers in Tokyo representing the Disciples of Christ were present. Mr. and Mrs. Madden reached the city the night before, and were on hand to be introduced to the workers and the work. After a brief address by President Guy, E. S. Stevens read a paper on "Entering upon the Work." He dwelt upon the need of a holy life, and enlarged upon some missionary methods. It was a thoughtful paper. The discussion was lively and profitable. Prof. Azbill called attention to the use of such phrases as "Our Church," "Our Plea," and "Our Position." He prefers to speak of Christ's position, and plea, and church. Miss Scott read a paper on "Charity School Work." She gave an account of her own school, as she knows that better than any other. Her school is in one of the poorest quarters of the city. Here are lepers and people with other terrible diseases; the blind and the lame; children clad and unclad, looking hungry and wretched. When the people get up in the morning they carry off and pawn their bed for enough to buy food or drink. If they can earn enough in the day to redeem the bed, they have it to sleep on during the night. The boys called the workers "foreign fools" and "foreign cats." They threw stones into the houses and made noises about the place, or abused and teased the children coming out of the school. Buddhist priests circulated falsehoods about Christians. But the work grew and prospered. She has now over one hundred children. They are in three grades. They are taught reading, writing, composition, geography, arithmetic, physiology, and practical Christianity. The Bible is taught every morning, and Christian songs are taught once a week. A new spirit has crept over the valley. The policeman speaks of the children as quiet and orderly, whereas they had been the bane of his life. The teachers are known and respected. C. E. Garst read a paper on "Industrial Work in Missions." Great care must be taken not to pauperize the people by doing too much for them. The better plan is to give them some work while in school, so that they may pay their own way. At the creation every tree had its "seed in itself." So Christianity is intended to be self-propagating. At the close I spoke about the work at home, and my impressions of what I had seen since reaching the field. We had a good day together. The workers in Japan are of one heart and one soul. They keep the unity of the Spirit in the bonds of peace.

On Saturday morning the Advisory Committee held a session for business. Later in the day we visited the Garst family. One of the many joys of this visit was a talk with Dr. Verbeck. He was born in Holland and educated in a Moravian school. After coming to America he entered Auburn Seminary. On his graduation he was sent to Japan. That was in 1859. He was one of the first four to enter Japan as soon as the doors were opened. He could not preach publicly, but, like Paul, he dwelt in his own hired house, and received all that came in unto him, preaching the kingdom of God, and teaching those things which concern the Lord Jesus Christ. An old priest brought three young men to him. He said he was too old to begin the study of Christianity, but asked him to take his young friends and teach them. An old doctor came by night to talk and to get many books for friends in the country. Dr. Verbeck baptized the second convert in Japan. He told us about it. The first convert died a few hours after his baptism. The commander of an army found a copy of the New Testament in Nagasaki Bay. Through an interpreter he learned that it was a good book, and that he could get a copy in Chinese in Shanghai. Being ordered to return home, he kept up the study of the Bible, and got four others to join him. He sent to Dr. Verbeck, and asked him if he would give him instruction in this book. Once a week he sent a trusty messenger to Nagasaki with an account of his progress, and with a request to explain some difficult passages. He sent, because he could not leave home himself. This went on for over two years. One day the commander appeared before his teacher and asked for baptism. After due examination he was

Miss Oldham. Miss Rioch.

CLASS IN ENGLISH IN TOKYO, JAPAN.

baptized. Then he told of the New Testament that he had found twelve years before. The baptism was private. The commander was ready to die for the faith, but if it was known that he was a Christian, his whole family would have been exterminated. At that time Christianity was "the vile doctrine," and its acceptance was a capital crime. This man kept the faith till the last. Every day he took his family into a private room and read and expounded the Scriptures. Fourteen years later a daughter and a female servant sought baptism. Dr. Verbeck had much to do with education in Japan. Two young men came to him to study the English Bible. About a year after they came to him bringing two sucking pigs as a thank offering for his teaching. They had been examined that morning and had carried off the highest prizes. The success of these young men led the government officials to seek Dr. Verbeck's services in an English school to be opened in Nagasaki. Afterward he was invited to Tokyo. Here he became the adviser of the government in all matters pertaining to education, and in other matters as well. He was principal of a school that had over a thousand pupils. This school is now part of the Imperial University. His influence for good has been immeasurable. Several years ago he severed his connection with the school and returned to the work of an evangelist. He is in great demand as a preacher and a lecturer. He is called for in all parts of the Empire. One of his greatest works was his share in translating the Scriptures into Japanese. Dr. Verbeck is a hale and joyous old man, and a fine specimen of the Christian gentleman. He is as young in spirit and as full of fun as a boy. He has seen the Empire opened, and has seen the day when 40,000 souls believe that Jesus Christ is Lord of all. In recognition of his great services to the nation, the government has granted him and his family a special passport, giving them the right to trade, sojourn and reside in any part of the Empire. Dr. Verbeck's life is an illustration of the words, "Always abounding in the work of the Lord." To meet such a man and to hear him talk makes one feel proud of his race.

At the request of the General Secretary, I delivered an address before the Young Men's Christian Association. There were over three hundred present. In that audience there were more brains and more promise than in all the priests and worshipers I had seen in the temples. Most of them could understand English. For the sake of those who could not, the Secretary interpreted for me after I had finished. All our own workers were present. The Association has a fine building. It cost $30,000, silver. Most of this money came from America. A number of eminent men, among them the Chief Justice of Japan, are among the directors.

It was a busy and happy week. I saw all the charity schools, and some of the work in the meetings for women. I met the Christians for conference and visited the workers in their own homes. As scarcely any two live within five miles of each other, this took time. There were many callers at the home where I was entertained. They came early and late. Sometimes there was no leisure, no, not so much as to eat. I think I saw and heard about every side of the work. The week closed with a service of song and thanksgiving to God for his loving kindness.

XII.

MISSIONARY METHODS IN JAPAN.

THE work of a missionary is clearly defined. He is to make disciples and teach them to observe all things that Christ commanded. This task is not so simple and so easy of accomplishment as many suppose. The people are not standing on the shore waiting for the evangelist, and eager to hear and obey his message. They are not hungering and thirsting after righteousness. Our Lord said, "No man having drunk old wine desireth new; for he saith, The old is good." Myriads are satisfied with what they have, and do not wish any change. In other minds there is an inveterate prejudice against a foreign faith. To secure a favorable hearing for the message requires wisdom, tact, patience, and love. The work of a missionary is a many-sided work, and it needs a many-sided soul. I wish to give an account of some of the methods employed in Japan.

I. PREACHING THE GOSPEL.

A missionary is to go and preach. It is God's good pleasure through the foolishness of preaching to save them that believe. Our Lord was a preacher. He went about all Galilee and Judæa teaching in their synagogues and preaching the Gospel of the kingdom. His apostles were preachers. They filled the Empire with their doctrine. There is no substitute for the living voice of the living man. The presence of an evangelist challenges attention and calls out inquiries. At once the people become curious as to his appearance and business and motives. It is for him to take advantage of this natural curiosity and supply the information desired. A missionary is not long on the ground before he begins to preach. He begins with an interpreter. As soon as he is able he begins to speak without this aid. Dr. McAll began with two sentences: "God loves you; I love you." The work may be begun in his own hired house, or in a hotel, or on the street, or in a chapel, or in a temple. Wherever people are found who wish to learn something about the faith of Christ, he is ready to speak. Paul made several long missionary tours. He said that from Jerusalem and round about, even unto Illyricum, I have fully preached the Gospel of Christ. The world was his parish. His example is followed to-day in Japan. No missionary remains in one spot, like an oyster. His labors are not confined to one neighborhood. Confucius said: "A philosopher need not go abroad to proclaim his doctrine; if he has the truth, the people will come to him." A missionary must go out on preaching tours. He may be gone a month or two at a time. It is not difficult to get a hearing. By announcing that he is going to speak in some temple or in the theater, he can call from five hundred to a thousand people together. The audience is in no hurry to go home. He can preach for an hour, or for five hours, as he prefers. In this way he advertises Christianity. Many will call upon him at his hotel to hear more. They will come before he is awake in the morning, and will remain till long after he ought to be asleep. Some may be drawn by the idlest curiosity. They may be like the Athenians, eager to hear some new thing. Some may come to oppose. A few may come to inquire what they must do in order to be saved. In any event, he has the chance to apply the truth to the heart and the conscience, and to make clear what in his address was not understood. An audience at home has a thousand years of Christian history behind it. The hearers understand allusions to Biblical history, geography, and social customs. Not so here in Japan. One man inquired of a speaker if John the Baptist was a place or a person. Such misconceptions are not uncommon. On these tours the evangelist is brought face to face with multitudes who otherwise would never care to inquire concerning Christianity. He has thus unrivalled opportunities of disarming prejudice, of explaining difficulties, and of publishing far and wide the message of salvation.

II. SUNDAY-SCHOOLS AND WOMEN'S MEETINGS.

The children are gathered on Sunday in the chapels or in the buildings used by the charity schools. Some of the workers have two and others three schools a week. The exercises are conducted as at home. The same lessons are studied and the same songs sung. The results can not fail to be good. On the seats are small children with babies strapped to their backs. The parents are busy and can not come; the children are glad to attend. Once a week each of the ladies of the mission has a meeting for women. This meeting is held either in their homes or in the chapels. In the two that I attended the women were studying the "Life of Christ." Songs were sung, prayers were offered, the Scriptures were read and explained. There is more need of such meetings here than in America. The reason is this: The women do not use the same language as the men. A woman may go to church and hear the sermon and understand very little of it. If the preacher wishes to display his learning, and uses Chinese words freely, the women will not be edified. In the meetings for women the leaders use Japanese words and phrases, and their explanations are clear to all.

III. CHARITY SCHOOLS.

In Japan there are public schools in all parts of the Empire. The intention of the Government, as stated in an Imperial edict, is that education shall be so diffused that there may not be a village with an ignorant family, nor a family with an ignorant member. But the schools in Japan are not *free*. It is true that the tuition fee is small, but a fee of fifteen or twenty cents a month is more than many families can pay. Hence the need of charity schools. In these no fees are charged, as a rule. Sometimes a small fee is charged; this is done only when the families are able to pay it. In these the course is substantially the same as in the Government schools. The difference is that the Bible and Christian songs are taught. By this means distrust and dislike are broken down, and hearts and homes are opened to the Gospel. For centuries the people of Japan were taught that foreigners were no better than the beasts of the field. It was said that missionaries were sent out to teach the people to disobey the laws. This care for the children of the poor attracts attention. Persons that engage in such a work, with no promise or prospect of reward, cannot be so very bad at heart. The strongest evidence our Lord could give that he was the Messiah was this: "To the poor the gospel is preached." This evidence is as cogent and convincing now as it was then. Acquaintance with the teachers dispels many foolish notions about them. They are seen to be possessed of ability, culture, refinement; they are kind and gentle and patient. It is impossible to hate or despise such workers. By their consistent lives and unselfish conduct they commend the Gospel to all who know them. The good seed is sown in the hearts of their pupils. Bishop Hughes said: "Give me the children till they are eight years of age, and I don't care who has them after that." Some of the children are won to the faith. All are more favorably disposed towards Christianity and Christian people than otherwise they naturally would be. Whole communities have been changed by a charity school. The pupils were brought into a new atmosphere. The boys were taught to serve their country and to grow up into good men. They were prepared to be heads of households. The girls were better daughters, wives and mothers because of the instruction and inspiration received. These schools build up the nation; they contribute to the advancement of the Lord's work in this land. One boy taught by one of our workers sends his mother to the meeting for women. He keeps the baby in her absence. Once his mother was going to a temple to pray that her sore eyes might be healed. The lesson that day was, "Thou shalt worship the Lord thy God, and him only shalt thou serve." He urged her not to go. She did not. Afterward she wanted to unite with the church, but her husband opposed.

IV. TEACHING ENGLISH.

The demand for this is not so strong as it was once, but it is strong enough to tax the energies of the missionaries. Once it was proposed to adopt English as the national language. That was a dream of the Restoration. No one thinks of that now. Then every man that could speak English was employed as a teacher. Men smoked and swore in the class-rooms. One article in the contract made with W. E. Griffis was that he should not get drunk. There was a reason for this clause. There is yet a great demand for English among the students. This helps the work. I think it was Duff that said that no one could get a knowledge of the English language without getting a knowledge of Christianity. No one can read Shakespeare, or Emerson, or Tennyson, or Lowell, without discovering many of the concepts that are peculiar to the Gospel. English literature is saturated with Christian thought. One can not read long without learning of God as a personal Being, of Jesus Christ as the Savior of men, of the worth of every human soul, of the value of freedom. No man can read English without coming to know that it is a shameful thing for men to lie; that it is a noble thing to be pure, and just, and generous, and self-sacrificing.

V. BIBLE CLASSES.

These are taught in the Sunday-schools and elsewhere. Young men come to the homes of the missionaries. The principal of one of the great schools of Japan said to his pupils, "You can not understand English civilization without a knowledge of the English Bible." Many read it for this purpose. They do not regard it as a revelation from the Father. They do not read it to make it the rule of their lives. They read it as they would read Longfellow, or

Hawthorne, or Milton, or Burke. No matter what the motive, if only they do read it. Dr. Gordon took a class of Buddhist priests through a course in the New Testament. That so many want to study the English Bible is a hopeful sign. It is a great and effectual door. Nothing but good can come from such classes. Many may not be convinced that it is the Word of God, but their erroneous views will be corrected and their mental attitude changed. As they read they will become familiar with some of the great truths and eternal principles that underlie Anglo-Saxon civilization. They will learn that, not the Emperor only, but every man is a son of Heaven; that all men are equal before God; and that all are sinners; and that Jesus the Christ is mighty to save.

VI. BIBLE DISTRIBUTION.

The people are glad to get a New Testament or a Gospel. After a large meeting in a theater many are willing to buy. Their interest is excited, and they are eager to know more. One of our workers at the close of such a meeting disposed of five hundred portions of the Bible. As they read they are convinced that this is not "the vile doctrine" reputed, and that it cannot corrupt the people. They are convinced that it cannot fail to do them good. It is the basis of ethics and the foundation of good government and of the greatest material prosperity. The distribution of the Scriptures cannot fail to bring forth good fruit. The printed page can go where no evangelist has ever gone. In connection with this work is that of tract distribution. Workers usually carry an assortment with them while touring. They give them to pilgrims in the temples, to passengers on the trains, to coolies on the street, to those who attend the services in the chapels. Some keep a supply on their desks, and give a copy to every caller. Some may be wasted, but all cannot be. The Japanese are great readers, and will make good use of any literature that comes into their possession.

VII. TALKING WITH THE PEOPLE.

The missionary may call to see a man by appointment, or a man may call to see him. At home people know their duty. They have no doubt about the inspiration of the Scriptures, or about the validity of Christ's claims. The one thing to do is to urge them to accept Jesus as Lord. It is not so here. Christianity is a new faith and has a foreign aspect. Much of it they do not understand. They hear of the resurrection and of miracles, and they are perplexed. They want to learn more. One morning in Tokyo a policeman called to make inquiries. He was from the country. He had heard several sermons, and he brought four friends and a list of questions. Mrs. Garst called to see a man dying of consumption. She urged him to put his faith in Christ. He was troubled about miracles and wanted help. There is not a question of Biblical criticism or a theological vagary in Europe or America which is not repeated here, and often in an aggravated form. Men are troubled and they call to talk the matter over. It may take a month or a year, or a series of years, to satisfy the heart and the reason. The missionary gives days and weeks to this work. He takes time from reading, and from meals and from sleep for this purpose.

On the trains missionaries talk to the passengers. They are surprised and pleased that foreigners can talk Japanese. They are affable and easily approached. They talk with the priests in the temple. Dr. Neesima urged a Cabinet Minister to confess Christ. They talk to men anywhere and everywhere. They sow beside all waters. They have one work on hand. The methods may vary, but the end in view is the same. They are fishers of men. They may have to change the net or the bait, but they must catch fish, or the nets and the bait avail nothing. Paul preached sometimes. At other times he held dialogues with the people. Whatever the form of speech, his aim was that by all means he might gain some. It is so now.

Other methods are employed. Thus schools are opened for girls. The higher education of women is not popular now. It is thought that it causes them to be less modest and more self-assertive than formerly. There are those who think differently, however. One statesman said: "Give me the women of the country, and you may have the army, and the navy, and the police, and all the rest." A daimyo said to a missionary: "If you have the best welfare of our country at heart, the best thing you can do is to educate our women." Medical work is still carried on in the interest of evangelism, but there is not the need of this that there once was. There are some mission hospitals in Japan. In connection with these nurses are trained. Orphanages have been established. The children in them are brought up in the nurture and admonition of the Lord. In the recent war with China, missionaries went into the hospitals and served the patients in every way they could. The missionaries feel that the people must be reached and won to

CHRISTIANS AND MISSIONARIES IN TOKYO, JAPAN.

the faith. If one method will not answer the purpose, another is adopted.

It will be seen, I think, that missionary work is more difficult, and calls for men and women of greater ability, than is generally believed. Savage people are ready to accept what they hear. A missionary digs a well in a dry season, and they regard him as a supernatural being. They never heard of a well. They are ready to say, "The gods have come down in the likeness of man." In Rome it is said that two priests could not meet without laughing at the way they were fooling the people. The Gospel spread like wildfire. In Japan it is different. Here are ancient and venerated religions, magnificent temples, and priests without number. Christianity was under the ban for centuries. Its advocates were said to be barbarous and devilish. The missionaries have to show that it is a rational faith, and that it is worthy of all acceptation. They have to present its claims so that men and women, born and bred in Buddhism, Shintoism and Confucianism, may be convinced, and may confess that Jesus Christ is Lord to the glory of God the Father.

XIII.

THE WORK OF THE DISCIPLES OF CHRIST IN JAPAN.

THE Indianapolis Convention of 1881 urged that Japan be occupied as a mission field. George T. Smith and Charles E. Garst and their wives were the first missionaries. Mr. Smith was born in Cincinnati; served in the army; was in Libby Prison for a time; was severely wounded. He was educated in Bethany College; preached in Swampscott, Bucyrus and Warren. Josephine W. Smith was born in Cornwallis, Nova Scotia, and was married in 1874. Mr. Garst was born in Dayton, Ohio; was educated in the Iowa Agricultural College, in the Military Academy at West Point, and at Butler University. M. D. Todd, who baptized him, urged him to devote his life to the ministry of the Word and to prayer. For some time he directed his studies by mail. Laura De Laney Garst was born in Hopedale, Ohio; was educated at Union Springs and Rochester, New York; was married in 1881. After their marriage Mr. and Mrs. Garst thought much of mission work. At one time they thought of going to Africa at their own expense. The Society heard of their thoughts and plans, and asked them to go to Japan.

These four workers sailed from San Francisco for Yokohama September 27, 1883. On their arrival they engaged rooms at the Temperance Hotel, and within a few days began the study of the language. They were kindly received by the missionaries on the ground. Among those to whom they were under special obligation for advice and assistance were Mr. Goble, who had been in Japan thirty years; Mr. Loomis, of the Bible Society, and Mr. Bennett, of the American Baptist Union. They remained in Yokohama till they mastered the language sufficiently to be able to take care of themselves in the interior. They found that the treaty ports were occupied. There were more missionaries in the Concession of Tokyo than in the same area anywhere else in the world. After looking over the whole country they decided to begin work in Akita, the capital city of the province by the same name. Akita is on the northwest coast. It has a population of about 40,000, while the province has a population of 600,000. At that time there were no Christian workers, either native or foreign, in that province. Most of the people had never heard of the Christ. For several months the missionaries lived in a Japanese house as one family. Mrs. Garst was the first American woman to live in Akita, Mrs. Smith having remained behind in Yokohama on account of sickness. The people were greatly amused when she and her husband walked the streets arm in arm. They had never seen anything like that before. Many called to inquire about their purpose, and about the faith which they came to preach. The neighbors used to come in to attend family worship.

Four months after their arrival in Akita there were two baptisms. Two months later there were four more. A church was organized and the ordinances were observed. The services were conducted in Japanese. In the autumn of that year Mr. O. H. Gulick, of the American Board, visited Akita. The theater was engaged and meetings were held. Messrs. Gulick, Smith, Garst, and Kudo, the Japanese teacher and evangelist, spoke. The audiences were large and attentive. They listened from two to three hours. In this way the missionaries were able to get the claims of the Gospel before the minds of the Japanese. The next spring Mrs. Smith died. Her patience and goodness caused her to be greatly beloved. She was possessed of that meek and quiet spirit which is of great price. A chapel was built by the children in America as a memorial to her. The bell rings out several times every week and invites the people to hear the Gospel. The day Mrs. Smith was buried Dr. Macklin reached Nagasaki. He had received his medical training in Toronto and in New York. Ascertaining that there was no special need of a medical missionary in Japan, owing to the proficiency of the Japanese physicians, he went to China and opened a mission in Nankin. The next year Miss Kate Johnson and Miss Calla Harrison joined the band in Akita. They had been efficient teachers in Madison, Indiana. They began the study of the language and taught in the school which had been opened. Soon after they reached the field almost the whole of Akita was destroyed by fire. The school building was opened to receive the homeless. The mission fed the people and did all in its power to relieve distress. Their conduct in that crisis was not without good effect. That summer the work was hindered by cholera. More than 200,000 died in Japan that season. All meetings were discontinued for a time.

While carrying on the work in Akita, the missionaries did not neglect the regions beyond. They made evangelistic tours into the surrounding country and towns. Honjo was the first out-station. Here was a town of 30,000 people without any Gospel privileges. Here a number of believers were gathered into a church. About the same time some work was done in Tsuchizaki, the port of Akita. At Arakawa a church was established by a Japanese Christian. He had been a cook in Mr. Smith's family. There he became a believer. He went to Arakawa to work in the copper mines. He had little culture but much zeal. He talked the Gospel to his associates and led several of them to Christ. With some help from the mission they built a small chapel. Here they meet and observe the Lord's Supper and exhort one another. Churches were established at Innai and at Shonai. Meanwhile believers were added to the Lord in Akita. Regular preaching services, Sunday-schools and other services were held about the city. Bible-classes were organized for women, and were productive of good fruits. The women were poor and ignorant, but the Spirit helped their infirmities. Some died in hope of eternal life; some live and adorn the Gospel of God their Savior.

In 1888 G. T. Smith returned from America, whither he had gone the year previous. He had been married to Miss Candace Lhamon, and she accompanied him to the field to assist in the work. Mr. and Mrs. Eugene Snodgrass came with them. P. B. Hall came out that same year. He remained in Japan till failing health compelled him to resign. After these arrivals it was deemed expedient to scatter the forces. C. E. Garst and Eugene Snodgrass and their families, and Miss Johnson, removed to Shonai. This was a city of 25,000 people, and the center of a vast and neglected district. Here a chapel was built at an expense of $300. One man had been a notorious drunkard. He accepted Christ as his Savior, and became a wonder to all his neighbors. They said that if the Gospel could work such a mighty change, it is worthy of all acceptation.

Two years later it was decided to make Tokyo the central station. It was a good thing in many ways that they went to Akita in the beginning of the work. Mr. Greathouse, American Consul-General to Japan, said that this was one of the causes of the more general dispersion of missionaries over the Empire that took place from that time forward. It was a good thing for the workers themselves. The experience gained was invaluable. They were able to preach sooner than if they had remained in a large city where the audiences are more critical. Nevertheless, Tokyo was the natural center of the work in Japan. People are constantly going there from all the provinces. From Tokyo they could go out in all directions. The fact that they came from the capital would give them a standing that they could not have otherwise. Before leaving the north they placed the work in the hands of Japanese evangelists. At the present time Saito San has charge of the work in Akita. Noto San lives and conducts services at Tsuchizaki. Kudo San is at Innai. Yokotsura San is at Arakawa. Tashiro San is at Honjo. Shonai is vacant, but expects to be supplied soon. Kawamura San is at Akodzu. There are chapels at all these points except Innai and Akodzu, and they are arranging to build. The workers in Tokyo visit these churches from time to time. Lately Miss Johnson spent forty days on such a visit and addressed many people. Mrs. Garst spent two weeks, and so spoke that ten were baptized.

Several of the workers sent out are no longer on the field. Those in Tokyo and their work are about as follows: C. E. Garst preaches in the city and makes tours into the country. He prepares tracts for general circulation, and does whatever else he can to advance the interests of the kingdom. Mrs. Garst teaches the women and the children and assists in all the services. Miss Johnson has a charity school, a meeting for women, a Bible-class, and goes out on tours. E. S. Stevens, Dr. Nina A. Stevens, Miss Lavinia Oldham, and Miss Mary Rioch reached Japan three years ago. Mr. Stevens has charge of one chapel, teaches a Bible-class, teaches English in the Young Men's Christian Association, and studies the language. Dr. Stevens teaches a Bible-class and carries on her medical work. Miss Oldham conducts three Sunday-schools, two charity schools, two Bible meetings for women and one English Bible-class. Miss Rioch has charge of the Girls' Home and Training School, conducts a charity school and a Bible meeting for women. Mr. and Mrs. Guy came out two years ago. He has charge of one chapel, teaches a Bible-class, teaches English in the Young Men's Christian Association, superintends the buildings in course of erection, and studies the language. Mrs. Guy has charge of a charity school and a Bible meeting for women. Three Japanese evangelists aid the work, namely, Nishioka San, Imai San, and Yoshida San.

Other workers have served in Japan. Five years ago Miss Loduska Wirick was sent out by the Belle Bennett Band of Drake University. She is now at home on furlough. She did a good work, and her praises are heard on all sides. Nearly three years ago W. K. Azbill, J. M. McCaleb and wife, Miss Lucia M. Scott,

Miss Carmi Hostetter and K. Ishikawa came out. Mr. McCaleb has built a chapel and preaches in it and at a station out in the country, publishes a Sunday-school paper and tracts, and conducts a Bible-class in his own house. Miss Scott assists in the Sunday services, teaches English ten hours a week, conducts a large charity school, teaches the children singing, assists in the meetings for women, and gives some time every day to the language. Miss Hostetter has a day school and conducts meetings for women. A suitable building has been erected. She teaches in the Sunday-school and has a Bible-class for young men in her own home. In addition, she teaches English ten hours a week in a large school. Ishikawa San teaches in a college for girls; teaches English to several, and aids in preaching. Mr. Azbill returned to America within a year. His purpose was to secure more workers. He is in Japan again. He has a preaching place where meetings are held three times a week. He gives lessons to two Bible-classes in connection with the Meiji-Jo-Gakko, and gives instruction three times a week to a gentleman who is making a special study of Christianity. As he can find time he engages in literary work. He has in preparation two small volumes—one on Baptism and one on the History of the New Testament Books. With the assistance of Miss Scott and Miss Hostetter, he is arranging to put up a chapel. Miss Alice Miller reached Japan last April. She teaches three Bible-classes a week; has a class in English in the Sunday-school; with the help of several Christian girls conducts an afternoon Sunday-school, and teaches English four hours a week in the Meiji-Jo-Gakko. If the time needed for correspondence and entertainment and the study of the language is considered, it will be seen that these workers have their hands full.

The Disciples of Christ stand for precisely the same thing in Japan that they do at home, namely, the union of all believers to the end that the whole world may be evangelized. It is true that most Protestant missionaries coöperate. Still there are differences in faith and in practice that can not be hid. It is no answer to say that Buddhism has many sects. Then there are the wider differences between Protestants and Roman Catholics and Greeks. If all who call upon the name of the Lord could unite, the chief hindrance to the spread of the Gospel would be taken out of the way. The Japanese want the very thing for which we plead. They want the Christianity of Christ, and not the creeds, or dogmas, or theologies, or customs of men. One of the ablest men in Japan says that there are hardly any of his countrymen who are loyal to the creeds and dogmas which constitute the foundations of the several denominations. Common believers, he adds, have been ignorant, from the beginning, of sects and denominations; but never before have these been so coldly disregarded by the ministers and officers in the churches as now. One prevailing current throughout all denominations is church union, and this current is growing stronger and higher and swifter. Leading men in the churches pay most diligent attention to the practical question of church union, and utterly none to the preservation of the denominations. All are waiting anxiously for the time and the man to take the final step toward a glorious reformation in Japan. The Japanese desire and pray for what we desire and pray, that there may be one flock, one Shepherd. Now is the time for us to publish far and wide the truth which we hold, and thereby help the Japanese to realize that which they so devoutly wish.

XIV.

CHRISTIANITY IN JAPAN.

JAPAN was opened to the Gospel in July, 1859. Before the close of the year six missionaries, representing three American societies, were on the ground. One was here two months before the date named in the treaty. The Japanese signified their desire to receive whatever foreigners might bring, except opium and Christianity. A nation professedly Christian had forced opium on China. The Japanese thought these two things were one and inseparable. It is plain that they did not know what Christianity really is. The first workers were closely watched. All business with them was under the strictest surveillance. For a time no teacher could be engaged, and then only a government spy. For several years the people were not accessible on religious matters. When the subject was opened to one he would place his hand to his throat to indicate the extreme peril of the topic. It was impossible to find an audience that dared to listen to the preaching of the Gospel. For two hundred and fifty years it was a capital crime for a Japanese to confess faith in the Christ. Bulletin boards in all parts of the Empire were covered with edicts to that effect. The missionaries were believed to be persons who came to the "God-country" to seduce the people from their loyalty to the Emperor, and to corrupt their morals generally. Christianity was regarded with feelings of intense hatred and fear. Its advocates were exposed to insult and assault. The soldiers scowled on them as they passed them in the street, and would gladly have expelled them as barbarians from the sacred soil. The government was confessedly hostile. As late as 1868 several thousand Roman Catholics were torn from their homes and confined in prisons in different parts of the Empire. Lest any one should mistake its temper, and think that an era of toleration had begun, a new edict was placed on the boards: "*The evil sect called Christian is strictly prohibited. Suspected persons are to be reported to the respective officials, and rewards will be given.*" Years after this a book-seller in Kobe was asked if he would be allowed to sell English Bibles. His reply was that any book-seller who sold a Bible, knowing it to be a Bible, would have to go to

MISS KATE JOHNSON, TOKYO, JAPAN.

prison. It will be seen that the statement made after the signing of the treaties, to the effect that Japan was fully opened to the spread of Christianity, is far from accurate.

The missionaries were not cast down. They felt confident that in God's good time the Empire would be opened. They could not preach in public, but they did what they could. They studied the language, prepared grammars and dictionaries, translated portions of the Scriptures, and relieved the unfortunate. They opened schools and taught the English language and Western science. Dr. Hepburn opened a hospital and relieved the sufferings and attended to the spiritual needs of thousands. His surgical operations astonished the Japanese, and did much to create a demand for foreign medicine. They sought, above all, by pure and upright lives and kindness, to convince the people that they were not such beings as they believed. Dr. Verbeck was told that there were spies in his house. He said he was glad to hear it. The more spies there were about the better. There was nothing in his house or in his life to conceal.

The schools opened by the missionaries were the means under God of securing a measure of good will and toleration. The soldiers were the literary class, and they wanted to study English. They saw in English the key to Western science. Men of this class went to the missionaries and asked to be taught English. The government sent a dozen young men of rank to a mission school for the same purpose. That event marked an epoch. It indicated a change in the minds of the officials respecting the character and motives of the missionaries. It was a practical recognition of them and of their work. When schools were opened in Nagasaki and Tokyo, missionaries were invited to teach in them. We read of an English engineer and a French corporal being engaged to teach, but the missionaries were by far the most competent teachers available. They advised the government in all matters pertaining to education. They helped to secure able teachers from America and to locate the young men sent to America to be educated.

The first church was organized in Yokohama in 1872. That was thirteen years after the arrival of the first workers. It was still a crime, punishable by death, to become a Christian. The prohibitory edicts were still unrepealed. But there was a better feeling on the part of the people and the authorities. The missionaries had, by their Christian character and conduct and patient labor, dispelled many false notions. They had carried themselves before their pupils in the schools and elsewhere in such a way as to compel their respect. Embassies had been sent to Europe and America. They expected to find barbarous nations. They took a supply of salt along among their effects, thinking that they would not find that useful article for sale. They found a degree of material prosperity and a civilization far surpassing what they had anticipated, and far surpassing anything they had at home. They found that the ablest statesmen and the profoundest scholars regarded Christianity as the chief power working for righteousness and for national prosperity. They found that Christianity produced the highest type of manhood. These embassies were received by Christian nations with distinguished consideration. It was impossible for them to feel as they had felt. They could no longer regard Christian men with horror and aversion, and Christianity as a menace to the welfare of the nation. They could not but feel some reverence for the faith of Christendom. So, while the laws prohibiting Christianity were not repealed, it was believed that they would not be enforced. The laws against a Japanese returning were still in force, but they were a dead letter. It was felt that if there were any executions they would be the last. Eleven men united to form a church. Their expectations were not disappointed; they were not molested.

The next year the edicts were taken down. This was due to the work of the missionaries. In 1871, Mr. Gulick's Japanese teacher was suspected of being a Christian at heart. He was interested, but had not been baptized. At dead of night he and his wife were arrested and sent off to prison. The American Minister and Consul pleaded for his release, but their plea was without effect. After some time it was discovered that they had been imprisoned in Kyoto, and that the teacher died there. When the second embassy went to the United States to urge that the treaty be revised, Hamilton Fish told them that so long as Japan did not repeal the laws against Christianity, the United States would not consent to place its citizens under Japanese jurisdiction. The embassy denied that there was any religious persecution in Japan. Mr. DeLong, former Minister, mentioned the case of Mr. Gulick's teacher, and stated that the matter had been brought under his official notice. No answer was made to his statement, but in a little while the edicts were taken down. It was said that they were sufficiently engraved on the minds of the people. Oriental rulers are slow to admit any change of policy or any abrogation of law. The removal of the edicts virtually amounted to a declaration of liberty of conscience.

The people understood it so, and the government was quite willing that this construction should be placed upon its action. That was the last of religious persecution. The Roman Catholics that had been sent to prison five years before were liberated and allowed to return to their homes. That year twenty-nine new workers reached Japan. This was the largest number that had ever been sent out in one year. The translation of the Scriptures by a committee representing all the societies wishing to aid in the work was begun, and three years later the government ordered the observance of Sunday.

The Christianizing of Japan has grown steadily from the first. Different societies felt that they must do something in this field. Year by year the number of workers has increased. There are thirty societies operating in Japan. The whole number of Protestant missionaries is six hundred and twenty-five. There are four hundred organized churches. Of these ninety-one are self-supporting, and two hundred and seventy partially so. The Protestant Christians number thirty-nine thousand two hundred and forty. There are twenty high grade schools for boys, fifty-one for girls, and twenty theological schools, with three hundred and fifty-three students. There are two hundred and fifty-eight Japanese ministers, and two hundred and nine Bible women at work. There are fifty-seven Endeavor Societies, fifty Young Men's Christian Associations, eighteen societies of King's Daughters, twenty-nine orphanages, and one hundred night, industrial and special schools and classes. The Scriptures have been translated, and a million copies circulated; each year seventy-five thousand copies are sold. There are some forty weekly, monthly, or quarterly newspapers or magazines under Christian management. The American Board sent its first workers to Japan in 1869. This Board has more missionaries in Japan than any other. These workers have organized sixty churches with a total membership of eleven thousand. Of these churches forty are self-supporting. The converts are taught that the churches must be self-supporting and self-governing. The Roman Catholics and the Greeks are at work in this field. The Catholics report forty-nine thousand two hundred and eighty members, and the Greek Church twenty-two thousand. Once it was thought that Japan would be a Christian nation before the end of the present century. President Kozaki speaks of this thought as the air-castle of children. No one speaks now of the immediate conversion of Japan; no one doubts the ultimate triumph of the Gospel in this land.

It was the earnest desire of the missionaries that they should coöperate to form one native church. They wanted to secure unity of name and organization. They wished all converts to be perfectly joined together in the same mind and the same judgment, to all speak the same thing, and to wear the same name. They sought not to import the differences that exist at home. The Japanese cannot understand these. If they did, they have no interest in perpetuating them. Their desire was to reproduce the apostolic doctrine, the apostolic ordinances, and the apostolic life. Their purpose was opposed and thwarted by friends at home who wanted to be able to see and count results. Among the workers love and good will prevail. They respect one another's convictions. They unite as far as they can. Three bodies united to form one. These were substantially alike in doctrine and in polity. The preaching and teaching of the missionaries is pre-eminently Biblical. This brings them close together. In the presence of Buddhism or Confucianism and Shintoism and secularism, they feel the need of harmony and coöperation. The lengthy creeds of Christendom have no place here. Whether men like it or not, there is a necessity for a return to the simplicity of the apostolic church. It is worthy of special mention that the eleven men that formed themselves into a church in Yokohama called their organization a "Church of Christ." The missionary was a representative of the Reformed Church in America, but that was no reason for calling the church in Japan a Reformed Church. These men knew nothing of John Calvin or of his teaching as distinguished from that of Luther. The churches organized by the workers under the American Board call themselves "Churches of Christ." They are Congregational in polity, but that is not intimated in the name adopted. The three churches that united called the resultant the "Japanese Church of Christ." These churches are Presbyterian in their government, but that is an incident. In Japan what they wish to emphasize is that they belong to Christ, and stand for him. The church of the future will be a united church with a scriptural creed.

XV.

TRAMPLING ON THE CROSS.

In the Imperial Museum in Tokyo I saw some engravings representing Christ on the cross. The plates are of bronze, and are fastened to blocks of wood. These engravings have a history. Nothing in the museum stirred me so deeply. It is generally known that Christianity entered Japan about the middle of the sixteenth century. For a time it was regarded with favor. After a while, for reasons of state, the authorities decided to extirpate it. In the persecution resorted to with this end in view, these engravings were used to discover secret believers. The people were called upon to trample on the figure of Christ on the cross. As many as did so were not molested; those that refused were turned over to the tormentors.

Francis Xavier landed in Japan in 1549. In Malacca he made the acquaintance of two Japanese exiles. These were instructed and baptized. Xavier heard of a Japanese prince who desired that Christian teachers be sent to him that he might learn from their own lips the truths of Christianity. His heart had long been set on visiting Japan. The way now seemed open. Taking the two Japanese Christians as helpers, he sailed for Japan. The prince received him with marked courtesy. Xavier studied the language, but only a little. He was never able to preach in Japanese so as to be understood. Speaking through interpreters, he won many to the faith. Nobles, priests, scholars, and the poor and ignorant, were among the converts. Xavier went to the capital, but found it desolated by war and fires. He tried to preach, but could not get the attention of the people. He was disgusted, and left Japan disheartened by the realities of missionary work. He was in the country less than three years, but he left an impression that has never been effaced. He died soon after at the age of forty-six. The work did not cease with his departure. Others took up the task he abandoned, and won great success. Christianity spread rapidly in the South, and was carried to the farthest provinces of the North. In 1581 the converts amounted to one hundred and fifty thousand. The staff of workers numbered one hundred and thirty-eight. They were Jesuits without exception. Two years later an embassy was sent by the believing princes to Rome. In their letters they declared their gratitude for the happiness vouchsafed to them through the knowledge of Christ. They begged the Pope to look with favor upon them and upon all the Christians in their dominions. They declared themselves the vassals of the Holy See. This embassy was received in Rome with the greatest honors. At one time there were six hundred thousand Christians in the Empire. The Japanese say there were two million.

The Portuguese were the first to enter Japan as traders. The Jesuits came with them. The profitableness of this trade led the Spaniards to send ships to Japan. With the Spaniards came the Franciscans and the Dominicans. The priests and monks soon began to quarrel among themselves. The Jesuits were first on the ground, and regarded all others as interlopers. Each party circulated evil reports about the motives and intentions of the other. Soon after this the English and Dutch arrived on the scene. They wanted a share in the profits of this trade. They saw that it was largely through the influence of the Jesuits that the Portuguese had a monopoly of the commerce with Japan. They went to work to break down this influence. They confirmed the evil reports that the Jesuits invented about the Franciscans, and the evil reports that the Franciscans invented about the Jesuits. High Japanese officials became suspicious of all parties. A sea captain was asked how Spain was able to conquer so many nations. His reply was, "Our country sends missionaries to convert the heathen, and after a while we send the army. Then the Christians help us, and the victory is easy and complete." Hideyoshi, the greatest statesman and soldier of Japan, was in power at the time. He resolved that he would make such a course impossible. He issued an edict calling upon all foreign religious teachers to leave the country within twenty days, on penalty of death. He declared that it was wrong for God's country to accept a false faith from a foreign nation.

When the Jesuits had the power in Japan, they prevailed upon the princes to compel their subjects to follow their example and to adopt the Christian faith. One prince gave his subjects the option of conversion or exile. Another did the same, and robbed Buddhist priests of their temples and lands. Princes used their authority to advance the cause of Catholicism. Hideyoshi regarded the foreign religious teachers and their doctrine as a source of danger to the country. With him the question was purely political. The two systems could not live in peace side by side. His thought was that the simplest and safest course was to expel the weaker of the two. He gave orders that the European and Japanese members of the religious orders should be sent out of the country, that all churches should be torn down, and all the converts compelled to renounce their faith. The priests were prudent, and shut themselves up till the storm should become a calm. They gave attention to the preparation of books and to the education of a native ministry. Meanwhile they carried on their work quietly. The converts numbered ten thousand a year.

It was not long, however, until the persecutions broke out afresh. This was caused in part by the conduct of the Portuguese and Spanish priests. Their national and sectarian antipathies were aggravated by contact on the field. Each slandered the other. The Buddhist priests did all in their power to poison the minds of the rulers against the foreigners. The government went to work to destroy Christianity, root and branch. Rewards were offered to any who would inform where believers were to be found. Thus three hundred pieces of silver were offered to one who would inform against a father; two hundred to one who would inform against a brother, and fifty to any one who would inform against a catechist. Later these rewards were doubled. It is said by an historian that these persecutions have never been surpassed for cruelty and brutality, or for the courage and constancy of the sufferers. We are told how they were hurled from lofty precipices, of their being buried alive, or being torn asunder by oxen, of their being placed in rice bags and heaped together and set on fire. Others were tortured before death by having spikes driven under the nails of their hands and feet. Others were shut up in cages and starved with food in sight. In one year three hundred and eighty-four persons were tortured, including beating with clubs, and burning and torture by the boiling springs. The hot water was poured over them, and they were compelled to breathe the suffocating sulphurous air which the springs emitted. In some instances the back was slit open, and the boiling water poured on the raw flesh. Naked women were compelled to walk on their hands and knees through the streets of the city. Some were hung by the feet over a deep pit. The suffering was unimaginable. The pressure on the brain was terrible; blood was forced from the mouth and nostrils. The victims lived sometimes eight or nine days before death came to their relief. One girl lived fifteen days, and died in the faith. Twelve persons were captured in hiding, near Nagasaki;

they were branded with a hot iron on the forehead and then on each cheek, and then, because they would not recant, they were burned. Prices were placed on the heads of priests. If a priest was found in any household, the whole family was put to death. The early history of the church has no brighter pages than those that contain the records of martyrdoms in Japan. Parents took their children with them to death rather than let them be educated in the ancient faith.

Some were driven to desperation and raised the standard of rebellion. In connection with some political malcontents they seized and fortified a castle. It took an army of 160,000 men two months to reduce this fortress. Had it not been for the big Dutch ship and guns which the Japanese borrowed, it may have been that they would not have reduced it at all. Every man and woman and child in the castle was put to death. Then it was that the government resolved to exterminate Christianity at any cost. Hundreds of native priests and missionaries were collected and placed on board junks and sent out of the country. Buddhist priests were deputed to paganize the converts. An edict prohibiting "the evil sect" was published in all parts of the Empire. Another said that so long as the sun shines no Christian shall enter Japan and no native leave it. Griffis says that all over the Empire, in every city, town, village and hamlet, by the roadside, ferry, or mountain pass; at every entrance to the capital, stood the public notice boards, on which, with prohibitions against the great crimes that disturb the relations of society and government, was one tablet, written with a deeper brand of guilt, with a more hideous memory of blood, with a more awful terror of torture, than when a like superscription was affixed at the top of a cross that stood between two thieves on a little hill outside of Jerusalem. "That name would bate the breath, blanch the cheek, smite with fear as an earthquake shock. It was a synonym of sorcery, sedition, and all that was hostile to the purity of the home or to the peace of society. That name was Christ."

Nagasaki was the center and stronghold of the new faith. A governor was appointed and commissioned to root out every vestige of Christianity. He went to work resolved upon complete success. He selected a headman for every street and an overseer for every five houses. He held them responsible for their districts. Not content with that, he himself went through every street and into every house, and examined every person. If the inmates were not Christians, or had renounced their faith, he did not trouble them.

1. Josephine Smith's Grave.
2. Josephine Smith Memorial Chapel, Akita, Japan.
3. Sue A. Robinson's Grave, Hurda, India.

If not, they were sent off to be tortured. In order to make assurance doubly sure, he adopted the novel method already alluded to in this article to detect secret believers. He had a picture of Christ on the cross, and he required the people to demonstrate their unbelief by trampling on it. This picture was carried from house to house till the whole city was finished. The head of the house, the whole family, servants of both sexes, old and young, any visitors or sojourners, were called into the room. Each was asked to set his foot on the plate. Infants were carried by their mothers and made to place their feet on the image of the Crucified. The Japanese who worked in the Dutch factory were required to do the same. Before the persecution began, whole districts were virtually Christian; Nagasaki was distinctively a Christian city. In 1567 it is said that there was hardly a person within its borders who was not a Christian. In 1629 not one was left who would acknowledge that he was a believer. The governor was proud of the fact that he had accomplished the task assigned him.

Before the end of the seventeenth century it was believed that Christianity had been so completely eradicated from Japan that its existence was historical. It was regarded only as "an awful scar on the national memory." No vestige of it was believed to remain. The Dutch had one trading port near Nagasaki. Here less than twenty Hollanders lived under surveillance. They were allowed one ship a year to come and trade with Japan. They were granted this because they did not engage in any religious propagandism; their sole object was trade. But the fire smouldered for more than two centuries; it had not gone out. After Japan was opened, several thousand Catholics were discovered in the villages near Nagasaki. Chamberlain says that without priests, without teachers, without almost any published instructions, they had kept alive a knowledge of the religion which their ancestors had professed. They had the Lord's Prayer, and a few other prayers, and the ordinance of baptism. There was great joy over this discovery. But the old hatred and fear were still alive. In 1868 the government arrested four thousand of these people and sent them off to prison. They were scattered among thirty-four prisons, and condemned to hard labor. Lest any one should misunderstand the spirit of the Emperor, new edicts were put up. These said: "The evil sect called Christians is strictly prohibited. Such persons should be reported to the proper officers, and rewards will be given." These edicts were not taken down till 1873. Then these Christians were set at liberty and returned to their homes. The Constitution guarantees to every Japanese religious liberty.

This incident shows how useless it is to fight against God. It would be as easy to keep out the sunshine, or keep out the tides, as to keep out Christianity. Fire and sword cannot prevail against the Omnipotent. It is his purpose that the whole world shall be filled with his glory, and his purpose is never defeated. Tycoon and Mikado may issue prohibitory edicts, but their edicts shall come to naught. Yesterday I walked the streets of Nagasaki and saw Christians everywhere. The hilltops are crowned with Christian schools and chapels and homes. I looked into the homes of the people where the inquisitors did their work, and where the terrified inmates trampled on the cross. I saw the rock in the harbor from which those who refused to recant were thrown. In the bay are ships representing all Christian nations. The Shogunate, which originated and directed the persecution, has passed away like a dream of night. It shows, too, something of the indestructibility of Christianity. If a corrupted faith could survive for centuries in the absence of the Scriptures and qualified leaders, what may we not expect from Christianity in its purity and where its exponents have the Word of God in their own tongue? It shows us once more that the Japanese are not so fickle as is sometimes claimed. Perhaps no other people would have resisted unto blood with fewer cases of apostasy, or would have endured so long with so little to cheer and encourage them. No one can pay a higher tribute to the Japanese than to recite this chapter in their history. No other answer is needed when they are charged with being as unstable as water. This incident affords all who labor and pray for the evangelization of Japan sure ground for the conviction that their labor is not in vain in the Lord.

XVI.

SOME CURIOUS THINGS IN JAPAN.

For several centuries Japan had no intercourse with the rest of the world. As a result, her people differ in many respects from Western nations. One of the things that impress a stranger is the fact that mechanics and tradesmen sit at their work. A blacksmith has his forge and anvil and vise on the ground. He sits on the floor while using his hammer and tongs. He can blow his bellows with his hand or with his toes, as he prefers. A cooper sits at his work. He uses his feet to hold his materials in place. Carpenters, stone-cutters and cabinet-makers sit at their work. An American could do almost nothing in that posture. A Japanese does nothing while standing that he could do while seated. What is true of mechanics is true of merchants. They do not stand while waiting for customers, or while trying to sell their goods. They sit on their feet, and are prepared to bow to any one who calls to examine their wares. Hotel clerks and book-keepers in the stores sit on the floor behind their desks. The Buddha is represented as sitting on a lotus blossom. Having attained to perfect knowledge, and having conquered passion, he reposes in eternal slumber. He is never represented as "going about doing good."

One sees few labor-saving machines. The Japanese have not used their intellects to make life easier and more comfortable for themselves. They have not utilized the mighty forces of nature to bear their burdens and to do their work. There are a few high smoke-stacks, but these are confined to the large cities. These are of yesterday and represent foreign capital and foreign methods. Most of the articles produced in Japan are produced by hand and in a small way. Horses are used, but these horses are either weak or the people think they are. You will see a man in the shafts pulling with a breaststrap, while a horse is pulling ahead of him, and his wife or his boy leads the horse. The load may not weigh over six hundred pounds. An American horse would pull the load and the man and his family, and scarcely feel the burden. In the North of Japan I saw men driving piles by hand. A steam hammer would do more work in an hour than these men could do in a week. Men saw logs with a hand-saw. One of our workers told a carpenter how timber was sawed in America. The carpenter did not believe him. He said, "I have been in this business twenty-five years, and I know you are saying what is not true." As simple a thing as a wheelbarrow is not seen anywhere. Men carry clay and stone on their shoulders. Large junks are propelled by oars or poles. A steam tug would drive a fleet of such craft. Where labor is so cheap as it is in Japan men have not felt that it was necessary to make steam and electricity do their work. It has not occurred to them that the forces of nature are the cheapest and most efficient of all servants.

Policemen are everywhere. They are found on almost every corner in the cities. They are in the smallest villages. There are ten times as many policemen in Tokyo as there are in Chicago or London. The people are quiet and orderly. I saw but one drunken man and no fighting. The Japanese are easily excited. It is cheaper to prevent than to put down a riot. The police are feared and respected. They represent the imperial government. They do not bear the sword in vain. You see soldiers in all the streets. They are going to and fro all the time. An officer rides along, and a footman runs before to clear the way if need be. The footman carries his umbrella when the sun does not shine. In a monarchial country there is greater need of police and a standing army than in a republic. In a republic the people are rulers. That form of government could not exist if the people were not instinctively law-abiding. The home of the President of the United States is very much like the home of any other gentleman. It needs no deep and wide moats, no high walls, no gates and sentries.

The dress of the people challenges attention. The ordinary dress of a man is not unlike that of a woman, except that a woman wears a large bustle. This is worn as an ornament. In summer the people as a rule wear nothing on their heads. The women arrange their hair tastefully; they wear neither hat nor bonnet. I have seen one Japanese woman, and only one, wearing a hat. She was dressed throughout as a foreigner. The jinricksha men wear a hat that looks like a wash-basin turned upside down. It is cool and comfortable. Some wear a cloth tied about their heads. You will see tens of thousands with no covering of any kind. Nearly every man and woman carries an umbrella. In winter both men and women wear something to protect their heads against the cold. Their foot-gear is peculiar. Many wear nothing. Others wear straw sandals. They are said to be very easy on the feet. Many wear wooden clogs. They add about three inches to their stature. They are held on the feet by a thong which passes between the great toe and the next. Stockings are made with an apartment for the great toe. When several hundred people get off a train and walk on a stone pavement the noise is almost deafening. The clogs are a convenience in muddy weather. Soldiers, policemen, trainmen, mail-carriers and many others are dressed like Americans. In the interior the women that carry firewood and hay and truck on their backs are dressed like men. More remarkable than anything else is the scantiness of the dress of the multitudes. Thousands of men wear nothing but a loin-cloth. The low-necked dresses worn in some circles at home would not provoke any criticism or comment here.

The houses are unlike ours. There is no cellar; because of the frequent earthquakes, cellars are dispensed with. There is no chimney. The fire is in a pit in the center of a room. The smoke goes out in its own way. As the house is open more or less on every side, the smoke goes out without any trouble. The houses are small and low. In Tokyo there are only a few houses three stories high. Most of them are one story. The majority are of wood. It is not at all strange that the average life of a house is seven years. Because fires are so frequent, many families have a room that is fireproof. In this room the treasures are usually kept. It is only recently that the Japanese began to use glass. They used paper instead. There is almost no privacy about an ordinary home. The passerby can see into every room in the house. The family cooks and eats where it can be seen by all. The first thing a merchant does in the morning is to take down the whole front of his place. His goods are all virtually on the street. There is nothing that is not in view. In hotels the bath-tub is in a place to which men and women resort. The wealthy people live in a compound. In the castles of the nobles, the retainers occupied the front rooms and the families the rooms in the rear. If an attack was made on the castle, the retainers were expected to bear the brunt of it. The best rooms were in the back part of the building. But the houses of the common people are open on all sides.

The Japanese do not shake hands; they bow instead. Friends meet and bow. Christians meet in church and do the same. When the meeting is in a room where the people sit on the floor, the bowing surprises a visitor. They touch the floor several times with their heads. Everyone that comes in bows to those present. This bowing takes time, and seems somewhat tedious at first, but it is not so to them. They are not in such haste as we are. They are anxious that what is done should be done properly. They would rather sacrifice time than good taste. They do not demand that a sermon be compressed within thirty minutes or less. No matter how long one speaks, if he has a message for them, they will listen without manifesting any sign of weariness. They do not look at their watches and show by their restlessness that they are eager for the end. A friend told me of a service held in a temple on the invitation of the priest in charge, which lasted from nine one morning till one the next. Nothing pleases them better than three or four sermons in succession. The theaters are open from ten in the morning till seven in the evening. The Japanese are the most patient and polite people on the globe. They take time to be courteous. They would rather live on less than disregard the proprieties of life.

There are other strange things in this beautiful country. For example, you take off your shoes before entering a house or a hotel or a temple. It would be regarded as an insult not to do this. It would be the same as to walk on the table or a bed with shoes on. The floors are covered with mats that would be damaged if this was not done. The shoes are made with this end in view. They can be removed in an instant. At home we take off our hats. Children are carried on the back rather than in the arms. Sometimes they are tied in position. Sometimes a garment is worn with a place in it for the child. A sister or mother can play or work with an infant on her back. The child falls asleep. Its head swings about. The flies gather upon its face. It does not seem to mind these things. Men and women sèldom ride or walk together. The carriages are made for one person. Young men and young women do not associate as in America. The streets are full of people, but each one is under his own umbrella and managing his own affairs. Horses are led, and not driven. A man goes before and the horse follows. Books begin where ours end. Instead of beginning at the left of the page and reading to the right, Japanese begin at the right and read from the top to the bottom. What we call foot-notes are placed at the top of the pages. Titles follow the name, while ours precede it. Thus we say Mr. Tennyson; they say Tennyson Mr. These differences are on the surface, and are slight. There are many evidences that the Japanese are bone of our bone and flesh of our flesh. We differ in language and in methods of work and in habits of thought and in social customs, but we are members of one family. We are children of the same Father. We have been redeemed by the same sacrifice. We are heirs of a common inheritance. One is not long in Japan before one begins to feel that he is at home. He soon realizes that he is among friends and kinsmen.

Japan is becoming more like a Western nation every day. Dr. Greene says that Japan is in the East, but really belongs to the West. Changes are taking place all the time. Many men are adopting the foreign dress. The hat is worn by thousands who dress in the Japanese style. Foreign shoes are worn. The native dress, picturesque and comfortable as it is, is giving place. Labor-saving machines are coming slowly into use. Already we see the railway and the street-car taking the place of the coolies. The nobles used to be carried on the shoulders of men; now they are borne in special trains. The sewing machine is seen in many places. Modern tools are exposed for sale and are seen in use. Cobble-stones were once widely used to hold shingles in place; now wire nails are used instead, to a certain extent. The people are learning to shake hands. Husbands and wives go out together as they did not formerly. Some of the brightest men in Japan have been educated in America or in Europe. Others have traveled extensively. They are determined that their country shall in no respect be behind any other nation on the globe. The changes that have already taken place are great; the changes that are taking place now are even greater.

XVII.

FROM TOKYO TO KOBE.

THE original plan contemplated a visit to the South of Japan, after visiting the North, and after seeing the work in Tokyo. The South is by far the most populous part of the Empire. It is destined to become more and more so. There is some thought of opening a work in the South. Accordingly, C. E. Garst came with me as far as Kobe, that he might survey the field and ascertain its needs. Dr. Butchart, of China, had been in Japan for a few weeks, hoping to be able to expel the malaria from his system. He was on his way home, and joined us. The morning we left Tokyo the Christians began to call at an early hour. They accompanied us to the station. Some walked five miles to see us off and to say *farewell*. The Japanese welcome the coming and speed the departing guest. The missionaries were out in force. I took my leave of them, feeling that they had a difficult task in hand, and feeling that they are doing their best to perform it. When I left I had a greater admiration for them, if possible, and a higher opinion of their practical wisdom and persistency and faith and patience than I had when I arrived. God bless this faithful band.

Our first stop was at Kamakura. This place was once the capital of Japan. Once it had a population of a million souls; now it is a small village of fishermen. On the shore the ambassadors who came from Kublai Khan to demand the submission of Japan were beheaded. Here is a colossal image of Buddha. Once it was inclosed by a temple; now there is a temple inside. This image is nearly fifty feet high and ninety-seven feet in circumference. The head measures seventeen feet from ear to ear. Bayard Taylor spoke of it as the most complete work of the Japanese genius, in regard both to art and the religious sentiment. The body of the image is of bronze, the eyes are of pure gold. We visited the temple of the Goddess of Mercy and the temple of the God of War. The image of the goddess is thirty feet high, and is seen by the light of candles. Recently the priests of Kamakura announced the death of Christianity, and fixed the time for the burial. Such talk has been heard before. A Roman Em-

MRS. GUY'S CHARITY SCHOOL, TOKYO, JAPAN.

peror wrote on the coins of the Empire, "The Christian religion has been destroyed." Somehow Christianity has a charmed life and disappoints the predictions and the boasts of those who would destroy, and those who think they have destroyed it. Mr. Garst told a funny incident. A priest began his address in the usual style, "I am a fool, and my speech is folly and not worthy of attention." A Christian in the audience cried out, "Hear! Hear!" The priest got hot with anger, and called upon his assistants to put him out.

Having spent two hours in Kamakura, we took the train for Yokohama. We called first at the Bible House. The British and Foreign Bible Society, the Scotch and American Societies coöperate. These societies stand back of every evangelistic effort in Japan. They employ seventy colporteurs. The agent told us that the attitude of the government towards the sale of the Scriptures was neutral. Other books are sold under license; the Bible is not. To license it would be an implied indorsement. The government does not prohibit, and it does not encourage the sale. In the war with China, the highest officials gave the society permission to distribute Bibles among the soldiers. The agent feels that this permission is the harbinger of a new era. The Emperor has consented to receive a Bible. A copy is being prepared. It will be ready in a few months for presentation. One of the most hopeful things alluded to by the agent was the Bible Readers' Union. There are eleven thousand people in Japan reading the same lesson each day. About half of these are not believers; a number are priests. Yokohama is well supplied with missionaries and mission schools. That night we had an earthquake that shook the house and aroused the people. The girls squealed, but no harm was done. This is the third shock I felt in Japan.

The next morning we took the train and resumed our journey. Most of the day we were riding along the base of the peerless Fujiyama, the sacred mountain of Japan. We saw green fields, noble hills, beautiful rivers and the sea. There is no prettier country on the globe. We saw scores of quaint villages and the busy villagers. We stopped for the night at Nagoya. At this place there is one of the most famous castles of Japan. A friend in the foreign office sent us a ticket of admission. In the feudal times every lord had a castle. Most of these have been destroyed; several have been preserved. This one escaped the vandals. The deep and wide moats, the high walls flanked with towers, give one an idea of what war in the middle ages was. Before cannons came into use, one of these castles would hold an army in check for years. The garrison might starve; it could not be conquered. In this city we saw some of the porcelain and cloisonne work for which the Japanese artists are so justly famous. In the feudal times, the wealth was in the hands of a few. Human life was cheap. There were a few lines only in which genius could exert itself. The nobles wanted silk fabrics and vases for flowers, and scrolls and pictures to adorn their palaces. The Raphaels and Angelos and Bacons and Shakespeares were put to work to supply this demand. A man might spend his life on one picture or on one vase. In this way the arts that adorn life were brought into a very high degree of perfection. The Japanese are naturally artistic; otherwise they could not have produced so many beautiful things. We called at an orphanage, and found to our surprise that it was a Buddhist institution. The priests have been driven to engage in benevolent work in self-defense. They say, "Unless we stir ourselves, we cannot hope to hold our ground against such energetic, untiring propagandism." In one place they organized a kindergarten in opposition to one of our schools. In another, they organized their young people into an Endeavor Society. Here they were driven to establish an orphanage.

The next evening we were in Kyoto. This city was the capital of Japan for more than a thousand years. In 1868 the Emperor and his court removed to Tokyo. Since then, Kyoto has lost in political importance, but it is still incomparably the richest city in the Empire in historical associations. Kyoto was and is the religious center of Japan. There are 3,500 Buddhist temples, and 8,000 priests, and 2,500 Shinto shrines and priests. Some of these temples cost enough to endow a dozen colleges. Their grounds and buildings and altars are magnificent. In one there is an image of Buddha fifty-eight feet high. The face is thirty feet long. There is a bell that weighs sixty-three tons. It is fourteen feet high, nine feet in diameter, and nine inches thick. The finest temple in Kyoto is a new one. The old one was destroyed by fire. Several millions were required to rebuild. An appeal was issued to the nation. The responses were prompt and heavy. Women gave their hair to haul the timber. The main building is two hundred and ten feet by one hundred and seventy. The ridge of the roof is one hundred and fifty feet from the ground. This temple is a work of real genius. In another temple there are 33,333 images of the Goddess of Mercy. Kyoto is a city of temples. You see them in all directions. One street has almost no other buildings from end to end. The temple grounds afford the children a fine place for play. Families hold picnics under the shade of the trees. Birds build their nests under the eaves and in the altars. The temples, as such, are dreary places. The priests are the least interesting class of people I have seen in Japan. They smoke their pipes, drink tea and sake, recite their prayers, and do little else. Near one of the temples is the "Ear Monument." An army was sent to conquer Korea. Instead of sending home the heads of the vanquished, they cut off 10,000 pairs of ears and pickled them in salt and sake and sent them home. They were buried and a mound built over them and a monument placed on the mound.

We were fortunate enough to get permission to see the palace and the castle. The Mikado is said to be the Son or King of Heaven. The palace is built after the same general pattern as the temples. We saw the place where he worshiped his ancestors and the place where he was worshiped. We saw the rooms where he lived and the rooms in which he studied and transacted business. He was regarded as a god and not as a man. He never appeared in public. His subjects, except his wives and concubines and highest ministers, never saw his face. He sat on a mat on a throne behind a curtain. Messages were repeated to the women, and they repeated them to him. His feet were never allowed to touch the earth. When he went abroad in the city, he rode in a car closely curtained and drawn by bullocks. The people were taught that they would be smitten with blindness if they saw him. When he went out, the streets were deserted. The people went into their houses and closed the doors and windows. The greatest nobles threw themselves on the ground and allowed the royal cortege to pass by. Now the Emperor is a man. He is seen by the people. When he goes abroad the streets are thronged. Banners are everywhere. The cheers of the multitude are gratefully acknowledged. The castle is a far more splendid building than the palace. Here the Shogun held his court. Here the daimyos came to confer with their lord. I saw nothing in Nikko or in Tokyo so fine as this. It gives one some idea of the power and wealth and magnificence of the Shoguns. The moats have been filled; parts of the walls have been removed; but enough is left to show what this castle was before the Restoration.

More to us than temples, or palace, or castle, is the Doshisha University. This institution is across from the palace. Prof. Albrecht showed us the buildings and some of the work. The Doshisha was founded by Neesima. The story of his life is stranger than fiction. A Japanese lad got hold of an Atlas of the United

States. From this he got some knowledge of America. At once he wished to go to that country. He picked up a tract which gave a synopsis of the Bible. In this he read of God as a Creator. That was a new thought. He reasoned, "If God created me, he owns me." He so thirsted for knowledge that he often read till cock-crow. He managed to get a little English. He ran away from his master, got to Shanghai, and from Shanghai to Boston. Here Alpheus Hardy, a Boston merchant, took him as his own son. He sent him to Phillips Academy, then to Amherst, and then to Andover. While in the academy, he confessed his faith in Christ. While he was in Andover, the second Japanese embassy visited America. He was asked to serve the embassy as an interpreter. He did so. He visited all the capitals of Europe as well as the principal cities of America. He made a special study of the systems of education. After he left the Seminary, he wanted the American Board to establish a Christian school in Japan. He did not get much encouragement. At the annual meeting held in Rutland, he was allowed to make a plea for funds for this school. He spoke with a broken voice and tears. At that meeting $5,000 was pledged. That was the nucleus of the Doshisha. He was urged to open the school in Kyoto. He thought that center and citadel of Buddhism was the last place in Japan for a Christian school. He was told that he might as well try to fly to the moon as to put up buildings; it would not be allowed. After much thought and prayer, the school was opened in a few dingy rooms of an old mansion. There were two teachers and eight students. There was no course of study. The appliances were of the rudest character. When he sought permission to teach Christianity, he was told to teach it under the head of moral science. The priests and magistrates were up in arms. They were determined to crush the school. Neesima's connection with the Japanese embassy years before gave him friends at court. These friends never deserted him or turned a deaf ear to his appeals. He did what no foreigner could have done. He bought land and began to put up buildings. There are now five buildings on the grounds and eleven dormitories not far away. J. N. Harris, of Connecticut, gave $100,000 to found a School of Science. Mrs. B. W. Clarke, of Brooklyn, gave $10,000 in memory of her son, to build a Theological Hall. A cabinet minister invited some rich friends to dinner. He spoke to them about this school and its needs. These men raised $30,000 in silver for a school of Law and Economics. The whole number of students enrolled from the first is 3,358; the whole number of graduates, 296.

Of the graduates 106 are preaching. Of the graduates seventy per cent. are Christians. No other school in Japan has produced so many Christian workers along so many lines. The Doshisha is spoken of as the center of religious life and thought in the Empire. In connection with it are the Girls' School, a Hospital and a Training School for nurses. In the Doshisha there are thirty-five Japanese and eight foreign teachers. We visited Dr. Albrecht and Dr. M. L. Gordon in their homes and broke bread with them. Dr. Gordon told us an amusing incident. Talking once with a nobleman who had visited Japan, he asked him how he was impressed with the country. He replied that he thought the "billiard tables of Yokohama were better than those in Tokyo." That was all. We called to see President Kozaki. He is a Japanese and lives in Japanese style. We found him a genial gentleman, ready to give us any information needed. He told us that the Japanese are a religious people. There can be no doubt of this. There are 72,000 Buddhist temples and 56,500 Shinto shrines in the country. Dr. Gordon took us to Neesima's grave on a hill overlooking the city. We felt that we were on holy ground. An unhewn block of stone marks his grave. He wished no other monument. The Doshisha will perpetuate his name better than any monument of bronze or marble. His purpose was not merely to give instruction in English and other branches of learning, but to impart higher moral and spiritual principles, and to train up, not only men of science and learning, but men of conscientiousness and sincerity. He believed that a nation needs manners, but it needs morals more. He believed that pure morality must be based on Christianity. Near by is the grave of Lieut. George C. Foulk. He was born in Pennsylvania and educated at Annapolis. He resigned from the United States Navy, where he had won a reputation for brilliant scholarship, and returning to Japan from Korea, where he rendered his country important service, he became a most valued member of the Doshisha faculty and an enthusiastic evangelistic worker. The students placed a slab over his grave with this inscription, "The zeal of thine house hath eaten me up." This sentence fitly portrayed his life. As we left the cemetery full of thoughts concerning Neesima and his work, I remembered one of his sentences, "Advance on your knees."

Leaving Kyoto we came to Osaka. This city is the Chicago of Japan. It is the commercial center of the nation. We climbed to the top of a pagoda and saw the whole city and the country adjacent. After visiting a few temples we called at the penitentiary.

There are 3,000 convicts in this prison. Some are lads; some are in the prime of life; some are old and gray. It was a sad sight. We saw them fed. For supper they had a ball of cold rice and wheat, and a cup of hot water. We ran out from Osaka to Nara. This place was the capital of Japan for eight years. In one temple there is an image of Buddha larger than the one in Kamakura. In a Shinto temple we saw two dancing girls. The priest sang something like a dirge, and the girls made some movements and called them a dance. In a village on the way is the oldest existing Buddhist temple in Japan. It was built in the sixth century. There are pictures in it said to be thirteen hundred years old. One curious thing was shown us, namely, the left eye of the Buddha. Our next stop was made at Kobe. This is an open port, and is much like Yokohama. We visited the Girls' School of the American Board. The buildings are well adapted to the needs of the work. In Kobe we met, among others, a member of the celebrated Gulick family. Six brothers and one sister gave their lives to the work of missions. Their parents were missionaries in the Hawaiian Islands. Two members of the third generation are already in the field.

XVIII.

FROM KOBE TO SHANGHAI.

At Kobe we took passage on the Empress of China for Shanghai. The Empress is a fine ship. Her officers are courteous to all. This line is becoming deservedly popular. It follows the short route from America to Japan and China. I have never been on another ship where all the passengers seemed so comfortable and happy. There were between forty and fifty missionaries on board. Some one said that this was the largest number of workers that ever reached China on one ship. Some had been home on furlough and were returning. They were eager to reach the field and enter upon the work. Among these were Mr. and Mrs. Saw, of Nankin. It was a great joy to meet them. About half the number are coming out for the first time. A glance shows that they are above the average in ability and scholarship. An acquaintance deepens the impression. The societies select men and women with great care.

Among the veterans, Dr. William Ashmore is easily the Nestor. He has been on the field forty-five years. Long before Japan admitted any Christian workers, he was in the Flowery Kingdom. He has seen the number of Christians in China increase from three hundred and fifty to fifty thousand. His home is in Swatow. This city is the center of operations reaching many miles into the interior. Dr. Ashmore is a fine specimen of physical manhood. His head and face and voice reminded me of the gifted and lamented Isaac Errett. He is a large man in every way. In a busy career he has kept abreast of the best scholarship of the age. On one point he differs from many of his brethren. He believes that the work of missionaries is that of preaching the Gospel. He thinks that the medical work is a good thing in opening a district, but that, like the miraculous gift of healing in the early church, its value is temporary. He would use schools to train helpers and evangelists only. In his opinion, medical work and educational work are good things, but these are not the works a missionary should engage in. Dr. Ashmore said he knew he was regarded as heterodox on these points, but he is satisfied that he is right. Dr.

McGregor was born in Aberdeen, Scotland. He has been in Amoy, China, thirty-one years. He is yet young and strong. He has seen great things; he expects to see still greater. When he reached the field in 1864, there were one hundred believers in that district. There are three thousand now. There are nineteen self-supporting churches. The Gospel is preached at seventy stations. He told me of a young student who had heard the Gospel from a barber. When his father learned that he attended church he was greatly concerned. He followed him and dragged him out and beat him. He drove him out of his house. He felt that his son's prospects would be ruined if he became a Christian. The son confessed his faith in Christ, was educated for the ministry, and is now the pastor of a self-supporting church. Dr. Barclay has been in Formosa twenty-one years. He has lived in the southern part. His report is encouraging. He believes that the war will help Formosa. The country will be advertised, and people and workers will flock thither. He showed us a curious document. It is a passport issued by the Republic of Formosa. It runs thus: "This is to certify that the Formosa Republic grants protection to Thomas Barclay, of Great England, and calls upon all officials, gentry, soldiers and people to carry it out. Those who refuse will be prosecuted." A republic in the Orient! This shows how far American ideas have been spread. In Brazil, in Central America, in France, in Hawaii, and in distant Formosa, the influence of Otis and Adams and Hancock and Washington and Jefferson is felt. The day for absolutism is about over. Dr. Swan is from the great hospital in Canton. He is the associate of the distinguished Dr. Kerr. These two physicians and their assistants treat fifteen hundred in-patients and twenty-five thousand out-patients a year. They preach to all who seek relief. They follow up their patients and seek to win them to Christ. As an evangelistic agency this hospital is said to be invaluable. Dr. Main, of Hangchow, has one of the largest hospitals in China. He does not agree with Dr. Ashmore as to the place of medical work in a mission. He regards the medical department as most fruitful in leading souls into the kingdom. He can lay his hands on scores of converts that have been won through the hospital. Among the young men was D. Willard Lyon. He spent a year among the colleges of America in the interest of the Volunteer Movement. His father is a missionary in China. He was born on a boat between Shanghai and Ningpo. Mr. Lyon and wife are on their way to Peking, where they expect to live and labor for the furtherance of the Gospel.

LI HUNG CHANG.

A CHINESE MANDARIN.

Mr. Loomis, of the Bible Societies in Yokohama, is on board, and gave an account of the work among the soldiers. If any one had told him before the war began that the highest officials in Japan would consent to the distribution of the Scriptures, as they have done, he would have said, "If the Lord were to open the windows of heaven, might this thing be?" He was accorded the privilege of giving copies of the New Testament or of the Gospel to the soldiers in the army, to the sailors of the navy, and to the wounded in the hospitals and to the prisoners of war. The prince in command of the Imperial Guard was very glad to allow him to give a Gospel to each of his men. That prince is now Commander-in-Chief of the army. He was permitted to visit the Naval Academy and to give a portion of the Word of God to every cadet. When the Empress visited the hospital, the head surgeon called her attention to the work done by the missionaries, and spoke of it as one of the most valuable things done for the country. In Tokyo, Mr. Loomis held a service for the Chinese prisoners. There were one hundred and sixty present. They were very eager to hear. A Japanese officer reported that a Buddhist priest came to the prison. The prisoners told him that they were Christians, and did not want him. There were two thousand five hundred New Testaments, and one hundred and twenty thousand Gospels distributed. Prior to 1873 it was a capital crime to sell an English Bible. The change since then has been marvelous. It is the Lord's doing. The speaker was deeply moved. He is a man of prayer—a man of God. He was surprised at the ease with which doors were opened. God gave him favor in the sight of the officials. He said he felt as Moses did when the Lord hid him in the cleft of the rock while his glory passed by. Mr. Loomis is on his way to Korea in the interest of this work.

Among the passengers is the celebrated traveler and author, Mrs. Isabella Bird Bishop. She is not a missionary, but is deeply interested in missionaries. She was born in England. Her husband was a Professor in the University of Edinburgh. She has made that city her home for thirty years. Her health has never been good. Much of her writing has been done in bed. She has traveled all over the world. Her books were written in the form of letters to a sister. In Japan she lived once for six months on rice and eggs. She makes it a rule to carry no food and no books She carries a bed and a chair and a blanket or two and some clothing and a camera, and almost nothing else. She gets a servant who can serve her as an interpreter; she has no other escort. Not long ago she was in the interior of China. She was taking a picture when some men saw her. They began to cry out, "Here is a foreign devil; kill her, kill her!" She finished her work, took her camera and returned to the boat. Her life was in peril, but she did not think so at the time. She is now on her way to Korea, to finish a journey which was interrupted by the war. Mrs. Bishop is a friend of missionaries. She knows them and their work. Once she avoided them. At that time she had no confidence in them. She believed the evil reports that are heard in certain circles. In the providence of God her eyes were opened. She is impressed with the great need of missionaries. The world is dark and needs the Gospel. She has borne eloquent testimony on this point. She has described the sufferings of women and children in non-Christian lands. Her interest centers in medical missions. She is now making a journey in the hope of being able to assist this work.

No one can be with such a company without feeling that they are diligent students of the Scriptures. At the daily meetings for conference every one had his Bible. The book showed that it was read and studied. Not only so, but they are men of prayer. They live near God, and they delight to talk with him. Moreover, they are full of joy. Their faces shine. It would not be easy to find another group of the same number with so many happy countenances in it. They have heard the call of God and obeyed it, and he has blessed them with his wondrous grace. Once more, they have perfect confidence in the triumph of the Gospel. The reports of riots and massacres do not disturb their serene confidence. They are without a doubt as to the final issue. The Mandarins may oppose; worldly-minded people may sneer; the Lord God omnipotent reigns, and the whole earth shall be filled with his glory. There are medical men on board who have left a lucrative practice to serve the Lord in China. There is no one in the group who could not get a larger stipend at home than he will get on the field. At the present time a riot may occur anywhere. No missionary is safe. Those who are seeking pleasant berths are not coming to China. The workers are ready to glorify Christ by living or by dying for him.

Our course for part of the way was through the Inland Sea. This is the short route from Kobe to Nagasaki. There is no more beautiful scenery in the world than in and about this sea. The waters are studded with fishing boats and trading junks. The shores are lined with villages. These have a background of mountains. The Inland Sea resembles the St. Lawrence with its

Thousand Islands. One place of interest passed was Shimonoseki. This is the place where Li Hung Chang was shot, and where the treaty of peace was drawn up and signed. We entered Nagasaki Bay after daybreak. The Bay is narrow and about three miles long. The harbor is thoroughly sheltered, and affords anchorage for ships of all classes. The entrance is not more than one-fourth of a mile wide. Here are war ships representing all nations. Officers in gold lace are seen in every direction. Nagasaki is historic ground. Here it was that the Portuguese merchants and missionaries landed. Here it was that the Japanese became acquainted with Europeans, and Christianity, and firearms, and other things unknown to Chinese civilization. Here Christianity was extirpated. Here the Dutch had their factory, and here all business with the outside world was carried on for many years. In the Bay there is a rock called Pappenburg. From this rock Christians were thrown, it is said, because they would not deny their Lord. As we walked the streets of the city we thought of the time when the citizens were required to trample on the cross to convince the inquisitor that they were not Christians. As we saw the homes of men representing Christian nations and the mission schools and the churches, we thought of the folly of fighting against the Most High. At Nagasaki we coaled. This was an interesting performance. The ship was anchored out in the Bay. Small boats loaded with coal came out. Ladders were placed against the side of the Empress. Men and women formed a line and passed up the coal in baskets. There were several sets working at the same time. In a few hours the work was done. It seemed strange to see women in such a place, but they want to earn a living. We left Nagasaki in the afternoon, passed the frowning batteries that guard the harbor, and soon were out on the Sea of China. We stood on deck as long as there was any land in sight. Japan is a beautiful country. The Japanese are a great people. Their victories in war are great; their victories of peace are still greater. God has a high mission for this nation. It seems to me that Japan is to be the leader of all the peoples of the East. In order to fulfill this mission she must have the Gospel. The heart and institutions of the nation must be Christianized. What is done for her evangelization must be done quickly. This is the nick of time. Thirty hours from Nagasaki we cast anchor in the mouth of the mighty Yangtsze. The next morning we took a tug and went up the Whangpoo River to Shanghai. As the tug came near the dock I caught sight of the pleasant face of James Ware, who came down to welcome me to China, and to take me to his own home.

XIX.

A GLIMPSE OF SHANGHAI.

SHANGHAI is the chief port of China, and has a population of 400,000. The foreign port resembles a European city. It has all the modern improvements, except street-cars. The Chinese city proper is walled, and is one of the nastiest places in the Empire. Contact with foreigners has led to no improvement. This is another illustration of the truth that it is only as people are renewed in heart and spirit that they are ready to adopt the institutions which are the fruit of the Gospel. The old city was offered good water. They said the water offered had neither taste nor smell; the water in the moat has both. The people wash their clothes and food and their persons in it, and then use it for cooking and drinking. In another city pipes were put in and water supplied free. The people preferred water that had some body to it. They neglected the pipes, and the good intentions of the foreigners availed nothing. Those who allege that missionaries would do better work if they put in sewers and water pipes and teach the people something about sanitation, ought to take these and similar facts into account. The truth is that moral regeneration must come first.

Shanghai is the center of much religious activity. As my time was short, James Ware had a program arranged in advance. It was his wish that I should see as much as possible. Our first call was at the headquarters of the China Inland Mission. The buildings are among the finest in the city. They are built about a large court. This property cost not less than $75,000. The money was given by one man. Not a dollar given for the work of the mission went into the grounds or buildings. Here are the offices and store-rooms of the mission, besides living-rooms and a chapel. All the workers in Shanghai live here and eat at a common table. Those on their way to or from the interior find here a home. The China Inland Mission has a remarkable history. It is now thirty years old. Dr. J. Hudson Taylor is its founder and principal manager. We had the pleasure of an interview with him. This mission is pan-denominational and international. It accepts workers from all evangelical bodies. There are Churchmen, Baptists, Methodists,

Presbyterians, and others on the field. To prevent friction, the representatives of each body are grouped in one province. They are allowed to preach and practice what they have been taught. There are workers from Great Britain and Ireland, Finland, Sweden, Norway, Denmark, Germany, Switzerland, the United States, Canada, Australia, Tasmania, and New Zealand. No salary is guaranteed; they go out trusting the Lord to supply their needs. The mission does not borrow and does not go in debt. No personal solicitation is made or collection called for. The treasury is supplied by voluntary contributions. The work is managed by missionary directors, assisted by a council of experienced workers. There is one council in London, another in Toronto, another in Australia, and another in Scandinavia. These councils select workers and receive and forward money. The aim of the mission is to evangelize the whole Empire. At the present time sixteen out of the eighteen provinces are occupied. There are seven hundred men and women at work. Forty per cent of these are either self-supporting or are supported by friends. The increase in the number of workers has been wonderful. At one time eighteen were sent out. In two years seventy-six were added. In one year the reinforcements numbered one hundred. The extra offerings of that year aggregated $50,000. Dr. Taylor does not believe in "the gun-boat policy." If property is destroyed, no indemnity is sought. The mission takes joyfully the spoiling of its goods. The workers believe that if they do well and suffer for it, and take it patiently, that is acceptable with God. Some of the workers are now in the city besieged by the Mohammedans. Their friends do not know their condition, but prayer is made continually on their behalf. They believe that they will be preserved, or that grace will be given to bear whatever may come. Dr. Taylor is a man of child-like trust in God. He is a man of mark. All the workers in the mission partake of his spirit.

Our next call was on Dr. Ernest Faber. He is a German of solid merit and great attainments. He is one of the first men in China. Dr. Faber has been in this country thirty-one years. For twelve years he was an evangelist in and about Canton. His voice having failed, he gave his life to literature. He has written some thirty volumes. These are in Chinese, in German, and in English. His scientific works have been approved by the government. He has written on schools in the West. He used to be asked, "Have you any schools in your country?" He wrote to answer that question. In all his works he has kept steadily in mind the conversion of China. He told us of a man in Japan who wrote a book entitled, "How I Became a Christian." He had been a Confucianist. His son presented him with one of Dr. Faber's volumes. He was bigoted, and threw it aside unread. His son presented him with another volume. He read it, and was led to accept Christ as his Savior and Lord. Dr. Faber spoke of the prejudice against foreigners. The people are led to believe that they take out the eyes, and brains, and hearts, and livers of the Chinese, and make medicine of them. It is this medicine that makes the foreigners so wise and so strong. The native physicians see that their craft is in danger. The triumph of the Gospel means their overthrow. Dr. Faber has no doubt as to the issue of the conflict between Buddhism and Confucianism and Taoism and Christianity.

Leaving Dr. Faber, we called on Dr. Joseph Edkins. The name of this distinguished scholar and author is a household word in the republic of letters. His studies have been in the field of Comparative Religion and Philology. He has written many books, and these have been widely read. In addition to his work in the Customs and in the study, he preaches every week. He has been in China for nearly half a century. The country was opened only six years before his arrival. The changes since then are great. The thought of them fills the soul with gratitude and hope. There have been riots and massacres, but the good done is immense, and is worth all this suffering and loss of life, and more. Sacrifice is the condition of progress. The blood of the martyrs is the seed of the church. The conviction of all men I have met in China is that the riots are instigated by the officials. The people are kindly disposed and would make no trouble whatever, if their minds were not poisoned against the foreigners. They are told that these people can see three feet into the ground. They can discover and carry away the precious metals. Their aims and motives are represented as evil, and only evil. They want to overthrow the government and take the country. There may be more suffering than there has been; officials may write books and send out circulars to inflame the minds of the populace, but the work is of God and cannot fail.

We reached Shanghai on Saturday. Sunday was crowded with services. In the morning we met with the believers for the communion and for preaching. This was after the Sunday-school. There were three addresses in all. At the close of the service there was a sermon by Bishop Walden in the Union Church. In the afternoon there was a Bible class in Mr. Ware's study. Among those present was a girl without feet. When her feet were bound she cried so much that the people thought she had a devil and threw her out. It was cold and her feet were frozen. They dropped off in course of time. She is now a Christian. Miss Lyon expects to train her for a Bible woman. Dr. Butchart thinks a pair of wooden feet can be secured for about forty dollars. Perhaps some one will furnish this sum. Another had been thought a demoniac. She was found by one of our workers tied to a post. She was naked and raving. Under kind treatment she improved. She was prayed with and led to Christ. She is happily married and lives an exemplary life. After the Bible class, Mr. Ware examined ten candidates for baptism. One woman said, "I am deaf, very deaf; stupid, very stupid; but I believe in the Lord Jesus with all my heart." In the evening there was a second service in the Union Church. It was to the pastorate of this church that W. P. Bentley was once called, at a salary twice as great as he was receiving. He did not entertain the call for a moment. All the workers of Shanghai attend this church. The services are at such hours as do not conflict with their own. The union sentiment is fostered by these meetings. We went from the Union Church to the evangelistic service conducted by James Ware and Evangelist Ni. This was a strange but fascinating sight. Men and women and children came in. Some smoked all the while. They came and went, but the house was full. Some scoffed, others listened to the words that were spoken. The audience was different from that in the morning. Chinese Christians have bright and happy faces. Mrs. Ware says that women learn to read after their conversion so that they can take part in the services. Evangelist Ni has a fine head and face. He looks like a bald eagle. One feels on seeing him that he is worthy of one's love and trust.

On Monday we visited the rooms of the American Bible Society. Dr. Hykes, the manager for China, showed us through the building and explained the work. Last year nearly 500,000 Scriptures, or portions thereof, were sold. Few are given away. People prize more highly that which costs something. The books are sold below cost so as to bring them within the reach of nearly all. The Bible is printed in the twenty-eight Chinese dialects. In different sections of the Empire the dialects are different. A Cantonese would not be easily understood in Peking. A Nankin man is not easily understood in Shanghai. Colporteurs go out and distribute the Word of Life. The missionaries on their tours do the same. Dr. Hykes is an aggressive man. There was a very marked increase in the sales last year; the sales for the current year are still larger. Near by is the Presbyterian Press, the largest mission press in any field. This is one of the institutions of the East. It is known in all parts of the world. It was established in 1844. It cost $65,000. Never was there a wiser investment. It pays all expenses and more. It prints, binds, makes type, plates, and everything else that is done in a great establishment. One year it printed 30,000,000 pages. Every mission in China is helped by this Press. Not only so, but its work goes to all parts of the globe. The day we were there an order was received from the University of Berlin for a font of Chinese type. Mr. Fitch, the director, is an Ohio man, and a very clever gentleman.

From the Press we went to a baptismal service. The candidates that Mr. Ware examined on Sunday were present. There were ten in all. An address was delivered by Mr. Ni explaining the meaning of the ordinance. With the exception of one woman seventy years of age, the candidates were young and strong. They will form a valuable addition to the church. At the close of this service we hastened to the monthly prayer-meeting in the Union Church. Here we met many missionaries and several other noted personages. Reports were given from different parts of the field. It was a season of refreshing from the presence of the Lord. The unhappy divisions of Christendom were forgotten. All present seemed to be members of one body. That night the Christians came to Mr. Ware's house and gave me a reception and an address. The sentiments are too flattering to be printed in English. Perhaps that is the reason they are in Chinese. They brought their refreshments with them. A stranger here soon gets acquainted and feels at home. He cannot fail to realize that he is among kindred in Christ. The warmth of their welcome is unmistakable.

The next morning we visited the Anglo-Chinese College. We went early, that we might see the students in the chapel. This is the school of the M. E. Church, South. The teaching is in English and Chinese. The government takes the best students before they are graduated and places them in its technical and naval schools. It pays all their expenses and gives them a salary besides. Their knowledge of English and science makes them more valuable. The school has a very desirable property. The tuition fees pay all expenses, except the salaries of the foreign teachers. Some of the boys are Christians, but most of them are not. Many of them would unite with the church if their parents would give their consent. One mother threatened to commit suicide if her son confessed his faith in Christ. These boys are Christians in their con-

CHINESE PAGODA.

CHINESE PRIEST BEGGING.

duct. They are friends of the work. On the way to the school and back we went through a large market. It was curious to see every buyer using his own scales. He cannot trust the seller to use just weights and a just balance. That morning we went out to St. John's College. This is the school of the Protestant Episcopal Church. There are in the boys' school one hundred and thirty-five students; in the girls' school sixty, and in the orphanage forty children. The school has a splendid property. It cost not less than $100,000. Prof. Cooper showed us the buildings and the grounds. There are no cleaner and neater rooms in China. We saw the boys eat their rice at noon. It was a sight worth seeing. St. Luke's Hospital belongs to the same society. Dr. Boone began with two beds. The property now used is worth $50,000. This was bought by the Chinese, and given to the mission in recognition of the value of such an institution. Dr. Boone told us of the influence of the hospital. A member of the literary class living in Woosung was paralyzed by overwork. He was cross, cursed the children, and threw his crutch at them. He was the terror of the place. Dr. Boone was able to send him some medicine that healed him. His heart was full of gratitude, and he wanted to do something. He opened a school and soon won the confidence and love of the boys. He would take no pay. His conversion deeply impressed many. They said if the Gospel can change such a brute into such a man it must be a good thing.

The same day we visited Sicawei, the great Jesuit institution. There are two hundred orphans here. They are sent to school and taught trades. We were shown through the shops. We saw carpenters, printers, painters, tailors and shoemakers. These orphans are kept in charge till they are twenty-seven years old, lest they should go back to heathenism. In the nunnery is a school for girls. There is a seminary in which priests are trained. The Observatory furnishes Shanghai with the time and weather indications. We saw the model of a new cathedral. This will cost $500,000. It will be built in time. The priests could not have been more obliging. They were pleased to see us and to give us any information asked for. They showed us through this vast establishment. There are many other institutions in Shanghai that we did not see, on account of a lack of time. Mr. Ware drives furiously and accomplishes more than several ordinary men, but even he could not see all that is worth seeing in this great city in two and a half days.

One thing impresses a stranger out here, namely, the extreme cordiality of every one. I took a score of introductory letters with me. Dr. Ashmore told me I would not need them. He was right. I have not shown one. It is sufficient that one is interested in the work. Catholics and Protestants of all schools, and men who have no direct connection with missionary work, take delight in showing one every possible courtesy. Buddhist and Confucianist have invited me to eat and drink with them. With Tiny Tim I say, "God bless them, every one."

XX.

FROM SHANGHAI TO NANKIN.

MR. WARE arranged that we should call on the way at several out-stations in his district. This made it needful for us to go partly by water and partly by land. The first place which we wished to visit is Tsungming. This is a large island in the mouth of the Yangtsze, with a population of a million. We left Shanghai in the "Love," the boat which the English Sunday-schools, under the leadership of Mr. J. Coop, gave the mission. James Ware was captain, Dr. Butchart was surgeon, and I was the passenger. The wind was straight ahead and blowing so hard, that with all our efforts we made only seven miles in ten hours. We ran into a creek known as the Exalted Bridge Creek for the night. As the sun was setting we took a walk into the country. We saw graves in all directions. In one field I counted one hundred and fifty. Some coffins are uncovered. Others are enclosed in brick vaults, or have mounds of earth built over them. Half the field is thus occupied. The time and place of burial are fixed by luck-doctors. They get the date of birth and marriage and death of the deceased, examine carefully the contour of the country, the hills, valleys, canals, and water courses, and then consult their books and diagrams and work out the grand result. They fix the exact spot and the precise angle in which the coffin is to lie. It may take weeks or years to do this. The luck-doctors make a good living at this business. If any good befalls the family it is because the right man was selected to locate the coffin. China is one vast graveyard. You see graves along the roads and canals, near the temples, within and without the city walls, on every farm. One is never out of sight of these eloquent reminders of our mortality.

The next morning we weighed anchor and started. We had to stop at Woosung for the tide to turn. This place is at the junction of the Whangpoo and Yangtsze. We called at the chapel of the London Missionary Society. Here we met a man who had been a fortune-teller and an opium smoker. He gave up both, burned his books of magic, and is now a helper in the mission. We entered an opium den and saw a Buddhist monk enjoying his pipe. He was a dirty, ragged fellow. We tried to persuade him to abandon this evil and hurtful practice, but our words fell on deaf ears. Opium is the curse of China. Wherever we have been we have found its victims. We are asked every day for medicine to break the habit. The sad thing about it is, that it was forced on China by Christian England. When the Emperor was urged to legalize the trade and make it a source of revenue, he replied that he could not use as a revenue that which brought suffering and misery upon his people. As soon as the tide turned we tried again to make Tsungming, but failed. At dark we put into another creek and waited for the wind to change. At midnight Captain Ware started again, and at daybreak we were at the land. If the "Love" had an engine she would make this trip in six or seven hours. Instead, it took two whole days. An engine can be put in for one hundred dollars. Perhaps some good friend will write a check for this sum. In that case one can go to Tsungming and preach and return the same day. Now it takes the best part of a week. This accounts for the fact that, though this island is only forty miles distant from Shanghai, no Gospel work has been done on it before.

After breakfast we entered the city. We found Evangelist Ku in the chapel. He is a fine fellow. He is young and has not had much experience. He spends two days each month in Shanghai with Mr. Ware. There are services every day in the chapel. There is a reading-room open to all. So far as known there have been no conversions at this place, though there are some inquirers. It is difficult to trace the influence and to tabulate results. One man preached in Chefoo for years and saw no fruit. Afterwards he learned that four hundred were won in these seemingly unfruitful years. The promise is, "You shall reap if you faint not." One sows and another reaps. The time will come when the sower and reaper shall rejoice together. Love never fails. Like all Chinese cities, Tsungming is a filthy place. The streets are narrow and full of people. The houses are open summer and winter. The cooking and eating are in view of all who pass by. There is no privacy and no delicacy. The gutters are rank and smell to heaven. Stagnant ponds, covered with green scum, breed malaria and pestilence. The wonder is that people live at all. But they do. Children are remarkably healthy. I have seen but one puny child, and that was in a hospital. Doubtless many die, and only the fittest survive. We spent two hours in the chapel, and then continued our journey. In the evening we reached and crossed the river. It was late when we found our hotel. In ten minutes the place was full. Men and women and children came in and watched us. They felt and commented on our coats, shoes, collars, ties, eyes and hair. You cannot lock the people out and eat and drink and rest in peace. An attempt of that sort would be resented. The doors would be broken down in an instant. The Chinese reason that they have a right to know what a stranger is doing. If he wishes concealment it is because he is planning mischief. Workers open everything to those who wish to see. A Chinese crowd is not always attractive, according to our notions. One man took our tea kettle, and putting the spout in his mouth, slaked his thirst. The noses of the boys are not always nice. If by pre-arrangement with one's ancestors, one has a stomach that is not easily upset, one will find it more precious than rubies. My bed was on a box. The others had rough bedsteads. We had our own bedding. This is the universal custom here. Coolies, travelers, friends visiting friends, rich and poor, all carry their own bedding. People were coming and going all night, but they did not molest us. "China's millions" gave us a wide berth. We slept very well. For supper and lodging we paid about seven cents each.

As soon as it was light we started. We made ten miles before breakfast. Though we were off so early hundreds were out to see us. Our coming was an event in their lives. It was like a circus at home. We were the first foreigners many of them had ever seen. We traveled all day in wheel-barrows. There are no railways and no stage coaches or carts in this part of the Empire. The wheelbarrow is the sole method of transportation. Thirty miles is a day's journey. A wheelbarrow in China has as little romance and comfort as one at home. It could be made fairly comfortable, but that would not be Chinese. Any change would show disrespect to Confucius. At the close of the first day one feels pretty sore. The roads are narrow and poor; China has the worst roads in the world. It is only by courtesy that they can be called roads. They are like Indian trails. Men must walk in single file. The bridges are about two feet wide. Culverts are often not six inches. A single stone, or a piece of wood flattened on one side, answers the purpose. No cart or horse could go over the roads and bridges in this part of China. The coolies are great, strong fellows. One wheeled two men over thirty miles in a day, and seemed as fresh at the end as at the beginning. They go faster with a load than we could without. I never looked at them without admiration. Give these beasts of burden the Gospel and a good education, and they will be worthy to stand before kings.

At every village the people flocked out to see us. Women tottered out on their small feet. A thousand would gather in the twinkling of an eye. They were curious, but civil. We heard the words "foreign devil" once or twice, but they came from small boys. The men gathered about us and felt us, but they said nothing disrespectful. No sooner did we stop than Mr. Ware began to speak. He illustrated Christ's method, "As you go, preach." He talks like a native and secures the attention of all. Mr. Ku was by his side with copies of the Scripture in his hand. He took a large package from Tsungming. Long before reaching the last station every copy was sold. We would wait ten or fifteen minutes at a place. The coolies would get their breath and smoke a pipe or eat a bowl of rice. Then we hastened on. Sometimes we entered a tea-house. This is a Chinese institution. It answers to our saloon. For a cent or half a cent we can have a cup of tea. There are tables and benches and one can sit and rest. The floor is of dirt or brick. Pigs and dogs and chickens act as scavengers. Birds build their nests in the roof. People come here to gamble, to transact business, to hear or tell some new thing, or to eat and drink. Peddlers come in and sell cakes, peanuts, sweet potatoes, melon seed, candies, and smoke. A man has a pipe with a long handle and one can have a smoke for a cash. No sooner were we seated than the people gathered and the conversation began. It does not take an expert long to introduce spiritual topics. James Ware is a prince for this kind of work. He has an answer for every question. He keeps the crowd in good humor. Nothing ever ruffles his spirit. If the wind is ahead, he is sure it will soon change. If it rains, he is thankful it does not snow. If fleas abound, he is happy in the thought that they are not bed-bugs. It is a picnic to travel with such a jolly genius.

We were traveling in one of the best parts of China. The land is as fertile as in Central Illinois. Farmers raise two crops a year. And yet they are poor. Their houses are built for the most part of mud and thatch. There are no barns. Plowing and harrowing are done with the water buffalo. We did not see a horse all day. The people are industrious and economical. Nothing is allowed to go to waste. The grass along the roads and on the mountains and on the commons is cut for fuel. Living cheaply is reduced to a science. The Chinese do not drink milk or eat beef. Their lakes and rivers abound in fish. We saw men catching them in all sorts of ways. The most curious method we saw was by the use of cormorants. These birds are trained to dive and swim so swiftly that no fish can easily escape them. The owner places a collar around the neck of the bird to prevent it swallowing any large fish. He can tell by its weight whether it has taken anything or not. The birds are rewarded with a part of what they have caught, or are fed with other food. These fish, either fresh or salted, are used with the rice, the great article of food among the Chinese.

We reached Tung Chau a little after dark. This place is thirty-three miles from the place where we slept the night previous. Tung Chau is a walled city, and has a population of about 75,000. We went to the chapel and book-room and saw the evangelist in charge. We had been hearing of this work most of the day. At nearly every place we stopped we met with some one who had heard the Gospel or who had been treated in some mission dispensary or hospital. We rested for an hour or two in the chapel, and had supper. Mr. Ware and Mr. Ku remained there to preach for a day or two and then return home. Dr. Butchart and I left for the river. This was seven miles distant. We heard afterward that the magistrate, fearing that we might be attacked, sent a secret guard along to protect us. This may or may not be true. We reached our inn about midnight. We slept well and were ready for the boat the next morning. That night I saw the watchmen making their rounds. One was beating a drum; one carried a gun; the third carried a light. The drum and the light would warn the burglars in time to get safely out of the way. This performance resembles that of hunting with a brass band.

No missionary confines his labors to one spot. He has his center where he carries on a work. From this center he goes out into the adjacent country. This was Christ's method. He did not build a cathedral in Nazareth or Jerusalem, and say, "Let the people come to me." He went about in all Galilee, and Peræa, and Samaria, and Judæa. Once the people wanted to tie him down in their midst. He said, "I must preach the good tidings of the kingdom of God to the other cities also; for therefore I was sent." These tours break down prejudice and disarm fear. The natives see that the foreigner has not horns and hoofs, and does not go about like a dragon spitting out fire and death. All sorts of rumors are circulated. All sorts of notions are prevalent. Foreigners are believed to be spies or secret enemies. They have some evil work in view. At first the sick will not take medicine from them. They are afraid that there is some charm in the foreign remedy. They are told that the foreigners can give a pill that will make them become Christians. He can give another pill that will make them go to church every Sunday, whether it rains or shines. A pill answering to that description would be a priceless boon in America, and would sell like hot cakes. The people see the missionaries. They are unarmed. They are peaceful. They do good and not evil. They sleep in their houses and put their lives in their power. They see that they are men like themselves, bone of their bone and flesh of their flesh, and their fears and prejudices take wings and fly away. This work must be done before China can be Christianized.

We took passage on the good ship Sual for Nankin. Captain Scott is a Christian man and a friend of missionaries and their work. He did everything in his power for our comfort. There are men in the East, as in the West, who sneer at missionaries. I have found two classes that have confidence in them. They are the bankers and the ship-owners. With these classes the missionaries have almost unlimited credit. That speaks volumes for them, and outweighs all vulgar and carnal sneers. The next morning we were in Nankin. I went ashore, thankful for the insight into missionary work which I had gained, and for such pleasant companionship. In the Mission Compound we had a royal welcome.

1. Mrs. F. E. Meigs. 3. Frank Garrett. 2. Mrs. Frank Garrett.
4. Miss Mary Kelly. 5. Mrs. E. P. Hearnden.

NANKIN, CHINA.

XXI.

NANKIN AND ROUND ABOUT.

Nankin is two hundred miles from Shanghai. It was once the capital of China, and may be again. We had hardly reached the place before the work of sight-seeing began. The first thing on the list was Dr. Macklin's clinic at the South Gate. Mr. Williams and Mr. Saw volunteered to go with me. We got donkeys and started. No carriage could make its way through such narrow and crowded streets. The Viceroy has built a wide road from one side of the city to the other. Horses and carriages are seen on it, but nowhere else. A boy goes with each donkey to twist his tail to make him go, to make the appropriate remarks when things go wrong, and to clear the way when it is blocked. The sights and smells soon convince one that he is in a heathen city. Though there are half a million souls within the walls of Nankin, there are no sewers and no sanitary provisions whatever. Large ponds are covered with green scum. Gutters are filled with garbage and filth. Coffins and graves are everywhere in sight. Houses are plastered with charms to keep away evil spirits and disease. In times of pestilence the streets are lined with idols and altars. Cleanliness would do more to prevent the plagues than all the prayers and offerings.

We found Dr. Macklin preparing an address and the dispensary full of people. The building is imperial property. It is an admirable place for the purpose. It is in one of the busiest parts of the city. Tens of thousands pass by every day in the year. The building is large and well arranged for a chapel and dispensary. There is a room in the front that will hold two hundred people or more. The medical work is done in rooms at the rear. Before seeing any cases, Dr. Macklin preaches to the people. The medical work is auxiliary to the evangelistic. Christ meets all the needs of humanity. He has healing for the body, truth for the mind, and redemption for the soul. He asked me to speak a few words, which he interpreted. While he was seeing the sick, Mr. Williams and Mr. Saw made brief addresses. The patients were suffering from all kinds of diseases. There were in the group victims of dropsy, epilepsy, syphilis, rheumatism, itch, ague, running sores, enlarged spleen, hip disease, consumption, varicose veins, leprosy. Some of these answered to the prophet's description, "From the crown of the head to the sole of the foot there was no soundness, but wounds and bruises and putrefying sores." The scene reminded me of the saying about the Christ, "And they brought unto him all that were sick, holden with divers diseases and torments, possessed with demons, and epileptic and palsied; and he healed them." Only the worst cases come to the foreign doctor. The Chinese prefer their own physicians in trivial cases. The clinic averages about eighty. With his two trained assistants, the Doctor gets through in two hours. Each patient gets a tract or a Gospel. After the clinic we had luncheon, and then we went to a tea-house and had some more Gospel talk. At another time I attended a clinic in the dispensary connected with the Memorial Hospital. There was first the preaching and then the healing. It was interesting to watch the people. One woman tried to kiss the Doctor's feet. She felt as the woman did who said to another medical missionary, " Och, docktar darlint, may ivery hair of yere head be a candle to light ye to glory." Some of these patients come from places a hundred miles distant. In touring, the workers nearly always find men who have been helped in Nankin. These men are always friends. Mr. Hunt was accused by some soldiers of being a Japanese and a spy. His life was in peril. The captain recognized him and let him go. This man had been treated in the hospital. Though they are in daily contact with these diseases the physicians are not attacked. The promise is verified, "A thousand shall fall at thy side, and ten thousand at thy right hand, but it shall not come nigh thee." They are better fed and observe the laws of health, and hence resist disease as the natives in their poverty and dirt can not. The Doctor showed me through the hospital. It is a noble building, one of the best in Nankin. In the reception room are pictures of O. A. Burgess, A. M. Atkinson, J. M. Trible, and Joseph King. When this work began the neighbors were angry and disposed to drive the Doctor away. When the hospital was built they made a feast, and hung up congratulatory scrolls, and made an offering of one hundred dollars.

The boys in the school and the teachers heard of my coming, and wished to welcome me in their own way. They prepared a beautiful silk scroll and wrote on it an inscription far too complimentary to be exact. They presented the scroll, and one of the number made an address. One part of the ceremony was the explosion of a thousand fire-crackers. Afterwards I visited the school and saw its workings. Prof. Meigs has three assistants. The Bible is taught every day. The exercises begin with praise and prayer. The boys are taught the classics, mathematics, geography, history, and science. Every truth of science or history helps to cut the roots of superstition and prejudice. Chinese maps give almost all the globe to China. Other nations are insignificant in size and are vassals and pay tribute. A map showing the relative size of China and giving facts as to the size, population, resources, and form of government of other nations, opens the eyes of the Chinese. In the native schools the Chinese characters and classics are taught, and nothing else. Graduates ask, Are Japan and England neighbors? In what province is England? Is the Queen coming to worship the Emperor? Does the sun shine in your country? Do you till the soil? Do you have any rice? Is Jesus your King? An eclipse is caused by a dragon trying to eat the sun. Gongs are beaten and cannon fired to scare the monster away. A few lessons in astronomy are sufficient to make eclipses intelligible. The telescope and other scientific apparatus presented to this school by Captain Atkinson, and the microscope presented by President Loos, are of the greatest value. Prof. Meigs has as many boys as he can take. He needs a dormitory. This will cost about $1,500. He is preparing to start some industrial work. He feels that this department is absolutely necessary. In China the literary class is the highest of all. It has the whitest and softest hands and the longest finger-nails. It has the greatest aversion to labor. This feeling must be broken down. If pupils are taught to work with their hands an hour every day, their conception of the dignity of labor will be changed. In this school are several promising young men. It is hoped that they will develop into effective evangelists.

One day was spent with Mr. Williams on one of his circuits. This one was about ten miles in length. We left the city by one gate and came back by another. He spoke six or eight times. At each village we got down from our donkeys and ordered some tea. The people gathered about us and began to ask questions. They asked our honorable names and exalted ages, where our noble mansions are located, how many princely sons we had. Mr. Williams gave them the facts called for, and then began to speak on Gospel themes. As a rule, they listened attentively. Sometimes they would urge an objection or ask a question. This would give him a chance to drive some truth home to the heart and conscience. We spent an hour in a temple. The monks were very friendly. They knew Mr. Williams. He spoke to them about the idols, and about the only true God, and Jesus Christ whom he did send. The Hia Kwan chapel soon filled. While Mrs. Williams spoke to the women in a separate room, he addressed the men. It was such a crowd as gathered about our Lord or about Paul on his tours. The way they pressed to the front, and the eagerness with which they listened for an hour, showed that he had them in the hollow of his hand. His fluency is astonishing. Few men can speak in English with such rapidity as he can in Chinese. His knowledge of the people, their history, their customs, and their manner of life, served him well. When the books are opened it may be found written "that this man and that man were born there."

The next morning Mr. Meigs asked Mr. Saw and me to go with him on one of his circuits. We were gone two days. The first day we had five services. We spent the evening and night in a temple in a large village. Part of the building is used as a school. The monk in charge was glad to see us, and was assiduous in supplying our needs. He sent the boys home, and hastened to cook supper for us. While he was in the kitchen, we went out and held a service on the street, and asked all to come to the temple when the work of the day was done. While we were eating, an old woman came in to worship. She lighted a candle on the altar, burned some incense before each of the gods, then went back to the altar, beat the gong and kotowed ten times. Then she arose, blew out the candle and left. Meanwhile the men of the place were coming in. Messrs. Meigs and Saw sang and expounded a hymn. We asked them if they worshiped the gods. They said yes. They worship the gods of heaven and earth and many others. We asked them why they worshiped. They said their hearts prompted them. We inquired what benefit they received. They promptly replied, "None." We asked them if there was any connection between their worship and their conduct. They answered us that there was not. The pious man is the man that goes to the temples and worships the gods. It matters not how he lives. We tried to learn what they thought about sin. One old man said it was eating meat. He was a vegetarian. Another said that it was an offense done against a man by another. Others spoke of it as a breach of propriety. Others still spoke of it as a violation of the laws. They did not seem to think it had anything to do with the gods. We asked them if there were any reasons why men should not sin. They said that a man ought not to sin in order that he might not be beaten or beheaded. We asked them if they were sinners. They laughed at the thought, and told us that they were Chinese. They regard themselves very much as the Pharisees did when our Lord was on earth. They think that outside barbarians sin; they do not. Toward the close one man admitted that he was a sinner. He was the brightest man present. He was the principal speaker throughout. He was a man of ability and culture. The Spirit of God was at work. That man was convicted of sin. Mr. Saw asked him if he would not then and there accept Jesus Christ as his Savior. He pressed him to decide. The man was convinced, but for some reason was not willing to make the good confession. He said, "It is hard to decide." The service lasted three hours, and was one of the most impressive I ever attended. The light was dim. Hundreds of gilt idols were about us. Incense pervaded the room. The listeners filled every available inch of space. The faces of many indicated that they were in earnest. After the audience withdrew the teacher placed the desks side by side, and helped us make our beds. Before we rose the next morning the old woman came in and went through the same performance as on the evening before. She has done this for twenty-five years without missing a morning or evening. The teacher cooked some eggs and made tea, and sent us on our way rejoicing. He has no faith in the idols. But he burns incense and bows down. He wants us to rent a building in the village and come regularly. In all the villages we found the people willing to hear the Gospel. Mr. Meigs sold Scriptures and dispensed medicine. The people used to fear him. They regarded him with contempt and aversion. On a recent visit an old man said to the people: "These men have been coming here for years. We know them, and we know that they are good men." That night there was a feast in the Hospital. One of Dr. Macklin's assistants was married, and gave a feast in honor of the happy event. There were about thirty dishes. It was an elaborate affair. Each guest took delight in preferring the others before himself. It was a pleasant evening.

While in Nankin I visited several temples. They are not used much except during the great festivals. Some are used as barracks, others are stored with coffins. I spoke once at the South Gate, and once at the Drum Tower, and once at the Union Service. I saw Miss Lyon's work among the women and children. One evening was spent with Dr. and Mrs. Beebe. They have been very kind to our workers. They are most estimable people. Among many incidents told by the Doctor was one with a dash of humor. One morning he was called to one of the Yamens. The imperial chamberlain died, and his wife thought the proper thing to do was to commit suicide. She had swallowed gold. Her people were in consternation. The Doctor gave her some medicine and withdrew. The next morning he was called again. He found his patient much better. She wanted to know if any evil effects would follow. He assured her that there would not. The incident passed out of his mind in a few days. Some weeks after he was visited by some men from the Yamen and asked if they might put up a tablet in the hospital in honor of this cure. He said they could. They wanted to know if they could do it that afternoon. That afternoon was quite agreeable. About three o'clock a great procession came down the street. A magistrate in his official robes was in command. A company of infantry and a crowd of men bearing firecrackers attended the bearers of the tablet. Arriving at the place the soldiers fired a salute. Ten thousand firecrackers were exploded. The Doctor took the magistrate into the guest room and gave him tea, while the carpenters were getting the tablet in place. Then the guns were fired again, and ten thousand more firecrackers exploded. On the tablet were four characters in gold. They read: "Divine Perception of Mysterious Devices." All that Dr. Beebe had done was to give the woman *a dose of castor oil.* Mrs. Beebe said one thing of which I have thought much. It was to the effect that any one who can make them laugh is a benefactor. The soul is cast down by the pride, indifference, hypocrisy, absurdities, stolid ignorance and inveterate prejudice of the people. Poverty and disease make exhaustive drafts upon the sympathies. Virtue goes out. A hearty laugh brings relief and helps one to regain one's usual faith and hope.

XXII.

CHU CHEO AND LU HOH.

In company with Mr. Saw I started from Nankin on a visit to these two places. Chu Cheo is northwest from Nankin, and is forty miles distant. Lu Hoh is northeast from Nankin, and is thirty miles from it. Chu Cheo and Lu Hoh are forty miles apart. Mr. Williams went with us as far as Pukeo. He preaches here every week in the chapel rented by the mission. We were two hours in crossing the river. The Chinese are never in a hurry. Their parting words are, "Slowly, slowly go." It would be as easy to hurry a Court of Chancery as to hurry a coolie. The animals were gotten aboard the ferry-boat with much difficulty. A rope was tied about the neck and two men pulled on it; another took hold of the tail; another still used the whip. They were forced to jump up about four feet and then to jump down into the hold of the junk. It would be an easy matter to build a gangway. This would be a saving in time and trouble, to say nothing of the comfort to the animals. But their ancestors did it in this way, and any improvement is out of order. Truly, "the dark places of the earth are full of the habitations of cruelty." When a dying man is driven out of doors to breathe his last on the street, when a drowning man is left to perish unless he can pay some one to rescue him, we need not be surprised if mules and donkeys fare as they do.

Chu Cheo is on the great high road between Nankin and Peking. Imperial couriers go this way when they bear messages from the Emperor to the Viceroy. This road was once fairly good, but it has been sadly neglected. No wagon could go over it now. We met caravans of donkeys carrying rice and wheat and oil and merchandise. We met wheelbarrows without number and coolies carrying heavy loads, but we did not meet a cart or wagon drawn by horses or oxen or steam. The bridges are good but narrow. Night coming on, we put up at an inn. The place was well supplied with opium, but had neither rice nor tea. We went out to a tea-house and got some supper. We slept in a large room with a score or more of human beings, and pigs and donkeys and fleas. There was no lock on the door and no door to the establishment. We were weary and slept well. The lullabies of the donkeys were unnecessary. The fleas insisted on escorting us to the next station, and were loth to leave us then. While in this hotel and on this trip, I felt that the shadow had gone on the sun-dial several millenniums. We were in the Patriarchal age. The rude plows and harrows and harness, the method of sowing seed and reaping the harvest, are such as were in use in the days of Abraham. The ox still treads out the corn, or it is beaten out by hand. The farmer throws it up into the air that the wind may drive away the chaff. The millstone is turned by an ass or by the wife. In large towns flint and steel are sold to kindle the fire. Men and women haul boats along the rivers and canals. The next day, a little before noon, we reached Chu Cheo. We took Mr. and Mrs. Hearnden and Mr. and Mrs. Hunt by surprise. Their welcome was not the less cordial on that account. This town has a population of 20,000, and is the center of a district having a population of 4,000,000. From this center the missionaries evangelize the outlying cities and villages in a district of 5,000 square miles.

That afternoon we left for Yu Ho Tsz, arriving at eight o'clock. Evangelist Shi and wife soon had some refreshments on the table. Mrs. Shi was the first convert at this village. Soon after her baptism she determined to build a chapel. Her neighbors heard of her purpose and came to her help. The chapel is a very neat building. It is large enough. She was then a widow. Since that time she married Mr. Shi. He was once a story-teller. He made a living by giving dramatic exhibitions of ancient scenes in Chinese history. Dr. Macklin led him to Christ and urged him to cut loose from all foreigners and earn his support among his own people. In so doing he would convince the Chinese that he did not make a confession of faith in Christ in order that he might eat the church's rice. He preaches in this chapel every day when he is at home. His work is known as far north as Peking. Travelers spend the night in the village. They hear the bell and stroll in to listen to the message. They hear an eloquent address from a Chinese. They carry a report of the place and the work to their homes. Early the next morning we went out to apprise the people that there would be a service in the chapel at eleven o'clock. We called on a man of some local celebrity. Once he was a terror to the community. He was so harsh and cruel that two wives committed suicide. He felt the disgrace so keenly that he made up his mind to dispose of his property, cut off his tail, enter a monastery, and become a Buddhist monk. While in the village he heard the Gos-

MEMORIAL HOSPITAL IN NANKIN, CHINA.

HONG-KONG.

pel, became interested in it, and soon made the good confession. Now he is an earnest Christian. He has thirty tenants on his land. His desire is to lead them all to Christ. He told us he had been a great sinner, and had experienced a great deliverance. He had been forgiven much, and he loves much. I spoke and Mr. Hunt interpreted me. Mr. Saw spoke on the same theme and applied the truth to the hearts and consciences of all present. After the service we were invited by Mr. Shi to sit down to dinner. Several neighbors were also invited. It took longer to get the guests seated than to eat the dinner. At one time I feared that they would never sit down. Each one wanted the lowest place. Each one sought to press the other into the seat of honor. At the table each one selected the choicest morsels, and, with his own chopsticks, placed them in the bowl of his neighbor. This was all in accordance with Chinese etiquette. In some circles outside of China, each one wants the highest seat and desires to have the choicest morsels on his own plate.

Dinner being over, we returned to Chu Cheo. The man from whom the mission rented the buildings in which the missionaries live and work had invited us, on our arrival, to a feast in his house that evening. When the food was ready to be served, he came to call us. This man is a Confucianist. He had been a Taiping rebel. He was the only man in Chu Cheo that was willing to help our people when they first went to that place. The rest of the citizens would not rent their property, and wanted to chase them away. This man stood by them from the first day until now. He was imprisoned for his course. Because he was a police official and a man of influence, he was kept in confinement only a few weeks. He is now eighty years old. He has his coffin in his house ready. He shows it to his friends, and tells them proudly that it is a present from his sons. This is not an unusual thing in China. There is no way in which children can better show their love and regard for their parents than in presenting them with a suitable coffin. The feast was fit for a king. The viands were the best the market afforded. The cooking and the service were admirable. One thing was lacking. There were no ladies present. This, too, was in accordance with Chinese notions of propriety. The women of the mission were not invited. The women of the household ate their food in their own apartments. After the feast we had a service in the chapel.

We spent the next forenoon with the workers, and saw and heard much of the work. The fame thereof has gone out through that whole region. People come from distant towns and villages for medicine for their diseases. We learned some things of special interest. At first the workers could not go out on the streets, or go out on a preaching tour lest some of "the baser sort" should attempt to fire their home. They have no fear on that score now. The presence of a woman is a great help. Men can come and go like birds of passage; women come to make a home. The same is true of a child. The people gathered to see Mabel Hunt. They had seen "men devils" and "women devils," but they had never seen a "baby devil." Her parents were urged not to go to Chu Cheo. Mabel was a better protection than a battery of artillery. The Chinese said, "The gods must love these people, or they would not give them such a beautiful child." The officials heard of Mabel's birthday and made a great feast in honor of the occasion. Mr. Hunt talked to the magistrate and his assistants about the Christian religion. Mrs. Hunt presented the great lady with a copy of the New Testament. A house is now in course of erection. The ground was secured on a promise that it should be only one story high. The Confucian temple near by is a low building. It must not be overshadowed.

After dinner we started for Lu Hoh. We spent the night in an inn about one-third of the way. It was market-day and the village was thronged. We had some difficulty in finding a place to sleep. We were packed into a small storeroom. Men and donkeys filled all the space without. At one table some men gambled all night. They began before our arrival, and continued after our departure. In the evening we visited a tea-house and had a service. The villagers crowded about us to see and hear. They climbed upon the tables and wherever there was a place to stand. Mothers held up their babes that they might catch a glimpse of us. They listened attentively to what we had to say. On the way back we went to an opium den. We saw twenty smoking. It was a pathetic sight. We reached Lu Hoh the next afternoon. This is a solid business town. Many Mohammedans live here. They are bigoted and self-satisfied. They say they worship the true God, and are not idolators. They refrain from pork and from things strangled. We went out on the streets and visited several temples and stores. In the evening the chapel filled. Mr. Saw, Mr. Hearnden and I spoke. We prayed and sang as well. Mr. and Mrs. Saw did much good work here and made many friends. Several have told him that they believe, and will soon make the good confession. When they left on their furlough the enemies of the truth said that his Emperor had taken away his button. When Mr. Arnold left for Wuhu, some time before, they said that his Emperor was going to take his head off. They look upon missionaries as political agents of some foreign power. Mr. Saw is never weary in well doing. He preaches wherever there is a man to hear. He is a delightful traveling companion.

The next day Mr. Saw and I left for Nankin. Mr. Hearnden returned to Chu Cheo. We reached the Drum Tower that evening. We were gone a week on this tour. That day we stopped at a tea-house for breakfast. At a table near us was a school-teacher. He gravely assured us that the Japanese were whipped in the war, and all present confirmed his assertion. He told us that the Black Flags were bound to succeed in Formosa. They had already surrendered. To him all foreigners are alike. He understands the Chinese characters and classics, but nothing else. He knows no more than an infant of general history, or mathematics, or philosophy, or science. He wears immense goggles to make him look wise and dignified. One of this class explained to one of our men the cause of night: "The people live inside the earth. The darkness is caused by the two hemispheres coming together and shutting out the sunlight." We asked him about sin. He indignantly denied that Chinese sin. That is for outside barbarians. Mr. Saw quoted Confucius against him. He said Confucius lied to teach his followers a truth. On the way we wanted to take the picture of a buffalo plowing. The men in the field objected. A gatling gun would not have scared them more than a kodak. They were afraid we might take something out of them or put something into them. On almost every farm were shrines to the earth-god. We must have seen thousands of these that week.

The ignorance and poverty of the people are indescribable. These two evils are caused by bad government. Give the Chinese the Gospel and free schools, good roads, railways, convenient markets, modern farming implements, flouring mills, and they will be one of the greatest nations on the globe. They have vast resources, but they are not developed. They are taxed and oppressed to support a horde of corrupt officials. The mandarins are greedy cormorants. Once a woman went to a Chinese sage and told him that her husband and two sons had been devoured by tigers. He asked her why she did not go to some other place. She said that, though the tigers were numerous, the government was not oppressive. He turned to his hearers and emphasized the thought that bad government is worse than tigers. Give China a good government and her peace will be as a river, and her righteousness as the waves of the sea.

XXIII.

HANKOW, WUHU, NANKIN AND SHANGHAI.

In order to see the work in different parts of China, I went up the Yangtsze as far as Hankow. This city is at the junction of the Han and Yangtsze, and is six hundred miles from the coast. Directly across the Yangtsze is Wuchang, while across the Han is Hanyang. These three cities have a combined population of nearly two millions. Hankow is a Treaty Port and a great center for trade. The bulk of tea exported is shipped from this point. Wuchang is the seat of the provincial government. Here the literary and military examinations are held. Hanyang is the seat of the iron industry. Here cannon, steel rails and railway supplies of all kinds are produced. Millions of dollars have been invested in this plant. These cities are annually visited by thousands of officials, students, traders, mechanics and laborers, and so are brought within the reach of the Gospel. At the great examinations systematic efforts are made to reach every one of the twenty or thirty thousand who come to compete for degrees. Many of these carry some of the seeds of truth to their homes. It is plain that this is one of the most promising places for missionary enterprise in China.

Hankow is the home of a number of men of ability and experience. The first one I met was Mr. Arnold Foster, a graduate of Cambridge. Though he works in connection with the London Society, he is entirely self-supporting. He has been in China twenty-four years. He teaches and preaches every day. He and his accomplished wife have a school for Eurasian girls in their own home. The girls are members of the family, and are treated in all respects as if they were their own children. They are quick to learn and easily managed. This school is a source of usefulness and joy. Mr. Foster said: "People say China does not move, but China does move. Quite true, she does not move as Western nations do, but she does move, nevertheless." He has seen great changes in his own time. He has no fear and no doubt as to the final issue of the conflict between light and darkness. Dr. Griffith John works in connection with the same Society. He has been in the field over forty years. Dr. John is one of the great men of the age. He is known and honored by every missionary in the Empire. He has translated the New Testament, and published it with explanatory notes. His tracts have been sold by the million. In addition to his literary work he preaches every day. He has baptized three thousand. In a recent address Dr. John said he was full of confidence with respect to the future. He expected to see great things, and a forward movement, as a result of this fresh upheaval in China. It would doubtless open the country in a wonderful way, and, better still, would open the eyes and hearts of the people. "The missionary cause was making rapid progress. It had taken the first thirty-five years of Protestant missions in China to build up a church of six members, while the last thirty-five years had built up a church of about 60,000 members. Let us all take courage and go forward."

J. A. Ingle represents the Protestant Episcopal Church of America. He is from Maryland; Mrs. Ingle is from South Carolina. They could not have been kinder and more helpful if they had been life-long acquaintances and friends. Mr. Ingle gave some account of the methods of work adopted and the results. The Society which he represents has a school for boys and a hospital in Hankow, and a college and a hospital in Wuchang. He has no street chapel where the Gospel is preached to promiscuous audiences. Instead, he has a guest room. A sign at the door invites all to enter who wish to inquire concerning the Christian religion. Tea and the water-pipe are served in accordance with Chinese notions of hospitality. Speaking of the converts, Mr. Ingle said that he found more comfort in the First Epistle to the Corinthians than in any other part of the Bible. Paul wrote to his converts that they were washed, and sanctified, and justified in the name of the Lord Jesus Christ, and in the Spirit of our God; but they were not just men made perfect. Who is there in the home land that has not felt the same? Converts in every age and in every field are substantially the same. The Protestant Episcopal Society has noble buildings. The chapels, colleges, hospitals, schools and homes are convenient and beautiful. No money is spared. These buildings are excelled by those of the Roman Catholics only.

David Hill is a man of private fortune, laboring in connection with the English Wesleyan Society. He has been on the field thirty years. He and his brother support a dozen laymen in China. Mr. Hill dresses like a native, and lives on five cents a day. He has a tough constitution, else he would have died long ago. Few men can live as he has lived. He is superintendent of the work in and about Hankow. He makes long preaching tours into the country. Speaking of methods, he said: "After all, it is the man, rather than the method. Dr. John adopts one method, and makes a brilliant success. Dr. Nevius adopts a different method, and his success is equally great." The Wesleyan Society has a high school in Wuchang. The boys pay fees and pay for their food. These boys are under religious instruction every day. English is taught as a pacificatory measure. The Society has a hospital as well. The evangelistic, the educational, and the medical melt and blend into one another, and together present a complete revelation of the fullness, the symmetry and the perfection of the redemption that is in Christ. Year by year Mr. Hill's conviction that the work is to go on and prevail is strengthened.

At the headquarters of the American Baptists we met Dr. Adams. He has been in China twenty years, and in Hankow two. He gave one incident showing how God overrules events to the furtherance of the Gospel. Years ago, in another province, the members of one of the churches under his care were urged to visit a neighboring village and preach. The villagers gambled and drank, and did not want them or their message. They beat the believers and drove them away. The more they were beaten and threatened, the more they returned and preached. The villagers killed their cattle and poisoned their wells. These things did not stop them. Then they threatened to kill them and burn their property. They got an astrologer to fix upon a lucky time. Hearing of their purpose, Mr. Adams went to the magistrate and asked him for protection. He said: "Let them alone; there are rich men in that village, and I will make them pay dearly for any riot." Mr. Adams told him that that was not what he wanted; he wanted protection for the innocent whose lives and goods were in peril. The magistrate informed him that it was his duty to punish crime, not to prevent it. The villagers heard that the magistrate would not interfere, and proceeded with their preparation. The Christians put their cattle in one house and gathered in another for prayer and praise. Other churches hearing of their danger united in prayer on their behalf. Mr. Adams wanted to stay with them and share their fate. The Christians would not hear to this. They said his presence would only aggravate the villagers. The assailants gathered for a night attack. They marched with lanterns and gongs and shouting. The ruffians of other villages joined the procession. Reaching the village they found the houses vacant, and supposed that the people had fled. Just then they heard them singing, and drew near to listen. At the close of a song an aged man lifted up his voice in prayer. As they listened, a furious thunderstorm broke upon them, and they were scattered as chaff before the whirlwind. They ran in all directions. Some fell into creeks and ponds and were drowned. When they went to the astrologer he said: "This fellow Adams has lightnings bottled up, and can let them go when he pleases." He advised them to go by day the next time. They planned another attack and started. On the way they sat down to arrange the division of the spoils. One wanted a certain cow. His brother wanted the same animal. Each caught the other by the tail, and a general fight began. One man was killed. One had his head and another his leg broken. When the fight was over no one cared to go on with the attack on the believers. The magistrate cut off several heads, and made others pay fines of several thousand dollars. The villagers said: "It is no use to fight against these people." The Christians rented a house in that village, and soon a church was organized.

John Archibald is the agent of the National Bible Society of Scotland in Hankow. In the eighteen years he has been in China he has traveled all over the Empire. He was the first foreigner to visit many places where now there are flourishing churches. Sometimes he has been guarded by five hundred soldiers. The society whose agent he is publishes about three hundred thousand copies of the Scriptures annually. He told us that there are three stages in Bible work. First, all want it. Second, no one wants it. Third, a few want it. This last stage is the hopeful one. Mr. Archibald showed us some of the famous Hunan pictures. The artist represents Christ as a pig. The Romans represented him as an ass. He told us that the Yangtsze Valley is the most trying place on the globe. If one gets sick he must get out at once, otherwise he will die. The mercury stands at ninety-eight or one hundred degrees during the day. At night it falls a degree or two. Mosquitoes get too languid to bite. People must sleep under punkahs or not sleep at all. New arrivals will not take advice. They know more than the veterans. They propose to show them a more excellent way. As a result, many get sick and go home or die. He says that it does not pay to live below a certain standard. To do so is almost sure to impair health, to diminish usefulness and to shorten life. He spoke of some who live on native food and go mooning about and accomplish nothing. Speaking of the riots, he told of one man who disregarded his principles and ran away. When called to account, he said he would rather ignore his principles one day than be dead all the rest of his life. John Archibald is as genial a spirit as ever left Scotland. A stranger in Hankow could not fall into better hands. He and his good wife open their hearts and their home. The only complaint they make is that their visitor does not stay long enough.

Dropping down from Hankow we stopped at Wuhu. Though it was near midnight, T. J. Arnold was waiting for me, and took me to the home of C. E. Molland. As the day had been unusually cold and stormy, the warm welcome and bright fire were doubly pleasant. A union service had been arranged for Sunday morning. All the missions in the city were represented. The room was full. The audience was orderly and attentive. Mr. Molland acted as my interpreter. In the afternoon there was an English service in the Home of the International Missionary Alliance. The gunboats and the Customs were represented. The Alliance has ninety workers in China, and sixteen more on the way. Of these forty-five are beyond the Great Wall in Mongolia. The missionaries are from Sweden, Norway, England and America. D. W. Le Lacheur is the superintendent of the work in the Empire. This Home is also a school. The new workers spend six months or more here on the language. At night there was another service in English. Dr. Jellison, of the Methodist Episcopal Hospital, dropped in on his way home, and spent a pleasant hour with us. Wuhu is a walled city and an open port. It has a population of one hundred thousand.

Leaving Wuhu in company with Messrs. Molland and Arnold, I returned to Nankin for a conference with all the missionaries. James Ware came from Shanghai and E. P. Hearnden came over from Chu Cheo. A whole day was devoted to this conference. Many important facts were brought out bearing upon the health of the workers, the needs of the work, and the best disposition of the force. Dr. Macklin pointed out the danger of sunstroke, the danger of attempting too much and neglecting proper exercise, and the need of good food. The climate is hostile to foreigners. Some are better in China than at home. This is not true of many. Houses are needed for several families. More workers are needed to enter the doors which God is opening. As we had time, we visited the other missions in Nankin. Dr. Beebe took us through the hospital under his direction. President Ferguson took us through the buildings of the Nankin University. A Pennsylvania lumber dealer paid for one building. It is his ambition to spend a million

Miss Dr. Daisy Macklin, Nankin.

W. P. Bentley and Family, Shanghai, China.

dollars in support of Foreign Missions. Another building was erected by the family of Philander Smith. This family paid for Dr. Beebe's Hospital, and for another building in Japan. We called at the Presbyterian and at the Friends' Mission. We saw all the workers and some of their work. The evening before I left Nankin the ladies arranged for a reception. All the missionaries in the city were present. Brief addresses were made by Mr. Williams, Dr. Beebe and Mr. Houston. After the addresses, refreshments were served. It was like a family gathering. All agreed that it was one of the most agreeable evenings ever spent in Nankin. The next morning I bade farewell and started for Shanghai. Most of the workers accompanied me to the ship. It was a great privilege to spend a few days in the homes and to look into the hearts and study the methods of these saintly workers. It would be a good thing if some one could come out every few years. It would do one's own heart good for many a day to see the joy of the missionaries. His coming will give a new impulse to the work and will bless his own soul. I left Nankin with a high opinion of the wisdom, energy and consecration of the workers. The Lord's cause cannot fail in such hands.

In Shanghai I met Mr. Ferguson,of Tibet. He came from Tibet to Hankow, a distance of fifteen hundred miles, on horseback. He asked for an escort while traveling through the province where the Mohammedans are now in rebellion. The authorities could give him no escort. They told him he could not go. He said he must go. For six days he had only one meal. Some soldiers called his companion a Foreign Devil. He dismounted and seized one of them by the tail. The others fled like sheep. Mr. Ferguson is a Canadian by birth. He is a member of the church in Muncie, Ind., for which H. T. Buff preaches. He is supported by some friends in Canada and in the United States. From Shanghai I go to Peking. Mr. Williams goes with me as interpreter and guide. This trip reminds me of the time when we were students together in old Bethany's classic halls.

XXIV.

PEKING AND THE GREAT WALL AND RETURN.

WE TOOK ship at Shanghai for Tientsin. This is the port of Peking. There were four missionary families on board. Some had been home and were returning, others were coming out for the first time. The rules say that passengers are not allowed to go bare backed, or to dress their hair, or smoke opium, or spit on the floor, or talk loudly in the salon. With such specific instructions it need not surprise any one that we behaved fairly well. Our course was through the Yellow Sea, the Gulf of Pechele and the Peiho. We passed between the Promontory of Shantung and Korea. The province of Shantung was the home of Confucius and Mencius. These men, more than any others, have shaped the Chinese character. In every city in the Empire there is a Confucian temple. In every school there is a tablet to Confucius before which the pupils bow on entering. One of their poets has said:

> "Confucius! Confucius! how great is Confucius!
> Before Confucius there never was a Confucius!
> Since Confucius there never has been a Confucius!
> Confucius! Confucius! how great is Confucius!"

Shantung is the scene of some of the most successful work in China. Here Drs. Nevius and Corbett and Timothy Richard and others labored for years. Here new methods were adopted. The converts were encouraged to support themselves and not to look abroad for any financial aid. Some of these converts migrated to Shanse. They called the village they built the Gospel Village. It was a time of famine. It was difficult to put up houses for themselves. Remembering the teaching they received, they built a chapel and held services. We passed Port Arthur and Wei-hai-wei. These places became famous in the war with Japan. We passed the Taku forts at the mouth of the Peiho. These were captured by the British and French in the second Opium War. As the water on the bar was low we left the ship and went by train to Tientsin. This was a thrilling experience. Think of it! A train in China! After riding on donkeys and mules and wheelbarrows, it was refreshing to buy a ticket and board a train. When the engine rolled up to the station I took off my hat. The train is European. The filth and stenches are indigenous.

We reached our hotel after dark. Mr. Stanley, of the American Board, helped us to engage a cart to take us on in the morning. We were off at daylight. The cart was drawn by two mules, driven tandem. The body of the cart was about two feet wide and four feet long, and was covered with blue cloth. One sat inside, the other sat on the shafts. There were no springs to break the jolting. The roads were rough and full of holes. They became worse as we drew near to the capital. Peking is eighty miles distant. We were told that it would take two and a half days to make the trip. Robbers abound, and it is perilous to travel after dark or before day. When we were beyond the wall of Tientsin, Mr. Williams told the driver he would give him a dollar extra if he would reach Peking in two days. The effect was magical. The mules and cart felt the inspiration. We passed every vehicle in sight. The first day we made more than half the distance. A little after midnight the driver was knocking at our door and telling us that it was time to start. We growled and protested, but it was of no use. All fear of robbers had vanished. At once we left the inn. Bad as the roads were, we sped on. We made fifteen miles before breakfast. A little after noon we saw the walls of Peking. By three o'clock we were at our journey's end. The driver was as proud as if he had won a battle.

Dr. Lowry met us and took us to his own home. He and his family did all in their power to make our visit enjoyable. They are Ohio people, and represent the Methodist Episcopal Church. Dr. Lowry is President of the Peking University. One son has charge of the hospital and dispensary. Another is Secretary of the American Legation. We visited the University. In the literary department there are one hundred and forty students. Most of these are believers. The Girls' School has nearly as many enrolled. The Medical School is well attended. The first morning at chapel the boys sang, "King Jesus, reign for evermore." That was in sight of the Emperor's palace. This mission has a strong staff. The workers go out into the towns and villages for hundreds of miles. The work was opened in 1868. Last year the conversions numbered eleven hundred. One of the most interesting events on Sunday was the Ragged Sunday School. There were four hundred present. Dr. Lowry is superintendent. The teaching is done by the advanced students in the university. It was a treat to hear them sing. Their singing was wholly unlike the caterwauling that is called music in China. This school has changed the character of the community. Instead of calling the missionaries "foreign devils," they ask when Sunday and Christmas are coming. At the union meeting Mr. Williams and I were asked to conduct the services.

We met Timothy Richard. He is one of the noted men in China. He and Dr. Wherry presented a memorial to the throne the day before our arrival. They want the Emperor and his advisers to understand the aims and motives of the missionaries. They want to convince them that the missionaries are good men, and that the evil reports published about them are false. They ask that Christianity be placed upon the same plane as other faiths. The officials who are anti-foreign are so either on account of ignorance, or because they foresee that the triumph of the Gospel means an era of honesty and efficiency, and an end of squeezing and robbery and oppression. Mr. Richard is seeking to open the eyes of the rulers of China. He is better qualified for this work than any other man in the Empire. He has been decorated by the Emperor for his services in the time of famine. He is the personal friend of several of the highest ministers. The Emperor is reading his translation of McKenzie's "History of the Nineteenth Century." The Prime Minister asked him to point out the reforms which are needed. He has been assured by several members of the Emperor's Council that they are in fullest sympathy with him. A club of young men has been formed. They are pledged to seek reforms. They publish a paper, and hope to reach every official in China. An amusing thing occurred while the memorial was under discussion. Dr. Wherry and a member of the Council had a lively tilt over the question of original sin. Confucius taught that men at birth are by nature good. Calvin taught that they are totally depraved. Gilbert Reid is engaged in the same kind of work. He dresses and lives in Chinese style. He aims to reach the official class in hope of being able to teach them the truth. He visits them and they visit him. While all do not receive him, he says his success is ten times as great as he expected. He reaches new men every week. Mr. Richard thinks this a most interesting period in Chinese history. The Japanese war has revealed a condition of affairs that surprised and shocked the officials. They do not know what to do. They are willing to be taught.

We visited the workers of the American and Presbyterian Boards, and met the men connected with the London Society. We were told that there are one thousand believers in Peking and four thousand in the region round about. Mr. Ament took us to see Mr. Murray's School for the Blind. The founder of this school was born near Glasgow. While a lad he lost his left arm. He became a letter carrier. Part of every day he studied Hebrew and Greek. He wanted to engage in some form of mission work. He was engaged as a colporteur by the Bible Society. In the summer he sold Bibles in the highlands; in the winter he worked among the sailors on the Clyde. His success was wonderful. The society wanted a man for China, and William Murray was sent. He has sold one hundred thousand copies of the "Classic of Jesus" in Chihli and Manchuria. He became interested in the blind by seeing them go about in winter in Peking. He spent eight years in trying to adapt a system to the language of China. He gathered in one or two and tested his system. In two months one was able to read fluently. Another was able to read in six weeks. It seems miraculous to the Chinese that the blind should be thus cared for and endowed with what, to them, are supernatural powers. Some are being trained as evangelists and others as Bible readers. God's promise is being fulfilled: "I will bring the blind by a way that they have not known; I will make darkness light, and crooked things straight."

Peking has a population of one million three hundred thousand. The walls are high and in good repair. There are two cities, one Chinese and the other Tartar. Within the Tartar City is the Imperial City, and within that, the Forbidden City. The streets are wide, but are unpaved. In dry weather one is in danger of being blinded by the dust. In the wet season one is in danger of being drowned in the pools or in the streams that rush along the thoroughfares. There is an air of decay everywhere. It extends to the palaces and temples. Peking is the filthiest city in the world. When the Son of Heaven goes out it is in a closed chair. The streets are hidden from his sight. If he would get out and walk he would see what a sty his capital is. On one of the streets we saw a dead beggar. He had been stripped of the few rags he wore. No one seemed concerned. In the temples and other places we found the guardians rude and inhospitable. Doors were closed and locked as we approached. Exorbitant fees were demanded before they would be opened. Everywhere else in China the priests were glad to see us and to show us everything. We found it difficult to get into the Hanlin Academy. There was little to see, but the gateman did not want to admit us at all. It would have been a pleasure to see the Emperor, but he did not call or even send his card. That reminds me of an incident in the life of Pestalozzi. He and several others were sent to see Napoleon on some educational business. Napoleon turned them over to some of his subordinates. On his return his friend said: "Did you see Napoleon?" The great teacher said, "No, and Napoleon did not see me." Perhaps the Son of Heaven was busy with his wife and numerous sweethearts, or was trying to borrow money to pay the little bill he owes Japan. Dr. Lowry took us to see the astronomical instruments made by the Jesuits in the seventeenth century. They are used no longer, but they are worth seeing. These Jesuits were able men. One of them cast three hundred cannon for the Emperor. He gave to each the name of a female saint.

From Peking we went on to the Great Wall. The builder of this wall smashed the feudal system of China, and became Emperor in fact as well as in name. He called himself "The First Emperor." Not only so, but he burned the books that disproved this claim and cut the throats of the literati, lest they should reproduce the books. He built the Great Wall to protect the Empire against the northern tribes. It was a colossal undertaking. It took a million of men ten years to complete it. It is one thousand five hundred and fifty miles in length. The height is regulated by the ground over which it runs. There are high watch-towers from which an army could be seen approaching. These towers were once manned; now they are deserted. Towers and gates and wall are tumbling into ruins. No repairs are made. The wall served its purpose, but it is useless now. The Mongols and Manchus crossed it and possessed themselves of the Empire. Dr. Martin says that there is no man in Chinese history so execrated as the Emperor that built the Great Wall. He is remembered as the Builder, Burner and Butcher, rather than as the Founder of the Empire. The scholars charge him with seeking to reduce the people to ignorance that he might govern them with facility, in accordance with the maxims of Laotze—"Fill their bellies and empty their heads." The wall is forty-five miles distant from Peking. The road for most of the way runs over a sandy plain. The country is poor and the population sparse. In the hotels we could get neither rice nor meat. Had we not taken some food with us we should have fared badly. The rooms were cold, and had no way of warming them. The poorer the fare the higher the price. We paid four or five times as much for what we got as we would have had to pay for better accommodation in the South. No matter. The wall repaid us for all our discomfort. It was a great sight. It is one that can never be forgotten. It is something to look upon a work that dates back two centuries before the birth of Christ.

On the way back we saw the Ming Tombs. With one exception, all the Emperors of the last dynasty were buried here. The tombs were magnificent pieces of work in their time. They are from three to five hundred years old. They are neglected and are falling into decay. We were gone three days. One night we slept in a Methodist chapel. The evangelist in charge took us in and supplied our needs. He would not accept anything for his services. The Lord grant that he may find mercy in that day.

The next morning we were on our way to Tientsin. We spent a few hours in Tung-cho. The American Board has been at work here for thirty years. Dr. Sheffield showed us through the North China College. There are seventy-five students enrolled. Dr. Sheffield had been attacked some months before and left for dead. There were thirty-two wounds in all. Of these thirteen were on his head. Being a man of robust constitution and good health, and having good attendance, he got well. He can say with Paul, "I bear in my body the marks of the Lord Jesus." Tung-cho is the point at which goods sent up the Grand Canal are reshipped for Peking. They are carried from this place on wheelbarrows and on camels and on mules. The wheelbarrows frequently have three horses or donkeys pulling them and three or four men steadying them. Great caravans of camels are met. These carry about six hundred pounds and make about three miles an hour. On our way to the Great Wall we met thousands of these great animals. They were carrying tea and other goods to Siberia and Mongolia and coals from the mines to Peking. One train would carry more than all we saw.

From Tung-cho we went by boat to Tientsin. We were thirty-six hours on the way. Mr. and Mrs. Stanley had invited us to abide with them. No one could have wished for more pleasant entertainment. Tientsin has a population of nine hundred and fifty thousand. It was here that the treaty was framed at the close of the second war with England. The treaty provides for the protection of all persons teaching or professing Christianity. So long as they do not offend against the laws they are not to be persecuted or interfered with. Here Li Hung Chang built a hospital for Dr. McKenzie. Here Lady Li established a school in which girls should be educated. McKenzie was a rare man. His influence was boundless. He was decorated by the Emperor. He received the star of the Order of the Double Dragon. The Viceroy behaved badly after McKenzie's death. He built a hospital across the way and opened a medical school. He demanded that the money he had given for the work be refunded. We visited the hospital. Many things in it reminded us of the gifted man under whose auspices it was built. His aspiration could be expressed in the following lines:

> "O God, that I could spend my life for others,
> With no false aims of my own;
> That I could pour my soul into my brothers,
> And live for them alone."

After his death Dr. Fred. C. Roberts took up the work. He was equally brilliant, and almost equally distinguished. After six years of service he went to his reward. The thought of his heart was:

> "I ask no heaven till earth be Thine,
> Nor glory crown while work of mine
> Remaineth here, when earth shall shine
> Among the stars, her stains wiped out, her captives free,
> Her songs sweet music unto Thee—
> For crown, give, Lord, new work for me."

Dr. Smith is now in charge. He is a modest and genial Scotchman. He is a worthy successor of the saintly men who have preceded him in that high office. We called on Dr. King. As Dr. Howard, she was associated with Dr. McKenzie in the treatment of Lady Li.

On the boat from Tientsin to Shanghai a mandarin and his servants occupied all the cabins but one. One servant filled his pipe and kept it lighted. One supplied him with a wet rag with which to wipe his face and fingers after eating. One furnished him with a piece of brown paper when he wanted to blow his nose. When he ate he threw the bones under the table. When he drank soup he could be heard across a ten-acre field. In this way he showed that he relished it. At Shanghai there were a score of mandarins to meet him and to do him honor. This man represents the worst class of men in China. They stand in the way of all progress. They are the conservatives of the conservatives. We went as usual to the hospitable home of Mr. and Mrs. Ware, and were cordially welcomed, as usual.

MISSION BUILDINGS IN NANKIN, CHINA.

XXV.

FROM SHANGHAI TO HONG-KONG AND CANTON.

BEFORE leaving Shanghai, I called on Dr. Y. J. Allen. He is a veteran missionary and a remarkably interesting man. He has been an evangelist, teacher and editor. He aided the government during the Taiping Rebellion and received a "button" in recognition of his services. He is now engaged in literary work. He founded and still edits *The Review of the Times*. This is the most widely read magazine in China. The officials not only read it, but buy it in quantities and distribute it among their friends. Dr. Allen tells the Chinese that he has a right to speak. He is not a wayfaring man spending a week or a month among them; he has spent most of his years in China; all his interests are here. He speaks as one having authority, and he is heard.

Since the war with Japan, the government has been asking, "What must we do to be saved?" The Mandarins are at sea; they have no answer. Most of them are fatalists. These say that nothing can be done. Dr. Allen has undertaken to answer that question. He is telling the officials that they must accept the new order of things, and do it ungrudgingly and cheerfully. The foreigners are here to stay. They are too strong to be driven out, and too influential to be ignored. China needs to get rid at once and forever of her old notions of exclusiveness and fancied superiority. The nations she contemptuously styles "barbarians" are her peers, and more. Plato thanked the gods that he was born a man and not a brute; a Greek, and not a barbarian. This is the feeling of the Chinese. One of them felicitated himself that he was not born across the seas, where the people are ignorant of the domestic relations, clothe themselves with leaves, eat wood, dwell in the wilderness, and live in holes in the earth. Being born in the Middle Kingdom, he has infinite blessings and the highest felicity. China can never go back to her old civilization. Whether she likes it or not, she must take her place among the nations of the earth. The next thing China needs is truth. It is the truth that makes men free from error and superstition. The officials do not know their duty. It is not enough that they do no wrong; they do wrong when they do nothing. In the recent plague in Canton, officers were continually going to the temples to entreat the idols to stop the disease. Day and night were made hideous by the cries of the people, the beating of drums and gongs, and the burning of fire crackers. In time of famine, millions die before food can reach them. If the rulers would adopt sanitary measures and build railroads, these things would be at an end. China needs the Gospel. Look all around the world. Wherever you see progress, you see that it can be traced to the Gospel as its root. This is true of Europe, America, Australia, and Japan. Persia and Turkey are dead. Were it not for international jealousies they would perish in a day. China can not keep out the Gospel. She ought not to try. It is her only hope. Dr. Allen is telling the Chinese that they must be born again. The acceptance of the Gospel means the regeneration of her whole national life, sweeping reforms in the army and navy, the reconstruction of the executive and the purification of the civil service. Dr. Allen is the friend of China. He wants her to be strong and rich and wise and holy.

I took passage for Hong-Kong in the "Empress of Japan." The first missionary work in the Empire was done in the South, because the South was first opened. On our way we passed several cities in which much good work has been done. Foochow is a city with a population of six hundred thousand. It is the center of a populous district. Moule says that the workers toiled and prayed there for eleven years without a single convert, and when he wrote there were eight thousand. The number now, so Dr. Gregory tells me, is ten thousand. Bishop Walden has been there holding the annual conference. He speaks in high praise of the eighty native preachers, and of the work generally. One Chinese Christian gave $10,000 toward the educational work in Foochow. Not far away is Hangchow. Here the Church Missionary Society has built a large hospital. One man gave $360,000 for the building and the endowment. Dr. Main says, with the Gospel and steel as weapons, we fight sin and sickness. Farther south are Amoy and Swatow. In these cities the English Presbyterians, the American Baptists; the Reformed Church, and perhaps others, are at work. Dr. Lyall, of Swatow, was on the "Empress." He has charge of the medical work. He told me that the out-patients number from one to two hundred per day. These cities are the centers of the work. The missionaries and the Chinese evangelists go into the interior for hundreds of miles and carry on the work. The rivers and canals of China make this possible. The house boats draw little water.

Some one said they go on "a heavy dew." Formosa was to our left. Here Drs. McKay and Barclay have done great good.

Hong-Kong lies within the tropics. Since 1842 it has been a British colony. Before that time it had no commerce. It was the site of a village peopled by a few fishermen. Now it is one of the great ports of the world. The island of Hong-Kong has an area of thirty squares miles. It is mostly a mountain. The population numbers 250,000. Ships from all parts of the globe ride at anchor in the harbor. Hong-Kong is the most cosmopolitan place I have yet seen. One sees more varieties of people and more strange headdresses on the streets than even in Shanghai. Being a British colony, several regiments are here. Mr. Musson, one of the chaplains, asked me to make his house my home. He took pains to show me the points of interest in the city, and particularly the missionary work. The English are good colonizers. They build roads that will endure as long as those built by the Romans. The Chinese say their roads are good for ten years, and bad for ten thousand years. The English build for the ages. Wherever England establishes herself, she rules in righteousness. As a result the people prosper. English possessions are open to all races and all creeds. The London Society has two hospitals in Hong-Kong. Each was built by one man and handed over to the mission. One was built by a Chinese. He had been educated in England and married a rich English wife. She died soon after their marriage. He built this hospital as her memorial. Afterward he went back to his old ways, and now has five or six beauties in his harem. The two hospitals have accommodations for one hundred in-patients. The out-patients number twenty thousand a year. Dr. J. C. Johnson showed me through both. I met Dr. Chalmers. He is a famous Sinologue. He has been in China forty-three years. He told me that he has charge of thirty schools. The Government gives them grants in aid. These grants are sufficient to pay all the expenses of the school. The Wesleyan, the Basle, the Rhenish Societies are also at work in Hong-Kong.

Macao is thirty-five miles distant; Canton is ninety-five miles. Morrison, the first Protestant missionary to China, did his work at these two places. Macao is now a Portuguese possession. Its business and its glory have departed. It is a pretty place, with some scenes of historic interest. The chief of these is Morrison's grave. Canton is on the Pearl River. The approaches to the city were guarded by forts that were considered by the Chinese impregnable. The British gunboats easily silenced their guns and passed on.

Canton was ransomed by the payment of $6,000,000. This is the most prosperous city I have seen in China. The buildings are substantial. The streets are about six feet wide. Coolies go along carrying chairs or loads, and though the streets are full of people, there is no collision. Canton is the silk market of China. This is the source of its wealth. The people must be very religious. Before every shop or store is a place where incense is burned night and morning. The temples are full of idols, and are in good condition. In one I saw Marco Polo among the gods, and incense burning before him. Canton is the only place in China where I saw dogs and rats for sale as food. Old ladies eat rats as hair restoratives. These animals are not used in this way as much as is commonly supposed. The boating population is a curiosity. It numbers three hundred and fifty thousand. People are born, married, live and die on boats. They cook and eat and wash their clothes and worship the gods on the water. They have no other home. Some are owned and managed by women. On one boat I counted four generations, and not a man in the lot. These mermaids handle the sail or oar or rudder as skillfully as men. Dr. Swan, whose guest I was while in Canton, showed me through the hospital. Dr. Peter Parker opened a work here sixty years ago. Dr. Happer reached Canton in 1844. For a time he stood almost alone. He endured hardships and confronted difficulties such as now few men can appreciate. Drs. Kerr and Swan are now in charge of the hospital. Dr. Kerr has been here for forty-two years. He is one of the most eminent surgeons living. He told me that forty thousand in-patients and hundreds of thousands of out-patients have been under his care since his service began. Each year the in-patients number one thousand two hundred, and the out-patients forty thousand. There are thirty-one men and women connected with the mission of the Presbyterian Church in this district. There are four stations and thirty-two out-stations. The school for girls has one hundred and sixty-five enrolled. The college is across the river. It has eighty students. Fourteen of these are studying for the ministry. Mr. Beattie of this mission took me to many places of interest. One of these was a Buddhist temple. We heard the priests chant for nearly an hour. I called at the mission of the Southern Baptists. Dr. Graves was teaching a class of thirty theological students. He said to me that they prepare men to preach, and leave the Lord to call them. I visited the Berlin mission. Mr. Kollecker explained that most of their work was educational. There are ten day schools and one theological semi-

FOUR GENERATIONS IN CHINA.

BOYS' SCHOOL IN CHU CHEO, CHINA.

nary connected with this mission. There are eight workers on the staff, and about eight hundred believers. I called at the Wesleyan Compound and on the representatives of the American Board, but did not see their work. The Catholics have a large property and a majestic cathedral. The ground upon which it stands was once the property of the city. It is a constant source of irritation to the Chinese that it is not so yet. Most of the Catholic missionaries in China are French Jesuits. The French Government stands behind them. Years ago all missionaries were called upon to leave China. Their property was confiscated. When the French made their treaty with China, they demanded that all such property should be returned to its Catholic owners. Centuries had elapsed since the confiscation. Most of the property was held by persons who had come into possession of it honestly. That made no difference; they were obliged to vacate. So it came to pass that what was once Government property reverted to the Catholics and they erected their cathedral upon it.

For three years Canton was held and controlled by the British. These were three prosperous years. The people soon became reconciled to their new rulers. Taxes were collected and the money used honestly. This was a new experience in Chinese politics. The salaries of the officials are small; they are expected to squeeze the people for much more than their stipulated allowance. Those who are best qualified to judge say that the service is corrupt and venal from bottom to top. One prominent Chinese said he thought he knew three honest officials in the Empire. The mandarins are supremely interested in perpetuating the existing misgovernment. Unyielding resistance to change is their motto. They have a monopoly and want to keep it. The English are often supercilious and overbearing, but they are honest and capable, and people prosper wherever the administration is in their hands. It is their honesty that gives them their place and influence in all Oriental countries. There are many in Canton who wish the British had retained permanent possession of their city. After two days spent in looking into the work, I returned to Hong-Kong.

XXVI.

CHRISTIANITY IN CHINA.

Tradition says that the Apostle Thomas preached the Gospel in China. This is possible, but not probable. So far as is known, the Nestorians were the first to send missionaries to the Chinese. Their watchword was, "Christ for the whole world; and the whole world for Christ." The time of their arrival cannot be ascertained. Williams thinks there are grounds for placing it as early as 505. The now famous Nestorian monument discovered in Shensi in 1625, was erected in 781. Some writers have denied or doubted the genuineness of this monument, but without sufficient reason. The inscription gives a summary of the Gospel and an account of its entrance into China and the patronage extended to it by various Emperors. It states that Olopun made his way from the West to China and translated a portion of the Bible. The Emperor investigated the new doctrine, was pleased with it, and said: "Let it have free access throughout the Empire." A monastery was built and the Emperor's picture was painted in it. He gave orders that monasteries should be built in every prefecture in China. The new faith enjoying imperial patronage spread rapidly in the ten circuits into which the Empire was then divided. It continued to prosper till the Empress Wu usurped the throne. She was an ardent Buddhist, and persecuted Christianity during the twenty years of her reign. After her death the buildings which she caused to be destroyed were restored, and the number of missionaries was increased.

Meanwhile Buddhism, which entered China in the first century of our era, was making progress. The two native faiths, Confucianism and Taoism, united against the two foreign religions, Buddhism and Nestorianism. They prevailed upon the Emperor to issue a decree suppressing all foreign religions. He commanded that the Buddhist monasteries be destroyed throughout the Empire, and that the monks and nuns all return to the ways of common life. Nestorianism shared the same fate. The Emperor said the men who taught it were to be required to resume the ways of ordinary life, and their unsubstantial teachings were to be no more heard. Buddhism rallied and filled the Empire. Nestorianism received its death-blow. No doubt many of the converts proved faithful unto death. Many, so it is believed, were gathered into the churches planted later.

John of Mount Corvin was the first Roman Catholic to enter China. He reached Peking in 1293, and was kindly received by the Emperor, Kublai Khan. He was made an archbishop, and had seven suffragan bishops under him. These were turbulent times, and Catholicism did not make much progress. After the fall of the Mongol Empire direct overland connection with Europe was interrupted, and for about two hundred years China was almost completely isolated from the Western world. Francis Xavier attempted to gain an entrance for the Gospel, but died on the coast in 1552. Matteo Ricci is justly regarded as the apostle of Roman Catholicism in China. He reached the Province of Canton in 1581. Soon after he made his way to the capital. He was favorably received by the Emperor on the throne. Ricci is described as a man of great scientific acquirements, of invincible perseverance, of various resources, and of winning manners, maintaining with all these gifts, a single eye to the conversion of China, and the bringing of people of all ranks to the faith of Christianity. Ricci is highly extolled by the Jesuits for his learning, tact, skill and perseverance. Another writer of the same church paints a different picture. "The kings found in him a man full of complaisance; the pagans a minister who accommodated himself to their superstitions; the mandarins a pliant courtier skilled in all the trickery of courts; and the devil a faithful servant who, far from destroying, established his reign among the heathen, and then extended it among the Christians." Among the converts was an officer of high rank, a member of the celebrated Hanlin Academy. His daughter did what so many Catholic women have done since. She gave her fortune to help the work. She built thirty-nine churches and printed one hundred and thirty books. The influence of Ricci and his associates at the capital was very great. They corrected the calendar, made a survey of the Empire, and cast cannon for the Emperor. The Emperor, so it is said, was on the point of becoming a Christian. Had he changed his faith the history of China and her relations with other nations would have been very different.

There arose fierce disputes among the missionaries themselves. The Jesuits began the work, but they were not allowed to prosecute it alone and in peace. The Franciscans and Dominicans sent their men to the field. Directly the strife began. They differed on two points. These were the words that should be used for God, and the worship of ancestors. They appealed to the Pope and to the Emperor. These distinguished arbiters differed. The Pope, assuming that he was Christ's vicegerent, insisted that his decision should settle the matter. The Emperor was not accustomed to such lofty claims and such authoritative expressions. He said, "Who is this man who dares to make decrees for my subjects contrary to my will?" All thought of becoming a convert was dismissed. His successor issued an edict prohibiting the propagation of Christians in the Empire, and calling upon all missionaries to leave the country except such as were required in Peking for scientific purposes. Some obeyed and left; others did not. They hid themselves among their flocks, and lived and died among them. Roman Catholicism remained under the ban till 1842. Since that time the force in the field has been greatly strengthened. The latest published statistics are as follows: Bishops, 41; European priests, 664; native priests, 559; colleges, 34; convents, 34; native converts, 1,002,818. Their cathedrals are the finest buildings in the Empire. There are four of these in Peking. The church is immensely wealthy. She owns great amounts of property in the open ports and in ports that are certain to be open in a few years. She can afford fine buildings on eligible sites. With her, money is no consideration.

Robert Morrison was the first Protestant missionary to enter China. He reached Canton in 1807. It was a capital crime for a Chinese to teach any foreigner the language. He saw that it would not be wise for him to attempt to preach to the people. He entered the service of the East India Company, and spent his time between Canton and Macao. He undertook to translate the Scriptures, and to prepare a Chinese-English Dictionary. In 1814 he published the New Testament. In 1818, with the help of Milne, he published the Old Testament. In the years 1817-1823 he published a dictionary in six volumes. It has been said that there is no finer monument of human perseverance than the dictionary of Dr. Morrison. Some one has said, "The patience that refuses to be conquered, the diligence that never tires, the caution that always trembled, and the studious habit that spontaneously seeks retirement, were best adapted to the first Protestant missionary to China." He saw three or four converts, no churches, schools, or congregations publicly assembled. When he died in 1834 the prospect was nearly as dark as when he landed. He died as he lived, in faith. He was one of those of whom it is said that

1. Jas. Ware. 2. Dr. Macklin. 3. C. E. Molland. 4. E. P. Hernden. 5. T. J. Arnold. 6. E. T. Williams. 7. A. F. H. Saw. 8. Dr. Butchart. 9. F. E. Meigs. 10. W. R. Hunt. 11. Mrs. Macklin. 12. Mrs. Williams. 13. Mrs. Saw. 14. Miss Lyon. 15. Mrs. Hunt,

MISSIONARIES IN CHINA,

they did not receive the promises, but saw and greeted them from afar, and confessed that they were pilgrims and strangers on the earth. In one of his letters he said: "I patiently await the events to be developed in the course of Divine Providence. The Lord reigneth. If the kingdom of our God and Savior prospers in China, all will be well. Other matters are of comparatively small importance."

The Nankin Treaty provided for the opening of five cities to foreigners. This treaty was formed at the close of the first opium war. The five cities are Canton, Amoy, Foochow, Ningpo and Shanghai. These are all south of the Great River. The Tientsin Treaty provided for the opening of other cities in the north. Other conventions provided for the opening of cities on the Yangtsze as far inland as Chunking. The whole Empire is now practically open. There are missionaries in all the provinces except one. The Catholics were there three hundred years ago, and they have been able to hold their ground. Since the adoption of these treaties Christianity is on a very different footing from what it was before. Its advocates are free to go where they please, and the converts are not to be molested in any way. There are now seventeen hundred missionaries scattered throughout the Empire. The converts number about sixty thousand. There are schools and colleges and universities, with a total enrollment of twenty thousand pupils. There are schools for the blind and the deaf. Leper asylums have been established. The missionaries protest against opium and against foot-binding. In times of famine, or flood, or pestilence, they are among the foremost in ministering relief. The converts are, for the most part, from the poor and the middle class. This need surprise no one. It was so in Christ's time and in Paul's ministry. "Have any of the Pharisees believed?" That was the taunt then. The officials now, as a class, stand aloof. The fact is, no Christian can hold office.

To the Chinese it seems monstrous that barbarians should attempt to improve the inhabitants of the Celestial Empire when they are so miserably deficient themselves. What are the grounds of this opinion? They allow men and women to mix in society and walk arm in arm through the streets. They do not scruple to trample printed paper under foot. They bury their dead in coffins only an inch thick, and do not burn a bit of gilt money to support them in the future world. They allow the rich and noble to pass into office without standing a literary examination, and do not throw open the doors to the poorest and meanest in the land.

They send gunboats and seize the territory of their neighbors. They see the immoral and intemperate lives and cupidity of some from Christian lands, and then ask, "What good will accrue to us in case we change our faith?" It is in this strain that a Chinese tract speaks. The missionaries have to meet the age-long and inveterate prejudices of the people. Treaties do not change public sentiment and make bitter things sweet. Archdeacon Moule states that converts lose all share in lands attached to the ancestral halls, and the affection and respect of relatives. In some cases their names are stricken from the family rolls, and thereby their posterity are incapacitated for competing at the public examinations for literary degrees. They become aliens and outcasts. They find it harder to borrow money and to obtain help in time of need. If they keep Sunday, they lose a seventh of their wages and gains, and often their employment. It requires no small degree of courage and faith to confess Christ in such circumstances. There are those who take joyfully the spoiling of their goods, and who regard it a gift that they can suffer for Christ as well as believe on his name. There are those, and they are a large number, who have demonstrated the sincerity of their faith by enduring martyrdom.

There are sixty-one hospitals and forty-four dispensaries in the Empire. The patients number 358,000 a year. This work manifests in a very practical way the humane side of our religion. It does much to undermine opposition and to dispel prejudice, and open homes and hearts that would otherwise be closed to the missionary. Williams gives a letter written by a Chinese gentleman to a doctor in Macao:

"To knock head and thank the great doctor. Venerable gentleman: May your groves of almond trees be abundant, and the orange trees make the water of your well fragrant! As heretofore, may you be known to the world as illustrious and brilliant, and as a most powerful and skillful doctor. I last year arrived in Macao blind in both eyes. I have to thank you, venerable sir, for having by your excellent medicines cured me perfectly. Your goodness is lofty as a hill, your virtue deep as the sea. I return to my mean province. Your illustrious name, venerable sir, will extend to all time; during a thousand ages it will not decay. I return thanks for your great kindness. Impotent are my words to sound forth your fame and to express my thanks. I wish you everlasting tranquillity."

It should be said that the Chinese distrust and dislike of foreigners are not without cause. Emperors belonging to three dynasties were kindly disposed toward missionaries. Had the Pope manifested the meekness and gentleness of Christ, the prohibitory decrees would never have been issued. His lordly airs gave offense. His insolence was resented. The opium wars were the most unjust wars ever waged. When the Chinese asked the British to help them fight opium, the answer was: "If your people are virtuous and your officers incorruptible, no opium will be consumed. But your people will have it. If we do not bring it, some one else will. Better legalize it and make it a source of revenue." The English took Hong-Kong. France took a large slice of the South. Concessions were demanded in several ports. In these the imperial authority is practically nullified. The bearing of Christian nations has not always been respectful. The Chinese are a proud people, and they were hurt by the unjust demands enforced by irresistible gunboats. Had she been dealt with as Japan, it is likely that the results would have been equally happy. The Christian nations did not act in a way to commend the Gospel to the Chinese. On the contrary, their conduct made it a stench in their nostrils. Furthermore, the Taipings claimed to be Christians. They had the Scriptures, and were baptized. But they were not worthy of that holy name. Nevertheless, the fact that they made this claim had its weight.

In the face of all this prejudice and hostility, Christianity is making substantial gains year by year. Those who have been longest in China are most confident of the ultimate and universal triumph. I have seen no man who is dubious of this result. In 1842 there were six Christians in the Empire; now there are sixty thousand. If Christianity should advance in the next half century at the same rate that it has in the last, and there is no reason why it should not, the converts will number many millions. The work is of God, and it cannot fail. We have his word of promise confirmed by his oath that all the earth shall be filled with his glory.

XXVII.

THE WORK OF THE DISCIPLES OF CHRIST IN CHINA.

THOUGH there had long been a conviction that we ought to aid in the evangelization of China, it was not until 1886 that anything was done. Dr. W. E. Macklin had been sent to Japan. On his arrival he found that there was no special need of a medical missionary in that field. The Japanese physicians are numerous and competent. Taking counsel with his associates and with the managers at home, he left Japan for China. After spending six months in Shanghai on the language, he moved to Nankin. As soon as he was able to speak and secure a place, he began to preach the Gospel and to heal the sick. It was not long till A. F. H. Saw and E. P. Hearnden joined him. They came from the West London Tabernacle. They had been trained in doctrine and in work by W. T. Moore. The next year F. E. Meigs and E. T. Williams and their families arrived from America. They secured rooms in an old temple, repaired them, and began the study of Chinese. Other workers have been sent to reinforce them at different times. Thus T. J. Arnold and W. R. Hunt and their wives came from England, and Dr. James Butchart, W. P. Bentley and wife, and Miss Rose Sickler, and Miss Emma Lyon came from America. Several valuable workers united with them on the field. These are as follows: James Ware and wife. He had long been connected with the British and Foreign Bible Society. He is fluent in speech, up in the language, diligent in business, and fervent in spirit. C. E. Molland and wife. He is English; she is Irish. They are a vigorous and happy pair. The pleasure of the Lord is sure to prosper in their hands. There has been one death, and only one, in the Mission—that of Carrie Loos Williams. A dozen children have been born. These brighten and bless the hearts and homes of the missionaries.

Nankin, the first place occupied, is on the Yangtsze, and is two hundred miles from the coast. It is a walled city, with a population of five hundred thousand. There are thousands of villages and towns within a hundred miles. Shanghai was next occupied. This is the most influential commercial center in the East. Its importance is destined to increase year by year. Shanghai is a great literary center. Here the *Recorder*, the *Review of the Times*, and the *Missionary Review*, to say nothing of the *Herald* and other secular papers, are published. Peking has a larger population, but in the volume of business and in the influence exerted Peking does not compare with Shanghai. Not only so, but Shanghai is one of the most cosmopolitan cities in the world. Walk along the Bund any hour of the day, and you will meet representatives of all kindreds and peoples and tribes and tongues. Wuhu is an open port, fifty miles up the river from Nankin. It has a population of about one hundred thousand. Chu Cheo is on the great road from Nankin to Peking. It is a city of considerable political importance. Lu Hoh is not far distant. This district has an area of five thousand square miles, and a population of four million. Not far from Chu Cheo there are two other cities and sixty towns and villages. Yu-Ho-Tsz is a village. The young church there is almost self-supporting. These places are centers from which the workers go out and evangelize.

Several buildings have been erected. The Memorial Hospital in Nankin cost $6,000. It has accommodations for sixty in-patients. The dispensary and chapel are a few yards distant. When the medical work began, the people were angry and wanted to drive Dr. Macklin away. The college building is in the same compound, as are the three homes erected for the workers. The Carrie Loos Williams Memorial Building is in course of erection. It will be the home of the Girls' School and the center of the work among the women. In Wuhu a home has been built. It needs a wall to make it complete. This will keep the pigs away and discourage burglars and beggars. In Chu Cheo a home is going up. This will be a great improvement over the mud house in which the two families there are now living. The other buildings used are rented. Some are commodious and convenient; others are not. Rents are very high. It is much more economical to build than to lease.

The location and work of the several missionaries at present, are as follows: Dr. Macklin has charge of the medical work in Nankin. There are two dispensaries—one at the Drum Tower and one at the South Gate. The out-patients number about twelve thousand a year; the in-patients about five hundred. As a rule, only the worst cases come to the foreigner. The Chinese, naturally enough, prefer their own physicians when they can heal them. They prefer powders made from tigers' claws or bones, or decoctions made from bugs and maggots, to the drugs that come from

America. The native physicians know nothing about surgery. Dr. Macklin told me of a beggar he found on the street. Both feet were gangrened. He took him in, washed, dressed, clothed and fed him. He removed both feet, and nursed him till he was able to go about. Then he set him up in business and put it in his power to earn an honest living. He said the difference between the hospital and the cold street was the difference between heaven and hell. The man did not become a Christian. On the contrary, he went back to his opium. Was the doctor's work a failure? *Love never fails.* Dr. Macklin preaches to the out-patients every day, and conducts services with the in-patients in the hospital as well. He goes out into the tea-houses and villages and preaches as he can find time. He uses his spare hours in writing for medical journals and in the study of social problems. Dr. Butchart has been associated with Dr. Macklin in the work since he reached China four years ago. When Dr. Macklin was home on furlough, Dr. Butchart had full charge. They have decided that it is better to divide. One man with trained assistants can do all that is needed in Nankin. In consequence of this decision, Dr. Butchart is looking out for a new place. This is not so simple a matter as it may seem. Some cities are fully occupied from a medical point of view. The present hospitals can do all the work there. Other places are not open. Dr. Butchart has been placed under guard on entering the gates, and placed in the magistrate's yamen. After an interview he was escorted out and passed on from one band of soldiers to another till he was out of the province. There are cities that will allow no foreigner to remain within their gates. Dr. Butchart hopes to be able to find a place soon where he can open a dispensary and begin work, and after a time put up a hospital.

F. E. Meigs has charge of the college. This is a boarding-school. The rising bell rings at six; breakfast is at seven; the work of the day begins at eight. There are thirty pupils and three teachers. All business is in the hands of the President. This takes most of every forenoon. He teaches four classes in the afternoon. Six boys are Christians, eight are inquirers. Most are from non-Christian homes. This must be so in the beginning of a work of this kind. In addition to this, he conducts the chapel exercises. He preaches regularly on Sundays and at other times. He has charge of the Sunday-school, the Endeavor Society and the mid-week prayer-meeting. Twice a month he visits a station in the country, fifteen miles from Nankin. He is gone two days, and preaches ten or twenty times. He has his household duties and general reading and study besides. E. T. Williams goes to the South Gate three times a week. He conducts a Bible-class and the communion service on Sunday, and preaches to the people. He goes to Pukeo and Kwan Ying Mung once a week. On his way home from each place he stops and preaches at Hsia Kwan. He preaches at several other points while going and coming. He gives some time each week to the *Missionary Review*. He is editor of this magazine. When I was in Peking, Timothy Richard, the Secretary of the Society for Christian and Useful Knowledge, thanked the Foreign Society for the good work Mr. Williams is doing, and expressed his desire that the Society could see its way to allow him to give even more time to a work so urgently needed and for which he is singularly qualified. Dr. Allen edits the *Review of the Times*. He discusses political and scientific subjects. His magazine is a secular one. The *Missionary Review* is wholly religious. The native pastors must be supplied with information respecting the progress of the work.

Messrs. Hearnden and Hunt live in Chu Cheo. Mr. Hearnden has charge of the evangelistic work there, and of the boys' school. He preaches every day in the street chapel, and goes out into the towns and villages occasionally. The boys at school attend morning prayers in the chapel. Mr. Hunt goes to Yu-Ho-Tsz once a week. He has charge of the dispensary in Chu Cheo. He sees about twenty patients a day. The night before my visit, he was called to see a young wife who had taken poison. Her mother-in-law was cruel, and she wanted to commit suicide. She had to respect and obey her while living, but dead she could haunt her and make her life wretched. The old lady was alarmed and wanted help. His fame has gone out through all the district. He has taken lessons from Drs. Macklin and Butchart, and can handle most of the cases that come to him. He evangelizes in the country as he can command time. Mr. and Mrs. Saw have just returned from home. They go to Lu Hoh for the present. They have lived there and have many friends. By their preaching and teaching and by their blameless and beneficent lives, they did much to break down prejudice and opposition, and to pave the way for the triumph of the Gospel in that section.

James Ware lives in Shanghai. He superintends the work in the Central Church. He preaches on Sundays and teaches a Bible-class. He conducts evangelistic services in the new manufacturing district of Shanghai. He has the oversight of the schools and examines the pupils weekly. He has charge of the work at four out-stations as follows: Tseu Saw, fourteen miles distant, a walled city having a population of thirty thousand; Tsungming, another walled city on an island fifty miles from Shanghai, having a population of one million; Yung Shing Saw, a city sixty-five miles away, and Tung Chow, a walled city eighty miles distant, with a population of eighty thousand. He is a member of the committee for the revision of the New Testament. In addition to all these duties, he directs the labors of ten colporteurs, and is the treasurer of the mission. W. P. Bentley and wife are at home on account of sickness. Their home on the field is in Shanghai. He had work in Tsa-Sao and in Yang-King. He went out into the country twice a month. He edited the Chinese department in *The Intelligencer*, and was General Secretary of the Endeavor work in China. In Shanghai he had charge of the weekly prayer-meeting and of the mid-week preaching. C. E. Molland lives in Wuhu. He preaches every day in the street chapel and conducts all the regular services of the church. He superintends the teaching in the day school. As he has opportunity he goes out into the villages in the vicinity of the city. T. J. Arnold also lives in Wuhu, but works altogether in the country. He goes west as far as Wu Wei Cheo and Lu Cheo Fu. He usually goes in a house boat. His district has a population of six millions.

Miss Lyon has services with the women in the hospital every morning, and visits them from time to time. She teaches one class in the college. Every afternoon, except Wednesday, she goes to the chapel and talks to the women. On Wednesday she has a prayer service. She has a Sunday-school for small children. Some of the most advanced students in the college help. She receives visits from the women, and explains the Gospel and the aims and motives of the missionaries in coming to China. She returns the calls of the women. This takes no little time, as they come some days in a stream. Mrs. Rose Sickler Williams assists in the Sunday services at the South Gate, and teaches a Bible class after the communion. She makes weekly visits to Hsia Kwan and talks to the women. While she was talking recently, one of the women was so moved that she said she would bind her child's feet no more. Then and there she proceeded to take off the bandages. She superintends a Bible woman who works among the neighbors, and translates school books for the Educational Association. She gives six hours a day to Edward and Loos. There is no public school in Nankin to which children can be sent. Mrs. Ware has a

CHINESE GAMBLING.

A RAILWAY IN CHINA.

Bible class for women on Monday on Seward Road, and another on Wednesday on Yangtszepoo Road. She looks after the school for girls, and receives and returns the visits of Chinese women. Mrs. Hearnden hopes to start a girls' school in Chu Cheo. She and Mrs. Hunt work among the women as they are able. Mrs. Hunt goes with her husband into the country, and carries the Word of life into the homes of the people. Mrs. Meigs, Mrs. Macklin, Mrs. Molland and Mrs. Arnold have small children and household cares. They assist in the work as they can, but they find it impossible to do all they wish. They feel that they must not neglect their children.

Several evangelists are engaged. Thus Chu works at the South Gate, Nankin; Ni works at Seward Road, Shanghai; Shi works at Yu-Ho-Tsz; Ku is now at Tung Chow; Zi is across the river. Mrs. Ware has a Bible woman who has an interesting history. Her sons are able to support her. As she is old, they wish here to retire. She says, "I must tell the people of Jesus while I live; I shall have plenty of time to rest in heaven." She has led eighty or ninety into the church. Sometimes she weeps because the people are so indifferent. She says: "I don't mind their treating me roughly, but it makes me sad because they treat Jesus so badly."

The work has several needs. The college needs a dormitory. This will cost $1,500. President Meigs wishes to start an Industrial Department. He wants to teach the students printing or binding or engraving. An oil engine and a press will cost $300. The pupils must not be pauperized. They must be taught to work and to rely on their own resources. More workers are needed, so that if one or two break down the work may go on. Dr. Macklin needs a trained nurse for the hospital. Miss Lyon needs an associate. The work among the women and children is too great for her. Dr. Butchart needs an evangelist to go with him to the city where he is to open his work. Buildings are needed. Thus far four families live in rented houses. The rent would pay for buildings in a few years. Not only so, but the health of the workers would be better. Chinese houses have no floors, and are only one story high. It is expedient to sleep upstairs so as to get away from the malaria. Schools and chapels are needed. We have no property in Shanghai. Business men have invested millions in factories, banks, hotels, stores, godowns, clubs and homes. Anyone who walks through Shanghai, or Hankow, or Tientsin, or Hong-Kong, will be surprised at the magnificent buildings seen everywhere. The money invested in mission property is trifling in comparison.

We have reason to be grateful to God for the workers he has given us in China. They compare favorably in natural ability and education and consecration with any I have seen. The measure of success that has rewarded their labors calls for an enlargement of effort. We must send out more men and women, and thoroughly equip them for the most effective prosecution of the work. So shall we be blessed, and so shall we become a blessing.

XXVIII.

SOME CURIOUS THINGS IN CHINA.

ONE of the first things that strike a visitor as strange is the way the people dress their hair. The men shave all the head except the crown. The hair there is allowed to grow as long as it will. It is braided and allowed to fall down the back. Usually it reaches to the ground. The owner will piece it out if necessary. This is a Tartar fashion. The Chinese were compelled to adopt it as a sign of subjection. Now they are proud of their queues. Women wear their hair in different ways. One can tell at a glance at the hair whether the woman is a maiden "heart whole and fancy free," or is engaged, or is married.

Another curious thing is the way the women compress their feet. The smaller they are the prouder the owner is of them. They are bandaged in early life and their growth arrested. The Chinese say: "It is very important that the feet should be bound so that they can walk beautifully, with mincing step, swaying gracefully, thus showing to all that they are persons of respectability." The origin of this custom is in doubt. Some cynics say that jealous husbands invented it to keep their wives from gadding about too much. Another theory is that a favorite Empress had a club foot, and the women of the court crippled their feet that they might resemble hers. In marriage arrangements one of the first questions asked is as to the size of the woman's feet. This is of greater consequence than her beauty, or health, or fortune, or disposition. If the "golden lilies" are only three inches long the arrangements can proceed. Women belonging to the laboring classes do not compress their feet. If they did they could not do their work. The Manchu women do not follow this fashion. For two hundred and fifty years the court influence has been against this foolish and hurtful practice. But it has had no effect whatever. The Chinese women, when spoken to on the subject, say that Christian women compress their waists. No doubt this is more injurious than bandaging the feet. The one evil is as hard to cure as the other.

One of the strangest things seen in China is the long finger-nails worn by certain classes. It is not an unusual thing to see nails an inch and a half or two inches long. All the nails are not of this length. They could not well be. Silver sheaths are worn to protect them. These nails show beyond question that they do no manual labor. They belong to the leisure class. Work is for coolies and for those who have not taken literary degrees. School boys write essays on the "Dignity of Labor." That is very well. But aristocracies of all kinds prefer that all labor should be performed by other hands than theirs.

Men and women dress much alike. Both wear trousers and jackets. The skirts of the women are not as long as those worn by the men. The Chinese do not use stoves to warm their houses. The front of their houses is usually open. The family live largely in public. They carry small stoves in their sleeves and so keep their hands warm. When they sit down in their homes or travel, they have a stove at their feet. The brick platform on which they sleep has an opening under it. This is filled with dry grass and set on fire. In this way the bed is warmed. Instead of warming their houses, the Chinese put on more clothing. They put on one suit over another till they seem twice their real size. They have on five or six suits at a time. The suits are padded and so are very thick and warm. They take them off in the spring gradually. In summer most of the people wear nothing at all on their heads. Some wear a skull cap with a button on the top. The women never wear anything approaching the millinery of the West. There are no large bills for husbands to pay for spring or winter bonnets. A few wear a band around their heads, but it is a simple and inexpensive affair.

The Chinese have a superstitious regard for printed paper. In school-rooms, shops, private residences, by the roadside, and in the temples, are baskets or boxes designed for the reception of scraps of printed paper picked up anywhere. It matters not what it is that is printed; the characters are sacred. Men go about the streets picking up every scrap in sight. These are burned and the ashes thrown into the sea. The Chinese say that when letters were invented heaven rejoiced and hell trembled. "He who uses lettered paper to kindle the fire will have ten demerits, and will have itchy sores; he who tosses lettered paper into dirty water, or burns it in a filthy place, will have twenty demerits, and will frequently have sore eyes or become blind. He who goes about and collects, washes and burns lettered paper, has five thousand merits, adds twelve years to his life, will become honored and wealthy, and his children and grandchildren will become virtuous and filial." One of the things for which they reproach foreigners is that they have no regard for printed paper. They think this a sure sign of a want of right feelings.

The Chinese have many ways of laying up merit in the future world. Thus, one may buy crabs or shrimps or fish that are offered for sale and put them back into the sea. That can easily be done, as they are generally alive when sold. There are in China asylums for animals. One who wishes to perform a meritorious act can go to market and purchase sheep or pigs or fowls, and save them from the butcher's knife. These can be placed in the asylums. Free ferries have been established, schools and orphanages have been opened, the hungry have been fed, and all with a view to secure a higher existence in the life to come. Certain acts have an ascertained value. Thus, to dig a well or repair a road ranks as ten. To give enough ground for a grave ranks as thirty. To set on foot some scheme for the public good ranks still higher. Other acts are counted against the doer. If a man levels a grave he will be charged with fifty demerits; if he digs up a corpse, with one hundred; if he cuts off one's male heirs, with two hundred. I saw an old priest on his way from Peking to a famous temple in the south. He was making the pilgrimage on foot. When asked why he was doing this, he said he wanted to lay up a store of merit. He was afraid if he did not he would be an animal in the next life.

The Chinese have peculiar notions about suicide. If one has had a quarrel with another, or has been deeply injured by him, instead of killing the enemy, he will kill himself. If possible, he will destroy himself in the house or at the door or on the premises of the man who has done him the wrong. In that case he makes his enemy responsible for his death, and amenable to the law for the crime of murder. Not only so, but as a disembodied spirit he can have his revenge both while his enemy lives and after his death, as he could not while in the flesh. It is a most terrible thing to have one commit suicide on one's premises, or on one's account. No blame attaches to the dead. Suicide is honorable. This formidable weapon is always in the hands of the weak. It is a protection against many evils. If a wife is neglected on account of a favorite in the harem, she can have effective redress. If a secondary wife or a daughter-in-law is cruelly dealt with, she can have her revenge. Dr. Macklin saved a man who had tried to take his own life because of some real or fancied injury of a neighbor. I think his dog bit him. As the Doctor bound up his wound, he said, "If I had died I would have made it interesting for *him*."

Begging is a profession. The beggars have guilds as other professions have. Certain streets are assigned to certain ones. A merchant can secure freedom from their visits by paying so much a year. The beggars go about and ask for one cash. They go into the stores and ring bells or beat gongs. In Canton I saw a man with a snake six or eight feet long. This reptile was trained to dart out its tongue. As a last resort, the beggars begin to sing. If any one has heard Chinese music at its worst or best, he will readily believe that the merchant capitulates, sooner or later. Sometimes a man draws a knife and cuts himself. A crowd gathers, blood flows, and the shopkeeper gives him a cash to get rid of him. He goes to the next place and repeats the performance with the same result. In Peking I saw a hundred men in line before a bank. That day every beggar was entitled to a cash; other days they go to other banks. It is not creditable to drive them out or send them away empty. Moreover, it is not safe to do so. They will watch their opportunity. At a wedding or funeral they will pour in and fill the house and defile everything. Beggars sit on the roadside. Some are blind or deformed or diseased. Mr. Saw gave an old lady a liberal offering. She got down on her knees and kotowed nine times.

In China the aged are congratulated rather than the young. The older one is the more he is respected. A man with a long white beard is regarded almost as a god. It is not an uncommon thing for a man who has reached the age of four score to be reported to the Emperor. The Son of Heaven may permit his family or friends to erect a tablet in his honor at their own expense. In Western lands people try to keep young. Ages are marked down as are the prices of shop-worn goods. In China age is prized, not youth. If the record is falsified, it is done by adding several years. New Year is everybody's birthday. If a child was born the last day of the old year, he is counted two years old on New Year's day. A recent traveler in China states that he began as a stripling with neither child nor wife. In six months he had several wives, a dozen or two of children, and several grandchildren. He changes the records to please the people. The three New Year's wishes are for "children, rank and longevity."

It is customary when speaking to disparage everything belonging to one's self and to magnify everything belonging to the person addressed. More than any other people the Chinese obey the precept, "In honor preferring one another." When two men meet the conversation is about as follows: "What is your noble name?" "My worthless name is Li." "Where is your splendid mansion?" "My mean hut is in the next province." "What is your exalted longevity?" "My miserable years number only sixty-eight." "Is the distinguished lady still living?" "The addle-pated person of the inner apartments is still alive." "How many princes have you?" "Two stupid little curs." "Are the princes doing well at school?" "The contemptible puppies have learned a few characters." How much of this is formal, and how much is sincere, it is not for a stranger to say.

Chinese women do not count for much. When young they are required to wait on their parents. After marriage they are to wait on their parents-in-law. There are few schools for girls, except those founded by missionaries. The Chinese have a contempt for the capacity of the female mind. It is a rare thing for a woman to be able to sign her own name. It is exceptional when a man can not. Ask a father how many children he has, and he will not count his daughters. Boys are often dressed as girls. This is done to protect them against evil spirits. Girls are not worth carrying away. The ancients taught that boys and girls ought not to sit on the same mat or eat together after they are seven years of age. Even their clothes should not hang on the same pegs. She is married to a man whom she has never seen. She has no choice in the matter. A virtuous wife is taught not to go beyond the threshold of her husband's house alone. She needs some one to protect her against "water, fire and fools." She can marry but once. This rule does not apply to the male sex. The sages taught that man is as high above woman as heaven is above the earth. When a woman becomes a mother or a mother-in-law or a grandmother, her position changes greatly. She passes from a slave into a goddess. But even beyond the grave she is to wait on her husband. In churches men sit on one side and women on the other. In some churches there is a high screen in the central aisle to prevent flirtation and even seeing. This is in deference to Chinese sentiment.

There are many other curious things in this strange land. They clean the streets once in thirty years. Dirt superabounds. No one cares. Pestilence is caused by some evil spirit. Friends shake their own hands when they meet. A man keeps his hat on in token of respect to a caller. He takes off his glasses for the same reason. The Chinese locate the intellect in the stomach. A proverb says, "You can row a boat in the interior of a broad-minded man."

Soldiers carry fans and umbrellas on duty. Full-grown men fly kites. Women smoke as well as men. The left hand is the seat of honor. The host will not sit down before his guest. White is the color worn in mourning. Blue is worn when the mourning season is half over. Red is the color worn on festal occasions. Brides weep and wail, and pull out their eyebrows. The soles of shoes are whitened, whereas ours are blackened. Tea is drunk in all places and at all hours; the Chinese never drink cold water. Tea is served without sugar or cream. These people never use butter or cheese or milk, and are disgusted when foreigners do. It is not unusual to ennoble a man's ancestors. This is done instead of ennobling his descendants. Sir Robert Hart's ancestors for five generations were ennobled on account of his services. China has no hereditary aristocracy, or almost none. Men quarrel about one cash. Angry words are heard, accompanied with violent and threatening gestures. Meanwhile their eyes are in a fine frenzy rolling. You expect that bones will be broken and perhaps two valuable lives taken. But no. These men were talking to keep up pretenses. The storm blew over and the whole affair was as bloodless as a French duel. A Chinese will not admit that there is any limit to his information. He has an answer for every question. The Classics contain all truth. There is no need of any other book. A Western man will admit that there are some things that he does not know; a Chinese never does. He can not afford, as a citizen of the Middle Flowery Kingdom, not to be omniscient. On New Year's Day all debts are settled. The kitchen god is burned. Before this is done his lips are smeared with molasses that he may tell a sweet tale. Men plow with a cow and an ass; or with a cow, an ox, or an ass; or with a cow and two asses, or with a mule, an ass, and a calf. Much of the life of the people is out of doors. You see cobblers, tinners, blacksmiths, druggists, washerwomen, and caterers, plying their vocations on the streets. Books are different from ours. The first page is where we have the last. The lines run from the top of the page to the bottom. They begin at the right hand. Portals are erected to women who refused marriage that they might wait on their parents, or to women who committed suicide on account of a husband's death. If a son kills a parent he is put to death and the house torn down. His nearest neighbors are punished, his school-master is put to death, the magistrate of the district suffers, and the governor of the province goes down in rank. Many other curious things could be mentioned, but these are sufficient. In many respects they resemble the Anglo-Saxons. In their fancied superiority, in the energy and ability to adapt themselves to their environment, in their love of money and power to make and keep it, in their sins and sorrows and need of a Savior, in their capacity to accept Jesus Christ as Savior and Lord, and to be justified, and sanctified, and glorified through him, they make it evident that they belong to the same race as ourselves.

XXIX.

CHINA AND THE CHINESE.

AMONG the nations China ranks third in area and second in population. She is surpassed in area by the British and Russian Empires; in population, by the British only. China proper has an area of 2,000,000 square miles. That is to say, she is equal in size to all the States east of the Mississippi, with Texas, Arkansas, Missouri and Iowa added. Including Manchuria and her colonial possessions, China has an area of nearly 5,000,000 square miles. Her coast line is 4,400 miles in length. Three great river systems drain the country. These are the Yangtsze, the Yellow, and the Pearl. She has mountains covered with perpetual snow, wide and sandy plains, and fertile valleys. In size, in position, and in her water courses, China is not unlike the United States. The mineral resources are varied and abundant. Thus far they have not been developed on a large scale. A goodly part of the land yields two crops a year; certain parts yield three. The principal products are rice, cotton, sugar-cane, tobacco, wheat, millet, corn, tea, sweet potatoes, beans, garlic, peas, turnips, grapes, peaches, oranges, bananas, apricots, watermelons and peanuts. The chief articles of export are tea and silk. The Chinese are constantly fertilizing their fields. Nothing is allowed to go to waste. They collect bones, soot, hair in barber-shops, exploded fire-crackers, sweepings of the streets, mud from the bottom of canals, offal of every kind, and the sewage of cities. As a result,soil that has been under cultivation thousands of years is as productive as it ever was.

China proper is divided into eighteen provinces. These are subdivided into prefectures, and these again into districts. Each division has its own capital. A provincial capital has a population of about 1,000,000; a prefectural capital a population from 100,000 to 800,000, while district capitals may have only a few thousand. These capitals are all walled cities. According to Nevius, there are 1,700 of these in the Empire. In the great cities there are Tartar garrisons. The Tartars live in a part of the city walled off from the Chinese part. The Tartars are all pensioned, and are regarded as bulwarks of the reigning house.

It is believed now by scholars that the Chinese came from ancient Elam. Before Abram left Chaldea to go west, the ancestors of the present Chinese went east, and in course of time settled in the land in which they now dwell. It may have taken centuries to drive out or to absorb the aboriginal races and to appropriate their territories. If this view is correct, China saw the rise of Assyria and Babylon, of Persia, Greece and Rome. The nations of Europe are of yesterday as compared with her. There have been twenty-four dynasties, but the people and their institutions are substantially now what they were two thousand years before the birth of Christ. An empire containing one-fourth of the human family, an empire incomparably the oldest in existence, challenges the attention of all students of history.

In theory the government is an absolutism. The Emperor is the Son of Heaven. There is no Congress or Parliament representing the people. Two councils give advice to the Emperor. Under these councils are the Six Boards. These relate to civil office, revenue, rites, war, punishment and works. Beside the Central Government in Peking, there are a dozen Viceroys. These rule over one or two provinces. They levy armies, own and control gunboats, coin money, and do other things that are usually done by the supreme power. There are under the Viceroys Governors of provinces and other officers, and under these Prefects, and under the Prefects Hsiens. While the Emperor is the Son of Heaven, he is under laws which cannot be broken or evaded. The people know their rights, and, though they are patient under oppression and unjust taxation, they have more than a score of times risen against their superiors and changed the dynasty. There is no office below the throne to which the humblest child in the Empire may not aspire. There is no aristocracy in China save that of learning. Those who win the prizes in the competitive examinations, and they only, fill all the offices. The Emperor cannot appoint his favorites to these positions.

The Chinese prize learning above everything else. The scholars occupy the first place. After them come the farmers, the artisans, and the traders, and in this order. The Mandarins dress in silk, and are housed in palaces. When they go out they have an imposing retinue. The people gladly make way for their chairs to pass. The man in the chair was not born in wealth. He was not promoted by the caprice of the Emperor. He rose to that position by his own exertions. He passed the examinations, and now there is nothing that he cannot do. He can lead armies, direct navies, administer justice, supervise public works, sit in either of the Councils, and give advice to the Son of Heaven. These examinations are a unique feature of Chinese life. Once a year in each district an examination is held. About one in a hundred gets a degree. Once in three years those who won the first degree repair to the provincial capital for a far more searching examination. Of these again about one per cent. are successful. The next year in Peking those who won the second degree are examined a third time. Those that take the third degree are chosen by lot to fill the first vacancies that occur. Those that win the third degree compete for positions in the Hanlin Academy. This contest is under the eye and direction of the Emperor. About twenty of the best are selected for this honor. Out of the twenty that win this prize the best is appointed laureate. He is the one bright consummate flower of the nation. He is the ornament of the reigning dynasty. Dr. Martin says: "Provinces contend for this prize. The town that gave birth to the victor is noted forever. Swift heralds bear the tidings of his triumph, and the hearts of the people leap at their approach. We have seen them enter a humble cottage, and amidst the flaunting of banners and the blare of trumpets announce to its startled inmates that one of their relations had been crowned by the Emperor as the laureate of the year." The daughter of a laureate has been deemed worthy of being an Empress. In the same hall grandfathers, fathers and sons may compete. Men have succeeded when they were past fourscore. The prize is worth a life of study and toil.

While the Chinese prize learning, it is not what we mean by learning. They are not examined in arithmetic, grammar, chemistry, physics, general history, or natural science. In their examinations the competitors are to write essays and poems on some sentence in the Classics. They must write in a certain style to win the prize. One may be able to repeat the Classics word by word, and be able to write beautifully on a sentiment found in them, and know little else. With all their love of learning they are not well informed. It is not long since Chinese maps gave almost all the land on the globe to their own country. England, Holland, Portugal, France, Germany and India were small islands running from north to south. Africa and the Americas had no place. China was 1,500 miles square. It was bordered by the four seas. All other nations were tributary to the Son of Heaven. Japan is spoken of as "a rebel."

The Chinese are industrious and economical. They work as

1. Dr. J. C. Kerr, Canton, China. 2. Pandita Ramabai, Poona, India. 3. Francis Xavier.

THREE DISTINGUISHED MISSIONARIES.

hard and live on as little as any other people. They gather grass on the hills and by the roadside and bean-stalks for fuel. As merchants they are very successful. They seek to please their patrons. They have learned that honesty is the best policy. Three-fourths of the business of Shanghai is done by them. In Hong-Kong, Singapore, and all through the Archipelago, the Chinese are taking the lead. The recent legislation in Australia and America, if not a confession of defeat, is not a pæan of victory. Sir Frederick Bruce said that Chinese statesmen were equal to any he ever met in any capital in Europe. Dr. Williamson said: "The Chinese are the imperial race in the far East." Moreover, they are a literary people. Their works of history are numbered by the thousand. No one, I think, can be long with the Chinese and despise their mental ability. They are not an inferior race.

The Chinese are a religious people. Temples, pagodas and shrines are everywhere seen. The boats on the river, the kitchens and the wells have their deities. China has 300,000 temples, 4,000,000 idols, and spends $400,000,000 a year on idolatry. There are three religious systems, namely, Confucianism, Taoism and Buddhism. Confucius was born B. C. 551. He was a transmitter, not a maker. He emphasized the Five Relations. These are the relations of emperor and officer, father and son, husband and wife, elder and younger brother, and friends. He had nothing to say about man's relation to God. The Chinese say, "Worship the gods, as if the gods were there; but if you worship them not, the gods don't care." He said little about the future. "We do not know life, how then can we know death?" When asked for one word that would serve as a rule of life, he said, "Is not *reciprocity* such a word? Do not do to others what you would not have them to do to you." Confucius has a temple in every city and a tablet in every school in China. In the temples 62,000 pigs, sheep and rabbits, and 2,700 pieces of silk are annually sacrificed to him. Taoism is a superstitious system. It seeks the philosopher's stone and the elixir of life. It teaches that the heart is to be cultivated by retirement, austerity and meditation. The body is to be disciplined by sitting cross-legged, swallowing saliva, rubbing the flesh, rolling the eyes, and gnashing the teeth. The elixir of life is found by collecting all the materials and putting them to boil in a pot over a fire not too hot or too cold, for eighty-one years. The Taoists select lucky places for graves and the exact time to bury the dead. They understand all about the *Fung Shui*. If evil befalls a family, it is because the dead are unhappy. They were not buried properly or they are in the chamber of horrors in purgatory. In either case, the priest, for a consideration, will insure their comfort and a return of prosperity. The Chinese are full of superstition. In time of drought they will pray to a snake. At other times they worship the fox, the weasel, the hedgehog and the rat. To them the air is full of evil spirits. They believe that these spirits can cut off their tails. The priests furnish charms that will protect them against this loss. Bits of paper and bags of beans can be changed into soldiers. Foreigners can see millions of miles into the sky and far into the earth. With the eyes of the Chinese as medicine, they can turn lead into silver. Buddhism came to China A. D. 63. Buddhism proposes to give peace by eradicating desire. It teaches the transmigration of souls. One may rise to a Buddha or sink into an animal. A woman can enter heaven only by being born again a man. There are temples of the three religions. Chinese are Confucianists, Taoists and Buddhists at the same time, and feel no sense of contradiction or incongruity.

The principal religion of China is ancestral worship. The Emperor only can worship the Supreme God. The people have nothing to do with that; they worship their ancestors. Confucius taught them that of all the actions of men there is none greater than filial piety. They revere and obey their parents while living. There is no stigma so dreaded as that of "undutiful." When they are dead their children are to worship them. Man has three souls. One goes into the ancestral tablet, one goes into the coffin, and the third goes into the spirit world. Worship is carried on before the tablet, at the grave, and in the temples. The spirit needs clothes, food, houses, money, candles and incense. These are offered. Excepting the food, the other articles are burned. It is the duty of the eldest son to carry on this worship. The greatest of all calamities is to have no son. Parents seek to provide against this. They arrange for the early marriage of their children. If no sons are born in a reasonable time, men take secondary wives. It is this, the worship of ancestors, that makes the Chinese prefer sons to daughters. Girls are of little value. Frequently no name is given them. In cases of infanticide the victims are all girls. A daughter never inherits property. A bride is a dove because of her quietness and stupidity. There is no reason why her husband should mourn in case she dies; he can get another within a week. The ancestral temple is the most sacred spot on earth. Here repose the spirits of one's ancestors. Here his own spirit will repose for all time. If he dies in a foreign land his body is brought back. Otherwise, his spirit will be unfed, unclothed, unhoused, and wander miserably on the Plutonian shore forever. So important a thing is ancestral worship that the selection of an heir to the throne is regulated by it. The heir must in no case be older than his predecessor. The elder cannot worship the younger. Dr. Yates estimates that the Chinese spend $150,000,000 a year on this worship. Great quantities of gilt money are made and sold. It is exposed in every store. Dr. Yates holds that ancestral worship is the chief obstacle to the spread of Christianity.

It is said of the Chinese that their literature is pure. They do not sanctify vice as was done in Corinth and Phenice. This does not mean that they are a pure people, but it does mean that their standard is high. They do not call evil good. There are things done in secret that are not to be reported in public. They do not regard lying as we do. Tell a man from the West that he lies, and he will regard it as an insult. Tell a Chinese that he has a fatal facility for lying and he will take it as a compliment. As well expect to insult him by telling him that he is an inveterate joker. Polygamy is found in the higher circles. There is very little of it among the working classes, except where the wife has borne no sons. But even then there is only one lawful wife. The children of the secondary wife are her children, and she is the servant of her mistress, even as Hagar was the servant of Sarah. Dr. Williams says that polygamy is supported by the wives themselves. They like to have subordinates to wait on them and to do their work. The officials are polygamists as a rule. They are a sensual and unclean lot. All the daughters of the Manchu officers pass before the Emperor once in three years. He selects those that please him for his harem. The Chinese are a race of gamblers. They begin in infancy and keep at it till they die. They stake their property, their liberty, their wives and children for generations on a throw of the dice.

Above all other peoples, the Chinese are conservative. They do not believe the words of Tennyson:

> "The old order changes, giving place to the new,
> And God fulfills himself in many ways,
> Lest one good custom should corrupt the world."

They love the ancient. They seek the old paths and walk therein. So railways are opposed. One was built by foreigners. The Chinese bought it and tore it up. So in a land of abundance

3,000,000 starve every year. Transportation by donkeys takes time and costs immensely. The railway would put an end to famines. Troops could be moved rapidly. As it is, a war is over before some of the troops reach the field. China has one railway of some length and two or three other short ones, and is talking of building more. But the conservatives shake their heads and give their voice against them. China has no imperial post-office. There are hundreds of private postal systems. They are managed as express companies are at home. The Customs service forwards letters to open ports in China, but does not handle foreign mail. So it comes to pass that it takes six or eight months for letters to cross China. Strangest of all, China has no free public schools. There are a few technical and naval and military schools, but no provision is made for primary education. The government indirectly encourages education, but leaves the people to employ such teachers and to adopt such courses as they prefer. As a result, one man in twenty and one woman in ten thousand can read intelligently. This is Dr. Martin's estimate. There are thirty-one papers and periodicals. Of these sixteen are secular and fifteen religious. The roads are poor. Goods are carried in boats or on camels or mules or donkeys or on wheelbarrows. Men are carried in chairs or in mule-litters.

Dr. Williams says that a thousand years ago China was the most refined nation on the globe. Other nations have made progress; she has gone backward. Why? His explanation is that China has not the Bible. That makes the difference. China has ethics, but her system of ethics has no root in religion. The learned men are either "pantheists or atheists." They worship no personal God and are amenable to none. One would think the Mandarins would be the best men in the nation; they are the worst. With few exceptions they are devoid of patriotism. Officialism is corrupt from top to bottom. Men draw pay for a thousand soldiers and have a hundred enlisted. They take pay for services that are not rendered. Ashes are sold for gunpowder. Shells are filled with peas instead of steel. There are no checks upon official corruption. Even literary degrees can be bought. China needs the Gospel. She has tested the Three Religions for millenniums, and has found them insufficient. Like the woman in the Gospel, she has spent her money, but has grown worse instead of better. There is one and only one source of help. The Emperor is asking the old question, "What must I do to be saved?" The old answer is appropriate, "Believe in the Lord Jesus Christ and thou shalt be saved, and thine house."

MISS MARY RIOCH AND CLASS OF GIRLS, TOKYO, JAPAN.

XXX.

FROM HONG-KONG TO CALCUTTA.

I LEFT Hong-Kong on the *Preussen*. This is a German ship. She runs between Hamburg and Japan, calling at important points on the way. The Germans are securing a goodly share of the business of the far East. Their success is alarming those who have borne the heat and burden of the day. They are civil and obliging, and give strict attention to business. Their ships are large and comfortable. The stewards have organized a band, and play every day and night. This is a popular feature. The music breaks the monotony of the voyage and is a real refreshment. For several days the sea was rough. Quite a number of the passengers were sick. All sorts of remedies were suggested. One of the so-called infallible cures is lager beer. One man never knew it to fail. It did not help in this case. A victim of sea-sickness drenched himself with beer, but had to throw it up in a few minutes. Another suggested that if the sick man would lie down with his feet higher than his head, he would find relief at once. Dr. Butchart, of Nankin, says he knows of one sure cure, and only one, namely, the shade of a tree. For those like me, who are never sick, the rolling of a ship is rather pleasant. It is especially so at night.

> "Rocked in the cradle of the deep,
> I lay me down in peace to sleep;
> Secure I rest upon the wave,
> For thou, O Lord, hast power to save."

Our first call was at Singapore. The island on which this city stands was bought from the Sultan of Johore by the British in 1819. At that time the population numbered only two thousand; now it numbers two hundred thousand. Singapore is at the extreme southern portion of Asia. The Malay Peninsula extends from Burma to Singapore. In addition to Singapore, the British own Penang, the Province of Wellesley, Malacca and Dindings. Six of the native States are under British protection. Wherever the British rule the people prosper. In the parts of the Peninsula under their control the population numbers four hundred to the square mile; where they are not in control the population numbers only nine to the square mile. The roads and buildings, and aqueducts, and dock, and the ships in Singapore are sufficient to show that the natives are not in authority. They care for none of these things.

Singapore is a free port. People are here from all parts of the globe. On the streets one sees Chinese, Malays, Japanese, Hindoos, Sikhs, Madrasees, Parsees, Negroes, Armenians, Burmese, Egyptians, Siamese, Singhalese, Tamils, Jews, Arabs and Europeans. The Chinese predominate. They number one hundred and twenty-one thousand. They have the bulk of the land and wealth and business. There are several Chinese in Singapore worth their millions. Singapore is within eighty miles of the equator. The mercury never registers higher than ninety-four degrees in the shade. The weather is not so hot as one would expect, but it is hot enough. There are no seasons. Singapore is the land where eternal summer reigns. The perennial heat enervates the system. The natives are not as industrious as in colder climates. They need little clothing. Food is abundant and cheap. Dr. Oldham says a man can build a house on the bank of the river. He can sit at home, and out of his opened window catch all the fish he needs. The cocoanut tree never fails to yield a crop. Tapioca grows wild, and is so cheap that it does not pay to cultivate it. When urged to work and rise in the scale, the native shakes his head and says, "It is difficult." So it comes to pass that the Chinese come in from the North and take possession. In a few generations they may become as languid as those whom they have displaced. I have heard that bees taken to the West Indies work hard the first year, but finding the flowers in bloom all the time they cease storing up honey for a winter that never comes.

Missionary work is carried on in Singapore by the Church of England, the Catholics, the English Presbyterians, the Plymouth Brethren, and the Methodist Episcopal Society. The Church of England has a fine cathedral and a strong staff of workers. They preach and teach. The Catholics have all the methods that they have found useful elsewhere. The Methodists have a college for boys. They have six hundred enrolled. The Chinese gave $6,200 to establish this school. The government grants and the tuition fees pay all expenses. In the classes I saw Chinese, Tamils, Malays, Eurasians, Javanese and Arabs. The boarding school has forty inmates. The Principal of the college and several American teachers eat at the same table with the boys. The Deaconesses have two hundred girls in the school under their care. In their Sunday-schools there are over five hundred enrolled. This society has a dispensary. The physician in charge was an army surgeon. He resigned his position to take up this work. Another efficient worker had been one of the Royal Engineers. In connection with this work is a mission press. While I was there a wealthy young man from New York joined the mission. He proposes to start a Medical Training School, and to support himself and the work.

Dr. Gregory, of China, went with me to see the summer palace of the Sultan of Johore. It is the most magnificent building I have ever seen. Much of the plate is of solid gold. Polished ivory tusks are found in all directions. The vases are of the costliest material and the most exquisite workmanship. The tapestries are of silk and gold. It would be interesting to know how this magnificence was paid for. The people are heavily taxed to support this display. In the East the good things belong to the few. The many have few comforts and no luxuries. The money invested in this palace would have established a score of colleges and libraries. The Sultan, we were told, was popular in his time. He was fond of fast horses and delighted in sports of all kinds. But if he ever did anything to uplift his people, we did not hear of it. In the company of Prof. Wood, I visited the Tau Tock Seng Hospital. This was more to me than the palace. A rich Chinese gave $7,000 to found a hospital for the diseased of all countries. His son gave $3,000 more. The hospital has six hundred beds. The government grants amount to $40,000 a year. This man was not a Christian, but he was prompted to this by what he saw among Christians. In Canton the Chinese have built hospitals and dispensaries because of Dr. Kerr's work in that city. Buddhist monks preach to the patients as Christian men preach in Dr. Kerr's chapel. The leaven is at work, and no power can arrest it till the whole lump is leavened.

There are a number of places of considerable importance not far from Singapore. Of these the following deserve mention: Sumatra, Java, Borneo, Celebes, the Philippines, the Moluccas, and Siam. The Philippines belong to Spain. Part of Borneo belongs to Great Britain. Siam is an independent power. The other places named belong to the Netherlands. These are all large places. Sumatra has an area of 160,000 square miles; Java, 50,000; Borneo, 203,000; Celebes, 72,000; the Philippines, 114,326; the Moluccas, 42,000; Siam, 250,000. The Dutch East Indies have an area of 719,000 square miles, and a population of 29,000,000. The Philippines are as large as all Italy. Borneo is larger than Great Britain and Ireland. It is said that if Borneo was as densely populated as Java it would have 125,000,000, while all Malaysia would contain

250,000,000. These islands produce sugar, tea, coffee, rice, oranges, bananas, mangosteens, the durian, the king of fruits, pineapples, cocoanuts, pepper, hemp, tobacco, tapioca, cocoa, spices and tropical fruits of all kinds. Bishop Thoburn says one sago palm will supply a man with food for a whole year, and one such tree can be bought for three dollars. The Malay Peninsula has enough tin in its mines to supply the world. Sumatra is the richest of the islands in minerals. Borneo has minerals and timber.

Considerable missionary work has been done in this part of the world. The Dutch societies are at work in the Dutch Colonies. They report sixty-seven missionaries and 236,604 converts. The Church of England is at work in all parts of the Empire. Other societies are helping to turn these people from Mohammedanism and Buddhism to the living God. In Siam the Presbyterian Board has a staff of thirteen ordained missionaries, four physicians, seventeen lay workers, and thirty-three native helpers. They report twelve churches, 1,114 converts, twenty-one schools, 641 pupils, four hospitals and two mission presses. The Catholics are everywhere. They came to this field 300 years ago. The Portuguese were the first to explore these parts and to settle in them. The Pope gave the king all the land he might discover in the East. The king was as eager to build up the church as he was to add to his possessions. Every ship carried some missionaries to these lands. Francis Xavier did much of his work in the Archipelago. "He pillowed his head on a coil of ropes and ate what the sailors discarded; and there was not a seaman in that laboring vessel, there was not a soldier in that crowded troop-ship, who did not inwardly recognize the great soul that glowed beneath those squalid garments; no outward humiliation could conceal that knightly spirit, no sickness and suffering could quench the fire of that ardent genius." He rebuked sin; he added great numbers to the churches. The Philippines are under Spanish control. The Catholics only are allowed to work there. The British and Foreign Bible Society has its main office in Singapore. The agent told me that last year they sold 75,000 copies of the Scriptures. These sales were made in forty-two different languages.

Leaving Singapore and passing through the Straits of Malacca, we came to Penang. This city is nearly as large as Singapore. The same missionary societies are at work in both. We were there on Christmas day. The government offices and the foreign business houses were closed. The Chinese and Malays were at work, as if they had never heard of the Christmas carol sung by the heavenly

BUNGALOW IN HURDA, INDIA.

BEGGARS IN HURDA, INDIA.

host over Bethlehem. Dr. West, of the Methodist Mission, took us to the Public Gardens and told us about the work. There are five hundred pupils in the three schools under the control of the Methodists. After taking on board one hundred and thirty thousand cocoanuts and some other freight, we left Penang for Burma. In three days we were in Rangoon. Burma is as large as Texas and Massachusetts, and has a population of eight millions. The population is made up of forty different races. The four distinct peoples are the Burmese proper, Peguans, Shans and Karens. There are thirty tribes of these jungle people. They all worship evil spirits. The Burmese are called the Irish of the East. They like gay clothing and are a gay people. They believe that sufficient unto the day is the food thereof. As a result, Chinese and Hindoos are doing most of the work. Teak and rice are the chief articles of export. Rangoon has doubled its population in ten years. Since Burma was annexed to India there has been a degree of prosperity unparalleled in the history of the country. Burma is a great Buddhist stronghold. The fame of her pagodas has filled the world. There is one in Rangoon that is three hundred and seventy-five feet high. It is made of brick, and is heavily plated with gold.

Judson reached Burma in 1813. Felix Carey and two others had been there before him. They left the field to him. For seven years he preached in Rangoon before he found any to believe his message. He was arrested and thrust into prison, and kept there for nearly two years. Part of the time he wore five pairs of fetters. Of his wife it is said that she followed him from prison to prison, ministering to his wants, trying to soften the hearts of his keepers, to mitigate his sufferings, interceding with government officials or with members of the royal family. For a year and a half she thus exercised herself, walking miles in feeble health, in the darkness of the night, or under a noonday sun, much of the time with a babe in her arms. She died in her youth, while her husband was at the capital acting as an interpreter between the king and the British. Years went on, and the work began to prosper. In seventeen years the whole Bible was translated. Native evangelists went out and preached with marvelous power and success. Judson lived to see 20,000 won to the faith. Some people came to him and said, "Sir, we have seen a writing that tells of an eternal God. Are you the man that gives away such writings? If so, please give us one, for we want to know the truth before we die." Others came from the interior and asked, "Are you Jesus Christ's man? Give us a writing that tells us about Jesus Christ." Others came from the borders of Siam and China, and said, "Sir, we hear that there is an eternal hell. We are afraid of it. Do give us a writing that will tell us how to escape it." The most successful work was done among the Karens. These people were more noble than the Burmese, in that they received the truth with all readiness of mind. Mr. Boardman did his work among the Karens. After his death his wife took his place, "proclaiming Christ to the inquirers, conducting schools, and making long tours, often in drenching rains, through wild mountain passes, over swollen streams and deceitful marshes, among the craggy rocks and tangled shrubs of the jungle." She translated "Pilgrim's Progress," several tracts, twenty of the best hymns, four volumes of Scripture questions for Sunday-schools. She learned the language of the Peguans, and superintended the translation of the New Testament and the principal Burmese tracts into it. Several years after the death of his first wife, Dr. Judson was married to Mrs. Boardman. Her health failing, it was decided that she should visit America. He accompanied her as far as the Isle of France, and then returned to his work. She wrote at the time:

"We part on this green islet, love—
Thou for the Eastern main,
I for the setting sun, love,
Oh, when to meet again?

"My heart is sad for thee, love,
For lone thy way will be;
And oft thy tears will fall. love,
For the children and for me.

"The music of thy daughter's voice
Thou'lt miss for many a year;
And the merry shout of the elder boys
Thou'lt list in vain to hear.

"My tears fall fast for thee, love,
How can I say Farewell!
But go; thy God be with thee, love,
Thy heart's deep grief to quell.

"Yet my spirit clings to thee, love,
Thy soul remains with me;
And oft will hold communion sweet
O'er the dark and distant sea.

"But who can paint our mutual joys
When, all our wanderings o'er,
We both shall clasp our infants three,
At home on Burma's shore!

"But brighter shall our raptures glow,
On yon celestial plain,
When the loved and parted here below
Meet ne'er to part again.

"Then gird thine armor on, love,
Nor faint thou on the way,
Till Boodh shall fall, and Burma's sons
Shall own Messiah's sway."

The "farewell" was spoken. They parted to meet on earth no more. The ship was obliged to put into St. Helena. Here Mrs. Judson died and was buried. The third Mrs. Judson was worthy of the other two. She was a poet and an author of note before her marriage. "My Indian Bird," written after the birth of her first child, contains the following lines:

"There's not in Ind a lovelier bird;
Broad earth owns not a happier nest;
O God, thou hast a fountain stirred,
Whose waters never more shall rest!

"The pulse first caught its tiny stroke,
The blood its crimson hue from mine;—
This life, which I have dared invoke,
Henceforth is parallel with Thine.

"A silent awe is in my room,
I tremble with delicious fear;
The future with its light and gloom,—
Time and eternity are here."

The Baptists have now one hundred and forty-eight missionaries in Burma, and six hundred and one native preachers. They have six hundred churches with a total membership of thirty-three thousand three hundred and thirty-seven. They have four hundred and fifty-six schools, with twelve thousand two hundred and ninety pupils enrolled. Near Rangoon they have a Theological Seminary, with two hundred students in it preparing to preach. This is one of the largest schools of its kind in the world. They have a college in Rangoon. Other societies have entered the field in recent years. Dr. Smith, of the Methodist Church, told me that while they have some work among the Burmese and Tamils and Telugus, their work is chiefly in English. The Burman Church is Judson's monument. He labored, and others have entered into his labors.

All through the East one is surprised to see so many Eurasians. These are the children of European and Asiatic parents. Some of these are strikingly handsome. Coming out of a church in Singapore, I asked the pastor concerning the future of Eurasian girls. He sighed deeply and said, "Their future is very dark." I asked him if he meant that respecting those that were cultivated and attractive. He said that the comlier they are in person and the sweeter they are in disposition, the more they are sought after for immoral purposes. Better for such girls if they had never been born. In America we condemn the Chinese because they do not bring their women with them and establish homes. The Chinese are not the only people that do that. There are thousands of men in the far East who are doing the very thing for which we condemn the Chinese. Three days and a half after leaving Rangoon we reached Calcutta, the capital of the Empire of India.

1. Miss Hattie Judson.
2. Dr. C. S. Durand.
3. Mrs. H. L. Jackson.
4. Miss Mary Thompson.

XXXI.

INDIA AND HER PEOPLES.

The outline of India resembles a triangle. The Himalayas form the northern boundary. Cape Comorin, the extreme southern point, is within a few degrees of the equator. The western coast is washed by the Sea of Arabia and the Indian Ocean. The eastern coast is washed by the Bay of Bengal. Quetta, on the west, is nineteen hundred miles from the eastern part of Assam. From the Himalayas to Cape Comorin the distance is about the same. Burma is no part of India. It is separated from it by mountains and by barriers of race and language. But Burma has been annexed and is now part of the British Empire in India. Ceylon lies to the southeast, and, though it is almost joined to India by a bridge of islands, it is a crown colony and is independent of the government in Calcutta. Excluding Burma and Ceylon, India has an area of 1,587,000 square miles. It is as large as all Europe without Russia, or as large as that part of the United States east of the Rocky Mountains.

There are three natural divisions. The first is that of the Himalayas. For 1,400 miles this range averages 14,000 feet in height. Mount Everest is 29,000 feet above the sea, or twice as high as Pike's Peak. The base of the Himalayas averages 150 miles in width. The second division stretches from these mountains to the Vindhyas, and consists chiefly of three great river systems: that of the Indus, that of the Ganges, and that of the Brahmaputra. The Indus and Brahmaputra rise north of the mountains; the Ganges rises on the southern side. India is thus watered by streams from both sides of the Himalayas. The Indus is 1,800 miles long and drains a basin of 372,700 square miles. The basins of the Ganges and Brahmaputra are about the same in extent. That part of India lying between the Vindhya mountains and Cape Comorin is called the Deccan, or Southland. The Western Ghats run down the Malabar coast at some distance from the sea. The Eastern Ghats run down the Coromandel coast in the same way. These two chains of hills unite at the Cape.

According to Sir William Hunter, India is a continent rather than a single country. He speaks of it as a museum of races differing in language and religion. The people may be divided into two classes: the Aryans and the non-Aryans. The Aryans belong to the same stock as the Greeks, the Romans, the Germans and the English. Their ancestors dwelt at one time in tents in Central Asia. About the time our forefathers began their migrations westward towards Europe, it is likely that some members of the same family turned their faces and their footsteps in the direction of India. No one knows how long ago that was. The Aryans entered through the northwest passes and settled in the valley of the Indus. When we first get a glimpse of them they are in the patriarchal age. The head of the family is priest and king. The people are engaged in feeding cattle and in tilling the soil. The king lives very much like the others. He aids in clearing the jungle, tending the cattle, and marking the calves. All were bred to arms,so as to be able to defend their homes and their crops against the aborigines. The Aryans were proud of their fair skins and culture, and spoke of the people whom they found in the land as "lawless," "raw-eaters," "men without language," "without gods," "without sacrifices," "as gross feeders on flesh." Being better armed and better disciplined than the aborigines, they drove them into the deserts and hills and jungles. Many were exterminated and many more were reduced to slavery. For centuries the Aryans lived in what is known now as the Panjab. They advanced as they were able till they conquered the whole Ganges Valley. In course of time, as they multiplied and felt the need of more land, they extended their conquests to the south. They drove the aborigines before them as they advanced. There are many non-Aryan peoples still in existence. Among those in the north are the Santals, the Kols, the Ghonds, the Kurkus, the Bhils, and many others. Among the aborigines of the south are the Tamils, the Telugus, the Kanarese and the Malayalam. The aborigines of the south are far more advanced than those in the north. It is said that some of the Assam hill-men have no word to express distance by miles or any land measure. They reckon the length of a journey by the number of plugs of tobacco they chew on the way.

India has three hundred distinct languages and dialects. The Aryans formed a number of kingdoms. These kingdoms had little intercourse. As a result they came to use different dialects. These dialects are all from the Sanskrit, but they differ as widely as Italian and French, or as French and English. Some of the principal dialects are as follows: Hindi, Bengali, Gugerati, Mahratti,

Panjabi, Sindhi, Oriya. Hindustani is a mixture of Hindi and Persian and Arabic. It originated in the camps. The Mohammedan soldiers had to find some means of communicating with the people whom they conquered. This mongrel language is the result. The non-Aryan peoples had little or no intercourse one with the other. Living alone they came to use dialects peculiar to themselves. No doubt the Aryans and the aborigines borrowed from each other to some extent, so that the languages of each have been more or less modified by those of the other. While the non-Aryans have always been despised by their conquerors, they are superior to them in some respects. They are noted for their truthfulness, honesty and bravery. They are ready to lay down their lives for those whom they serve. They give a more willing ear to the Gospel. The greatest victories won in India have been among the aboriginal races.

Gracey speaks of India as the prize of the East. Certain it is that India has been a battlefield for many generations. In the time of the Buddha, Darius conquered a part and placed a satrap over it to rule in his name. Three centuries before the Christian Era, Alexander the Great crossed the Indus in his career of conquest. The Indians, under the leadership of Porus, went out to oppose him. They had more troops and elephants and war-chariots. But they were unable to withstand the discipline and the matchless strategy of the Greeks. Alexander asked the conquered Porus how he wished to be treated. He replied, "Like a king." It was the wish of the conqueror to go on and subdue Bengal, but his soldiers refused to go farther than the Sutlej. On the death of Alexander, India fell to Seleucus. He undertook to complete what Alexander had begun. The Bactrian Greeks ruled for a time a part of the west and northwest.

The Mohammedans invaded India early in the eleventh century. Their rule began in 1001 and lasted till 1857. They ruled over a large part of the country, but never over all. The period of their supremacy did not last much over a century. Before that time the Hindus began the work of reconquest. Mahmud of Ghazni invaded India seventeen times. His aim was to get the wealth of the country, and to convert the people to Mohammedanism. He smashed the idols and temples and carried away so much plunder that Ghazni became the richest city of the age. Hindu slaves were sold in the market for two rupees each. In one temple there was a huge idol which the Brahmans wished to ransom. The fierce iconoclast said, "I came to destroy, and not to sell idols." He struck the monster with his mace and an immense quantity of rubies and pearls and diamonds rolled out. These were worth much more than the ransom offered. For nearly two centuries after this little of the history of India is known. Mohammed of Ghor broke the power of Ghazni and undertook to conquer and to rule India. At his death in 1206, all north India from the delta of the Indus to the delta of the Ganges was subject to him. Several dynasties succeeded and ruled Hindustan with varying fortunes. In 1398 Timour sacked Delhi. He was afraid of insurrection at home and did not tarry long. Each of his soldiers carried away one hundred and fifty captives, and even soldiers' boys got twenty slaves apiece. The plunder was immense. Babar, the sixth in descent from Timour, was invited to India in 1524. Two years later he ascended the throne of Hindustan. He was the first of the Mogul Emperors. His son, Humayun, reigned for six years. Akbar, his son, was one of the greatest and most famous monarchs of his age. He conquered all Hindustan and part of the Deccan. He was a skillful soldier and a wise ruler. His son Jahangir, his grandson Shah Jahan, and his great grandson Aurangzeb, were three of the richest and most powerful monarchs of the world. One of them built the Peacock Throne at a cost of $30,000,000, and the Taj Mahal at a cost of $10,000,000. Under the last of the three the Mogul Empire in India attained its greatest splendor and its widest extension. By the time of his death it was rapidly falling into decay. There were other emperors, and they maintained a show of power until the Sepoy Mutiny, but the Indian peoples were gaining strength and were making inroads upon the Empire. The Hindus were not capable of self-government. Had they been they would have combined and driven out the foreigners. They could not unite even in the interest of self-preservation. The Mohammedan power was based on pride, hate and lust. It was never accepted by the people as a rightful supremacy. The peoples groaned under the foreign yoke and never ceased to wish to shake it off.

From ancient times the commerce of India enriched three continents. Goods were shipped by the Persian Gulf and by the Red Sea. Some found their way into Egypt. Some were carried overland to Alexandria and reshipped to Phœnicia, Palestine, Rome and Constantinople. In later times Genoa, Florence, and Venice profited by this trade. Six years after Columbus discovered America, Vasco da Gama sailed around the Cape of Good Hope and reached India. The Pope had given the King of Portugal all lands

SCHOOL CHAPEL IN HURDA, INDIA.

BUNGALOW IN MUNGELI, INDIA.

that might be discovered in the East, and the right to trade with Ethiopia, Arabia, Persia and India. Portugal was mistress of the seas and had a monopoly of this trade for a long time. The first settlements were made in Goa and Cochin on the west coast. The famous Albuquerque was sent out as Viceroy. New settlements were made in Ceylon, in Bengal, and in Chittagong. The Dutch sought to divide the trade of India with Portugal. In the struggle that ensued they drove the Portuguese from most of their settlements and took possession. Portugal still owns the island of Goa, and a small strip on the mainland, but her primacy in the East vanished like a dream.

In the year 1600 Queen Elizabeth signed the charter of the East India Company. Thirteen years later the Emperor gave them permission to establish factories in his dominions. The first places occupied were Masulipatam on the east coast and Surat on the west. Some years after they bought Madras and the site of Calcutta and Bombay. The French entered India in 1604. They bought Pondicherry on the southwest coast and obtained some settlements on the Hoogly above Calcutta. Dupleix, the French leader, formed the idea of driving the English into the sea and building up a French Empire in India. In the war that broke out the French were victorious for years. They took Madras. They set up triumphal arches and felt confident of the complete overthrow of the English. At the darkest hour in the Company's history, Clive appeared on the scene. His presence and efforts turned the scale. He broke the power of the French and practically terminated their career in India. They have still a few settlements, but they are insignificant. The conquest of India by the English began with the battle of Plassey. By the time of the Mutiny, a century later, most of the country had been acquired. What began as a factory grew into a vice-royalty. After the Mutiny England took India over, and the East India Company ceased to exist. There are thirteen provinces administered by the representatives of the crown. These provinces have an area of 944,992 square miles and a population of 221,-000,000. This part is known as British India Proper. There are 460 Feudatory States. These States have an area of 600,000 square miles and a population of 66,000,000. In some of these the ruling princes are practically absolute in all that relates to domestic affairs. Nevertheless they are vassals of the Paramount Power. British residents assist in the administration of the government and keep the authorities in Calcutta advised as to what is going on. The relations of these States to the Supreme Power are not uniform. All are pledged to good government.

Max Müller says: "If I were asked to look over the whole world to find out the country most richly endowed with all the wealth, power and beauty that nature can bestow—in some parts a very Paradise on earth—I should point to India." In this great and good land are 287,000,000 of human beings of our own kith and kin. Their forefathers and ours dwelt together in Asia, and before their dispersion spoke the same tongue and worshiped the same gods. With the same Gospel and equal advantages the people of India will be as enterprising and as prosperous and as great politically and otherwise as their European and American cousins.

XXXII.

CALCUTTA AND SERAMPORE.

CALCUTTA is on the east bank of the Hoogly, and is eighty miles from the sea. When the East India Company opened its first factory in Bengal, in 1686, Calcutta was a small village; now it is one of the great political and commercial centers of the world. Its population numbers 840,000, and its annual commerce amounts to $300,000,000. In the business part one sees great public buildings, large mercantile and manufacturing establishments, institutions of learning, churches and cathedrals, and palatial homes. These buildings are worthy of New York or London. Farther back one sees the shops and homes of the natives. These are small and mean as a rule. It has been said of Calcutta that it has palaces in front and pig-sties in the rear. Gradually, however, the natives are being educated and are competing for positions in the postal, telegraph, railway and government service. They sit on the bench and fill responsible and lucrative positions in the administration. They are constantly clamoring for a larger share of the offices. The cry is being heard, "India for the Indians." The Europeans complain that the natives are crowding them out, and filling positions which they once regarded as peculiarly their own.

The Hoogly is one of the many mouths of the Ganges, and consequently is a sacred stream. Along the banks thousands bathe daily. They plunge under again and again. They wash their clothes and their drinking vessels. They drink its waters. This is done to cleanse the defilement of sin. There are places where the dead are burned. Formerly people were brought to the river to die. Their mouths were filled with mud to hasten the process. Dead bodies were thrown into the stream. Children were offered in sacrifice. The government put a stop to these practices. At the edge of the city on the bank of the Hoogly is the famous temple of Kali. This goddess is the wife of Shiva, and is the chief object of worship in Bengal. She wears a necklace of skulls; for earrings she has two bodies; her clothing is a girdle made of human hands, and her tongue protrudes from her mouth. Her eyes are red and her breasts are smeared with blood. It was from this shrine that Calcutta took its name. Farther down the river on the opposite side are the Botanical Gardens. The main object of interest here is a banyan tree that covers a square mile. Farther up the river is Henry Martyn's Pagoda. In this he lived for a time and studied, and here a number of friends used to meet with him to pray.

Every one has heard of "the Black Hole of Calcutta." The Nabob of Bengal attacked the British. Most of the people escaped in boats. The garrison could not escape and surrendered. The prisoners, 146 in number, were thrust into a cell twenty feet square. The next morning only twenty-three were living. Clive came from Madras to chastise the Nabob and to recapture the city. The battle of Plassey was fought near Calcutta. Clive had only a handful of men. He trembled when he thought of the odds and the issue. The victory was complete and British prestige was restored. The battle of Plassey decided the fate of India, as the battle of Hastings decided the fate of England in the days of William the Conqueror.

Kiernander, a Dane, was the first missionary in Calcutta. He began work in 1758. He established schools and preached to Europeans and natives. Carey arrived in 1793. For five years he had charge of an indigo factory in Malda. Here he studied Bengali, translated the New Testament, and preached to the people. In 1799 Marshman and Ward joined him. Owing to the hostility of the Company it was deemed expedient to settle in Serampore. Other societies sent out representatives later. The Church Missionary Society, the Scottish churches, the London Society, the Methodist Episcopal and others are now at work in this field. The Protestant converts number 2,743; the Catholics, 1,358. The attitude of the government is very different now from what it was in Carey's time. Then orders were issued that preaching be discontinued, and the issue of any publication that had for its object the conversion of the natives was strictly prohibited. Now churches are open and the Gospel is preached, none forbidding.

I visited the General Assembly's Institution. This is the first college founded by Duff. This illustrious man came to India with a new policy. He proposed to reach the brain of India as well as the heart and conscience. He proposed to do this through an education saturated with Christianity. He proposed, furthermore, that the teaching should be done in English. He began with five boys. In a little while he had 800. This institution has now 1,000 pupils enrolled. The schools for girls have charge of about the same

1. Miss Mary Graybiel. 2. Miss Adelaide G. Frost.
4. Miss Alice Spradlin. 3. Miss Bessie Farrar.. 5. Dr. Rose Oxer.

MAHOBA, INDIA.

number. At the Disruption, Duff and his associates went out. This led to the establishment of a second college. This is a prosperous institution, but the attendance now is not quite so large as at the other. All the societies at work in Calcutta carry on considerable educational work. There are government schools of all grades. But in religion these schools are neutral. The mission schools are carried on with a view to aid the evangelistic work. Mr. J. C. White is working among the students. He is an agent of the Young Men's Christian Association of America. There are 6,000 young men in the different colleges in the city. Half of these are in government schools. He has on his books the names of 1,000 students. They come to him to read the Scriptures and to pray or to talk about the Gospel. Hindus of all castes and of no caste and Mohammedans are enrolled. He has a reading-room and a chapel. Thus far he has not dared to advertise his services, because he is unable to receive all who would come. He has a large and fruitful field and is greatly encouraged.

I attended as many church services as I could. The pastor of the English Baptist Church showed me the baptistery in which Judson was baptized. Carey served this church as its minister fourteen years. The East India Company gave him a communion set of solid silver. This is still in use. Mr. McDonald of the Free Church took me to an evangelistic service in the public square. He was associated with Duff for some time. A number of Bengalis spoke. Some spoke in English and some in Bengali. Several of the speakers were Duff's pupils. They have his theory and his pronunciation. In all the churches there are memorial tablets. They give the names and some account of the services rendered. On one of these tablets are the words: "Remember them that had the rule over you, which spake unto you the Word of God; and considering the issue of their life, imitate their faith." In the cathedral there is a statue of Heber. He was the happy possessor of all sorts of gifts and accomplishments. He had birth, wit, fame, high character and wealth. He gave up all for India. He died in the prime of life from overwork. In a poetic letter to his wife he wrote:

"If thou, my love, wert by my side,
My babies at my knee,
How gaily would our pinnace glide
O'er Gunga's mimic sea.

"I miss thee at the dawning grey,
When o'er the deck reclined,
In careless ease my limbs I lay,
And woo the cooler wind.

"I miss thee when by Gunga's stream
My twilight steps I guide,
But most beneath the lamp's pale beam,
I miss thee by my side.

"I spread my books, my pencil try,
The lingering noon to cheer,
But miss thy kind approving eye,
Thy meek attentive ear.

"But when by morn and eve,
The star beholds me on my knee,
I feel, though thou art distant far,
Thy prayers ascend for me."

Twelve miles from Calcutta is Serampore. I ran over to see this famous place. Once it was the chief educational and publishing center in India. It is so no more. The Baptists have a school with a hundred boys enrolled. The principal showed me through the building. I saw the pulpit in which Carey preached and the chairs used by him and his colleagues. I saw the house in which he lived and the room in which he died. Some one said of the house that it was built for the angels, so simple is it. The principal said: "Perhaps it suited the angels; it is a bit awkward for human beings." I looked for Carey's garden, but found no trace of it. Shortly before his death he was sad. When asked the reason he said, "After I am gone, Brother Marshman will turn the cows into my garden." Carey was one of the first botanists of his age. He took long walks in his garden every morning. Someone wrote of him:

"Thou'rt in our hearts, with tresses thin and gray,
And eye that knew the Book of Life so well,
And brow serene, as thou wert wont to stray
Amidst thy flowers, like Adam ere he fell."

In his last days, Daniel Wilson, Bishop of Calcutta, came to him for his blessing. Duff called. Carey said: "You are just buckling on the armor, I am almost out of the fray. Pray for me, pray!" When Duff was leaving, the dying saint called him back and said: "You have been speaking a great deal about Dr. Carey, Dr. Carey, Dr. Carey. I beg of you that, when I am gone, nothing may be said of Dr. Carey. Speak, I beg of you, of Dr. Carey's Savior." As the sun was setting, we walked out to the little graveyard where "the three mighty ones" are buried. Carey's tomb contains his name and the date of his birth and death and the words: "A wretched, poor, and helpless worm, on Thy kind arms I fall." He was seventy-two when he died, and had been in India forty-one years. Marshman's simple monument has on it the words: "They that be wise shall shine as the firmament, and they that turn many to righteousness as the stars for ever." Mrs. Marshman was a great woman, and deserves honorable mention. She taught a school for girls for forty years. She was the pioneer in female education in India.

The hotels of Calcutta in some respects differ from those in other cities. Every guest is expected to hire a "boy" to wait on him at table and to care for his room. Otherwise he will fare badly. As one can be had for sixteen cents a day, the expense is not very great. All through the East with Europeans dinner is a high function. They appear in full dress as at a ball. The amount of liquor drunk is enormous. There are four glasses at every plate. At our table there were over a hundred guests. So far as I could see there was only one without his bottle, and only modesty keeps me from recording his name. One man dressed like a clergyman drank as much as the rest. These men think they could not live without alcohol. Fools and blind! No wonder that the Hindus and Mohammedans think Christianity the droughtiest of all faiths. I rather like the idea of full dress at dinner, and have thought of adopting the spacious shirt-front and the swallow-tailed coat on my return. But as for the alcoholic beverages, I am unalterably and everlastingly opposed to them.

XXXIII.

INDIA AND CHRISTIANITY.

The Gospel was probably carried to India by merchants or colonists. In the second century the converts requested the Bishop of Alexandria to send them a Christian teacher. In response to their request Pantaenus was selected and sent. He was the head of the Christian School in that city, and was the greatest scholar and teacher of his time. He had trained Clement and Origen for their work, and missionaries for Northern Africa, Ethiopia and Southern Asia. After some time spent in confirming the churches in India, he returned to Alexandria and resumed work in the College.

The next missionaries came from Syria by way of Persia. It is generally believed that they had adopted the Nestorian heresy. Though Nestorius had been deposed and banished on account of his views, the community that accepted his teachings flourished and sent missionaries in all directions. Their motto was, "Christ for the whole world, and the whole world for Christ." One historian says of them, "Because their faith was dark, their message mutilated, their intellect darkened, and their life selfish, it was not possible for the colonies of Syrian and Persian Christians dispersed on its shores to bring India to Christ."

The Roman Catholics came to India with the Portuguese. They undertook to bring the Syrian Christians under the control of the Pope. At first they sought to conciliate them. A school for Syrian youth was opened in Goa. Those who passed through this school were ordained as priests. But the Syrians refused to admit them into their churches. Failing in this policy, they resorted to sterner measures. One Syrian bishop was shipped to Lisbon to be tried as a heretic. Another was sent to Rome for the same purpose. The Inquisition sent men to prison and to death, but the effort to bring the Syrians to acknowledge the supremacy of the Church of Rome failed. The census of 1891 gives the number of Syrian Christians as 200,467.

Xavier landed at Goa in 1542. He had been sent out by the King of Portugal. He found vice open and defiant and shameless. He rebuked it in high places and in low places. His method

ORPHANAGE IN DAMOH, INDIA.

Mrs. McGavran. J. G. McGavran. Miss Stella Franklin.
Mrs. Rambo. W. E. Rambo. Miss Josepha Franklin.

MISSIONARIES IN DAMOH, INDIA.

of evangelizing was quite peculiar. He had translations made of the Creed, the Lord's Prayer and the Ten Commandments. These he committed to memory. Then, with bell in hand, he went through the villages and called the people together. To these he recited the translations, and after each article of the Creed he asked them whether they believed. If they assented, he baptized them then and there. He wrote: "It often happens to me that my hands fail through the fatigue of baptizing, for I have baptized a whole village in a single day; and often by repeating so frequently the Creed and other things, my voice and strength have failed me." The Roman Catholics boasted that they made ten thousand converts in Travancore in a single month. The work there has been continued ever since. Catholic institutions and Catholic workers are found everywhere. In nearly every large city they have a cathedral. They have a strong staff. They have 619 European missionaries and 668 native priests. The converts in British India number 1,594,901.

The Danes were the first Protestants to aid in evangelizing India. Ziegenbalg and Plutschau reached Tranquebar in 1706. As soon as they explained their object, they were advised to return home at once. They were not wanted. They had been sent out by the king. Their commission had been sealed with the royal seal. That made no difference. These men studied the language; preached the Gospel to the people; translated most of the Bible into Tamil; prepared books, and did whatever they could for the furtherance of the Gospel. In fifty years 11,000 souls were added to the church.

The most distinguished of these early missionaries was Christian Frederic Schwartz. He was born in Prussia, educated in Halle, and came to India in 1750. Tanjore and Trichinopoli were the scenes of his abundant labors. For fifty years he went about doing good. The poor and injured looked to him as a friend and advocate. The great and powerful yielded to him the highest homage ever paid in that part of the globe to European virtue. In the midst of war in the Carnatic, Hyder Ali said to his officers, "Permit the venerable father Schwartz to pass unmolested, and show him respect and kindness, for he is a holy man and means no harm to my government." Once the Rajah of Tanjore wanted to send him on a political mission to Madras. He said, "Padre, I have confidence in you, because you are indifferent to money." He was revered by the natives of every degree and every sect. He lived in a room in an old Hindu building, which was just large enough to hold himself and his bed. He ate the food of the natives. His salary was about $250 a year. He lived to see 10,000 converts. His last words were: "O Lord, hitherto Thou hast preserved me; hitherto Thou hast brought me; and hast bestowed innumerable benefits upon me. Do what is pleasing in Thy sight. I commend my spirit into Thy hands; cleanse and adorn it with the righteousness of my Redeemer, and receive me into the arms of Thy mercy."

William Carey arrived in Calcutta in 1793. Before the time of his arrival, and long after, most of the Europeans in India were opposed to missions. Each factory had its chaplain and schoolmaster, and provided a decent place for worship. The Sunday sermon was followed by gambling, shooting, drinking and racing. The directors passed pious resolutions from time to time. They went so far as to adopt a form of prayer for their servants. They were concerned, so they said, that those Indian nations among whom we dwell, seeing our sober and righteous conversation, may be induced to have a just esteem for our most holy profession of the Gospel. But their agents were hostile, and wished to be let alone. Some of the leading officials lived in open sin. They had zenanas filled with black beauties, and amused them at times by serving their gods. Drunkenness was associated with Christianity as an almost necessary accompaniment of conversion. "What!" was the indignant answer of a man to a missionary who urged upon him the baptism of his son, "would you have me make him a drunkard!" Henry Martyn did not drink. The people said of him, "The Dinapore Padre has turned Mussulman." Sir Thomas Roe said the natives say, "Christian religion, devil religion; Christian much drink; Christian do much wrong; much beat; much abuse others." Everything from abroad was labeled Christian. Every European was regarded as a disciple of Christ, no matter how corrupt he might be in heart, in thought and in character. It was in such a community that Carey felt called of God to labor. At first he was ignored. He was an obscure vagrant, and consequently beneath official notice. When Marshman and Ward joined him, it was deemed prudent to make Serampore their home and the center of their operations. There they set up their printing-press in the name of the Lord; from Serampore they sent the Word of Life in many languages to the peoples of India. The feelings of these three men were expressed in their own words: "Let us give ourselves up unreservedly to this glorious cause. Let us never think that our time, our gifts, our strength, our families, or even the clothes we wear, are our own. Let us sanctify them all to God and his cause. Oh, that he may sanctify us for this service! Let us forever shut out the idea of laying up a dowry for ourselves or our children. If we are enabled to glorify God with our bodies and spirits which are his, our wants will be his care." Carey's salary as teacher and translator for the government was 1,250 rupees a month. His associates earned large sums in the printing office and in other ways. But Carey lived on fifty rupees a month; Marshman on thirty, and Ward on twenty. Carey needed more than the others because of his duties at the college and his appearance at the Government House. The rest of their earnings went into the fund of the mission.

At the present time there are over sixty societies at work in India. The foreign ordained missionaries number 868; the native ordained ministers, 797; the foreign layworkers, 118; the native layworkers, 3,491. The foreign women number 711; the native women, 3,278. According to the census of 1891, the Protestant Christians in British India number 648,843. The Gospel is preached in chapels, in the bazars, in the homes, and wherever the people will listen. Due emphasis is laid upon preaching. Not only is the Gospel preached, but the sick are healed. The foreign doctors number ninety-seven; the native doctors, 168. India has 166 mission hospitals and dispensaries. A Hindu said to Dr. Clark, "There are nine women in our house, and they are all donkeys but one; she is sick; come and heal her." He did so. Afterwards he asked this man what it was he feared most from the missionaries. He answered: "There are your preaching missionaries; we don't mind them, we needn't listen to them; and there is your educational missionary; we don't mind him, we needn't hear him; there are your books and papers, but we need not read them; what we really fear is your Christian women, and we are afraid of your medical missionaries, for by your Christian women you win our wives, and by your medical missionaries you win our hearts, and when that is done what is there for us but to do as you say?" Schools and colleges have been opened. In these young men are being trained for the work of the ministry. India must be evangelized by Indians. The girls in boarding schools number 7,302; the girls in day schools, 62,414; the pupils in Sunday-schools, 135,565. In addition to what is done in schools, 32,659 women are taught in their homes. The credit for the education of women belongs entirely to the missionaries. Not only so, but the Bible has been translated into most of the languages of India. An Anglo-Indian said: "The Bible is the best of all missionaries. It finds access through doors that are closed to the human foot, and into countries where missionaries have not yet ventured to go; and above all it speaks to the consciences of men with a power that no human voice can carry. It is the living seed of God, and soon it springs up, men know not how, and bears fruit unto everlasting life." Tracts are printed and scattered broadcast. Every method that promises good results is tried.

There is abundant evidence that the labor of the missionaries has not been in vain in the Lord. At the present rate of progress there will be ten million Christians in India in the next fifty years, and two hundred and fifty millions in a century. It may be said that the greatest success has been won among the lowest castes. This is quite true. It is now as it was in our Lord's time. The question then was, "Have any of the rulers or the Pharisees believed?" From these despised castes come men who compete successfully with the highest castes in every direction—morally, socially and intellectually. Under the Gospel these lower castes have advanced by leaps and bounds, and have taken their position almost in the front ranks of Indian society. Bishop Caldwell said that the Christians of India have no need to shrink from comparison with Christians in a similar station of life, and similarly circumstanced, in England or in any other part of the world. Lord Lawrence has said, "Notwithstanding all that the English people have done to benefit India, the missionaries have done more than all other agencies combined." The greatest of modern Indians has said, "The spirit of Christianity has already pervaded the whole atmosphere of Indian society, and we breathe, think, feel and move in a Christian atmosphere. Native society is being roused, enlightened and reformed under the influence of Christian education."

Most, if not all, of the large cities are occupied. But there remains much to be done. The great faiths of India are not disposed to yield without a struggle. Their champions are girding themselves for the conflict. If the churches do their duty, there can be no doubt as to the final issue. The divine decree has gone forth, "My word shall not return unto me void, but it shall accomplish that which I please, and prosper in the thing whereunto I sent it."

FIRST CHURCH IN HONOLULU, SANDWICH ISLANDS.

G. W. WHARTON AND HIS HELPERS, INDIA.

XXXIV.

THE WORK OF THE DISCIPLES OF CHRIST IN INDIA.

OUR first workers reached the field in October, 1882. They began their work in the Central Provinces. These provinces have an area of one hundred and sixteen thousand square miles, and a population numbering thirteen millions. The first stations were opened in Hurda and Bilaspur. Hurda is four hundred and seventeen miles from Bombay; Bilaspur is five hundred and three miles from Calcutta. As I entered India from the east, my first visit was made in Bilaspur. A ride of twenty-four hours brought me to the station. M. D. Adams and E. M. Gordon were waiting to welcome me. In a few minutes I was in the mission bungalow, where all my needs were supplied.

In the spring of 1885 Mr. and Mrs. Adams, Miss Graybiel, Miss Boyd and Miss Kingsbury made Bilaspur their home. There are in this district one million five hundred thousand souls. The work is conducted along the following lines: Evangelistic, medical, zenana, educational and orphanage. M. D. Adams gives his strength to preaching in the villages and in the church. He is assisted by two good evangelists. He superintends the boys' school and the Sunday-schools. The Sunday-schools have a total enrollment of about two hundred and fifty children. The boys' school has an average attendance of fifty-seven. The boys are Hindus, Mohammedans and Christians. The church has received seventy-five members. Some of these are dead; some have gone away; a few have gone back. Mrs. Adams has charge of the book-store, keeps house, visits the women in their homes, and renders efficient service in the day and Sunday-schools.

Miss Boyd gives her time to work among the women. At first she had to seek for an entrance into the homes, and to encounter many rebuffs. Men and boys used to follow and mock and jeer. Now she is sought or called in as she is passing, and asked to teach in their homes. Rebuffs are less frequent, and the boys are respectful. She visits all classes, from the Brahman and Mohammedan to the outcast sweepers. She does not exclude even the leper. At each visit she teaches the Scriptures. In some instances she has taught the women to read and write. Many houses are still closed against her. Miss Kingsbury has charge of the orphanage. There are thirty-one girls under her care. Their ages range from three years to nineteen. They are taught to cook, sew, wash, sweep, and to do all kinds of useful work. Their dress is becoming; their faces are clean and bright. They look as if they belonged to a different race from that seen on the street. The day begins with a scriptural lesson. On Sunday they study the same lesson as the schools at home. The aim is to train the girls to live faithful lives among their own people. The transforming power of the Gospel is evident here. Lying and abuse are giving place to truth and gentleness. Moral thoughtfulness takes the place of selfishness and carelessness. Twelve of the girls have become Christians; three are married.

Mrs. Lohr has charge of two schools for girls. The school first opened has one hundred enrolled and an average attendance of eighty. Children from Brahman and Mohammedan homes, as well as children from low castes, are found in this school. The girls in the orphanage are sent here. They are taught all the common branches. In addition, they are taught to sing, to sew, to knit, to draw, and many other useful things. The Bible is not neglected. In 1894 three went up for examination as teachers. Two passed. These are from the orphanage, and they are now helping Mrs. Lohr in the work. The next year she sent up three more; all passed. Two of these are now taking a normal course. The government gives a grant-in-aid of about seventy dollars a year. It has promised $125 towards the enlargement of the building. Mrs. Lohr is a born teacher. Her ability, education and experience qualify her for the place she fills. The Inspector has acknowledged that she is doing a noble work. A Brahman told her that the people could never be sufficiently grateful to her for her services. The second school is in a poorer part of the town. Nevertheless, it has grown year by year. Beginning with fifteen pupils, it now has thirty. Women do not count for much in India. As a result, the education of girls is not prized very highly. This is specially true of the poor. Besides her other duties, Mrs. Lohr has a Sunday-school at the station for English and Eurasian children.

Dr. E. C. and Dr. Lillian B. Miller are giving most of their attention to the language. They have been wisely advised to do this. In their leisure hours they superintend the grading of the hospital grounds. They are arranging their medicines and surgical instruments, and are planning for their work after they return from the hills next autumn. In the meantime, though they are not seeking a practice, they have to treat many cases. People come to them every day, and they cannot send them away without relief. The report has gone out that two new physicians have come to take up the work of Drs. Merrill and Baldwin. I heard complimentary remarks on all sides of these good missionaries, who are now at home on furlough.

There are two bungalows in Bilaspur, two schools, an orphanage and a hospital. One school building is used as a chapel. The orphanage has been enlarged and will accommodate fifty girls. It will soon be full. The hospital consists of three buildings. The materials and workmanship are of the best. Missionaries are learning that it pays to put up good buildings. The first cost may be greater, but it is cheaper in the end. The great enemy of buildings in India is the white ant. If walls and floors are of hard brick or stone, and rafters and joists of iron, the white ant can do nothing. But if the walls are of sun-dried brick and the rafters of wood, the occupant must be on his guard, or he will have the roof about his ears.

During my stay in Bilaspur I visited all the schools, and was pleased with what I saw of the work. On Sunday I spoke through Mr. Adams. The house was full. At the close we had the communion. It was a season of refreshing from the presence of the Lord. One evening I went out to the bazar and heard the evangelists preach. The audience came and went. Some listened intently, others turned away as soon as they understood the nature of the message. We visited the temples and shrines. One priest sitting on a tiger skin under a huge umbrella assured us that if we wanted children our prayers would be granted, if we made an offering to his god. This seems to be the great wish of Orientals. We met one man offering flowers and pouring out water over every idol. He had been praying for children for ten years, and in vain. One evening the ladies gave a supper in native style. The orphans and all the Christians were present. There was no table, or chair, or knife, or fork, or spoon. We sat on the floor. Curry and rice and dhal were served on a banana leaf. We ate with our fingers. Cakes and sweets were served at the close of the feast. Then one of the Christians made an address of welcome, to which I responded as well as I could. There were about seventy present. It was an evening long to be remembered. One could not look over that company without feeling that the missionaries are helping to make the kingdom of God come in India.

From Bilaspur I visited Mungeli. This place is distant thirty-one miles. The bungalow was built and work begun by G. W. Jackson in 1887. Four years later his health failed, and he left for home. E. M. Gordon was engaged the same year. The next year W. E. Cooper joined the mission. It was at this point that Dr. Hitt was stationed. The people speak of him with affection. In 1894 Mr. Cooper resigned and Dr. Hitt left for home. Since then Mr. Gordon has been alone. One year he had only one visitor. He evangelizes in Mungeli and in one hundred and fifty villages within a circuit of five miles. He uses the magic lantern to attract the people and to impress the truth. There are seventeen Christians in Mungeli. Though poor, they are collecting a fund to pay for a place of worship. One of the members is blind. He was taught to read by Mr. Gordon. For three years he has been in the Training School in Hurda. Mr. Wharton speaks of him as one of the brightest young men he has ever met. Two schools are conducted. One is a night school and is for those who cannot attend by day. Last year the teacher became a Christian. The parents became alarmed and took away their children. They are now returning. Dr. Miller and Mr. Adams went with me and added much to the profitableness of the visit. We called to see the school. We met the Christians in two services and exhorted them to cleave to the Lord. The work in Mungeli is said to be in some respects more promising than at any other station. The converts are aggressive, and are earnestly seeking to win others to the belief of the truth. Mr. Gordon stands at his solitary post like a sentinel. When I was there he was anticipating that he would have an associate within a few weeks, but his hopes were dashed for the present. Miss Graybiel said to me later, "Mr. Gordon is the hero of our mission."

Every hour was full of interest. The children came in and gave us an exhibition. They sang and declaimed. We asked some questions, and were gratified with the knowledge which the answers evinced. We left the shepherd and his little flock with admiration and hope. Such fidelity cannot but bear much fruit. On our return to Bilaspur we had a service of prayer and exhortation and song. All the missionaries were present. That evening I left for Damoh. They all came down to the train to send me on my way rejoicing. I shall long cherish the remembrance of this visit. I have reasons for profound gratitude, but I need not publish them. The children were as kind as their parents. May the Lord make his face to shine upon them and give them peace.

It took three days to get from Bilaspur to Damoh. The train

GIRLS' ORPHANAGE, BILASPUR, INDIA.

GIRLS' SCHOOL IN BILASPUR, INDIA.

brought me as far as Jubbalpur. At this point John G. McGavran met me. He escorted me the rest of the way. We had to go sixty-six miles in a horse tonga. It took a day and a half to cover this distance. John was one of my students in Bethany. The hours passed rapidly as we talked of old scenes and old friends, and of the work in this district. He was married recently, and is the happiest man in India. A railway is being built through Damoh. When it is opened this station will be easy of access.

The work in Damoh began about a year ago. Mr. and Mrs. W. E. Rambo and Mr. McGavran were the first workers. Miss Josepha and Miss Stella Franklin and Mrs. McGavran joined them later. Damoh was selected on account of its healthfulness, and on account of its central location. The workers live in tents and in a house built of mud and thatch. They have had much difficulty in getting land. This delayed the building and hindered the work in other ways. Damoh is the site of the orphanage for boys. The foundation of the first building is nearly done. The plans for the bungalow are almost ready. The work on both will be pressed to completion.

I found Mr. Rambo and family ready to leave for Bombay, and perhaps for home. He was taken down with typhoid fever in August, and has not been well since. The doctors are doubtful of his recovery. He goes to Bombay to consult with the physicians in charge of the General Hospital. If they agree with Drs. Durand and Quinn he will go home. It was expected that he would take charge of the orphans. That work will now fall into other hands. Mr. McGavran had equipped himself for evangelistic work in the villages. Now he has the oversight of the boys and of the building operations. He has to go to the quarry for stone, and to the jungle for timber. He conducts Sunday-schools in the town, and preaches as he is able. Miss Josepha Franklin teaches the orphans. She aims to do the same grade of work that is done at home. The boys sit on the floor. The school has almost no apparatus. Nevertheless the boys are making good progress. The Bible is taught every day. The teaching throughout is essentially Christian. Mrs. McGavran teaches them to sing. Some of the orphans are too young to attend school. Miss Franklin has these in a little house next to the one in which she lives.

The orphanage work began in Bilaspur. Last July the boys were removed to Damoh. Then there were twenty-four in all. Before the end of the year over thirty more were added. Scarcely a week passes without some coming. The crops have failed for four years in succession. Parents die of famine, and leave their children to be cared for by others. Some brought their little ones and said, "We are dying of hunger; we have had nothing to eat for days; take our children and give us some food." Officials have sent children to them. Some of these have a pathetic history. They wandered about eating refuse left by animals, or subsisting on such fruits as they could find in the jungles. At night they slept beside a tree, or a stone, or in a ditch. Their hair grew long and matted. Their bodies were encrusted with dirt. Their blood has been impoverished. As a result, running sores break out, and maggots breed in their hair, and in almost every part of their bodies. Their eyes are sunken. The skin lies in wrinkles over the bones. These children are devoid of energy, and sit listless for days. Some come crawling, because they are too weak to walk. In a few weeks, if they are not too far gone, they begin to improve. They gain in flesh and in animal spirits. Several were pointed out to me. They came to the orphanage resembling a bag of bones; now they are stout and strong, and give promise of long life. The aim of the workers is to take these children and train them for lives of usefulness and nobleness. An industrial department has been started. The boys are taught to sweep, to dust, to draw water, to tend cattle, and to work in the garden. As soon as practicable, they will be taught trades, so that they can earn their own living and help support the Lord's work in India.

I visited the day and Sunday-schools. Miss Franklin loves these boys and they love her. It was Topsy who said that Miss Ophelia would as soon touch a toad as to touch her. It is not so with Miss Franklin. She is not afraid to touch her boys. She is deeply interested in all that concerns them. They respond to her interest and affection. Lying and stealing and cruelty are abandoned under the influence of her life and teaching. The boys are remarkably well informed in the Scriptures, considering the time they have been in the orphanage. Some have confessed their faith in Christ and have been baptized; others are inquiring. Mrs. McGavran was born in Bengal. She is familiar with mission methods and mission work. She knows much of the language spoken in Damoh, and is able to render valuable service in the schools and in other departments. Miss Stella Franklin is giving her whole time and energy to the language. Within a year after her arrival she will be able to undertake some work.

I left Damoh for Bina. The work at this station is about a year and a half old. The staff consists of Mr. and Mrs. Ben Mitchell,

Miss Mattie W. Burgess, Miss Ida Kinsey, and the native helpers. Since locating here Mr. Mitchell has given most of his time and strength to the erection of the bungalow and out-buildings and to preaching. The bungalow is a very convenient and substantial building. The walls are of stone, the roof is of tiles, and the rafters of steel. He has planned and built for the centuries. building in India is a serious matter. The workmen must be constantly watched. Every stone must be inspected. The most reliable contractor cannot be fully trusted.

Mr. Mitchell has regular services for the English and Eurasian people of Bina. Once a month he goes to Mahoba. He is preparing to build a chapel. He hopes to raise the money on the ground. Mrs. Mitchell speaks with the beggars at the gate, and sees that the hungry are fed. She makes temporary provision for the orphans sent to the bungalow, and forwards them either to Damoh or Mahoba. Besides she directs the labors of two evangelists and goes with them to the villages and towns whenever possible and addresses the people. In addition to her other duties, she keeps house. This is an important item, as the efficiency of the workers depends upon their health. Miss Burgess spends most of her mornings in the villages. The native preachers often go with her and assist. In one village she has regular meetings with a number of girls and women. In the afternoon she works among the women of Etawah. She is admitted to fifteen houses; before others she reads and sings. Frequently she sits down with the women in the street to tell them of the love of Christ. She has found only two or three that can read. Their minds and hearts have been starved from birth. They listen while she talks, but when she goes back they have forgotten most that she has said. Miss Kinsey has charge of two schools; one for boys, and one for girls. The parents are not concerned about the education of their daughters; consequently their attendance is irregular. The largest boy in the school is making good progress, and says he is going to become a Christian. These schools are self-supporting. Miss Kinsey has a Sunday-school with about sixty enrolled. She has met with some opposition from the Mussulmans, but this is dying down.

I went with Mr. and Mrs. Mitchell and Miss Burgess out into the villages. They stood under a tree and sang. At once the people began to assemble. The women were a little shy and looked around corners and out of doors. They were near enough to see and hear. The evangelist spoke. In most cases the attention was perfect. One man said, "We did not send for you; we have our own gods and are content." As of old, Christ is found of them that sought him not. We went from place to place all day. The services were deeply interesting. The day reminded me of what was said of the Master, "He went about through the cities and villages, preaching and bringing the good tidings of the kingdom of God." I called to see the schools, and heard the little ones sing, and saw their slates. Miss Kinsey has reason to feel gratified over the work of her pupils. Mr. Mitchell went with me to see the local Rajah. He is a little wizened bit of humanity. Though he has never been out of India, he speaks English well. He has been kind to the mission. He gave it ten acres of ground for an annual rental of less than a dollar. He has helped the workers in many ways. He playfully speaks of Miss Kinsey as "the superintendent of public instruction." He gave us some perfume and a betel nut, and offered us the use of his hookah. He gave us a ride on his elephant, and sent us some sugar cane as a present. One evening there was a social in the bungalow. The friends and neighbors gathered, and filled the parlors and halls. Before leaving one man made a little speech. He thanked the workers for the interest taken in the children, and for the pleasures they gave them on Christmas. Referring to the preaching, he said it was almost as good as he heard among the Catholics. He meant that for the highest compliment he could pay. After two full and delightful days in Bina, I took the train for Hurda.

Hurda is ten hours by rail from Bina. G. L. Wharton and his son Lawrence came out a distance of twenty miles to meet me. Mrs. Wharton and Miss Grace and Dr. Durand were at the station to reinforce the welcome already received, and to take me to the mission bungalow. The other workers had their schools to look after, and could not come. Hurda is our oldest station in India. The staff consists of Mr. and Mrs. Wharton, Dr. and Mrs. Durand, Mrs. Nellie L. Jackson, Miss Hattie L. Judson, Miss Mary Thompson, and the native assistants. Mrs. Durand is in America at present on account of sickness. Miss Thompson is from Australia, and is supported by the churches in that country. The work of each is somewhat as follows:

Mr. Wharton has charge of the Bible and Training School. He teaches twenty hours a week. He superintends the evangelistic work in the bazar and in three out-stations. In addition to these duties he preaches for the church and teaches a Bible class in the Sunday-school. Mrs. Wharton has charge of the book-shop, conducts an English Sunday-school, does zenana work and looks after

E. M. Gordon. Dr. Anna M. Gordon.

MUNGELI, INDIA.

the sick women, especially in the church. Nathoo Lal evangelizes in Charwa and neighboring villages, and has charge of two Sunday-schools. His wife goes with him and teaches the women. Jagannath preaches in Rahatgaon and teaches a day and Sunday-school. Dr. John Panna has a weekly dispensary, and preaches to the people in Timarni. There are fourteen Sunday-schools in Hurda, with four hundred and seventy-seven pupils enrolled. Dr. Durand visits the hospital twice a day and attends to the in-patients; does out-door dispensary work at the hospital and in the bazar; gives four hours a day to a medical class; attends to thirteen lepers, giving them food and medicine; conducts services with the converts and non-Christians twice a day; and superintends a Sunday-school near the hospital. Most of the evangelistic work is done by Jeremiah. The wounds are dressed and medicines dispensed by Samson and other assistants. The average number of in-patients is ten, and the average of out-patients each day is about fifty. Last month the prescriptions numbered one thousand three hundred and seventy-one. The conversions numbered eight. Mrs. Jackson has two boys' schools. She superintends the teachers and teaches some classes herself. Scarcely a day passes that she does not have to doctor somebody. Children and adults go to her for relief. She spends an hour and a half with her boys on Sunday in the study of the Scriptures. Her blackboard illustrations make the truth clear and memorable. Her household duties, the care of her own babies and of several orphans, and the temperance work among the Europeans, fill up the other hours of the week. She is a musical genius, and sings the Gospel into many hearts that otherwise would be shut against it. Miss Judson teaches in and superintends a school of girls. There are thirty-eight enrolled. On Sunday they have a special lesson in the Scriptures. Three days in the week she teaches a woman reading and arithmetic. After the reading lesson twelve of her neighbors meet with her for a Bible lesson. Several of these are seeking the true way. Every day she gives remedies for coughs, fevers, skin and other diseases, to the girls, their parents and other people in that district. Miss Thompson, in the cold season, goes twice a week to some of the villages near Hurda. She is accompanied by a Bible woman. The other four days she visits the women in Hurda, several of whom are learning to read. On Sundays she has a school for boys. The average attendance is twenty-one. She has on that day also a class for beggars. Every day she has religious exercise with the servants. She is constantly called on by the people among whom she labors for simple remedies. Sarubia and Bhaktibai also visit the women in their homes and go to the villages near. There are six hundred villages waiting for the Gospel.

I went to all the schools and saw the work. I examined the pupils and was pleased with their understanding and answers. Dr. Durand took me to the hospital. The building is clean and large enough. The land was given by the head man of the town. Under a tree, Jeremiah was preaching to the patients. The lepers are in another place. They are in a pitiable condition. Their toes and fingers are dropping off. The good doctor has cured several as bad as these, and hopes to cure many more. Dr. Wharton took me to see the grave of Miss Robinson. It is in one of the prettiest spots in India. A slab of marble gives her name and age and the words, "Until the day dawn." In the same lot, Norman Kent Durand, the child of Dr. and Emma Durand, is buried. One evening we went out into the bazar to hear the singing and preaching. The students of the Training School sang, and several spoke. Near by a cow-protector spoke in the interest of this sacred animal. One audience heard of Christ and the great salvation, and the other heard about the sanctity of the cow and the crime of eating beef.

When I was in Hurda there was a gathering of workers from all stations to discuss questions relating to the work. The first meeting was in the nature of a reception. The house was full. There were several addresses of welcome and as many responses. That evening the Magistrate and the Municipal Council called at the bungalow and spent an hour talking about India and America. After they left the missionaries came together for a season of prayer and song and conference. We had a time of refreshing from the presence of the Lord. The next morning we had a sunrise baptism. One of Dr. Durand's patients made the good confession and was baptized. We then repaired to the church and spent two hours in prayer and listening to addresses. Being in Hindi I did not understand what was said; but the earnest faces of the audience showed that they were interested. That afternoon I left for Mahoba. The workers and the Christians came down to the station. As the train pulled out the scene reminded me of the breaking up of one of our State Conventions. As the familiar faces faded in the distance I thought, "These are chosen vessels to bear the name of Christ before the heathen. It must be that the pleasure of the Lord shall prosper in their hands."

The railway crossed the Narbadda river. This is one of the sacred streams of India. The people say that the Ganges is sacred on one bank only, but the Narbadda is sacred on both banks. By noon the next day I was at Mahoba. This is a new station in the Northwest Provinces. The staff consists of Miss Graybiel, Miss Adelaide Frost, Miss Bessie Farrar, Miss Elsie Gordon, and a native evangelist and his wife. Miss Graybiel is housekeeper, architect and builder, and general superintendent. She has been able to get land at once, and with no trouble. In Hurda they have been trying to get some ground for years, and thus far have failed. She got her deed in a few days. The rental is ten cents a year. The people asked her as to her object. When she explained that the mission wanted to teach their women and children they said, "We will help you." They have done so. She has found a reliable contractor, and so was saved much anxiety. The bungalow and other buildings are as good as any I have seen in India. Miss Frost has charge of the orphanage. She had forty-four then, and new ones are coming in every day. She will need room for a hundred. That district is suffering from famine. For three years the crops have failed. The little ones come in with pinched faces, and legs and arms like pipe-stems. In a few months they are fat and rosy, and as full of play and mischief as could be desired. They call her "Mamma," and gather about her when she appears, and climb her knees, the envied kiss to share. They are as fond of love and kisses and sweetmeats as children at home. They are her joy and crown and reward. Some have died. Be it so, but "love never fails." The Sunday I was there five of the girls were baptized. Miss Frost's cup of joy was full. Miss Gordon and Miss Farrar have recently joined the mission. Miss Gordon helps with the little ones. Miss Farrar is studying the language and helping as she is able. The bungalow is surrounded by temples, shrines, idols, sacred trees, old palaces and suttee mounds. It is a light in a dark place. Miss Graybiel is planning for a school, a widows' home, and a hospital. There are some twenty believers now; she is praying that there may be fifty before the year closes. There are seven hundred and fifty-three villages in Mahoba. I was unable to visit Deoghur and Madhupar. Miss Adam has been at work in this field for seventeen years. Her prayer was that she might be sent to the darkest spot in India. For nine years she lived in a little house on wheels. Those who know her say that she thinks of herself last. She has been praying for a hundred women to help her. Though over sixty years of age, she has no thought of retiring or relaxing her efforts. Miss Alice Spradlin is now associated with her in the work. Miss Farrar will join them in September. After three pleasant days in Mahoba, I left for Allahabad and Benares.

XXXV.

BENARES.

To THE Hindu Benares is the most sacred place on the earth. What Jerusalem was to the Hebrew, what Mecca is to the Mussulman, that and more than that Benares is to the Hindu. All who die within its limits, no matter what their creed or character, enter at once into everlasting bliss. Curiously enough, if one should die on the opposite bank of the Ganges, in the next transmigration he will be born an ass.

Benares is the center and citadel of Hinduism. If any one thinks that this ancient faith has lost all vitality, a visit to this city will change his opinion. The crowds of pilgrims that flock here from all parts of India, and the earnestness they display in their worship, make it evident that Hinduism is a living faith. Benares is a place of interest to the Buddhists also. Here it was that the Buddha began to preach. A naked ascetic met him and asked him why his face was so joyous. He said, "I am the all-subduer, the all-wise, the stainless, the highest teacher, the conqueror. I go to Benares to dissipate the darkness of the world." He gathered about him a small band of disciples, and said to them, "Go ye out and travel from place to place, for the welfare of many people, for the joy of many people, in pity for the world, for the blessed welfare of gods and men." Buddhism was crushed and driven out of India by the Brahmans. But Buddhists remember that Benares was the place of its birth.

The first place I visited was the monkey temple. This building is sacred to Kali. Within the temple is an image of the goddess. She is represented as a woman with a silver face and a red tongue. She was formerly worshiped by the blood-thirsty Thugs as their patroness. She is said to be the only deity in India who is worshiped with bloody sacrifices. The goat is the animal usually offered in sacrifice. The head goes to the priest, the body is eaten by the worshiper. In some way monkeys took possession of this temple. They come and go at pleasure. They climb up into the trees and run over the roofs of the buildings near. The worshipers acquire merit by feeding them. After I had seen the place and

BUNGALOW IN BINA, INDIA.

HOSPITAL IN BILASPUR, INDIA.

was about to depart, a crowd of men and women surrounded me and began to ask for money. One was the high priest of the temple, and must be paid. One was a Brahman, and on that ground pressed his claim. Another was the keeper of the monkeys, and wanted money to buy them food. Then beggars of every description were waiting their turn. Some were lepers, some were blind, some were deformed; all cried, "Great King, give me something." They had the beastly habit, which I have seen in all parts of the country, of uncovering their stomachs that I might see that there was nothing in them.

Leaving this place I went to the Golden Temple. The roof is plated with gold, but the interior is sloppy and nasty enough. Not being a "Hindu gentleman" I was not able to enter and go about where I pleased. All that I could do was to stand at the entrance and look in. The sight was one never to be forgotten. The place was thronged. The worshipers rang the bells, made their offerings, and repeated their prayers. As they were leaving a priest stamped their forehead with red paint, and they went on their way rejoicing. Near by is the "well of knowledge." Water from this well gives the knowledge of salvation. The people are constantly casting in fruits and flowers. To keep the water pure the authorities have covered over the mouth of the well. A Brahman sits by and ladles out some of the sacred fluid to those who pay for it. Another well of still greater sanctity is the "well of the ear-ring." This well was dug by Vishnu. His sweat filled it. Shiva looked into it, and so trembled with rapture that from one of his ears a jeweled ring fell, thus making the well doubly sacred. Pilgrims come here. A Brahman tells them of the cleansing efficacy of this water. The price demanded is reasonable. They hand him their hard-earned coins and then descend the steps and plunge into the pool and all is over. Every stain of sin is removed. "The liar, the thief, the murderer and the adulterer, may here wash and be clean."

Other temples are not far distant. I visited one sacred to the cow. A dozen cows were going about among their devotees. Pious Hindus feed them and kiss their tails and pray to them. I visited the temple of Ganesh. This god has the head of an elephant. The explanation is this: One night his father returned home drunk. Ganesh did not recognize his voice and refused to let him in. His father became enraged and struck him and knocked his head off. His mother was greatly distressed. The father took an elephant's head and put it on the boy and comforted his mother with the assurance that he would be the most popular god in India.

Benares has over two thousand temples and two hundred and seventy mosques. It is wholly given to idolatry, and such idolatry as Paul never saw in Athens or Corinth. The emblems of Shiva are everywhere. There are more of these in the city than there are human beings. Benares is a veritable paradise for the Brahmans. They are omnipresent, ever ready to guide the pilgrim in his devotions and to relieve him of his money. Naked fakirs smeared from head to heel with ashes are seen on all sides. The dirtier they are the greater their holiness. Sacred bulls swarm in the streets. They are fed by the people, and go wherever they choose.

Next morning Dr. Lazarus sent a guide with me to see the bathing in the Ganges. He took a boat and rowed up the stream to the edge of the city, and then floated down with the current. Benares is built on a high bluff, and stretches four miles along the Ganges. Palaces have been built by wealthy men for themselves and for their relatives. Stone steps lead down from these palaces, and from the streets to the water. At sunrise tens of thousands come here to bathe and to worship. Men and women of all ages plunge in and wash themselves thoroughly. Then the men wash their loincloth, make their offerings, pray, and go home. "A pathetic feature of this jostling, bellowing crowd, is the large number of tottering, aged women, with scanty white locks, coming out of the cold water, crawling feebly up the steep steps with their wet clothes clinging to their poor, shivering lean legs, shrinking into some recess lest the shadow of a passing Englishman or Mussulman should fall on them, a calamity that spoils the effect of the sacred cleansing, and renders it needful to creep back once more to the chill water." At one point is the burning ghat. As soon as a Hindu dies his body is carried to this place. The bearers shout as they run, "The name of Rama is true." When they come to the ghat they lay the bier in the water. In due time a platform of dry wood is prepared. The body is laid thereon and covered with faggots. A torch is applied and the whole reduced to ashes, and the ashes swept into the stream. If the men in charge are in a hurry, they do not wait for the fire to do its perfect work. I saw one body not more than half consumed. A crow was feasting on it as it floated down the river. To die in Benares, and to be burned at this famous ghat, is considered the highest felicity possible. We left the boat and visited the mosque of Aurungzeb, the tallest and most imposing building in the city. I ascended one of the minarets and saw the whole city and its numerous temples and shrines and worshipers, and thought of the saying, "The idols he shall utterly abolish."

I visited some of the missions and tried to learn what I could about the work. The English Baptists work among the girls and women. The Church Missionary Society has an orphanage, a school for girls, and a large school for boys. The London Society has a boarding school with five hundred boys, several schools for girls, a high school and a church. The Wesleyans have a preaching place, a school for girls, and keep several catechists at work. The Zenana Bible and Medical Mission has two centers of work and several dispensaries. The work is hard and the progress slow. Mr. Parker, of the London Society, said to me that it was not like hitting a stone wall, but like beating against a wall of rubber. Nevertheless, good work is being done, and the ultimate and universal triumph of the Gospel is assured.

XXXVI.

CAWNPORE AND LUCKNOW.

From Benares I went to Cawnpore. This city became famous in 1857. Here the crowning tragedy of the Sepoy Mutiny was enacted. Several causes led up to the mutiny. The people were dissatisfied with the rule of the East India Company. Some hoped to restore the Mogul rule. Some aspired to office and power. Some thought they would be able to enrich themselves by plunder in a time of anarchy. Evil reports were circulated and readily believed by the soldiers. It was said that the cartridges were greased with the fat of beef and pork, and that the soldiers would have to bite off the ends before loading. The Hindus would be defiled by eating beef, and the Mussulmans by eating pork. Sepoys were made to believe that the bones of cows and pigs had been ground to powder and mixed with their flour and butter, in order to destroy their caste and religion, and to compel them to become Christians.

The massacre that took place in Cawnpore was inspired and directed by Nana Sahib. This man was the adopted son and heir of the old king. The Government denied him the pension which he claimed was his due. He saw a chance for revenge and embraced it. At first he pretended to be the friend of the English. He assured them of his support in case of an attack. When the Sepoys rose and butchered their officers and committed their usual atrocities, he threw off all disguise. General Wheeler had a small force of soldiers in Cawnpore. He pitched his camp in an open field and threw up some entrenchments. All the English residents flocked to him for protection. There were nearly a thousand persons in the company. Nana persuaded the Sepoys to open fire on the English. For three weeks the attack and defense continued. The hot season was coming on: supplies of food and ammunition were running low; the besiegers numbered eleven thousand. All hope was given up. Nana offered to send them safely by boat to Allahabad, if they would lay down their arms and surrender their treasure. They accepted the terms and marched down to the Ganges to go on board. They suspected no treachery or bad faith. When the boats were full, guns were run out of ambuscade and

Jew Hawk and Family.
PORTLAND, ORE.

Miss Ida Kinsey. Ben Mitchell.
Miss Mattie Burgess. Mrs. Ben Mitchell.
BINA, INDIA.

firing began. Escape was impossible. Some were killed; some were drowned; the others were brought back to the shore. The men were dispatched at once. The women and children were preserved for a worse fate. They were sent for confinement to a house in the native city. Two strong swimmers escaped. Nana heard of Havelock's approach and sent his butchers to kill the women and children. There were two hundred in all. The butchers used hatchets and swords. They cut off arms and legs and heads. The next morning they returned and found a few still living. They threw these with the dead into a well near by. They had hardly finished their devilish work when Havelock's men appeared on the scene. They were horrified by what they saw. Kneeling there on that bloody floor, with arms and legs and heads all about them, with their swords in their mouths, they swore to be revenged.

The guide pointed out the well from which the besieged got water. The Sepoy guns were trained on this well, and water was drawn at the peril of life. He took us to the well where those who were killed or died during the siege were buried. This well is now filled and has a monument over it. The inscription runs: "Our bones are scattered at ye graves' mouth, as when one cutteth and cleaveth wood upon ye earth; but our eyes are unto thee, O God the Lord." A memorial church has been built. It cost $100,000. On its walls are the names of all who fell. We went to the other well. This too has been filled, and a monument erected over it. The soldier on guard pointed out the tree on which several hundred natives were hung. He told us that many had been shot from cannon. The vow of Havelock's men was kept. Those who were hung were compelled to drink the blood of their victims, and then were led out to the fatal tree.

I called at one of the mission bungalows. Mr. Conklin, the missionary in charge, told me that several societies are at work in Cawnpore. There is quite a colony of Europeans. Cawnpore is becoming a manufacturing and commercial center. The native Christians can earn good salaries, and so are able to contribute to the support of the Gospel. He told me of a Brahman boatman who found a Bible in the Ganges. He did not know what it was, but he felt that it was a good book, and he read it to his associates. He is now a Christian and a man of much influence. He is a boatman still, but he preaches as he is able.

At Cawnpore I took the train for Lucknow. Here I saw the palace of the last king of Oudh. It is not what it was once, but it is worth seeing. This king had two hundred wives. We went through their apartments. They are empty and silent now. We saw mosques and temples and tombs without number. President Mansell took me to see the Residency. It was here that the English community were shut up during the mutiny. Here for more than four months they made as brave a fight as history records. Six hundred men withstood sixty thousand, armed with three hundred cannon. Sir Henry Lawrence was killed soon after the siege began. His last words were, "Whatever you do, never surrender." His words were heeded. The Residency is a ruin. It is as it was when the besieged were rescued. The places where great deeds were done and where brave men fell are marked. Among these were some native soldiers who remained loyal to the government. Havelock and Outram cut their way through the besiegers and relieved the garrison. The pent up feelings of the garrison burst forth in deafening cheers, so it is said, and even the wounded soldiers in the hospital crawled out to join in the chorus of welcome. The bearded warriors, who had just fought their way through the city, shook the hands of the soldiers of the garrison with frantic joy, and took the infants out of their mother's arms and kissed them with the tears running down their cheeks and tossed them up into the air in their exultation and delight, whilst they thanked God that they had come in time to save the survivors from the fate that had befallen the victims at Cawnpore. In the graveyard near the Residency is the tomb of Sir Henry Lawrence, the man who tried to do his duty. The garrison was relieved, but that was all. Havelock's force was not strong enough to rescue the besieged. Later Sir Colin Campbell came with an army of sufficient strength to drive back the Sepoys and carry away the garrison. Havelock died and was buried at Alumbagh. There was something of Cromwell in him. His saints could always be depended upon in any emergency. These were thrilling times. The heart beats faster while reading Whittier's stirring lines. When the garrison had given up all hope a Scottish maiden cried out, "Dinna ye hear it? Dinna ye hear it? The pipes of Havelock sound!"

"Oh, they listened, dumb and breathless,
And they caught the sound at last,
Faint and far beyond the Goomtee
Rose and fell the piper's blast.
Then a burst of wild thanksgiving
Mingled woman's voice and man's,
God be praised! the march of Havelock,
And the piping of the clans.

"Louder, nearer, fierce as vengeance,
Sharp and shrill as swords at strife,
Came the wild McGregor's clan-call
Stinging all the air to life.
But when the far-off dust clouds
To plaided legions grew,
Full tenderly and blithesome
The pipes of rescue blew.

"Round the silver domes of Lucknow,
Moslem mosque and Pagan shrine,
Rose the air to Britons dearest,
The air of Auld Lang Syne.
O'er the cruel roll of war-drums
Rose that sweet and home-like strain,
And the Tartan clove the Turban
As the Goomtee cleaves the plain."

I visited the Mission Press and found one hundred and fifty men at work. This Press issues thirty-five million pages a year. It is self-supporting, and more. Miss Thoburn has one hundred and forty-three girls in her boarding school. In other schools three hundred girls are being taught. The English and Hindustani churches are self-supporting. The boys' boarding school has fifty enrolled. Reid Christian College has twenty in the regular courses. I visited the Widows' Home. A Hindu may marry a wife to-day and divorce her to-morrow. There are widows in India who have never been wives. These are taught and trained to serve as nurses or teachers. Some become wives of the native evangelists. One came to the deaconess in charge and said, "You gave my neighbor a good wife; can you give me one as good?" She said: "Yes; do you want to see her?" "That is not necessary. Name the day when I can come and be married." The Church of England is at work in Lucknow with a strong staff. The next point at which we are to call is Delhi, once the capital of the Mogul Emperors.

XXXVII.

DELHI AND AGRA.

Delhi is an old city. Tradition states that parts of it date back as far as the Exodus. For miles and miles beyond the limits of the present city there are traces of fortresses, palaces, tombs, temples and mosques. Each king wanted to build a capital that would eclipse that of his predecessor. The new city was built beside the old. The abandoned city in course of time fell into ruins. The ruins about Delhi cover forty-five square miles.

The first place to which the stranger is taken is the Fort. The inclosing wall is of red sandstone, and is a mile and a quarter in length. The government has taken possession of this property and keeps it in repair. Within the Fort is the Private Hall of Audience. This is of white marble. Once it was inlaid with all manner of precious stones. Most of these have been carried away by vandals. The place is shown where the Peacock Throne stood. This throne was so called because its back was formed by jeweled representations of peacocks' tails. It was of solid gold inlaid with gems, and cost $30,000,000. When Nadir Shah, the Persian, invaded India, he took away the Peacock Throne. The Mahrattas took the silver filigree ceiling as part of their spoil. On the wall may be read a Persian inscription, "If on earth there is a heaven of bliss, it is this, it is this." We saw the Public Hall of Audience, the baths of the Emperor, his wives, and children, and the mosque in which the imperial family worshiped. From the Fort we went to the Great Mosque. This building is situated on a rocky eminence. There are magnificent flights of steps leading up to three lofty and handsome gateways. The court is 450 feet square and is paved with red stone. In the center is a reservoir for water. Being built on so high a rock the domes and minarets lift themselves high into the air and are seen from afar. I was shown a hair from the beard of Mohammed, one of his slippers, and a print of his foot in marble. These things are guarded with the most jealous care. The custodians appear to think that they are genuine and of the greatest value.

Eleven miles from New Delhi is the Kutub-Minar. This tower is

WATER CARRIER.

JAIN PRIEST.

238 feet high, and dates back to the thirteenth century. It was built on the ruins of a Hindu fortress by the first resident Mohammedan king of India. Whole chapters of the Koran are cut in relief upon it. Though the Kutub was built six hundred years ago, the carving and masonry are as fresh and as perfect as if they had been finished but yesterday. I went up to the top and looked out in all directions. As far as the eye could reach the landscape was filled with ruins. Another tower of the same pattern was begun but not completed. The foundations of a great mosque were laid and the walls partly erected when the work ceased. The builder died or changed his plan. On the way back we stopped to examine the tomb of Humayun, the father of Akbar the Great. The mausoleum is of red sandstone inlaid with marble. It was here that the two sons of the last Mogul Emperor took refuge in the Mutiny and were shot. We glanced at Indrapat. This fortress is said to be the oldest part of Delhi. It reaches back to the time of Joshua. We saw Ferozabad in the twilight. Within it is one of the columns of Asoka, on which his edicts are inscribed.

On Sunday morning I went to the Episcopal Church. It was a military parade service. The officers of the garrison wore their swords, the soldiers carried their guns. Before the Mutiny they left their arms outside; since the Mutiny they take them in. The sermon was ten minutes by the clock, but owing to the sing-song tone of the preacher it seemed an hour. Delhi is the home of the Cambridge Brotherhood. The members are celibates and live as one family. They carry on evangelistic work and teach in the college for boys in Delhi and do work in the outlying district. In the evening I went to the English Baptist Church. The missionary in charge was out in the villages. One of his associates preached. The Baptists carry on evangelistic and educational work here.

Delhi was the center of the Mutiny. Here the old Emperor lived in retirement as a pensioner of the government. His partisans brought him out and placed him on the throne. Soldiers gathered from all parts of Hindustan. Thirty thousand disciplined troops held the city. The English did not have as many as ten thousand. It was felt that Delhi must be taken at any cost. The post of danger and of honor was assigned to General Nicholson. He was to blow up the Cashmere gate and storm the city on its most deadly side. Soldiers carried bags of gunpowder through shot and shell and placed them in position. All were either killed instantly or fatally wounded. The train was fired and the gate blown into atoms. The assailants rushed in and charged the Sepoys with the bayonet. More than a third of the British force fell. General Nicholson was shot in the hour of victory. In a little while the British flag waved over the citadel. The neck of the Mutiny was broken, and India was saved to England. The valor displayed in and around Delhi has never been excelled.

I left Delhi for Agra. This city was built by Akbar. The walls inclose eleven square miles. Dr. Colin Valentine, a Scottish worthy, took me to his own home. After breakfast he took me to Sikandra. Here the great Akbar is buried. Three thousand men spent twenty years building his tomb. The lower stories are of red sandstone; the upper one is of white marble. He is buried in a dingy vault. There is a cenotaph in the upper story. Around it are the ninety-nine names of God. At the head is a pillar in which the Kohinoor was set. The jewel has passed into other hands; the glory of the Mogul Empire has departed. Across the road is an orphanage for boys and girls under the control of the Church Missionary Society. The government gave this Society the tomb of one of Akbar's wives for this purpose. This is the best use I have seen made of any tomb in India. The orphans are taught to read and write and to work with their own hands. Among other things they are taught printing and binding, and do very creditable work. After our return we went to the Fort and saw the Pearl Mosque, the Palace, the Public and Private Halls of Audience, the Tilt-yard, the Palace of Glass, the rooms occupied by the numerous wives of the Emperor. Bayard Taylor says of the Pearl Mosque: "To my eye it is absolutely perfect. It is a sanctuary so pure and stainless, revealing so exalted a spirit of worship, that I felt humbled, as a Christian, to think that our noble religion has never inspired its architects to surpass this temple to God and Mohammed." The Palace of Glass is a bath, the walls of which are adorned with thousands of small mirrors. Akbar's judgment-seat is as he left it. It is a block of black marble. The guide points out a crack in it, and gravely tells you that blood came from this crack more than once. Another seat of white marble was used by the King's fool.

I went twice to see the Taj Mahal. This is the most renowned building in the world. Twenty thousand men spent seventeen years in its construction. The ends of the earth were searched for precious stones to garnish it. The Taj is the tomb built by Shah Jehan for his favorite wife, the lovely Noor Jehan, the Light of the World. It rests on a plinth eighteen feet high and three hundred and thirteen feet square. The tomb proper is one hundred and eighty-six feet from side to side. It is surmounted with a central dome eighty feet high and fifty feet in diameter. At each corner there is a smaller dome. The whole of the Koran is inscribed on the walls. There are four minarets one hundred and thirty-seven feet high. The entire building is of white marble. On either side there is a mosque of red sandstone. The Taj is approached through a lofty gateway. The avenue is lined with trees and flowers. In the midst of it a stream of clear water runs. The Taj baffles description. One can give its materials and dimensions and decorations, and leave the reader little the wiser. He can say that the walls are covered with tulips, lilies and oleanders; that the tombs of the Emperor and his beautiful wife are inlaid with flowers made of the costliest gems; but no one could get from such words an adequate conception of the graceful proportions and exquisite beauty of this building. We may call it a dream in marble, we may say that it is the perfection of beauty; we may get photographs of it. These help a little, but not much. It would be as easy to gild refined gold as to describe the Taj. Heber said, "The Pathans design like Titans, and finish like jewelers." They do. It is significant that the finest tomb ever erected was erected to a woman, and that in a country where women are lightly esteemed.

The thought of these great buildings and their builders fills one with sadness. The Mogul Emperors were little better than savages. When one ascended the throne he blinded or strangled all his near relatives. Brother rose up against brother, and son against father. Shah Jehan built the Taj, but that did not keep him from seeking solace in the company of dancing girls. He spent the last seven years of his life as a prisoner. The Taj was built by men who were not paid for their services. The Emperors built tombs and palaces and mosques to perpetuate their own names, but no provision was made for the common people. They were not taught; roads and bridges were not made so that they could take their products to market. "For a less sum of money than they spent on their palaces, two tombs and a throne, the British government has made 4,500 miles of irrigating canals, watering 3,000,000 acres, and giving employment and food to fifteen or twenty millions of population."

Dr. Valentine is the head of a medical missionary school in Agra. He has students from all parts of India. Every evening they gather in his home and listen to his expositions of the Scriptures. In Jeypore he healed one of the wives of the Maharajah. This gave him a standing at court and in the community that he could not have had otherwise. He is a man of God, and he is doing the work of God. I called to see St. John's College. This is a thoroughly Christian School. Nothing is left undone to bring the students to Christ. The classes are full. New buildings are needed. The Agra College has about the same number of students. The Principal is a Scotchman and a Christian. But there is no religious instruction in the classes. I called to see all the missionaries and heard from them about their work. I left Agra for Bombay by way of Jeypore and Baroda.

1. Miss Kingsbury. 2. Dr. Merrill. 3. Dr. Baldwin.
4. Miss Boyd. 5. Mrs. Lohr. 6. M. D. Adams.

MISSIONARIES IN BILASPUR, INDIA.

XXXVIII.

BOMBAY, POONA AND NELLORE.

BOMBAY is the chief commercial city of India. Its harbor is one of the finest in the world. The population numbers 805,000. The great buildings and crowded streets remind one of an American seaport. Mr. Wharton came down from Hurda to meet me and to go with me through Southern India. With such a genial and accomplished guide my visit to this part of the country could not fail to be both pleasant and profitable.

We went first to the office of the *Bombay Guardian*. Mr. Dyer, the editor, belongs to the Friends, and therefore is pledged to seek peace and to pursue it. But let no evil think it can flourish in Bombay on that account. He will smite it with both hands earnestly, and will consent to no cessation of hostilities till the evil ceases to exist. He is a pronounced and persistent assailant of vice and crime. For his outspoken words against the opium traffic and other iniquities he was sent to jail. But even that experience did not subdue his spirit or cause him to abate his zeal for the Lord of hosts. Mr. Dyer is a moral force in India. His influence for good is felt throughout the Empire. Vice knows and fears and hates him.

Eleven missionary societies are at work in Bombay. The whole number of missionaries is forty-four. The work of the American Board is said to be the most prosperous in the Presidency. Mr. and Mrs. Hume, the missionaries in charge, received us most kindly and showed us the premises and the work. They began a school in 1876 with one pupil. They have now 165. The dormitories and class-rooms have been outgrown. Recitations are held in all sorts of places. The pupils are all Christians or are from Christian homes. Because they are, they meet and recite in the same classes. This is the only place in India where I saw this done. We were there on Washington's birthday. Mrs. Hume had an American flag and gave a short talk on Washington. She gave the school a holiday in honor of the occasion. The address and the holiday were loudly cheered. Mr. Hume told us that the church is entirely self-supporting. The members collect and disburse the funds and manage their own affairs.

The Parsees are the most influential class in Bombay, though they number only 70,000. When the Mohammedans invaded Persia, twelve hundred years ago, some of the Persians migrated to India. The Parsees are their descendants. One of the priests told us of their worship. They follow the teachings of Zoroaster. He taught the necessity of good thoughts, good words, and good deeds. In their temples the sacred fire never goes out. Sandal wood and incense are kept burning all the time. But they do not worship the fire or the sun. These are symbols of God and are helps to the mind. We visited the Towers of Silence. These are the places where the Parsees expose their dead. The dead body is carried up into the Tower and left there perfectly naked. The mourners remain below in the house of prayer. As soon as the bearers are gone the vultures swoop down on the corpse. In less than ten minutes the bones are stripped bare. After some time the skeleton is thrown down a well in the center of the Tower. Here rich and poor meet together. Pipes lead from the central well to four other wells. When the bones become dust the rains carry the dust into these reservoirs. The Parsees are rich, intelligent, and public-spirited. They build schools and hospitals and infirmaries and endow them. Their women dress with admirable taste. In this respect they excel all the peoples I have seen on my travels.

In the hospital for the deaf we saw Gulali, one of the students from Hurda. Mr. Wharton says that he is not only the brightest mind in the class, but one of the brightest men he has ever met. He is totally blind and recently has been growing deaf. One ear has gone and the other is going. The doctors think they can arrest the disease. His face shone when we spoke to him. He said that as Paul's imprisonment led to the Gospel being preached in the imperial palace, so his confinement in the hospital was being used to carry the Gospel to those who had never heard it. The physicians and the patients gathered about him as he read the Bible for the blind. He had read to them most of the Gospel by John.

After seeing Bombay we went to Poona and spent Sunday there. T. H. Marshall and family, formerly of Hurda, live there and took us to their home. Poona is an interesting city. Here Pandita Ramabai lives and carries on her work. Ramabai belongs to the highest caste. She was taught Sanskrit by her father and mother. At sixteen she was married. She said her parents did not throw her down the well of ignorance by giving her in marriage in infancy. She became an advocate of female education. In Calcutta she was examined and pronounced "a prodigy of erudition." When she was eighteen she was left a widow and an orphan with a daughter to support. She took the platform and advocated the cause of Hindu women. She formed a society to promote female education and to discourage infant marriages. Feeling her need of more training she went to England. There she became a Christian and went to college for several years. Then she went to America and stirred many by her eloquence. She returned to Poona and opened a home for high caste widows. India has 23,000,000 widows of all ages. The law is, "once a widow, always a widow." Their heads are shaven, they are starved and beaten, they wear special garments and no jewels. These are "badges of shame." Ramabai opened her home with one child widow. The number increased to sixty-nine. We called to see her. We found her surrounded by a group of girls. She was reading and explaining the Scriptures. She showed us through the compound. Her home is a beautiful one. There are many evidences of taste, but none of wealth. We saw the class-rooms and the library. She has fifty girls now; of these, forty are widows. Several became Christians. A storm was raised and some were withdrawn. No effort is made to turn the inmates from Hinduism. But the atmosphere of the place is decidedly Christian, and girls do give themselves in love and trust to Christ. Ramabai is a quiet, modest, gentle soul. It is plain that she lives in the Spirit, and walks in the Spirit.

R. P. Wilder and Max Morehead are at work in Poona among the college students. There is a daily lecture. On Sunday there is a service of song, and this is preceded by a season of prayer. A daily paper sounded an alarm. It said, "The love of the missionaries is more dangerous than the sword of the Mohammedans." A Brahman was baptized. He came to the hall and told his experience. He said, "You may beat me; you may kill me; I care not." Then he told them that he had been baptized. There was a fierce outcry at once. The meeting became a mob. They beat him and spat in his face and tried to kill him. He was offered good positions if he would deny the faith, but he remained steadfast and immovable. The missionaries were stoned. The building was saturated with oil and set on fire. Two men stood at the door and refused admittance to the young men. They were obliged to seek another hall. One student who manifested some interest was caught and locked up and his clothes taken away. He got out and came to Mr. Wilder almost naked. He is undaunted. The evening we were at the service there were several weddings near by. There was a score of brass bands. It was as if bedlam and pandemonium had broken loose. The speaking was interrupted, but the hall was full and the attention good. Mr. Wilder feels greatly cheered in the work.

We called to see the Bernard sisters. They are nieces of Lord Lawrence. One has charge of the educational work, one is at the head of the medical department, and the third superintends the orphanage. They are all women of ability and education and consecration. They are fitted to adorn any sphere. They work at their own charges. They are as great and effective in their way as Ramabai is in hers. They are remarkably happy in their work. Their joy is such as no butterfly of fashion or belle of society can ever know. Our day in Poona was one to be long remembered.

Our next halt was made at Nellore. Most of the country through which we passed is rocky and poor. The population is sparser than in Bengal or the Central Provinces. Mr. Downie, of the American Baptist Missionary Mission, was at the station and constrained us to abide with him. He and Mrs. Downie and their associates contributed in every way to our enjoyment. The great work of the Baptists among the Telugus began at Nellore. The plant here is a large one. The whole district has been evangelized. The church in Nellore has 700 members. There are 225 boys and girls in the schools on the compound. The industrial department is in charge of Mrs. Downie, and is self-supporting and more. The demand for the work is greater than the supply. Dr. Gould has the work in the hospital and dispensaries. Dr. Downie has been in Nellore since 1872. He took part in the relief in the famine of 1877. He told us that as much relief work was done in Nellore as in Ongole, but the ingathering that followed was not so large. Still it has been very gratifying. With such a staff and with such workers as preceded them, it could not have been otherwise. One evening the children came over and sang and recited for us. The kindergarten songs were as entertaining as any such songs at home. We saw all the work and were greatly pleased with it. We left Nellore for Madras.

BUNGALOW IN MAHOBA, INDIA.

TAJ MAHAL.

XXXIX.

FROM MADRAS TO COLOMBO.

Madras has a population of 500,000, and is the capital of the Presidency. The most noted institution here is the Christian College. This school was founded by the Free Church of Scotland. The Wesleyan and Church Societies contribute to its support. Professor Kellett showed us through the buildings. There are nearly 2,000 students enrolled. More than half are in the primary department. One student in ten is a Christian. There are ten European teachers on the staff and about seventy natives. Dr. William Miller is the principal. Some are not satisfied with his attitude toward Hinduism and Mohammedanism. They feel that he and his associates do not do all they ought to win the students to the faith of Christ. Dr. Miller is a strong man. He is the most accomplished and successful teacher in India. He gives reasons for his course. The calendar states that what the college desires is to make education an instrument of opening men's minds to moral and spiritual and Christian truth, and thereby to take a humble but useful part in the mighty work which Christ began and which his body, the universal church, is bound by every means within her power to further. While we were in Madras there was a conference of the colleges of Southern India. The conference was held in one of the halls of Christian College. Forty schools were represented. J. R. Mott, J. C. White, R. P. Wilder, Max Morehead, and J. H. Forman were present. The advancement of the cause of Christ in the colleges was the one aim of the conference.

We visited several missions and inquired concerning the progress of the work. We heard here, what we heard in other cities, that the work was hindered by representatives from Christendom. This is not true of all, but it is true of many. We called to see Dr. Murdock. He has been in India over forty years. His books are everywhere. They are widely read and cannot fail to do much good. We heard of an American convict and went to see him. He is not an American by birth. It is not clear that he is one by adoption. He has had a half dozen different names. There were tears in his eyes and in his voice. He cries too easily. His term will soon expire. He admits that he has been a bad man, but promises to mend his ways.

We left Madras for Colombo. On the way we stopped for a few hours at Tanjore. This was the home of Schwartz for years. His church is in the fort. The Rajah took a great interest in him and his work. No doubt the favor of royalty contributed to his success. The people saw that Schwartz was able to protect and to assist them. Mr. Blake, the missionary in charge, showed us through the church and the schools. There are 600 boys in the college. In the same compound there is a large school for girls. Near by is a Christian village. Mr. Blake is a High-church man, but he was extremely obliging and gave us all the time and attention we could desire. We crossed the street and visited the Leipsic Mission. This mission carries on evangelistic and educational work. Caste is not recognized in the church or at the Lord's table. In the homes it is. People of different castes do not marry. The missionaries regard this as a social regulation and do not interfere with it. These two missions inherit the work of Schwartz. We saw his grave in the church. When the old Rajah was dying he sent for the man of God and entreated him to become guardian for his young son. He said to him, "This is not my son, but yours; into your hand I deliver him." When Schwartz died the young prince wrote the following lines, which were placed upon his tomb:

"Firm wast thou, humble and wise,
Honest, pure, free from disguise;
Father of orphans, the widow's support,
Comfort in sorrow of every sort.
To the benighted, dispenser of light,
Doing, and pointing to, that which is right,
Blessing to princes, to people, to me;
May I, my father, be worthy of thee,
Wisheth and prayeth thy Saraboji."

Our next call was made at Trichinopoly. The Society for the Propagation of the Gospel has a school here with 1,500 boys in it. Of these 700 are in the primary department. This is the largest school south of Madras. In the church we saw the grave of Heber. He died here while on a tour of Episcopal visitation. His grave is very simple. The temples in the south of India are wholly unlike anything seen in other parts of the country. The gates are huge and high. They and the temples proper are covered with tiers of images of gods and goddesses. The buildings are filled with rude carvings. There is no beauty or utility anywhere. The temple in Trichinopoly covers a vast space. People inside sell all sorts of merchandise. The inclosure looks more like a market than a house of prayer. Crowds of priests want to serve as guides. They follow visitors about and then demand pay for imaginary services. They press their claims with an importunity worthy of a better cause. We found the missionaries kind and helpful. They regretted that we could not stay longer and see more of their work.

The next day was spent in Madura. This district is as large as Massachusetts and is worked by the American Board. We heard a sermon in Tamil in the morning. At Mr. Herrick's request I spoke in the evening. After the service Mr. Chandler took us to the monthly missionary concert. Here Mr. Wharton spoke. There are two self-supporting churches in Madura. They pay all their own expenses and aid the work elsewhere. The next morning Mr. Chandler showed us over the spacious compound. We met Dr. Van Alen in the hospital and Miss Swift, Miss Root and Miss Noyes in their buildings. The work has outgrown the premises. In the afternoon we rode out to Pasamulai to see the college. We made the acquaintance of Drs. Washburn and Jones and Professor Zumbro. We saw the buildings and the classes. There are about 700 students here. Most of these are believers. The representatives of the American Board are able men. This is true in Japan and China as well as in India.

Our last visit was made at Palamcottah. This is in the Tinnevelly district. The two societies connected with the Church of England are at work in this field. The work began more than a century ago. Schwartz was the pioneer. He was succeeded by Rhenius, Ringeltaube, Jaenike, Kohlkoff, Thomas, Ragland and others. Bishop Sargent was here for fifty years. He saw the number of converts in his diocese increase from 9,000 to 55,000, and the number of missionary agents from 184 to 768. No wonder that on his deathbed he said, "If I had a thousand lives they should all be devoted to missionary work." Mr. Walker, the leading missionary, put us in the way of seeing the schools and other places of interest. We spent some time in the Sarah Tucker Institution. Miss Askwith has 300 girls under her care. Some are blind, others are deaf and dumb. This school is affiliated with the Madras University. Mrs. Kember has ninety-five girls in her building. Professor Keyworth has 200 boys in the High School. Professor Schaffer has 400 in the college in Tinnevelly. A great work is being done here. In this district there are 465 schools with 16,000 boys and girls enrolled. Miss Askwith has the oversight of fifty of these schools. Miss Blythe directs the labors of forty Bible women. Large sums of money have been invested in this mission. The returns are very gratifying. At this point Mr. Wharton left for Hurda. He had been my guide for two weeks and helped me to see Southern India with profit. Mr. Mead, a distinguished Baptist preacher from Adelaide, joined me here. He had been in India in the interest of missions, and was on his way home.

I have found English clergymen very pleasant socially. They are as hospitable as one could wish. But they are priests, and they alone are qualified to minister in holy things. Not only so, but I have found that to Europeans in the East America is practically non-existent. When I would introduce the subject they would say, "Really," or "O," and begin at once to talk about something else. They do not know that nearly half the missionary work of the world is done by Americans. They know as little about the New World as the average American knows about the Old, if they know as much. Going into a store to buy a hat, the salesman said, "Americans can't make stiff hats." I said, "Americans can make anything." He said, "They can make soft hats, but not stiff hats." Mine was once stiff. He said, "You must go to London for stiff hats." I told him if he would look into the hat he was disparaging he would see that it was made in London. He had no more to say.

As we sailed from Tuticorin for Colombo, and as India faded from sight, I thought that that great land belongs to Christ, because he died for its redemption, and he shall have it. The struggle with the powers of darkness will be a long one. But it must be continued

"Until that land, so dear, so sorrowed o'er,
With all its load of misery and sin,
After long ages of transgression, turn,
And, pierced in heart with love, the shaft of Kings,
Fall down and bathe His blessed feet with tears;
Then rise, and to the listening world tell out
Her deep repentance and her new found joy."

BUNGALOW IN BILASPUR, INDIA.

BOYS' SCHOOL IN BILASPUR, INDIA.

XL.

LARGE INGATHERINGS IN INDIA.

In some parts of India large numbers have become obedient to the faith. The workers in other missions have been as faithful and diligent in holding forth the word of life, but the results that rewarded their labors and cheered their hearts have not been so great. The large ingatherings have been, without exception, in missions that have long been established. A bountiful sowing has preceded a bountiful reaping. Bishop Thoburn says that it requires a generation to get laborers settled and fairly at work. Distrust and dislike must be lived down, and confidence and good will secured, before the people will listen attentively to the Gospel. In several instances the relief given in time of famine contributed to the large results. I propose to give brief accounts of some successful missions in India.

The Gossner mission in Chota Nagpur has recently celebrated its Jubilee. This mission works among the Kols, an aboriginal tribe. Their religion consists in the worship of evil spirits. They think they please the gods best by feasting, drinking and dancing. All diseases are attributed to demons or to witches. The reports show that the converts, from the first, number 52,246. In fifty years many have died, or have gone back, or have gone to Assam or elsewhere. Of the whole number of converts, 40,000 are living and known. The missionaries met with much opposition. The converts were plundered by armed bands. Their rice, their money, their ornaments and the roofs of their houses were seized and carried away.

The Arcot mission is inseparably connected with the name of Scudder. Dr. John Scudder was one of the first physicians of New York City. He read a paper on "The Conversion of the World; or, The Claims of Six Hundred Millions, and the Ability and Duty of the Churches Respecting Them." He offered himself to the American Board and was accepted. In 1819 he sailed from Boston for Ceylon. He decided to work among the Tamils and to make Madras the center of his work. Dr. Scudder was a versatile man. He served the people as preacher, teacher, physician, translater and editor. He was instant in season and out of season. He realized his own desire to be one of "the inner circle about Jesus." His children and children's children to the fourth generation have walked in his steps. For his eldest son Silas his prayer was that God would make him a Christian and a missionary. Silas wanted to make a fortune as a physician in New York. He founded the Women's Hospital in that city and was making money. But God touched his heart and he went to India as a medical missionary. Dr. Henry M. Scudder selected Arcot as his field. There are now in the mission nine missionaries, eight native pastors, sixteen catechists, seventy-five readers and teachers, 124 congregations, a Christian community of 6,504 souls, and 122 schools with 4,517 pupils. Since the mission was opened, railways, bridges, macadamized roads, houses of brick and tile, have been built; electric wires have been strung; streets have been cleaned and walls whitewashed. In all these improvements the missionaries have been in the lead.

The Methodist Episcopal Society opened its first station in India in 1857. In recent years its success has been marvelous. Not less than one thousand a month renounce idolatry and put themselves under Christian instruction. Dr. E. W. Parker, of Lucknow, gave me an account of the work. Some low caste Sikhs came to the missionary in Bareilly and told him that they had heard the Gospel on the banks of the Ganges at one of their feasts, and they wanted to hear more. Some were led to confess their faith in Christ. These were sent back to their own people with the message of salvation. In course of time the whole caste, consisting of about 10,000, was won. From these converts, preachers, catechists, railway clerks and civil servants have come. The work among the Chamars began in this way: A religious teacher was led to Christ in the Church mission. He wanted to go home and preach to his own kindred. That mission had no work in that part of the country. He went to the Methodist mission and told his history. He was so revered by his pupils that they would wash his feet and drink the water. He felt confident that many of these would listen to his words. He wanted to preach. Dr. Parker took him with him on his tours among the towns and cities. He was able and eloquent, and so spoke that many believed. One day he said, "This is not the work I want to do. Do you see these villages? I have disciples in them all. They will believe what I say." Dr. Parker said to him, "Go." Soon after a delegation returned with him and said, "We want this man to live with us. We will feed, and clothe, and house, and protect him." He went with them that very day. Many thousands have avowed their faith in Jesus Christ. This particular caste numbers 500,000; there is reason to believe that the whole caste will be brought over. The largest ingathering has been from the sweepers, the lowest of all castes. Some boys asked to be taught. The teachers did not stop to inquire as to their caste. Schools were opened in their villages and myriads have believed. Caste is not recognized in the churches. But the work, in the main, has been along caste lines. One family has been used to reach other families. Converts find it easier to work among their own kindred than among strangers. Bishop Thoburn told me that the converts connected with the Methodist Society exceed 55,000. Dr. Parker thinks that at least 90,000 have broken away from idolatry.

The Madura mission of the American Board was established in 1836. Two men came from Ceylon to occupy a field as large as Massachusetts. These two were soon joined by several others. The present staff consists of thirteen missionaries, sixteen assistant missionaries, 543 native agents. Schools have been opened for girls and boys. Teachers and preachers are trained for service. Hospitals and dispensaries have been provided for the sick. Twenty-eight Bible women are employed. They meet with many rebuffs. The people whom they seek to help and bless say, "It is not our custom to learn to read; it is not our custom to sing." Custom in India is law. Miss Swift gives an account of what these women meet. One enters a house and her pupil says, "O, I can't study to-day! We are in *such* distress, we haven't eaten anything to-day! Early this morning a cat jumped in at one window and out at the other! We are quite sure it must have been a demon, and something terrible is going to happen." Some hill people said to a missionary, "We die like beasts, and are buried like dogs; ought you neglect us?" That is not the mental attitude of the majority of the people in India. Of almost every convert it can be said, "Is this not a brand plucked from the fire?" When we remember the obstinate opposition to Christianity it will be seen that the Madura mission has been eminently successful. The adherents number 14,810; the youths in school, 6,873.

The work in Tinnevelly began more than a century ago. Schwartz sent his agents to preach the Gospel throughout all Southern India. In 1816 Chaplain Hough found three thousand Christians in Tinnevelly. He did what he could for them himself and applied to the Church Missionary Society for evangelists.

Two were sent out. Whole villages expressed a desire to be taught. As the years went on, the workers were reinforced. Schools of all kinds were opened. Workers were trained. The Gospel was preached far and wide. After a severe famine multitudes turned to the Lord. They were impressed and led to examine the claims of the Gospel by the kindness shown them in distress. The greatest success was in one caste, that of the palmyra climbers. These people have been wonderfully improved since they accepted Jesus as their Savior and Lord. The Christian community connected with this society now numbers 55,571; the youth under instructions, 19,564. The Society for the Propagation of the Gospel represents the same religious body and has worked in one part of this district since 1825. The success of this society has been almost as large as that of the Church Missionary Society. It reports 42,170 adherents, and 15,764 scholars. The converts of the two societies aggregate nearly one hundred thousand souls. The London Missionary Society has been at work among the same people and among their neighbors in Travancore. The place last named is the stronghold of Brahmanism in Southern India. At one festival the Maharajah officiates for a short time as one of the bearers of the palanquin of the chief Brahman. After doing so, he washes his feet and drinks some of the water. The London Society has 41,000 converts under its care, and 17,240 pupils in its schools.

Perhaps the work of the American Baptists among the Telugus is more widely known than any other work in India. This work began in 1840. Four years later a church of eight members was organized in Nellore. At the meeting of the Board in 1848, the question was, Shall the Telugu mission be continued or abandoned? The decision was in its favor. Five years later the same question was discussed. The results had been discouragingly small. Some one proposed that Dr. Jewett be instructed to close the mission and remove to Burma. The Corresponding Secretary asked, "And who will write the letter? And who will write the letter?" His tone indicated that whoever would do so, he would not. One speaker referred to the mission as the one mission east of the Bay of Bengal. He spoke of it as the Lone Star Mission. The decision went over to the next day. That night Dr. S. F. Smith wrote the famous lines:

"Shine on, Lone Star! thy radiance bright
Shall spread o'er all the Eastern sky;
Morn breaks apace from gloom and night;
Shine on and bless the pilgrim's eye.

G. W. Coffman, Damoh.

Dr. A. C. and Dr. Lillian B. Miller, Bilaspur.

WORKERS IN INDIA.

"Shine on, Lone Star! I would not dim
The light that shines with dubious ray;
The lonely Star of Bethlehem
Led on a bright and glorious day.

"Shine on, Lone Star! in grief and tears
And sad reverses oft baptized;
Shine on amid thy sister spheres;
Lone Stars in heaven are not despised.

"Shine on, Lone Star! Who lifts his hand
To dash to earth so bright a gem,
A new 'lost Pleiad' from the band
That sparkles in night's diadem?

"Shine on, Lone Star! The day draws near
When none will shine more fair than thou;
Thou born and nursed in doubt and fear
Wilt glitter on Immanuel's brow.

"Shine on, Lone Star, till earth redeemed
In dust shall bid its idols fall;
And thousands whom thy radiance beamed
Shall crown the Savior Lord of all."

The poem saved the mission. It was unanimously resolved to reinforce the workers. Several years later, owing to a lack of success, the old question recurred. Dr. Jewett said that even if the Board declined to aid him, he would go back to live and die among the Telugus. Some said, "If that is your feeling, we must send some one back with you to give you Christian burial." John E. Clough was appointed to go with him. When the great famine came in 1876, relief works were opened. The missionaries did what they could to save the people alive. Mr. Clough was an engineer. He was asked to superintend the cutting of one section of the Buckingham Canal. While the men were eating and resting the native evangelists preached to them. For fifteen months there were no baptisms. It was not till the famine was over and no further pecuniary favors were expected that Mr. Clough consented to baptize any. He was afraid of unworthy motives. Again and again he told the people to go home and wait a few months longer. The time came when they would not hear his request for delay. They demanded baptism as their right. He and his associates began to examine them. In six months 9,606 were baptized. There were 2,222 baptisms in one day. The work began at six in the morning. After prayer, two native evangelists took their place in the water. When they grew weary, two others relieved them. They rested from eleven till two, and at five they were done. Two men in eight hours baptized over two thousand. Had six officiated they could have completed the task in less than three hours. The people of one village asked for baptism. The missionaries tried to send them away. They said, "We don't want any money; we will not ask for any, either directly or indirectly, either now or hereafter. As we have lived thus far by our work,—by the blisters on our hands we can prove this to you,—so we will continue to live, or if we die we shall die, but we want you to baptize us." The result was that in three days there were 3,536 baptisms. In another field Dr. Clough visited ninety-eight villages and baptized 1,068. In the mission there are ninety-eight missionaries; 266 native preachers; eighty-three churches; 56,683 native Christians; 577 schools, and 8,112 pupils in them.

These large ingatherings are cheering, but we must not be cast down because there are not many of them. In most missions the results are quite as great as we have any reason to expect. If societies have reaped sparingly, it is because they sowed sparingly. If we will strengthen the staff of workers and supply their needs, we shall see most gratifying returns. Nothing can be truer than the words of Carey, "We are sure to take the fortress, if we can but persuade ourselves to sit down long enough before it. We shall reap if we faint not."

XLI.

THINGS INDIAN.

One is surprised to find the skin of the people so dark. Foreigners speak of them as if they were negroes. This is a mistake. They are black, or nearly so, but their features are unlike those of the negro. They belong to the Aryan race. They are of the same stock as the nations of Europe. Some are darker than others. The aborigines are, as a rule, the darkest; the Brahmans are the fairest. The color of these people is due to the climate. The aborigines live more in the open air than the Brahmans, and consequently are darker. The Jews in India are much swarthier than in Europe or America. Most of the sheep are black.

Children wear little or no clothing. Boys and girls go about the streets and attend Sunday-school as naked as when they were born. They may have on a bracelet or anklet or ear-ring or nose-ring, but nothing in the way of clothing. Like our first parents, they are naked and not ashamed. Working people wear scant covering. A loin-cloth costs not over three cents. Nothing more is needed for a man. He needs neither hat nor shoes. Working women wear more than men, but not much. Ten cents would pay for an average outfit. As for changes of style to accord with the season, that is something of which they have never heard. The poor sleep at night in the clothes they wore during the day. Servants sleep at the doors in the halls and on the verandas, or wherever they can find room to stretch their wearied bodies. Rich people spend more thought and money on dress. They delight in bright colors. In Calcutta and elsewhere one sees men dressed in green, or blue, or white, or red, or yellow, or crimson. Men go about in the heat of the day with no covering on their heads. This would be fatal to an American. The natives are used to the sun and do not mind its fiercest rays. The climate of India is warm, and clothing is not needed as a protection, as it is in the north.

The common people live in clay or stone buildings. They spend most of their time in the open air. The cooking is done out of doors. In the rains the family sleep in the house, the rest of the year they sleep outside. In winter they sit in front of the house to keep warm. The heat comes from the sun. The houses have no furniture. A bed is a luxury. It costs fifteen cents. There are no tables or chairs. There is no carpet on the floor and no paper or pictures on the wall. Knives and forks and spoons are not considered among the necessaries. The rich keep their women indoors. Those who wish to be fashionable do the same. I was in the house of one man of wealth and social position. I cannot say that I envied him his home. Americans study comfort and conveniences as no other people on the globe. One of our mechanics has more of both in his house than an Indian Maharajah has or than Solomon in all his glory had.

Mechanics sit at their work. This is true of the blacksmith, the carpenter, the stonecutter, and the carriage-maker. Bricklayers sit on the wall as they build. Those that carry mortar and brick stand, but no workmen do this if they can possibly sit. The barber sits and his victim sits opposite him. They look like a pair of fighting cocks. People sit in the bazars and in the stores to sell goods. Neighbors sit and gossip. They never seem to grow weary or change their positions. When they talk they sit on their heels; they do not sit on chairs or on the ground. They might work to better advantage and accomplish more if they stood on their feet, but they are never in a hurry. Time is nothing. What cannot be done to-day can be done to-morrow. It is a matter of no consequence if it is never done.

The tools used are of the most primitive character. The plow only tickles the ground. Their animals are not strong enough to go down deep. They cut with a sickle. In one field I counted sixty persons. The threshing is done with oxen. They spin with the rudest kind of a wheel. They never heard of the spinning-jenny. If they have they have no desire to adopt it. They prefer that to which they and their ancestors have been accustomed for ages. They do not use as simple a thing as a wheelbarrow. Instead they use a basket and carry it on their heads. They use a long hoe instead of a shovel. Water is drawn by hand, and not by pumps. The people are conservative and reject our Western inventions. They admit that these things may be very good for us, but they do not want them. Labor is abundant and cheap. They have no capital to invest in machinery.

The people of India delight in jewels. Long before children begin to wear any clothing, they wear necklaces. Women wear rings on their ankles and toes and arms and in their ears and noses. The girls that cut grass in the jungles and sell it wear a dozen rings

AN INDIAN PRINCE.

AN INDIAN MAHARAJAH.

on their arms. Their anklets are often large and cumbersome. Men wear ear-rings and nose-rings so large that they will go over their heads. You will find bells on horses and bullocks. Most of these jewels are glass or iron or some other cheap metal. Yet the people are as proud of them as if they were children. India has more goldsmiths than blacksmiths. Much of the wealth of a prosperous family is put into jewels. These can be easily hid or sold in case of need. These are the last things that the family will sell. One officer in the famine district was telling me that the people could not be very poor as they had been sending considerable amounts of gold to London. A missionary said that that meant that they were in the last ditch. It was an indication, not of wealth, but of extreme need.

They wash their clothing in a peculiar way. They have no steam laundries. There is one caste that does all the washing. Wherever you see a river or lake or pond you will find some men of this caste at work. They stand in the stream while they pursue their calling. They do not use hot water. They have a flat stone and they beat the clothing on this stone. They have a kind of soap or some substitute for soap. In this process the clothes are washed clean. At the same time they are cut worse than in a hotel laundry.

Women work on buildings and in the fields as men do. They draw water, mix and carry mortar and brick and stone. They help to make the roadbeds for railways. They go into the jungles and collect fuel and bear it on their heads to the bazars. They reap in time of harvest. They are paid less than men. Not being so strong, perhaps they do not do so much.

The number of servants in a European household surprises a stranger. This is an old custom and it cannot be changed. One servant cooks, another sweeps, another carries water, another cuts grass for the bullocks, another washes, another sews, another waits on the table, another looks after the children. An ordinary family needs ten servants and cannot get along with less. One will do one thing and on no account will he do anything else. These are paid from ten to five rupees a month. A rupee is worth less than thirty cents. On this small sum they support themselves and families. One good servant in America will do as much as the ten and give better satisfaction, and will cost about as much. The foreigners can not do differently. They take things as they find them. Some have tried to get on with one or two servants and found it impossible. It is not strange that the people are poor. If ten men, in order to observe caste regulations, do the work of one, they must divide the wages of one among themselves. They are only playing at work. There is little manufacturing done in India. The people hold to the old methods, foolishly thinking that machinery would make havoc of all their social arrangements and throw multitudes out of work. It might do this for a time, but after a little it would increase their wealth at a rate that would astonish their political economists.

The hours of eating are unlike ours. In the hotels in Calcutta and Bombay you can have tea and toast and fruit in bed at any hour. Breakfast is served at half-past eight, tiffin at half-past one, tea at four, and dinner at eight. The missionaries have the small breakfast of tea and toast about seven. They work till nearly noon and then have breakfast. In the heat of the day they religiously keep out of the sun. They have dinner at six, and may have tea in the afternoon. The people of India eat twice in the day. They have one full meal and one luncheon. Their main article of food is rice. In addition they eat bread and sweets. Most of them lie down and rise up hungry. They are better off than ever before, but their condition is pitiable. There is always famine somewhere. The government opens relief works and remits taxes. Men are paid less than four cents a day and women less than three. This is all they have to keep their families on.

India is the paradise of idolatry. In Athens it was easier to find a god than a man. The same is true here. India has a population of 287,000,000 and 330,000,000 objects of worship. There are sacred plants and trees. The people hang rags and bits of paper on the branches. Under the trees there are stones painted red. They pour water or scatter leaves and flowers over the symbols of deity. Much of their worship is indecent. Most of it is unworthy of human beings. They worship birds and beasts and creeping things. The monkey is a god. In Benares there is a temple set apart to monkeys. The cow is specially sacred. One of their grievances against the English is that they kill the cow and eat her flesh. There is a society whose aim is the protection of the cow. Its agents preach in the bazars and carry on their propaganda everywhere. The purpose of this worship is, not to make the worshipers pure and perfect, but to ward off some peril or evil, or to secure some coveted good. Of India it can be said that darkness covers the land, and gross darkness the people. The Hindus are wholly given to idolatry. The men on the streets have marks on their foreheads or breasts or arms. These marks are made of red or white clay or paint. Some are parallel lines, others are in the form of a trident. They have been to the river and bathed and worshiped, and the marks are to certify to this fact. An expert can tell the god they worship by looking at these marks.

The roads are very good. The English built them. They will last for ages. All through India, in the towns and along the roads, there are government bungalows. In these there are places where you can spread your bed and sleep. Food can be had at moderate prices. The Hindus do not want people to enter their homes. The shadow of a stranger would defile their meat and drink. They have *serais* in which their own people can sleep, but they make no provision for other travelers. At all the railway stations one can get food and a place to sleep. In India, as in Japan and China, every traveler carries his own bedding. The government provides a cot and he finds the rest. These bungalows are a great convenience. The railways are not managed like ours. The conductor does not see that you get on or get off at the right station. He does not collect the tickets. His business is to see that the train runs on time. As you get off the station-master collects the tickets. The door is locked while the train is in motion. One can be fined for getting off before it stops. Ice-water is sold to passengers. In the first and second-class coaches one can sleep on the seats. There is no extra charge for this. There are no sleeping cars.

Every native carries a brass vessel when he travels. This is called a "lota." In it he carries water to drink or to wash in. Water men with pigskins go up and down the platform with water for passengers. The natives get what they want from them or from a pump on the grounds. In the morning they go out and wash. They use sand instead of soap. No Hindu goes anywhere without his lota. He takes it with him to the Ganges and carries home water to drink.

The country is poor. In no city, aside from Calcutta, Bombay and Madras, did I see any signs of wealth. There is famine all the time in some parts. The people are not provident. They spend much on silly customs. Marriages are a great tax. Feasts must be given and presents must be made. The people bury money. They are afraid to trust the banks or to loan it at interest. Agriculture is the main source of wealth. There is little mining or manufacturing.

The women of India are degraded. The caste women are shut up and know nothing of what is going on in the world. The outcaste women have more freedom, but they are just as ignorant and superstitious. On two things all Hindus are agreed, namely, "The cow is a sacred animal; woman is an unclean animal." In ancient times it was not so. Then she was not married in infancy and without any choice in the selection of a husband. She was married at a reasonable age, and it was her privilege to choose the man to whom she was to be joined in wedlock. If her husband died she could marry again. One of the poets said,

> "A wife is half the man, his truest friend—
> A loving wife is a perpetual spring
> Of virtue, pleasure, wealth;—a faithful wife
> Is his best aid in seeking heavenly bliss,
> A sweetly-speaking wife is a companion
> In solitude; a father in advice;
> A mother in all seasons of distress,
> A rest in passing through life's wilderness."

Since then her lot has been changed for the worse. She is married in infancy. She has no voice in the selection. No matter how debauched and unfaithful a husband may be, his wife is taught to revere him as a god. Until recently if he died she was burned alive with his body. She was taught that she would have 45,000,000 years of bliss with her husband after being burned with him. Even now she may not marry. Being a widow, her jewels are stripped off, her delicate clothing is taken away. She must eat one meal a day only, and twice a month she must fast. She is made a drudge and regarded as a harlot. She regrets that she can not be burned and escape a world of misery and disgrace.

The most peculiar thing in India is caste. Many centuries ago the people were divided into four classes. The priests, or Brahmans, sprang from the head of Brahm, the soldiers from his shoulders, the cultivators of the soil from his thighs, and the Sudras or servants from his feet. The priests became the dominant class. They taught the others that they existed by their permission and to minister to their needs. The three highest castes wear the sacred thread, and are known as the twice-born. There are many sub-divisions of each caste. The Sudras now rank pretty high. Beneath them are the out-castes. The Brahmans still hold that they are to be regarded as supreme divinities. The people delight to honor them. A low caste man will go up to a Brahman with a basin of water. The Brahman will thrust his foot into the water, and the low caste man will go away and drink it. A Hindu may believe anything and do anything; he may be an atheist, a pantheist, a polytheist; he may be guilty of lying, theft, uncleanness, or murder, provided he holds fast to caste and worships the Brahmans. Let him have all the virtues and yet go to England, or eat beef, or dine with a person of another caste, or marry a widow, or even take a glass of water

LEPERS IN HURDA, INDIA.

PREPARING TO BURN THE DEAD.

from the hand of a Christian, and he is put out of caste at once. He may be restored by taking penitential pills made from the five products of the cow and paying the Brahmans handsomely. Caste is a curse. It prevents any aspiration. One can never rise out of the sphere into which he was born. It stifles compassion. Men going along a road may find a man smitten with disease and dying; he may ask for a drink of water; they pay no more attention than if he was a dog. He may be an out-caste; if so his presence is a pollution, and they will not play the part of the good Samaritan. This evil system is doomed. God is smiting it with both hands and it cannot long survive. As one of her own sons has said, "India belongs to Christ, and he alone shall have it." Everything in India "that is bad in custom, false in creed, and all that makes the boor and mars the man, shall pass away forever."

XLII.

FROM CEYLON TO AUSTRALIA.

Ceylon has been called a pearl-drop on the brow of the Indian Continent. Its greatest length is from north to south, and measures 270 miles. Its greatest breadth is 140. Its area is 25,000 square miles. Four-fifths of the island are comparatively level; one-fifth is mountainous. Lying wholly within the tropics, Ceylon is clothed with perennial green. The verdure extends from the tops of the mountains to the sea. Rice is the principal grain. Among the fruits are oranges, bananas, guavas, mangoes, cocoanuts. It is said that the cocoanut trees number 30,000,000. There are a hundred uses to which this tree may be put. The leaves, stems of the leaves, sap, nuts, oil, shell of the nut, fibre and trunk, are all utilized. The palmyra is scarcely less useful. From it the natives draw their toddy, make their oil, kindle their fire, carry their water, store, cook, and sweeten their food. From this tree they build entire houses. Cinnamon was once the leading article of commerce; it is now the fifth on the list. At one time coffee was by far the most valuable of all the exports; it is so no longer. Tea is now the chief product. The crop of one year is worth 25,000,000 rupees. The cinchona tree, from whose bark quinine is made, is also grown extensively and yields a handsome profit. The population numbers 3,007,789. Of these two-thirds are Singhalese, 750,000 are Tamils, or Malabars, 200,000 are Arabs, 18,000 are Berbers, 10,000 Malays and 5,000 are Europeans. The last-named class, though the smallest numerically, is incomparably the most influential and the most useful.

The Portuguese discovered Ceylon in 1505. Thirteen years later they settled on the island and built forts to protect their interests. The natives deemed it prudent to maintain friendship with a people armed with guns that could send balls for leagues and then break castles of marble or iron. It was not long till the principal king became a vassal of Portugal and agreed to pay an annual tribute of cinnamon, rubies, sapphires and elephants. Within eighty years after their first visit, the Portuguese were the undisputed masters of all the maritime provinces. Meanwhile, the followers of Xavier were busily engaged seeking to win the people to the Catholic faith. In a few years almost the whole population professedly gave up idolatry and were baptized. One of the local kings called in the Dutch to aid in conquering and expelling the Portuguese. In return for their assistance, the Dutch were to have the sole trade in pepper and cinnamon. The Dutch drove out the Portuguese; not content with that, they made themselves masters of the people whom they came to deliver. Being Protestants, they undertook to bring all the people to the acceptance of their faith. No native could hold office or rent land who was not a member of some Protestant church. As a result, several hundred thousand people became nominal Christians. Even Brahmans made a profession of conversion. The English appeared on the scene in 1589. When war broke out between England and Holland, in 1705, the Dutch lost their hold on Ceylon. It was not until 1815 that the whole island became a British possession. It is now a crown colony. Since the advent of the English, roads and railways have been built, schools have been established, and many other improvements have been introduced. The English attitude toward religion is that of absolute neutrality. The spread of the Gospel has been left to private enterprise. The Baptists began work in 1812; the Wesleyans in 1814; the American Board in 1816; the Church Missionary Society in 1818; the Society for the Propagation of the Gospel in 1840. At the present time the Catholics number 215,000; Protestants, 68,000. The missionaries and ministers number 422. Notwithstanding all that has been done, one-half the population are Buddhists; 500,000 are Hindus, and 200,000 are Mohammedans. The Buddhist priests number 6,279. Most of the people are demon-worshipers. They suppose that they are surrounded by evil spirits, who lurk behind rocks and trees seeking to do them harm. They believe that by flattery or force they can compel the gods to obey them.

At Colombo we took the Himalaya for Australia. This ship belongs to the P. and O. Line. She is one of the largest and altogether the swiftest boat in the fleet. The first cabin is more stylish than the second, but is not any more comfortable. In the first the passengers are called to their meals with a bugle; in the second with a bell. The food is the same. Some of the richest men on board are in the second cabin; some of the poorest are in the first. There are three bars, so that no one need go thirsty. I venture that the profit on liquor exceeds that on freight or on the passenger list. Concerts and sports help to break up the monotony and to pass the time.

Among the passengers is J. R. Mott, the General Secretary of the World's Student Christian Federation. He states that there are organizations for Christian work in five hundred of the leading colleges and universities in the United States and Canada. Over thirty-three thousand students and professors are united in this movement. More than thirty thousand young men have been led to accept Jesus Christ as Lord. The study of the Bible has been promoted. Not only so, but seventy thousand have been trained to work as Christian laymen, four thousand have been led to enter the ministry, and an equal number have been led to volunteer for work in the foreign field. This movement has extended to Great Britain, Germany, Scandinavia, Turkey, Syria, Egypt, South America, South Africa, Ceylon, India, China and Japan. He is going to Australasia to enlist the schools there. Mr. and Mrs. Bowie, of Aberdeen, are on the way to the New Hebrides to carry on the work of Paton and Geddie. Some are going to the gold fields of West Australia. Others are going out seeking fame or fortune in the great Southland. We have on board some of the best and a few of the worst people I have ever met. Two men and two women are drunk most of the time. One man was threatened with being put in irons if he did not conduct himself properly.

While we were in the neighborhood of the equator the days were insufferably hot. The heavy awnings were some protection, but not much. As we steamed on we found the polestar getting lower, till it disappeared altogether. We were under a new sky. The sun was in the north. The farther south we went, the cooler was the atmosphere. The Southern Cross is a disappointment. It is neither so large nor so brilliant as I expected. The albatross followed us for days. What a graceful bird it is! It seems to put forth no effort whatever. Its wings are motionless; yet it ascends and descends, goes ahead or comes behind the swift ship. I have read on the voyage Coleridge's "Rime of the Ancient Mariner," and after seeing the albatross can understand his feeling that it was "a hellish deed" to shoot such a bird. It was fitting that his victim should be hung about his neck for days. The lesson of the poem is one that all would do well to take to heart.

> "He prayeth well, who loveth well
> Both man and bird and beast.
> He prayeth best, who loveth best
> All things both great and small;
> For the dear God who loveth us,
> He made and loveth all."

BENARES, INDIA.

THE GREAT MOSQUE, DELHI, INDIA.

Ten days after leaving Colombo we entered King George's Sound and called at Albany to set down passengers and take on the mails. It is at Albany that men going to the gold fields of Coolgardie leave the ship. They go the rest of the way by rail. Three days after leaving Albany we came to Adelaide. As we drew near, I was wondering if anyone would be on the dock to receive me. I had sent no positive promise that I would visit Australia. I had made up my mind to go to some hotel, and go to church the next morning and make myself known. Before we dropped anchor a boat came out to meet the ship. On the deck were T. J. Gore, D. A. Ewers, H. D. Smith, and A. C. Rankine. They were waving their hats and welcoming me to Australia. On the pier J. C. Dickson and M. W. Green were waiting to repeat the welcome. Mr. Gore took me to his own house and made it my home while in Adelaide, and a most delightful and restful home it is.

XLIII.

ADELAIDE.

Adelaide is a beautiful city. The streets are wide and straight, and well paved. Provision has been made for numerous parks. The government buildings, the university, and the business houses are worthy of the capital of a large and flourishing colony like South Australia. The homes remind one of the stately and happy homes of England, of which Mrs. Hemans sang so beautifully. Schools and churches abound. No one need grow here in ignorance, or be without religious privileges. On one side of the city is a high range of hills, on the other side is the sea. All the fruits and flowers that grow in Palestine grow here. Adelaide has no winter. The population is given as one hundred and thirty-four thousand.

We arrived on Saturday. My first Sunday service was with the Unley Church. M. W. Green is the evangelist. He will be remembered by many in America. He visited many of our churches in the interest of a Bible College in Australia. His eloquent addresses will not soon be forgotten. He was born in Manchester, and emigrated to New Zealand. He was a builder and preacher for years. Because of his gifts as a public speaker, he was urged to give himself to the ministry of the Word and to prayer. He served the people of that colony in the pulpit and on the platform as a lecturer on temperance, and in Parliament. He was spoken of as "Green with a conscience." He met in debate and vanquished many a doughty champion of error. The church that morning was full. The singing was led by a trained choir, and was admirable. In the afternoon the Sunday-school, under the accomplished leadership of Mr. Ernest Green, gave a cantata, which was so much enjoyed that its repetition was called for.

That evening I spoke in Grote Street. This is the oldest of the South Australian churches. The membership is about five hundred. The buildings are large and convenient. T. J. Gore, the pastor, was born and raised in Kentucky. He came out here twenty-nine years ago. He has all the virtues of his native land and of the land of his adoption, and, so far as I could see, the vices of neither. His praises are heard on all sides. I found only one fault—he spends too much money on his guests. He is so obstinate in this that all appeals are in vain. Mrs. Gore is a daughter of the lamented Philip Santo. She is as good and as wise and as efficient as her husband, and that is saying much. The singing of the great audience was like the sound of many waters. It seemed to me that everybody sang. No one slept or manifested any sign of weariness. Young men and old men were present in force. Australia is the first place I have seen where the males outnumber the females in the churches. Nothing could exceed the cordiality of the people. Hundreds came up to shake hands and to bid me welcome. My arm was wearied, but my spirit was refreshed. Their greeting was like that of a Texas or a Missouri convention.

On Monday evening we had a meeting in Norwood. A. C. Rankine is in charge there. He is an Australian, but was educated in Lexington. Many of the students of the Bible College will remember him and will be glad to hear of his good work. He began in Norwood seven years ago with twenty; the church now has three hundred and fifty members. The building has been enlarged once or twice. It will have to be enlarged very soon, or the church must swarm. Though it was a week night, every seat was full. The people caught the enthusiasm of their leader. Because of his representations, they gladly came to hear of the work in the regions beyond.

The next evening the Unley Church had its annual tea-meeting. This is an English institution, I believe. The people have tea at six. As soon as the tables are cleared the speaking begins. Mr. Green read the reports of the year. Addresses were made by J. Colbourne, J. C. Dickson, A. C. Rankine and William Burford. Mr. Burford had been the Sunday-school superintendent. The programme was so arranged that I should have all the time I wished. At all such meetings I have had the "right of way." The evening passed pleasantly. The congregation and members of other congregations and friends came together to renew or to form acquaintances and to rejoice over the progress of the work. It was a time for sociability and for instruction and worship.

On Wednesday we had a service at Hindmarsh. This is the second largest church in Adelaide. Its register contains the names of over four hundred members. H. D. Smith is the preacher. He is the Secretary of the Foreign Committee, and is the friend and advocate of every good work. The night I was there he was absent at a wedding. Here, as elsewhere, people marry and give in marriage, no matter who speaks or what the subject of his speech. The large audience was a proof of the fact that the pastor's heart is in the cause of world-wide evangelism. Mr. Gore went with me and presided. At the close, the usual vote of thanks was proposed and carried. An Australian audience would think itself lacking in courtesy and kindness if this part of a service was omitted.

One morning we went to Glenelg to call on William Burford. He is a friend of preachers, and is a liberal contributor to every worthy enterprise. He is the main support of the work in Glenelg. He supports Nathoo Lal in India, and one of the workers of the China Inland Mission. He and his family were preparing to start on a European tour. They expect to be gone a year or two. He goes in search of health. It is hoped by thousands that he will find it. He talks of visiting America. I trust he will do so. J. Colbourne has just taken the work at Glenelg. The church meets in a hall. Before long it will have a building of its own. Mr. Colbourne was born in England. He was a Baptist when he reached New Zealand. Here he fell in with M. W. Green and was led by him to unite with the Disciples of Christ. He studied under T. J. Gore and H. S. Earl. He says he owes more to Mr. Gore for the gentle and Christ-like spirit which he manifested and for his instruction, than to any other living man. He has preached around Adelaide, in Victoria, and in Sydney.

Part of the day was spent in the home of A. T. Magarey on Mount Lofty. The name of his father, Thomas Magarey, is familiar to many in Europe and America. He is a man of mark. In any assembly he would be picked out as a man of exceptional ability. He did much to plant and establish the cause in the Colonies. In recent years he has left us and joined another communion, much to the regret of those who know his moral worth and his valuable services. He has two sons who are useful Christian men. Dr. S. J. Magarey is a leading physician in Adelaide. He is a member of Parliament, and might have been a member of the Cabinet. He is an elder in Grote Street, and is faithful and diligent in that high office. A. T. Magarey is a business man, an antiquarian, a promoter of exploring expeditions, a preacher, and I know not what besides. His week days are full of work and care. He has charge of two churches, and preaches twice every Sunday. He is one of the best-informed and most entertaining men I have met. As was said of Burke, no one could be with him five minutes without learning that he was no ordinary man. Mrs. Magarey is a

PARSEE GIRLS.

KING OF SIAM AND CHILDREN.

daughter of Col. Campbell, of Bethany. I knew her when a student, and was very pleased to meet her in her own home.

It was not possible to speak for J. C. Dickson. I met him several times, and heard much about the work the Lord is doing through him. He and Dr. Verco carry on the work in North Adelaide and in Prospect Street. Dr. Verco is the most distinguished physician in South Australia. Not only so, but he is one of the most active Christians in the colony. He manages his work so that he can attend church three times on Sunday, and preach once or twice, or oftener. He built the chapel in North Adelaide, and rents it to the church. He has paid for a chapel and a home for John Thompson, who is at work among the Kanakas in Queensland. I asked him how he was able to do so much Christian work. He said he saw his patients on Saturday and on Monday. They knew that he wanted Sunday for other duties.

H. D. Smith informed me that we have twenty-seven churches in South Australia. In these there is a total membership of two thousand six hundred and twenty-one. There are seventeen Sunday-schools, with one hundred and ninety teachers, and two thousand one hundred and forty-one scholars. Most of the churches have Endeavor Societies. There are eight of these churches north of Adelaide. G. D. Nesi is the evangelist in that district. Six are south of Adelaide. R. G. Cameron is the evangelist in charge. The churches in South Australia contribute to the work at home, to John Thompson, and to Mary Thompson, in Hurda. They give $1,200 for Foreign Missions. They are talking of sending another worker to India. Hindmarsh sent H. H. Strutton to Poona to work in an undenominational mission. Among the pioneers spoken of are J. C. Verco, W. H. Burford, Philip Santo, Dr. S. Kidner, John Chambers and Henry Warren.

At the close of one service several came to me and thanked me for what I had said. Among those was one who said, "Do you know what I was thinking about all the time you were speaking?" Several thoughts passed through my mind. Perhaps he was thinking of making a handsome offering to the work. Or perhaps some lofty sentiment stirred his soul. At the very least he was thinking of something complimentary to say about the address. Judge of my surprise when he said, "*I was wondering whether you were chewing gum all the time you were speaking.*" He had heard that Americans chewed gum, and supposed that I was no exception. I left Adelaide for Sydney. On my return I am to deliver several addresses more. My visit will last only one month. I return on the ship on which I came.

XLIV.

FROM ADELAIDE TO SYDNEY.

AUSTRALIA is a place of magnificent distances. Sydney is over a thousand miles from Adelaide. Going by rail, one must needs pass through Melbourne. The train service is so arranged that passengers must rest in that city for seven hours. On my arrival at the station I was surprised beyond belief to find a committee waiting for me. The committee consisted of D. A. Ewers, Malcolm McLellan, A. B. Maston, F. G. Dunn, Isaac Selby, F. M. Ludbrook, Joseph Pittman, W. C. Thurgood and J. A. Davies. They took me to the Coffee Palace for breakfast. About forty men and women sat down and partook of the smoking and savory viands. After doing ample justice to the meat and drink the speeches began. D. A. Ewers, President of the Missionary Conference, presided. He called upon A. B. Maston to speak as an American; upon F. G. Dunn, as the representative of the press; upon Isaac Selby, as the representative of the preachers; upon Mrs. Joseph Pittman, as the President of the Women's Conference; upon F. M. Ludbrook, as the representative of the Foreign Missionary Committee; upon James Tully, as President of the Sunday-school Union, and upon F. McClean, as Superintendent of the Chinese Mission, and upon Joseph Pittman to lead in prayer. Mr. Maston expressed a wish, in which all concurred, that more men from America would visit the colonies. He mentioned J. W. McGarvey as one of a class that would be particularly welcome, and that would do much good. Mr. Selby spoke of the Americans that had spent some time in Melbourne, and of the debt of gratitude which the churches owe them. These good men are held in loving remembrance. At the close, I was asked to say a few words. Being weary from traveling all night without sleep, and being taken unawares, and being bewildered by the reception accorded me, I tried to speak, but could only utter a few words in response. Out of the abundance of the heart the mouth speaks. Out of its superabundance the tongue stammers. After this performance was over, I was hurried off to be photographed for the public good. Then J. A. Davies took me home with him. He and Mrs. Davies had compassion on me, and put me to bed for two hours. That evening I took the train for Sydney. I left Melbourne with the understanding that I was to return for the Victorian Conference, beginning on Good Friday and closing on Easter Monday. The conference is held at this time because it is a holiday season.

It was nearly noon on Saturday when I reached Sydney. Here a dozen men and women were on the platform to take charge of me. Among the number was C. F. Forscutt. I knew him years ago when he was a student in the College of the Bible. He is now Principal and proprietor of the Rockdale College. He opened this school five years ago. He prepares young men for business careers and for the university. Mrs. Forscutt looks after the table and the beds and teaches music and some other branches. The school is flourishing. The Principal preaches on Sundays, but gives his time and strength to the college. His home was mine most of the time I was in Sydney. The first afternoon he took me in his carriage to see Botany Bay. He pointed out the spot where Captain Cook landed when he discovered that part of the continent. Botany Bay is a fine body of water, but Sydney Harbor is so much larger and better as a port that all ships go that way.

On Sunday morning Mr. Forscutt took me to the Enmore church. This is the largest church in the colony. It has on its muster-rolls the names of three hundred and fifty members. The venerable and revered Dr. Joseph Kingsbury presided at the Lord's table. I was told that he had given two or three fortunes to the Lord's work. He is hale and hearty, an eloquent speaker, marvelously gifted in prayer, and manifestly a deeply religious man. On his snowy hair and beautiful character, the splendors of eternity are falling thick and fast. The Enmore church has been without a pastor for some time, consequently the audience was not large. There were about one hundred and fifty present. After the Lord's Supper I spoke for thirty minutes. We went home with John Bardsley to dinner. He is the Timothy Coop of New South Wales. He is a prosperous wholesale grocer. He has a large home and a large heart. Mrs. Bardsley was born in Scotland, and has the hospitality characteristic of her race. On Sunday their home is open to all comers. Food is provided in abundance and served without stint. These two good people are unspeakably happy when their long table has no vacant chair. In the afternoon we went out to the Public Domain. This is a favorite resort for speakers of every kind. The first speaker we heard was a woman belonging to the Church of England. She was preaching to a large crowd. Her topic was the Words of Jesus on the Cross. Her spiritual face and clear and tender voice added emphasis and charm to her words. Preachers representing nearly all the denominations were speaking. Advocates of temperance, politicians of different schools, Socialists and Anarchists, promoters of fads of every variety had their rostrums and their sympathizers or opponents. Preaching on the streets and in the parks is very common. That evening I spoke in the building just purchased by the church in the city. It was built by the Free Thought people, but they were not able to pay for it. The church bought it for less than half what it cost. It is a fine building. The auditorium will seat about 800. There is a large basement that can be used in many ways. There are all the separate rooms needed for Sunday-school and other purposes. The building is new, and has all modern comforts and conveniences. This church, like the church in Enmore, was without a pastor when I was there. I learned that George T. Walden was on his way from London to take the work at Enmore, and that P. A. Dickson was coming from Brisbane, in Queensland, to Sydney. Both these men are known by many in America. Under their ministry these churches are certain to enter upon careers of renewed prosperity.

On Monday the women of New South Wales held their annual conference. They are not organized into auxiliaries as are the women at home. But they have an organization to whose funds the members are asked to contribute a penny a week. They do something for home missions. They do temperance and charitable work as well. Mrs. Clapham presided and did her duty gracefully and acceptably. Reports were read showing what progress had been made in the different departments. Business was transacted, papers were read, and appropriate songs were sung. At night the house was well filled. I was asked to tell something about the way the women in America did so much. I did so, and urged them to send some one of their own number to India or China. In no other way can they do so much to help the work at home. I think they will do this.

The next morning Mrs. Forscutt and her sister took me to see Sydney Harbor. William Clapham and Robert Gilmore went with us. They are two faithful preachers. They know the place and the history of the work in the colonies, and were therefore intelligent and agreeable companions. Sydney Harbor is said to be the largest and grandest harbor on the globe. The fleets and navies of all nations could find room and shelter in its ample waters. The

TEMPLE IN SOUTHERN INDIA.

KUTUB—MINAR, DELHI, INDIA.

heads are high and bold, and are a mile apart. If one should undertake to walk round the bay he would have to travel two hundred miles. All the way down the guides pointed out the palatial homes of the city magnates. On the highest point is the Catholic College and the palace of Cardinal Moran. This harbor is one of the wonders of the world. It is as well worth seeing as Niagara or Mt. Everest. We steamed down for about seven miles. When we came to the swell of the ocean we turned aside to Manly Beach. We crossed the narrow neck of land and came to the ocean. Mrs. Forscutt had brought luncheon along. We sat down under the shade of a tree and partook of a bounteous repast. Towards evening we started towards home. We saw the magnificent harbor again. It grew on us as we studied it. This day will ever stand out in my mind as a mountain peak stands out from a plain. We parted from Mrs. Forscutt with many expressions of sincere gratitude for the picnic she gave us. We took tea with Mr. and Mrs. Gole. He is the Secretary of the Foreign Mission Committee, and a very genial and intelligent man. At night there was a union service in the Enmore Church in the interest of world-wide evangelism. The audience was not so large as I had expected, but those that did come seemed deeply interested. The next morning my friends of the day before took me to see the Botanical Gardens. There is an endless variety of tropical trees and flowers. The site slopes down to the bay. This is one source of their great charm. Sydney is a century old. It is laid out like a European city. The streets are narrow and crooked. This is especially true of the oldest part. It is a substantial city, and has a population of four hundred and twenty-one thousand and thirty. That evening I took the train for Melbourne.

The first church established by the Disciples of Christ in New South Wales dates back to 1851. The leading men at that time were Albert Griffin, George Taylor, Henry Mitchell, Joseph Kingsbury and Edward and David Lewis. Dr. Kingsbury told me of his conversion. He heard a man preaching in the Park. He did not know his name, but he presented the truth so clearly that all doubts were removed. He went home in rapture and kissed his wife, and said: "Darling, I have found that for which I have been seeking for ten years." He began to preach as soon as he was baptized. The church was spoken of as "Kingsbury's Mob." There are now twenty churches in the colony, with a total membership of two thousand and forty-two. There are seventeen Sunday-schools. In these there are eighty-eight teachers and eight hundred and ninety-four scholars. The number of preachers is given as three. The churches are not growing as one could wish. In the absence of a sufficient number of able and educated men to give themselves wholly to the ministry, it is difficult to see how they can grow in numbers and in spiritual power. Our churches in America learned this lesson fifty years ago.

XLV.

THE VICTORIA MISSIONARY CONFERENCE.

THE first day of the Victoria Missionary Conference was occupied by the women. They met on Wednesday in Swanston Street Chapel to transact business and to render a very interesting programme. They are organized in the same way, and for the same purposes, as the women of New South Wales. They assist the cause of temperance; do relief work such as is done by Dorcas societies; visit prisons and hospitals, and contribute to the support of the evangelists in the home field. The young ladies are organized into bands. Last year the women gave $380 to Home Missions. In ten years they collected and disbursed $3,225. Mrs. Joseph Pittman is the Acting President and Miss Emma Hill is the Secretary. They are enthusiastic and efficient workers. Mrs. Antoinette K. Thurgood, of Pittsburg, is the perpetual Honorary President. She was the first to move in the matter of an organization, and keeps in touch with the society, though so far away. She is held in the very highest esteem by all for her worth and work.

Thursday was devoted to temperance. By all accounts it was a field day for this most worthy cause. The large auditorium was comfortably filled during the day; at night it was packed. John Barnacle and W. J. Phillips were the leading spirits. At the evening service an address was made by a man who has been on the platform as a temperance advocate for over half a century. He is yet hale and hearty. The children gave an exercise that was greatly enjoyed. The principal address was given by A. R. Edgar, a Wesleyan minister engaged in rescue work. He and his remarks called forth unbounded applause. In most of the churches in Melbourne and round about there are Bands of Hope.

The Conference proper began its sittings on Good Friday. The address of the President, D. A. Ewers, was brief and pithy, and was well received. He reviewed the work of the year, and called upon the churches to raise the standard of giving, and to do more in every direction. Though times are hard, he urged that all should take heart and hope, and make greater sacrifices, and put forth greater efforts. I caught two of his ringing sentences: "Any so-called Restoration of Primitive Christianity which does not prominently develop the spirit of missionary self-sacrifice is deficient in its most vital element, however sound and orthodox it may be otherwise." "The avowed and supreme reason for our existence as a Conference is the extension of missionary work in order to the salvation of souls." The Secretary, Malcolm McLellan, had the Annual Report printed and distributed in advance. It was not read as a whole and referred to committees, as at home. Each paragraph was read and discussed separately. Most of the speakers were not evangelists. The discussions were more protracted than in our conventions in America. Three men had been kept in the field throughout the year. Their names are: W. D. Little, Thomas Hager, and G. H. Browne. They were present and supplemented the report with verbal statements. The whole amount raised by the churches for Home Missions was $2,483. The year closed with a deficit, but it was so small that no one was distressed by it. One evening there were several addresses on Home Missions. D. M. McCrackett spoke on "The Author of the Gospel;" W. D. Little, on "The Definition of the Gospel;" Isaac Selby on "The Object and Power of the Gospel;" and Joseph Pittman on "The Conditions and Promises of the Gospel." The Conference has under consideration the establishment of a Church Extension Fund. A. B. Maston offered to visit all the churches in Victoria during the year in the interest of missions on condition that his traveling expenses were paid. He is the manager of the Austral Publishing Company, and preaches on Sundays. He is not a millionaire, and if he did not have a great soul and a good wife, he could not make such a generous tender of service.

The report of the Victoria Biblical Institute was discussed at considerable length. The Principal, J. K. Henshelwood, stated that there were thirty-two young men enrolled; of these only one is preparing for the ministry. He made an eloquent appeal on behalf of the Institute. The discussion was somewhat acrimonious. Unfortunately, the Principal does not command the undivided confidence and support of the brethren. It is clear that the Colonies should be preparing a larger number of consecrated young men to preach the Gospel. Several religious bodies have built schools near the University, and so get the advantage of that great institution. The reports bearing upon the hymn-book, on temperance, and on Sunday-school work, were read and emphasized.

The election of officers occupied a whole afternoon. Nominations were made in open Conference. When the ticket was com-

1. T. J. Gore, Adelaide.
2. A. C. Rankin, Adelaide.
4. Mrs. J. A. Davies, Melbourne.
3. J. A. Davies, Melbourne.
5. Isaac Selby, Melbourne.
6. Dr. Joseph Verco, Adelaide.

AUSTRALIAN FRIENDS.

plete the balloting began. They are familiar with our method of having a special committee to nominate officers, but they prefer their own, and desire no change. To many this is the most interesting part of the programme. Nevertheless, it is a trifle monotonous and wearisome to one accustomed to see a ticket elected in as many minutes as here it requires hours. As business increases, and time becomes more precious, some more expeditious way will be adopted.

One sitting was devoted to foreign missions. Miss Mary Thompson sent a report and a letter to be read. G. L. Wharton sent an address. Miss Thompson went from Melbourne. She was a member of the Collingwood Church. Milner Black was the preacher in charge at the time. It was largely through him that she was led to volunteer. John Thompson sent an account of his work among the Kanakas in Queensland. The Kanakas are natives of the islands in the South Seas. They have been brought to Australia to work on the sugar plantations. Mr. Thompson has been engaged in this work for eight years. Half of the time he has worked at his own expense. He has led seventy-three to Christ. He reports thirty-three meetings in the district each week. Recently four have gone out as missionaries. One was sent to the New Hebrides and three to the Solomon Group. Ferdinand Pittman gave a racy account of his experience as a worker among these people. He spoke in high praise of the faith and zeal of the converts. The Chinese Mission School gave an exercise. This school is under the superintendence of F. McClean. Sam Ah Wong gave an address. It fairly bristled with good points. No other address was more vigorously applauded. The Conference raised $1,214 for Foreign Missions in the year.

The Conference Essay was written and read by F. G. Dunn. His theme was "Our Position and Mission." He set forth the things that are most surely believed amongst us. He alluded to the communion and money questions, taking the ground held by many in the Colonies. He filed his objections against the Endeavor Society. He found fault with the pledge, and with associate membership. In the discussion that followed some favored the essay throughout, and expressed a wish that it might be published as an authoritative statement of what the Disciples of Christ believe and teach. Others declared that the essay, as a whole, did not embody their convictions. The Endeavor cause had its champions. All agreed that the essay was an able production. The author is the editor of the *Australian Christian Standard*. He is a man of scholarly tastes and wields a trenchant pen. Whoever crosses swords with him will find a foeman worthy of his steel. The Conference Sermon was preached by Isaac Selby. He spoke on "The Kingdom of God." He took the position that the kingdom of God was historically manifested in three forms: As the kingdom of Israel, as the Church of Christ on earth, and as the Church triumphant. Mr. Selby is the pastor of the Lygon Street Church. He is a speaker of marvelous fluency. He spent several years on the Free Thought platform. He has been with us seven years. He knows why he is where he is. He talks of visiting America. If he comes he will be warmly received. Mrs. Selby was reared a Catholic. She, too, has been on the platform as an advocate of Free Thought principles, and as an opponent of the faith in which she was born. She has the wit of the Irish race. A visit to their home is an event, and is sure to be followed by many sunny memories.

Monday was wisely given up to a picnic. But even at the annual picnic the Anglo-Saxon love of religious discussion was manifested. A wagon was used as a platform. A chairman was appointed and rules adopted. The Essay and Sermon were discussed in all their bearings. After the brethren had exhausted these subjects, one or two men came forward to exploit their pet fads. I listened for a time, and then turned aside to see some girls skip. The graceful skipping of the girls was more edifying than the advocacy of some novel and inconsequential negations. Bodily exercise profits little, but some religious controversies profit nothing.

I blush to think of the number of speeches I made in the Conference. Every sitting some one wanted to hear from me. The audience was pleased to listen to all I had to say. I do not suppose that every soul present believed every word I said; in fact, one or two told me that they did not. But I am convinced that on the points of difference the majority of the people were with me. In any event, I can bear witness that at no convention anywhere have I been listened to more sympathetically or with more demonstrations of approval. I was told that in Australia there is no opposition to missions or to missionary societies. The most conservative believe in both as heartily as any others. The conservatism that exists here operates in other directions. As most that I had to say related to the evangelization of the world, I had the moral support of all. But there were those who wanted to know what the brethren in America held on the points that are in dispute here. After hearing all I had to say, the Swanston Street Church, the most conservative church in the colony, gave me a call. When the orthodoxy of the American brethren was challenged, I pointed to this call as the most triumphant refutation imaginable.

On Tuesday evening the cantata, entitled "Jacob and Esau," was rendered by three hundred voices, under the leadership of Ferdinand Pittman. The audience filled the large building, and hundreds were turned away. The cantata closed the Conference.

XLVI.

A BRIEF CAMPAIGN IN MELBOURNE AND VICINITY.

A SPECIAL committee arranged a series of meetings for me in and about Melbourne. On Tuesday evening I went to Doncaster. This is the home of D. A. Ewers. He is the minister of the church, editor of the *Pioneer*, and the friend and champion of every worthy enterprise. His friends think he is doing too much. That evening the Mission Band invited the officers of the church to take tea with me in the vestry. After tea we had a service in the chapel. Doncaster Mission Band supports Jeremiah in Hurda. Some of them wish he had a more cheerful name. But if they saw his bright face and heard his hopeful words, they would be satisfied. The next evening there was a meeting at Cheltenham. This is another suburb with a prosperous church of one hundred and fifty members. G. B. Moysey is the evangelist. He is a man of ability and a diligent student. The meeting was well advertised. The people came out to hear what I had to say about world-wide evangelism. On Thursday night it was arranged that I should visit the Chinese Mission School. F. McClean is the superintendent. The register contains thirty-five names; of these five are Christians. There is a teacher for each pupil. The class meets three times a week. The superintendent read a brief and cordial address of welcome. Short addresses were made by Thomas Hager, F. M. Ludbrook and Isaac Selby. There was a Bible lesson, and then a lesson in English. The boys prepared refreshments for the large company present. This school is one of the most Christlike and encouraging things I have seen in Australia. The boys write home and tell their parents and friends of what the church is doing for them. The people at home will get a better conception of the spirit of Christianity than they would otherwise. The missionaries will find that their lives and property are more secure, and their work more fruitful, because of the work done in this upper room in Lygon Street.

The next day there were two services. The women met in Swanston Street and wanted an address. I spoke to them about the way the sisters in America are organized for missionary work, and told them of what they have done and are doing. I urged

MAORI WARRIOR.

MAORI CHIEF.

them to effect a similar organization in the colonies. That night there was a service in North Fitzroy. The audience, the singing and the attention were all that could be desired. Saturday was observed as a holiday. John A. Davies took Messrs. Maston, Selby, McLellan and myself to Ferntree Gully and Black Spur. He wished me to see something of the Australian bush and ferns and big trees. After a ride of four hours in the train we took a wagon and rode for twenty miles through the primeval forest. The trees are tall but not as large as those in Gippsland or as those in California, but they are large enough. The fern-trees are exceedingly beautiful. We saw tens of thousands of them. The day was delightfully spent. Our host insisted on paying all expenses. On the way home we passed a hearty vote of thanks to him for his kindness. As opportunity afforded I saw the public institutions of the city. Mr. Selby took me to see the Zoological Gardens and the University. We saw the kangaroo, the emu, the wild dog, and many of the birds belonging to this continent. He showed me the ornithorhynchus. This is one of the missing links in the Darwinian system. It lays eggs and suckles its young. It is partly bird and partly mammal and party reptile. Mr. Davies took me to see the Library, the Art Gallery, the Exposition Buildings and the Aquarium. From the main tower of the Exposition Buildings we saw the city in all its magnitude and glory, and the fertile country round about, and Port Philip in the distance. Mr. Dunn took me to see the Botanical Gardens. These institutions are worthy of "wonderful Melbourne."

Sunday morning Mrs. Davies drove me to Collingwood. This is the home of Mary Thompson. Ferdinand Pittman is in charge of the work. Collingwood has the finest building in the city, but it is heavily burdened with debt. A. B. Maston was present and presided, and, after service, took a number of us home to dinner. In the afternoon I spoke at North Carlton, and in the evening at Swanston Street. Sunday was a good day. At all the services I had "liberty" in speaking. The right words to express my thoughts came at my call. The eager and rapt attention was an inspiration. The next morning I called to see T. H. Jennings. He was in Bethany College in my time. He and Mrs. Jennings and their daughter made my short stay very pleasant. He attended all the meetings and helped me much by his presence and interest. That night I went to New Market. John Morris and his good wife are from Dundee. He manufactures shoes on a large scale, and preaches for the church. The singing was excellent, even for Australia, and that is saying much. On Tuesday morning I visited the mission training-school of Dr. and Mrs. Warren. They have ten young ladies in the class, and thirteen have gone out. They are in China, Japan and India. This work is a work of faith and love. The motto is, "My God shall supply all your needs according to his riches of glory." From the first there has been no debt and no lack of any good thing. Mrs. Warren and her pupils know how to sing and how to pray. They pray for the workers by name. They correspond with them, and so keep in touch with them and their work. In the evening I went out to Brighton with Dr. Ludbrook to tea. The large parlor was full of church people. They came to meet and talk with me, as I could not speak in that suburb. Dr. Ludbrook is a cousin of Sydney and Milner Black. His mother is a daughter of the sainted Mr. Wallis, of Nottingham, England. After tea we went to North Melbourne. D. M. McCrackett is the minister here. As a result of his enthusiasm and efforts we had a good audience and one of the best meetings in the series. On Wednesday night all the churches came together for a grand farewell. An hour before this service those especially interested in the evangelization of the world met for a conference. Many questions were asked and answered. At eight o'clock W. C. Craigie, the new President of the Conference, took the chair. After singing and reading of the Scriptures, Joseph Pittman led in prayer. The chairman made a short talk, and then called on Brethren Dunn, Ewers, Moysey, Selby, Maston, Davies, Martin and Ludbrook. Mrs. Maston and Mrs. Ludbrook spoke for the women. Miss Nellie McClelland and Mrs. William Wilson sang solos, and added greatly to the joy of the feast. The speeches were kind and complimentary. One of the speakers said they did not all subscribe to everything I said, but the points of difference were few and of small moment when compared with those on which we were all agreed. A vote of thanks to the brethren in America, for enabling me to make this visit, was passed. Nor was this all. A generous sum of money was handed me toward the expense of the trip. The next morning I left Melbourne for Ballarat. A number of brethren came down to the train. I recall the names of C. G. Lawson, T. S. and Robert Lyall, A. B. Maston, F. G. Dunn, Isaac Selby, W. J. Phillips, W. C. Thurgood, T. H. Jennings, M. McLellan, John Morris, D. M. McCrackett, W. C. Craigie, and Mr. and Mrs. J. A. Davies. Mr. Dunn gave me enough books to read till I should reach London.

All the time I was in Melbourne, the home of Mr. and Mrs.

Davies was mine. No weary pilgrim could wish to fall into better hands. Mr. Davies was born in Wales. He was a member of the church in New York when U. C. Brewer was pastor. He is now a prosperous merchant miller. Mrs. Davies was born in the colonies and educated in Scotland. Their home was to me like rivers of water in a dry place, as the shadow of a great rock in a weary land. They went with me to all the meetings and paid all expenses. Not a day passed that they did not present me with a book or some other object of value. Their generosity reminded me of the words, "All that I have is thine." The Lord bless them and keep them. The Lord make his face to shine upon them and be gracious to them. The Lord lift up the light of his countenance upon them and give them peace. The hospitality of the people was boundless. My limits will not permit me to mention the names of those who fed me and ministered to my needs. But if I forget their kindness, may my right hand forget its cunning.

The work in Melbourne began in 1853. John Ingram, T. S. Lyall and H. G. Picton and their wives met to break bread. After six months they moved to Prahran. Here they worshiped in a tent and in a brickyard. The next year they returned to Melbourne. They met in a building down a narrow passage. The preachers announced the meeting, and sat down to wait for an audience. One evening the hour passed and no one came. Suddenly many footsteps were heard approaching. The preachers waited anxiously for their hearers, when in marched two goats. They looked up and said: "Ma, ma." The preachers laughed heartily, and decided not to preach. There are now twenty-seven churches in and about Melbourne, with 3,309 members. There are fifty-nine country churches with an aggregate membership of 1,816. Robert Service was a pillar in the church for twenty-five years. One of his sons has been Premier of Victoria.

XLVII.

FROM MELBOURNE TO THE SHIP.

Ballarat is a prosperous city with a population of forty thousand. It was here that gold was discovered in 1851. The output of gold in Victoria since that time considerably exceeds a billion dollars; the output of all Australasia exceeds two billions. Ballarat has had many public-spirited citizens. The monuments of their liberality are seen on all sides. They made their money easily and spent it generously. Charles Martin met me at the train. He was born in England, and has been in Ballarat since 1857. He has been a teacher in the public schools. His pupils are in all parts of the world. He is now on the retired list and receives a pension. He preaches for one of the churches in the city. As he advances in life, he thinks more and more of the lines of Trench:

"I say to thee, do thou repeat
To the first man thou mayest meet,
In lane, highway, or open street,
That he, and we, and all men move
Under a canopy of love,
As broad as the blue sky above.
And ere thou leave him, say thou this,
Yet one word more: They only miss
The winning of that perfect bliss
Who will not count it true that love—
Blessing, not cursing—rules above."

As I arrived early, my guide took me to the Art Museum and to several of the mines. The ground under Ballarat is honeycombed. The mining proceeds and the supply of gold is as great as ever. In the evening we had a service in the Dawson Street Chapel. After an hour's address many said they were surprised when I stopped; they wished I had talked for another hour. There are two churches in Ballarat; both are weak. It would be well if they could unite. I made the acquaintance of George Morris, a leading merchant and an elder in the church. He shares in the preaching. The next morning we visited the School of Mines. The principal spared neither time nor pains to explain everything. He took us through a mine and showed us how the quartz was obtained. Then he showed us how it was crushed and how the gold was collected. He took us through the Museum and showed us its contents. There are under a glass case models of the great nuggets that have been found at different times. He told us that some burglar had broken in and carried off similar models, thinking that they were pure gold. In the afternoon we visited the Public Gardens. The gardener is a genius; his work is of a very high order. That evening Professor Martin and Mr. Morris went away to attend a tea meeting. A. E. Lilburne, the clerk of the church and a pleasant and well-informed gentleman, took charge of me and placed me on board the train for Adelaide.

The next day about noon I reached my destination, and found T. J. Gore waiting for me with a carriage. The Australian trains are not the most comfortable in the world. Every half hour an inspector comes in to examine tickets. Sleep is murdered. In consequence of this pernicious system I was weary. After luncheon, my good host and hostess sent me to bed to rest and recuperate. On Sunday morning I spoke at North Adelaide. Dr. Verco presided. When he speaks, no one would think that he is a busy physician. He talks as if he did nothing but preach. Dr. Verco is a many-sided man. He does several things, and does them all well. On Sunday afternoon the Grote Street Sunday-school and the mission connected with that church met to hear an address on the condition of children in the heathen world. The children voted to observe Children's Day, and to help in sending the Gospel to the Christless nations. That night I spoke to a great throng in Grote Street. On Monday evening this church had its annual tea. The preachers in Adelaide and vicinity were present in force. Many friends of the church attended and manifested their interest in its welfare. Grote Street is first, and last, and always a missionary church. The Mission Band has supported a young man in Hurda who is preparing for the ministry. The Sunday-school room is adorned with photographs of our missionaries. One or two young people are ready to go out. Anything relating to missions is heard with unusual eagerness. Several addresses were made after the tea. The pastor read the annual report. This showed substantial gains in all departments. On Tuesday night there was a farewell meeting in the hall of the Young Men's Christian Association. Dr. Morton was asked to preside. He is at the head of a school in which candidates for the mission field are trained. He brought his whole class to the service. Mr. Gore wanted me to see everything and to get as much work out of me as possible. The people are hungry to hear about the work. They want to know how they can most effectively contribute to its support and enlargement. One afternoon was devoted to a conference. Men and women belonging to all the churches came together to inquire about the missionaries and their methods and difficulties and needs. One morning I was taken to the Botanical and Zoological Gardens and to the Academy of Fine Arts. One evening we went down to Glenelg and dined with Dr. Magarey. On the way we called to see Pastor Abbott. He has been in Adelaide from the beginning. There are seven congregations in South Australia known as Christian churches. They are very much like our people. They baptize as we do, on a confession of faith in Jesus as the Christ, the Son of God. They break bread every week. The points of difference are these: They are Calvinists; they lay special emphasis on the pre-millennial coming of Christ; and some of them hold to the theory of conditional immortality. They are friendly to us; their pastors and our evangelists exchange services; but they do not unite in any association or in any work. Pastor Abbott belongs to these people. Henry Hussey is another of their pastors. He jocularly boasts that he is more orthodox than any of our people, as he went all the way from Australia to Bethany to be baptized by Alexander Campbell.

The next morning a number of men and women came down with me to the ship. Mrs. Gore had a box of choice fruit placed in my cabin. The Australians know how to welcome the coming and how to speed the parting guest. They omit nothing that has a tendency to make him feel grateful that he has been able to visit them and to make him desirous of visiting them again. They pay all expenses and load him with costly gifts and slip into his hand a goodly number of guineas to help meet the cost of the trip. The only discomfort is in the thought that they do too much; they do far more than one could wish. I met some men and women in Australia who raised my estimate of the race as a whole. I took leave of them with a fervent prayer that they, being rooted and grounded in love, may be strong to apprehend, with all the saints, what is the breadth, and length, and height, and depth, and to know the love of Christ which passeth knowledge, that they be filled unto all the fullness of God.

Before leaving there H. D. Smith gave me the names of the Americans who have preached for the churches in the colonies. These are: H. S. Earl, T. J. Gore, G. L. Surber, H. L. Geeslin, O. A. Carr, W. H. Martin, J. F. Floyd, J. J. Haley, A. B. Maston, J. H. Edwards, W. S. Houchins and J. W. Shepherd. In Adelaide they still tell how the papers advised all the preachers in the place to go to hear Mr. Earl as a study in pulpit eloquence. In Melbourne they talk of the great sermons preached in the Music Hall by Mr. Haley to the thousands that flocked to hear. All these men did good work, and left a good name behind them. Speaking of different ones, the people say, "He led me to Christ." Of the men that came from the colonies and preached, or now preach in America, the names are: Mark Collis, T. H. Capp, C. A. Moore, J. W. Webb, A. M. Growden, M. Gunn, T. H. Bates, C. L. Thurgood, Hugh McLellan, B. C. Black, E. T. Edmonds, G. M. Anderson, J. J. Irvine, G. T. Walden, and H. Goodacre. Of those that went to America to be educated and returned, the names are: P. A. Dickson, J. C. Dickson, F. W. Greenwood, A. C. Rankine, C. T. Forscutt and T. H. Jennings. There are about a dozen men in America now preparing for the ministry. The day should come, and come soon, when the colonies will establish a school of their own and train their own men.

XLVIII.

CONCERNING THE AUSTRALIAN CHURCHES.

THE Australian Christians have some admirable traits. All bring their Bibles and hymn-books to church. They follow when the Scriptures are read, and turn to the text and other passages as they are announced. All join in the singing. They sing with the spirit and with the understanding. All contribute toward the expenses of the church. I tried to find out the methods employed to secure a consummation so devoutly to be wished, but failed. All say that this is the fact, but no one is able to account for it. The converts are expected to give, and this expectation is not disappointed. In America a minority bear all the financial burdens. There are exceptions, but this is the rule. In Australia no one would be regarded as being in good standing and full fellowship unless he bore his part of the current expenses. A large number of business men can exhort and preach and pray acceptably. There are men who are engaged all the week in secular pursuits who conduct the public services on Sunday. The churches feel that their existence does not depend upon having a preacher; in his absence the work can go on. Congregations listen most intently. There is no sleep or slumber or weariness. No one consults his watch. They are quick to see a good point and to respond. Some audiences are cold and sluggish; they would quench a seraph's fire. If one had the tongues of men and angels, he could not speak effectively in their presence. Others inspire a speaker, and call out the best that is in him. If one can speak at all, he can speak well to an Australian audience.

Wherever I went people said, "I suppose you find things here different from what they are in America." In most things, and in the most essential things, there is no difference. An Australian would find himself very much at home in any American church, and an American would find the same in Australia. I detected some differences that are verbal only. The preacher is called the "evangelist." The term is more classical than the one we use. I detected some real differences. The Sunday morning service is for the members only. No effort is made to secure the attendance of non-

1. John Bardsley, Sydney. 2. Mrs. John Bardsley, Sydney.
3. J. Colbourne, Adelaide.
4. D. A. Ewers, Melbourne. 5. William Burford, Adelaide.
6. A. B. Maston, Melbourne. 7. F. G. Dunn, Melbourne,

AUSTRALIAN FRIENDS.

believers. They are not debarred, but they are not expected, and they do not come. The Lord's Supper is the main feature of this service. This usually occupies an hour. There is an unwritten law that the entire service must not exceed an hour and a half in length. The speaker has from twenty to twenty-five minutes for an exhortation. Sometimes the evangelist speaks; more frequently some one else. At one time any one who wished could speak; now the officers determine who shall occupy the time. The Sunday morning service is very like a mid-week prayer-meeting at home.

One of the Melbourne elders asked me how we conducted our meetings. When I told him, he said, "Perhaps that accounts for your rapid growth in America." I think it does. The Sunday morning service is the best service in the week for preaching the Gospel. It is easier to get strangers to attend in the morning than in the evening. In the churches of which I have knowledge there are more confessions in the morning services than at any other. In Australia the pressure of the Gospel upon the world is reduced one-half. In my opinion, they would do far better if they would seek to fill their houses and preach the Gospel at every service. They could give saint and sinner a portion in due season. I think the results would be more gratifying. Last year there was a *net* loss of five churches and thirty-six members in Victoria; the year before there was a loss of two hundred and eighteen members. New South Wales had a gain of only one in the year. These losses are explained by saying that some have removed to West Australia, and that several church rolls have been revised. The explanation accounts for a part of the losses, but not for all. Christianity is a conquering faith. If in any field it does not run and is not glorified, there must be some reason for it. It is for those in charge to inquire what the reason is. I believe the Melbourne elder laid his finger on the weak spot. I am sure that the churches in America would lose immensely if they were to adopt the Australian system. Our churches magnify the Lord's Supper, but they do not lose sight of the unsaved. At every service people are urged to believe on the Lord Jesus Christ and to confess him publicly.

In the Conference one or two speakers were constantly talking against taking money from the unimmersed. Their remarks always called out some applause. One man said that some Sunday-schools had made offerings to the work. He spoke of this as a violation of a principle of the Church of Christ. The President explained that a resolution had been adopted three years ago providing that all such offerings should be used for benevolent, and not for evangelistic, purposes. I was asked if it was true that the American churches took money from "all and sundries." I told them that in America money for the Lord's work came from the Lord's people. The world loves its own and spends its money on its own. If any money came from the outside it was so infinitesimal that it was not worth talking or contending about. We are in no danger from this source in America, and do not need to put up any safeguards. John Bright used to tell of a mountebank who sold pills to prevent earthquakes. We are in as little peril from one source as from the other, and do not need to take any preventive. We make our appeal to the churches and we get our money from the churches. I learned that the churches in Australia are not a unit in their opposition to taking money from the unimmersed. Some take any that is offered and make no remark. They call to mind the words: "The silver is mine, and the gold is mine, saith the Lord," and if any one wishes to pay to the Lord that which he owes, they do not object. Others can see no difference between taking money for evangelistic and for benevolent purposes. They think this is a distinction without a difference.

No unimmersed person is invited to the Lord's table. I was asked more than once as to the views and practice of the churches in America. Here again it seems to me that this matter is dwelt upon with undue insistence. The fact is, that people of other communions are not pressing in and claiming the right of sitting down with them at the Lord's table. There is no need of fencing the tables, as there is no one seeking to obtrude himself where he knows he is not welcome. Even if their position was scriptural, this is not a practical issue, and all that is said about it is a waste of breath. On the question of instrumental music there is as much diversity as at home. Some use the organ at all the services; some at the evening services only; two or three that I visited do not use it at all. Some speak of the morning service as for worship, the evening service as for preaching the Gospel. I think, speaking broadly, the churches in New South Wales are the most conservative in Australia; those in South Australia the least so, and those in Victoria are between the two.

There are 12,850 Disciples of Christ in Australasia. Of these 150 are in West Australia; 2,621 in South Australia; 5,150 in Victoria; 2,129 in New South Wales; 300 in Tasmania; 2,500 in New Zealand. This number should be doubled in ten years. To do this, more preachers are needed to give their whole time to the work. At one time any form of paid labor smacked of ecclesiasticism and was supposed to have the mark of the beast. That feeling has largely died out. These churches are learning what other churches had to learn, namely, that they must have an able and educated ministry, and that those who preach the Gospel must live of the Gospel. It is well to have business men capable of preaching on Sunday, but that is a small part of the work. With every pulpit supplied and every pew filled on Sunday morning and evening, we may confidently expect the churches of Australasia to enter upon careers of unexampled prosperity.

XLIX.

FROM ADELAIDE TO ISMAILIA.

We left Adelaide on the twenty-second day of April. Commissioner Coombs and family and Colonel and Mrs. Dowdle, of the Salvation Army, were among the passengers. The Salvationists were out in force to see them off. About a hundred men and women accompanied them to the ship. They sang and prayed on board, and listened to some parting counsels from the Commissioner. He had been in charge of the work in Australia for six years. Under his wise management the Army grew and flourished. He goes to take charge of the work in England. Herbert Booth takes his place in the Colonies.

The cabins and tables were full. The passengers proved quiet and orderly. Most of them are Christian people. There was no gambling, and little drinking to excess. In this respect the passengers are widely different from those on the ship on the voyage out. I found the Colonials very friendly. Some of these had been in the Colonies for fifty years, and are wealthy. They are going back to visit the land of their birth. They still speak of England as "home," but they have no thought of remaining there. Their homes and their interests are under the Southern Cross, and they mean to return after seeing their friends and kinsmen.

There are twenty-nine children on board. Some of these are not at all backward in coming forward; none of them are angels; but they add not a little to the amusement and enjoyment of their associates. They go everywhere, ask all sorts of questions, and laugh and play in calm and storm. The voyage would be dull and dreary without them. Blessings on you, little folks!

"You are better than all the ballads
 That ever were sung or said;
For you are the living poems,
 And all the rest are dead."

One passenger is a dog. His mistress washes and combs his shaggy hair, feeds him, and kisses and caresses him. His master carries him about when he needs air, and walks the deck with him when he needs exercise. This poodle is a lucky dog. Few children are cared for so tenderly.

Soon after starting, the usual committee on entertainment was appointed. The committee sought to please all classes. Accordingly, they arranged for debates, lectures, concerts, cricket and field sports of all kinds, chess, cards, draughts, moot courts, and dances. A weekly paper was published. This gave all the home news and contained imaginary cablegrams from all parts of the world. The Colonials nearly all play whist, euchre and cribbage. Cricket is the great English game. It is much less violent than base ball. Saturday night was reserved for dancing. No one looked upon this as disqualifying the participants for worship the next day. The captain danced with young and mature girls till midnight, and read the service on Sunday with the solemnity of a bishop. Neither card-playing nor dancing is regarded as unbecoming in a Christian. One aged lady wanted some one to help her dance the Highland Fling. Usually I feel impelled to assist persons of this class when I find them traveling alone. But as I do not know the Highland Fling from a waltz, or a waltz from a hornpipe, I was obliged to remain silent. The young fellows who could dance were not gallant enough to volunteer. Had she been young and beautiful, there would have been no dearth of partners.

There being no English clergyman on board, we had no sermon in the morning. The Captain read the service of the English Church and dismissed the audience. It seemed to me that he was going through with a disagreeable duty, and was glad when he came to the end. The service is wondrously beautiful. Its charmed words fell on the ear and heart like music. But I missed the sermon and the Lord's Supper. We were dismissed before we came to the true conclusion. We went away as from the first course at a feast. The soul's thirst was unslaked, its hunger unfed. The evening services were conducted in the second saloon. The people gathered on the deck and sang and listened. The Salvationists spoke twice. The first address was somewhat of a surprise. I did not suppose that such antiquated theology was preached anywhere. I had many talks with these godly men, and found much pleasure and profit in their society. They explained to me the management and work of the Army. Each division is self-supporting. The officers receive a certain amount, provided they raise it. Collections are called for at all the services. A part of the money raised in this way is sent to London for general expenses. One week in the year is set apart for self-denial. The soldiers in Australia gave $70,000 in this week. The whole Army gave $200,000. General Booth has never drawn a dollar of salary. Some wealthy friends supply his needs and pay all his traveling expenses. In starting a work in India or Japan, grants are made, and the officers in charge are expected to use these as economically as possible. I talked with them about the ordinances. The Army observes neither baptism nor the Lord's Supper. The explanation given was, that these are symbols, and that, if they have the realities symbolized, the symbols can be dispensed with. One of their mottoes is, "Don't argue." I regard their treatment of the ordinances as an error and as a weak point. Our Lord understood human nature, and he gave no ordinance that does not have its place and use. Consequently it can not be set aside without loss. No one denies the zeal and devotion of the Salvation Army. Their motto is, "Blood and Fire." The army was organized, so it is said, to save sinners, to save the worst sinners, and to save the largest number of the worst sinners. The soldiers go everywhere, and bear testimony wherever they go. The joy of the Lord is their strength. General Booth is not afraid to tackle any evil. He has attacked sin in its strongholds; he has undertaken to deal with poverty in the great cities; to rescue fallen men and fallen women; to assist discharged convicts; in short, to hasten the coming of the new heavens and the new earth wherein dwells righteousness.

At the request of the passengers I spoke on two Sunday evenings. I gave two lectures besides. I spoke once on my travels and once on America. In a public address, the speaker spoke slightingly of Americans. He said that in America human life was lightly esteemed. He did not know that there was an American on the ship. After the service I challenged his statements. Others joined in the conversation. They talked of the bad way in which Americans usually acted. One man blandly said, "Everybody knows that your officials from the President down are corrupt." Judges, Congressmen and customs officers were all included in this sweeping condemnation. As a result of the evening's talk I was asked to give a lecture on America, with a view to remove existing misapprehensions. The people in the East and South know almost nothing about America. I searched the book-stores of Colombo for an American history or for any book on America, but found none. The most popular works at home are unknown by name here. When the time came, I gave the audience some idea of the extent of our territory, the character of our people and their contribution to the welfare of humanity, of the stability of our government, of the incorruptibility of our public men, and of the problems we are trying to solve. I spoke for an hour and a half. Some were so interested that they said they could have listened all night.

We were three days crossing the Great Australian Bight. Our first stop was made at Albany in West Australia. We set down and took on some passengers at this point. Our next stop was at Colombo. Some of the natives claim that this was the site of Eden. It is a veritable paradise. One may travel over the world and not find another spot so beautiful. The people have not yet forgiven Heber for speaking of Ceylon as the place "where every prospect pleases, and only man is vile." He was not far wrong. The place swarms with beggars. Children are taught to beg and to lie as soon as they are born. They all have the same story: "Me no fader; me no moder; me no broder; me two sisters to feed; good papa, give me something to buy rice and curry." Bearded men and young children follow strangers for miles repeating this story. When one has heard it ten thousand times, he wonders if all the youth of Ceylon are really orphans; and if so, what epidemic carried off all the parents and spared all the children.

The next land we saw after leaving Colombo was the large island of Socotra. To us it appeared a barren rock. We saw no signs of life of any kind. We learned, however, that there are ten thousand people on the island, and that they cultivate spices of different kinds. Socotra is a British possession. Our next call was at Aden. This is the Indian Gibraltar. The British own thirty-five square miles of Arabia. They have here a military establishment and a coaling station for the navy. The population, excluding the garrison, numbers thirty thousand. The town and fort are in the crater of an extinct volcano. The feature that interests strangers most is the system of tanks made to catch and hold water. Sometimes it does not rain for years. Long ago these tanks were begun. They hold in all thirty million gallons. One sees almost no vegetation. The beggars here are as numerous as in Colombo, and they have the identical story. Ostrich feathers, tapestries, boxes and baskets of various kinds are pressed on the passenger for sale. If a seller gets a third of the first price, he gets as much as he ought. The British and Foreign Bible Society has a depot here. The Church Missionary Society has a chaplain. The Roman Catholics have a strong staff. In the English graveyard rests all that was mortal of Ion Keith-Falconer. He was a son of the Earl of Kintore. At Cambridge, where he was educated, and where he taught Arabic, he was neither a prig nor a Pharisee. He delighted in all athletic sports. He was the best amateur cyclist in England.

He was a helper in mission work at home. He heard General Haig plead for some one to work in Aden. Thousands came from all parts of Arabia to Aden, and they could but contrast the peace and order and liberty of the place with the misrule and despotism of their own homes. Here was a great opening for a good work. This young man, living in a pleasant home with a happy bride, in the midst of the culture and refinement of an ancient university, with a splendid career opening before him, left all at the call of God to work in Arabia at his own expense. He took the Aden fever and died. Behind his grave are the gloomy hills of darkness, to whose people he came with the message of Gospel light; before it the white Arabian shore, with the ocean stretching away into the limitless distance. The Free Church of Scotland has taken up his work and has resolved to prosecute it vigorously.

The day before we reached Aden one of the passengers died. She was sick when she boarded the ship in Melbourne. Sixteen years ago she left Scotland to marry a prosperous colonist. She was then one of the happiest girls that ever breathed. Her life since has not been without sorrow. She and her husband parted. Feeling that her end was drawing nigh, she started for Scotland. She wanted to put her little daughter under the care of some relatives. Her prayer was that she might reach the home of her youth. This prayer was not answered. Most of the way she was in the hospital. Some of the passengers took care of her and supplied her needs. One of them took charge of her daughter. I have always noticed that where God sends sorrow or sickness, he also sends some good woman to comfort and to nurse. Her body was placed in a coffin heavily loaded with iron. As the sun was setting, the coffin, draped with a flag, was placed on a platform. The captain read the burial service. When he came to the words, "We therefore commit her body to the deep," the seamen raised one end of the platform. The coffin slid down and sank like a stone. The engines, which had been stopped, were started again, and the ship continued her course as if nothing had happened.

Ninety miles west of Aden we entered the Red Sea. This sea is not red, but blue. The entrance is known as the Straits of Babul Mandib, or "The Gate of Tears," so named from the number of ships that have been wrecked in this region. Soon after we passed the Island of Perim. The English flag flies over it, and a small garrison is stationed there. This island commands the entrance to the sea, somewhat as Gibraltar commands the entrance to the Mediterranean. We were three days on this sea. Much of the time we could

THE PYRAMIDS.

SUEZ CANAL.

see no land on either side. We saw many ships. The Red Sea is now one of the great highways of the nations. All ships bound for the East pass through the Suez Canal and the Red Sea. As we entered the Gulf of Suez we saw the mountains of Arabia and Africa. In the far distance is Sinai, where the law was given to Moses, but we could not see it. The days and nights were cool and refreshing. Usually on the Red Sea the heat is suggestive of Tophet. We had nothing to complain of in this respect. People sat on deck with their wraps about them, and slept at night under covers. We had heard much of the hot blasts from the Sahara, but we felt none. In fact, we had no oppressive heat at any time in the voyage. The tropics behaved beautifully. There was no time when we could not work or play, according to our mood. When we crossed the equator we saw the polestar and the Great Bear. In the Red Sea we lost sight of the Southern Cross.

After a brief stay at Suez we entered the canal. This ditch is eighty-seven miles long and is deep enough for the largest ships. It cost nearly $100,000,000. One wonders why English engineers declared that a canal here was impossible. The Isthmus is level. The Bitter Lakes lessened the cutting. One of these is fifteen miles long; another is seven. There is an enormous amount of digging, but that is all. There are no triumphs of engineering genius. The cutting of the Suez Canal is child's play compared with the building of the Southern Pacific or the Denver and Rio Grande Railway. I left the ship at Ismailia. The passengers gathered about me and expressed their regret that I was not going with them to London. No one could wish to travel with a nicer company of people. I shall always cherish pleasant memories of these colonials. The captain is a little snob. He did not wish to be intimate with any one who was not distinguished by a title or wealth or genius. One good woman, an invalid too, wished to be introduced to him that she might thank him for some privilege accorded her. He said, "No; if I consent to be introduced to her, I shall have to be introduced to others." Perhaps he has a drop of blue blood in his veins or some blue milk in his stomach. The company to which the ship belongs is rich and pays large dividends. At the same time its treatment of its men is simply scandalous. The stewards get no butter; they eat standing about; they sleep like cattle down in the hold; some of them are on duty for twenty-four hours without intermission. Such shameful treatment of men should be impossible under great England's flag and on a ship receiving large subsidies from the British government.

L.

FROM ISMAILIA TO ALEXANDRIA.

Ismailia is on the Isthmus of Suez, about midway between the Red Sea and the Mediterranean. This neck of land connects Asia and Africa, and has associations of the greatest historic interest. Over it Abraham and his family passed when they went down into Egypt in the time of famine. Over it Joseph was carried when he was sold by his brethren to a company of Ishmaelites. They came from Gilead, with their camels bearing spicery, and balm, and myrrh, going to carry it down to Egypt. Over it Jacob and his household passed when at Joseph's invitation they went to sojourn in Goshen during the years of famine. Over it the Assyrian, the Chaldean, the Persian and the Arab passed on their way to conquer Egypt, and over it the Egyptian armies marched on their way to invade western Asia.

At some point in our course through the Red Sea and the canal, we must have crossed the path of the Hebrews on the Exodus. One place on the Gulf of Suez was pointed out as the actual spot. There are high hills on either side of a plain large enough to accommodate the host of Israel. The sea there is seven miles wide. Sir William Dawson and others are of the opinion that, at that time, the Red Sea extended as far inland as the Bitter Lakes, and that the crossing took place not far from the present Ismailia. But as we scanned every inch of the way for two hundred miles, we must have seen the place where the people at the commaud of God went forward, and where the seas parted and gave them an easy and safe passage, and where the Egyptians, undertaking to capture them and bring them back to their cruel bondage, were drowned. It was easy in imagination to call up the great scene and the actors.

The enemy said, "I will pursue, I will overtake, I will divide the spoil; my lust shall be satisfied upon them; I will draw my sword, my hand shall destroy them." God blew, the sea covered them; they sank as lead in the mighty waters. In the psalm of victory, the people said, "Who is like unto thee, O Lord, among the gods? Who is like unto thee, glorious in holiness, fearful in praises, doing wonders?" Miriam and all the women took timbrels and danced and said, "Sing ye to the Lord, for he hath triumphed gloriously; the horse and his rider hath he thrown into the sea."

At Ismailia two other passengers left the boat for a brief stay in Egypt. In the morning we walked out to see the town. The donkey boys discovered us and insisted that we should have a ride on their animals. One was named "Yankee Doodle;" one, "Mrs. Langtry," and one the "Grand Old Man." These lads are shrewd, and understand human nature better than many philosophers. By wit and flattery and importunity they seek to worm a few extra piasters out of their patrons, and seldom fail. They are civil and attentive and point out everything that has any historic interest. Ismailia is a dull place. It originated when the canal was in process of construction. It depends wholly upon the canal for support. All around is desert. From Suez, we saw scarcely any green thing. Where springs are found or where sweet-water canals have been cut, one sees feathery palms, grain, fruits and flowers, but these are scarce. In the afternoon we took the train for Cairo. For miles we saw only a sea of sand. One station is named Tel-el-Kebir. It was here that General Wolseley smashed the power of Arabi, and saved the Egyptians from a great evil and the foreigners from a grave peril. After Tel-el-Kebir the verdure increased till the whole country became a garden. Central Illinois is not more fertile. We passed through the ancient Goshen. Pharaoh said to Joseph, "The land of Egypt is before thee; in the best of the land make thy father and brethren to dwell." The king added, "Ye shall eat of the fat of the land." This district answers to the description. Though the country is naturally fertile, and yields several crops a year, the people are indescribably poor. They herd together in mud huts, and are destitute of almost every comfort. The whole family live in one room. The same apartment is shared with the dogs and goats and fleas. England is in Egypt, and there is a sense of unwonted peace and security. I trust that England will abide in Egypt, and so preclude a return of the misgovernment of the Khedive. In case she does so, the inhabitants of this "garden of Jehovah" will enter upon a period of unprecedented prosperity. The railway leaves Zoan and Rameses on the right. Zoan was founded seven years before Hebron. It was a town of some importance before the migration of Abraham. Zoan was once the capital. It was to this place that Moses and Aaron went to demand of Pharaoh that he let the children of Israel go. Rameses was the place of the first encampment. It was here that they rendezvoused and kept the Passover with their feet shod and loins girded. Every foot of this journey was absorbingly interesting.

We reached Cairo two hours before dark, and were surprised to find it such a fine city. In modern Cairo the buildings are large and substantial. The streets, though not wide, are well paved and lighted. There is an old Cairo. This is the Arab quarter. There the streets are narrow and crooked and foul. There the cholera microbes breed and spread. But much of Cairo is clean and wholesome. The hotels are as good as those in Bombay or Melbourne. The city is well supplied with mosques. There are two hundred and sixty-four of these places of prayer. From any elevation one sees minarets in all directions. At intervals the shrill cry of the muezzin is heard calling "the faithful" to prayer and reminding them that there is no god but God, and that Mohammed is the prophet of God. The Mohammedans founded this city in honor of their conquest of the land, and named it "The Victorious." Most of the people are Mohammedans; the other faiths are represented by two hundred and twenty-five chapels.

Being a semi-tropical climate the people live much in the open air. They need little clothing and little shelter. It was a common thing to see men sleeping on the streets or in the parks or wherever they could find room to stretch their bodies. In the morning and evening tables and chairs were placed out on the sidewalks, and hundreds sat down and played games and drank coffee or whisky, according to their taste and religion. The bright colors worn by the people attract the attention of strangers. Men dress in all sorts of styles, but more and more the European style is becoming prevalent. Nearly all wear the red fez. We saw many women walking the streets, but never in the company of men. The men go together, each holding the hand of the other; the women do the same. The wives and daughters of Mohammedans and Copts in good circumstances are always veiled; only the eyes are seen. Black women are as careful on this point as white. The veil protects them against insult. Rich women always dress in black. Poor women and the wives and daughters of Europeans go uncovered. They have not been born to blush unseen. We made long excursions into the city by night and by day. The people everywhere were invariably quiet. We saw no drunkenness and no disposition to do us any violence. We were unarmed, and felt as secure as we could have have felt in Boston or London.

Securing a dragoman and a carriage we drove out to see the Pyramids. On the way we got our first view of the Nile. The bridge across it is guarded by British lions at both ends. The guide pointed out an island in the river, and told us that tradition says that it was there that Pharaoh's daughter found Moses in the ark of bulrushes. A ride of seven miles brought us to the Pyramids—one of the seven wonders of the world. They are built on a rock of considerable height on the edge of the Great Desert. The largest covers thirteen acres, and is four hundred and sixty feet high. The next largest is on higher ground, and appears to be the higher of the two, though it is much smaller. The others are insignificant in comparison. They were once covered with smooth stones. These smooth stones were taken away by the Arabs and used in building mosques. The surface now resembles a staircase. The Bedouins took us in charge at once. With one holding each hand the ascent was easily and speedily made. Several times we stopped to take breath and to study these great works. From the top we got a view of the whole country adjacent. The longer we gazed at the Pyramids the more wonderful they appeared. They grew on our thought and assumed colossal proportions. On our descent we went in and explored the different chambers. We saw some empty coffins, but nothing else. We felt relieved when we got out. Evidently, the Pyramids were built as royal sepulchres. There are other tombs on the same platform. These are above the flood of the Nile, and not far from Memphis, one of the ancient capitals. The Bedouins were clamorous for pay and for backsheesh. Those who rendered no service wished to be paid for their good intentions. Every man thought we ought to satisfy him before leaving. They see the stranger but once, and they think that it behooves them to make the most of that one opportunity. From the Pyramids we walked over to see the Sphinx. This great figure has the head of a woman, and the body of a lion. Once the head was adorned with a helmet and a beard. Near by we saw the foundations of a temple. The size of the stones that are still in place give one some conception of the grandeur of the building. These huge blocks of granite were brought down the Nile from Assouan. On our return to Cairo we learned that the Syrian ports kept all passengers from Egypt in quarantine ten days. This is on account of the cholera in Cairo and Alexandria. I did not know this till I was in the trap. The problem now is how to get out. I must go up to Jerusalem, but I do not like to remain in quarantine on board a ship, or in a lazaretto in Beirut for ten days.

I visited more than once the missions of the United Presbyterians of America. I met all the workers. I attended their mid-week prayer-meeting, visited their school for boys, and saw the chapel. Like all such buildings in the East, the men sit on one side and the women on the other. There is a screen between. Drs. Harvey and Watson and their associates gave me many facts about the mission. Some of these I add: The mission began forty-two years ago. Since that time the workers have been increased, stations occupied, schools opened, Scriptures distributed, preachers trained, and churches organized. In all the principal cities of the Delta missionaries are stationed, and the smaller places are visited by evangelists and colporteurs. In the Upper Country the work is in a flourishing condition. The missionaries number forty-one; the native ordained pastors, nineteen; the whole number of workers, three hundred and sixty-seven; the communicants five thousand and four; churches, thirty-seven; other preaching places, one hundred and fifty-three. Of the converts seventy were Moslems. In one hundred and twenty-five Sunday-schools there were six thousand six hundred and twenty-two pupils. There are one hundred and sixty-one day schools—one hundred and thirty-six for boys, and twenty-five for girls. These schools have ten thousand eight hundred and seventy-four pupils enrolled. There are three high schools for boys, with seven hundred and eighty pupils, and five for girls, with one thousand and fifty-seven pupils. One-fifth of the scholars are Mohammedans. In ten years the attendance has doubled. The mission has a college at Assiout. This college began in 1865 in a stable; the donkeys were at one end and the boys at the other. Now it has substantial buildings and four hundred and twenty students. This school has trained pastors, teachers, doctors, lawyers, journalists, authors, newspaper correspondents, interpreters, merchants, farmers, mechanics; it has prepared men for the postal, railway, telegraph, police, justice, finance, and war departments. The Theological Seminary is in Cairo; it has a three years' course. The mission was not content with educating boys; it desired to raise up a generation of educated Christian women, who should build up Christian homes in Egypt. In addition to the primary schools, there are two advanced boarding schools for girls with two hundred and fifty enrolled. The largest school of this kind in Egypt is in Cairo. It has seventy-nine boarders, and two hundred and fifty-three day pupils. In these schools many wives have been trained. The hearts of their husbands do safely trust in them. In 1854 there was scarcely a woman in the land able to read; now there are two thousand three hundred and thirty-two girls attending school. The mission employs twenty-seven colporteurs. These sold last year sixty-two thousand one hundred and thirty volumes. These serve as pioneer evangelists as well. There are forty-nine special workers among the women in their homes. They have one thousand seven hundred and seventy-two regular pupils. They reach Mohammedans, Copts, Jews and Greek Catholics. In the hospitals, fifteen thousand are annually treated. The patients are brought under Christian influences while in the hospitals. Papers are printed and scattered far and near. The mission received last year from the people of Egypt for the support of the work, $38,468. The native church pays about one-half the entire expense of the mission. Ninety schools are self-supporting. The gain in converts and in liberality is constant. I rejoiced with these saintly workers, and came away feeling increasingly confident of the regeneration of Egypt.

It was in Cairo that Miss Whately did her great work. She went there expecting to remain a few months. Seeing the degradation of the women she opened a school for poor girls. Until the work outgrew her means she bore all the expense. She began with nine girls. On their first appearance they were not very attractive. Cleanliness is not an Arab virtue. Mothers think that plenty of dirt protects the child against the evil eye. For a time work was carried on in the face of great disadvantages and discouragements. It is hard to teach people who are utterly ignorant and who do not prize knowledge. Besides she could not then speak fluently in Arabic, and she had no efficient helpers. But God sent her two qualified teachers. It was not long till a school for boys was opened. By practicing the most rigid self-denial she was able to pay the rent and teachers. Her assistants preached the Gospel in the surrounding country and in the towns along the Nile. She hired a boat, and with her sister engaged in the same work. On one of her tours the people were so impressed with her message that they said, "Bring out the aged, that they may hear the word of God before they die." A hospital was opened and several thousand patients were treated annually. She pleaded with the Bedouins to accept Christ; she went into the streets and slums and told the people of the love of God; she induced story-tellers to read and repeat the Gospel message. The work grew in her hands. God sent her friends and helpers and means. When the Prince and Princess of Wales visited Egypt, the Khedive gave her some ground. On this suitable buildings have been erected. She became widely known and profoundly respected. In streets where once she was pelted with dirt and reviled as the "cursed Nazarene," she was met by the salutation,

"Blessed be thy hands and feet, O lady." Some people said of her and her associates, "These women will surely go to Paradise, even though they are Christians." Her death was mourned by all who knew her. Miss Whately did good work, and "the day shall declare it." She spent thirty years in that delightful service. She was one of the first to labor among Mohammedan women in Egypt. She died, but her work lives and grows. In addition to the missions already alluded to, the Church Missionary Society is at work in Cairo. I saw a German and an English Church. These are for the people of these nations living here.

Two other places were immensely interesting, namely, the Museum of Gizeh and the Mohammedan university. The museum is stored with Egyptian antiquities. One sees innumerable mummies. The Egyptians embalmed not only human beings, but sacred bulls, and crocodiles, and goats, and fish, and birds. In the tombs they placed jewels, grain, clothing, money, gods and other things. This museum is worth many visits. One feels curious as one looks on the face of the king who oppressed the Hebrews and upon the representations of men who lived at the same time as Joseph, and perhaps long before. I saw the Rosetta Stone. It was by the study of the trilingual inscription on this stone that the hieroglyphics were deciphered. The university was founded by the Caliphs in the day of their power, and has changed little in spirit or form since. It is the principal Mohammedan school in the world. The pupils come from all Moslem countries except Persia, and number 12,000. At the door we met with men who put slippers over our shoes lest they should touch the sacred floor. We listened to several lectures and recitations. Teachers and scholars sit on mats. There is no furniture whatever. Children of all ages were writing on tin slates or telling what they knew. The Koran is the one textbook. It is supposed to contain all knowledge and wisdom. All laws are taken from it. We saw some of "the faithful" engaged in prayer. Others were chatting in an undertone. In one place barbers were plying their vocation. Some were eating bread and onions or curd. Hundreds spread their mats on the floor of the mosque, which is the home of the university, and sleep. This institution is, without doubt, one of the most remarkable sights in Egypt. We also saw the Citadel, the Alabaster Mosque, Joseph's Well, the Tombs of the Caliphs, and the Tombs of the Mamelukes. I wanted to visit Memphis, Luxor, Karnac, and Thebes, but could not afford the time.

From Cairo I went to Alexandria. There I met John Johnson,

MOHAMMEDAN UNIVERSITY, CAIRO.

DANCING DERVISHES.

of England. He is now working with the North African Mission. This mission has stations in Egypt, Tunis, Algeria, and Morocco. There are, in all, about a hundred workers. The mission is interdenominational, and is on the same lines as the China Inland Mission. The support is meager, but the workers live simple and joyous lives. They have schools and hospitals, and preach Christ in season and out of season. On Sunday we went to the Church of Scotland. The minister prayed for the great American republic, for the officials and the people. He preached on the Galatians, taking Professor Ramsey's view, that the Galatians were the churches of Derbe, Lystra, Iconium and Antioch in Pisidia. He urged his hearers to guard against legalism, and to stand fast in the liberty wherewith Christ had made them free. In the evening I went to the Church of England. The rector has a weak voice. I heard a word now and then. Like Tennyson's "Northern Farmer," I thought he said what he should have said and came away. On Monday Mr. Johnson and Mr. Somers went with me to see the city. We went to the top of the light-house and got a bird's-eye view of Alexandria and the country round about. We passed the site of the ancient Pharos. The light-house was one of the wonders of the ancient world. It was built for the guidance of those who travel by sea. We saw Pompey's Pillar. This is a shaft of granite seventy-three feet high and thirty feet in circumference. It must have been floated down the Nile from Assouan. We examined the catacombs at the base of the pillar, but saw nothing remarkable.

Alexandria was founded in 333 B. C., and was for a long time the greatest city on the globe. Nineveh and Babylon had fallen and Rome had not risen to be the mistress of the world. For two hundred years it was the residence of the kings of Egypt. Under the Ptolemies it was a city with five hundred thousand inhabitants, and was adorned with the wealth of Egypt and the arts of Greece. Omar described it as a place with four thousand palaces and a like number of baths, four hundred places of amusement, twelve thousand gardens, and a Jewish quarter occupied by forty thousand people. Its schools were the best in existence. They inherited the fame of the schools of philosophy in Heliopolis, the city that had been the resort of Greek sages and students. Alexandria became the seat of learning and the repository of all the wisdom of the Egyptians. It was the home of Pantaenus, Hipparchus, Theon, Hypatia, Clement, Origen, Athanasius, Cyril, Dionysius, and others famous for all time. Here was the great library, having on its ample shelves seven hundred thousand volumes, and whose loss is still deplored. Here the Old Testament was translated into Greek. From this place the eloquent Apollos went to build up the church in other regions. But the glory has departed. The rise of Cairo and the discovery of the passage around the Cape and the Suez Canal have taken business and wealth from Alexandria. The population now does not exceed three hundred thousand; at one time it was only six thousand. Owing to its situation it will never sink into insignificance. The United Presbyterians and the British and Foreign Society have workers there.

For the student of history Egypt has a strange fascination. It is the oldest kingdom of which we have any record. It has been called a land of wonders and monuments, a land of ruined cities, palaces, temples, pyramids, obelisks and hieroglyphics. Once it was the granary of the world. All Egypt has an area of 382,523 square miles, but by far the greater part of this is desert. Egypt proper, consisting of the Delta and the Valley of the Nile as far as the First Cataract and the oases in the Libyan Desert, "the islands of the blessed," has an area of about 14,000 square miles. From Cairo to the First Cataract the valley is about ten miles wide; from Cairo to the sea it spreads out like a triangle. The base on the Mediterranean is one hundred and sixty miles long and is five hundred and fifty miles from the First Cataract as the crow flies. The cultivable part of Egypt is, as Herodotus said, "the gift of the Nile." This river was once honored as a god. The being and the well-being of the nation depended upon it. There was an inscrutable mystery as to its source and the cause of its annual rising and falling. Any impossible enterprise was spoken of as an attempt to seek the source of the Nile. Now all mystery has been cleared away. Its source has been discovered and the cause of its rising ascertained. None the less is it a noble stream, and the source of life and wealth to the people. The Nile is nearly as long as the Mississippi. At Khartoum the blue and the white streams unite. From that point to the sea it receives only one tributary; for a thousand miles it receives none. All through Egypt its waters are trained off into canals and irrigating ditches. The most common sight along its banks is the shadoof, the rude instrument used for raising the water into the ditches.

The population numbers 6,821,413. The Arabs represent the conquerors of the seventh century. The Bedouins live in tents and despise civilization. The Copts represent the ancient Egyptians, and constitute one-tenth of the population. Beside these there are Berbers, Soudanese, Turks, Levantines, Jews, Gypsies, Greeks,

Italians, French, Austrians, English, Germans. It is said that six million two hundred thousand are Mohammedans and six hundred thousand Christians. The Copts are Christians, but like the Abyssinians, Greeks, Maronites, Druses, Jacobites, Nestorians, Armemians and Bulgarians, they have lost their first love. They hold some essential truths, but they are mixed with much error. Egypt has most of these sects, and perhaps many more. They cling to their errors as a limpet to a rock, and are not willing to be aroused out of their lethargy. The Roman Catholics are here in force. Whatever we may think of some of their tenets, we must admire their zeal. Women are held in slight esteem. The Koran allows a man four wives and as many slaves as his right hand possesses. A recent Viceroy had five hundred women in his harem. There is no discrimination on account of color. One Bedouin asked me if I was married. When I told him, he said, "I have two wives and will sell you one for twenty pounds." I was afraid to offer him twenty piasters lest he should accept. From what I have seen of the veiled houris they are not distressingly adorable. The women are married in childhood, and live and die in ignorance.

The Biblical student finds much said about this land in the Scriptures. It was here that God molded his chosen people into a nation. Here Moses was trained for the great task to which he was afterwards called. Here God wrought signs and wonders, and delivered his people with a mighty arm. Here the child Jesus found shelter when Herod sought to destroy him. The world owes much to Egypt. Here, according to Dawson, it learned its first lessons in geometry, chemistry, medicine, architecture, and sculpture. Yet for some reason, Egypt was "the basest of kingdoms," "a servant of servants," and was trodden under foot by many, by the Assyrian, the Chaldean, the Persian, the Greek, the Roman, the Arab, the Frank, the Briton. She has now the best government she has ever had, and all signs indicate the dawn of a better day. With the advantages of good government, with schools in every town and village, with the Gospel preached everywhere, the words of Jehovah will have a new application and a new significance, "Blessed be Egypt, my people."

LI.

FROM ALEXANDRIA TO JAFFA.*

I LEFT Alexandria thankful that I had been kept from the pestilence that walks in darkness and from the destruction that wastes at noonday. Our small ship was crowded with people rushing away from the cholera. The cabins were full and the decks covered. On a boat with a carrying capacity of seventy-five, we had 267 passengers. The officers had never seen anything like it. There was a fresh breeze and the sea ran high. Most of the people were sick in consequence. For a time they were afraid that they would die; then they became afraid that death would not come to their relief. On occasion the Mediterranean can be as rough as the Atlantic.

We called at Port Said and spent a day there. This place has a bad name. It is said to be worse than Sodom. Some captains do not allow women to land. I saw little wickedness. I went about the streets for hours. The place is quiet, even to dullness. I fancy the young bloods who see so much wickedness in Port Said take pains to look for it. A salesman said to my cabin-mate that he had some pictures that he would show him if he would go into a back room, and asked him if he wished to see them. He said "no," with such indignant emphasis that the fellow looked at him in amazement and sneered, "*missionary*." He is a commercial traveler, an agent for a wholesale liquor house; he is not a missionary, but he has no relish for nastiness. This sneering epithet was the highest compliment he could have paid this class of Christian workers.

We visited the British and Foreign Bible Society and the Seaman's Rest. In the Rest we met a Miss Van Zandt, of California. She and a Miss Shaw, from the same State, came out here to do missionary work. Miss Van Zandt feels that she has been definitely called of God to Port Said. She is in the very place where he wants her, and she is unspeakably happy. She said she is like a tree planted by the rivers of waters, that bringeth forth fruit in its season; its leaf also shall not wither; and whatsoever she does shall prosper. She has had so many unmistakable evidences of God's favor that she can not doubt that she is in the right place. She is learning Arabic, that she may be able to work among the natives. There is no other mission work here. There is an English church,

*The Joppa of the Bible.

AN ARAB SCHOOL.

but it is for the English; it does nothing for the Egyptians. Port Said is at the entrance to the Suez Canal. It is a commercial port, and is destined to grow in numbers, in business and in wealth. It is a strategic point, and should be occupied by a strong staff.

Instead of going to Jaffa directly, we went to Beirut, in Syria, to spend ten days in quarantine. Jaffa has a bad harbor and no quarantine accommodations. We spent a night and a day on the Mediterranean. We saw few ships. Yet we were sailing in front of the most interesting of all lands and in front of what was once the commercial center of the globe. The first land we saw was Mt. Carmel. We were reminded of Elijah's contest with the priests of Baal, and of the cloud no larger than a man's hand, seen by the servant of the prophet. Toward evening we dropped anchor in St. George's Bay. Here, according to tradition, St. George killed the dragon. Before us lies Beirut. The buildings belonging to the American Mission occupy a conspicuous position and can be seen from afar. In the background is "grand old Lebanon with a diadem of stars around his snowy turban, looking for all the world like some august monarch of the universe, with his head in heaven and his feet on the sea." In Beirut, it is said, Christianity early gained a foothold, and became the seat of a bishopric. An earthquake shook the place and ruined the city, overthrowing colleges, churches, theaters, palaces, and burying many hundreds of all classes under the debris. Many villages are seen on the sides and crest of Lebanon. Sixty miles distant is Damascus, and near Damascus are Baalbeck and Palmyra. It would be a pleasing experience to visit these places, but we are in quarantine, and can not go ashore for any purpose. For several days the sea was rough. The eating saloon is fitted up with berths, and the men and women and children that occupied them were in all stages of sea-sickness. They were groaning and vomiting all the time. The sights and sounds and smells were not conducive to comfort or appetite. A strong stomach and philosophic mind are worth more to a traveler than rubies. The food was abundant, and not bad; the cooking suited those to the manner born better than strangers; but the toothpicks were the best I have seen since leaving home. In fact, I do not see how they could be better. One bottle of wine is served to each passenger at luncheon, another at dinner, and rum and cognac at tea. The rules say that if anyone wishes a greater quantity, or at different times, he must pay extra for it. The supply would seem to be ample. The rules amused me. One states that passengers, as persons of education, are expected to treat each other with respect and to pay due regard to *the fair sex.* When women smoke and drink as much as men, which sex is fair? And which is foul? I wish to know. We have on this ship a most unique collection of fat women. There is nothing like it on the planet. On what meat do they feed that they have grown so great? The men cannot compare with their affectionate spouses.

To spend ten days on a ship in quarantine is not the most delightful experience imaginable. We had the consolation of knowing that the thousands in the lazaretto on the shore are immeasurably more uncomfortable. Some read and write, and read and sleep. Others play cards, sing, talk, and long for the close of the tenth day. The words of the hymn have new meaning, "Fly swifter round, ye wheels of time." The experience is all the harder because we know that there is no need of any quarantine. Neither England, nor Austria, nor Italy feels any danger. Cholera microbes could not live in this atmosphere ten seconds. The stenches would poison them in an instant. One day we were taken ashore to be fumigated. As the ship had no bath-room and no soap, it would seem that something of the kind was necessary. We were taken to some rickety sheds and were obliged to wait there for hours. There was no bench or chair on which we could rest. The bedding and clothing of the deck passengers were steamed. The sailors were asked to put on some clothes belonging to the station while theirs were being cleansed. The clothes offered them were so foul with vermin and filth that they refused to put them on. This resulted in a dead-lock which lasted for an hour. The first and second-class people were taken into a room and sprayed. One man held the nozzle and the other turned the crank. In ten seconds the work was done. The quarantine officers themselves needed to be soaked and scraped. They were filthier than any on the ship. The whole performance was a roaring farce. We were pronounced "clean," but we were no cleaner than before. Those who pronounced the word ought to have placed their hands on their mouths, and their mouths in the dust and cried, "unclean, unclean." When, on the last day, officers came on board to collect twelve francs from each passenger, we understood why we were kept in quarantine. The government is bankrupt, and here was a chance to get some ready money. The nation loses more than it gains; the policy is short-sighted and opposed to all good sense. No matter for that. It yields some money to-day; to-morrow can take care of itself. The night before our release we had an illumination. The passengers and crew bought fireworks, and turned night into day. When the yellow flag was hauled down and we were free to go ashore, our joy was boundless.

I called to see the Presbyterian missionaries. Americans have been at work in Syria for seventy years. There are now sixteen men and twenty-three women on the staff. Some of the best known men are: Drs. Bliss, Porter, Van Dyck, Post, Jessup, and Schauffler. Others equally noted have been connected with the mission in former years. There are five central stations: Beirut; Tripoli, with twenty-seven out-stations, and reaching to Aleppo; Abeih, in Mt. Lebanon, with twenty-eight out-stations; Zaleh in Cœle-Syria, with nineteen out-stations; Sidon, with twenty-four out-stations, and reaching nearly to Galilee and Nazareth. The methods of work are: Preaching, teaching, publishing, and healing the sick. The Gospel is preached at ninety-one places. In the 127 primary schools there are 6,384 pupils, while hundreds are being trained in the high schools, seminaries and academies. The Syrian Protestant College has 292 students in the Preparatory, Collegiate, and Medical departments. The Theological Seminary has a strong corps of teachers. The large hospital belonging to the Knights of St. John is under the control of the medical men in the mission. Last year 10,314 patients were treated in the polyclinic. An industrial school and an orphanage for boys have been organized in Sidon. The Mission Press prints 25,000,000 pages a year. The Bibles circulated by the Levant Agency in sixty years number 1,550,000. The Church of Scotland has a mission to the Jews in Beirut. The Society for the support of British Syrian Schools has seven schools and a training institution; the Kaiserwerth Deaconesses have an orphanage and a boarding school for girls, there are schools for blind men and women. Miss Taylor has a school for Moslem girls. The United Presbyterians are at work in Latakia, and the Irish Presbyterians in Damascus. I visited the college in Beirut. The buildings are large and suitable. The hospital is all that could be desired. This mission has been greatly blessed in its workers and in its work. The Syrians speak in high praise of the American mission.

It was hoped by many, years ago, that the missionaries could reform the churches of the East from within. These churches were not willing to be reformed. When Bird and Goodell came to Beirut, the Patriarch of the Maronites launched his curse on the man that rented them a house. The whole family was excommunicated. "Let the curse envelop them as a robe, and spread through all their members like oil, and break them in pieces like a potter's vessel, and wither them like the fig-tree cursed by our Lord himself. And let evil angels rule over them, to torment them day and night, asleep or awake, and in whatever circumstances they may be found. We permit no one to visit them, or employ them, or do them a favor, or give them salutation, or converse with them in any form, but let them be avoided as a putrid member and as hellish dragons." When the Friends began work in Palestine and Syria the priests said, "Cursed be you if you look at this English missionary, because he is not sent from God, but by the devil." When they bought a plot of ground on Mt. Lebanon for a training house they said, "Cursed be this place! Let no grass grow upon it, nor flower bloom upon it; let no tree grow upon this cursed place; cursed to eternity, because it belongs to the English people." The place flourished, nevertheless. But those priestly anathemas reveal the mental attitude of these churches toward all who may seek to arouse them out of the slumber of ages.

I found T. R. Gibson, the American Consul, a very genial fellow. While I was in quarantine he wrote me a kind letter and sent me a bundle of papers. Mr. Gibson is from Augusta, Georgia, and knows the Lamars, and the Pendletons, and George Darsie, and Z. T. Sweeney, and C. S. Lucas. He has the hospitality of the Southland. I spent several pleasant hours with him and Dr. Schauffler in the consulate. I shall remember their kindness many a long day.

As the sun was setting, we weighed anchor, and steered away toward Jaffa, reaching our destination at daybreak. Though Jaffa has a bad harbor, it is the best on the coast of Palestine. Here Hiram sent the timber for Solomon's temple. From Jaffa, Jonah started on his memorable voyage. Here all pilgrims going to Jerusalem land.

JERUSALEM.

ST. PETER'S, ROME.

LII.

FROM JAFFA TO JERUSALEM AND RETURN.

It was in Jaffa that the Lord taught Peter that he was to call no man common or unclean. He was on the housetop of Simon, a tanner, at the time. This house is still pointed out. On the roof I read the account of Peter's vision. The guide took me to the site of the home of Dorcas. It was in this city that she did her good works and alms-deeds. Her return to life caused many to believe in the Lord. The influence of this woman has been felt in every part of Christendom. J. E. Hanauer, an agent of the London Jews' Society, is stationed here. He preaches to those who will listen, meets inquirers in the Book Depot, visits the people in their homes, and goes out to the Jewish colonies near Jaffa. He has Jewish blood in his veins, was born in Palestine, speaks several languages, and, as far as I could judge, is a capital man for the place. I found him an intelligent and agreeable gentleman. The Church Missionary Society is at work among the Moslems and others. Mr. Wolters is at the head of the mission. In the boys' school there are one hundred and thirty pupils and four teachers. Miss Arnott, a Scotch lady of means, has undertaken to educate the girls at Jaffa. She has a large boarding school and five day schools. The Church Society has several deaconesses here. I met Miss Armstrong and Miss Newton only. They visit the women in the city and in the district. The British Hospital is the principal religious institution in Jaffa. It was built by Miss Bessie Mangan, the daughter of an Irish clergyman. She had a small fortune, and came to Palestine to work at her own charges. Within a year after her arrival she started a medical work. She learned dressing, bandaging and dispensing. She opened the hospital with twenty patients. The new building has forty-five beds. The in-patients number four hundred and seventy-eight; the out-patients nearly thirteen thousand. The staff consists of one physician, six deaconesses, one dispenser, and two ward attendants. In the chapel there is a service before every clinic. Most of the patients are Moslems. A few are Jews, Druses, Roman Catholics, Protestants and Maronites. The walls are adorned with texts in different languages. The

New Testament is within the reach of all. Miss Watson took me all over the premises. The wards are clean and neat and cheerful. The faces of the nurses are bright and joyous. The patients manifest their gratitude in many ways. They kiss the hands and feet of those who care for them. Some are hard to manage. They swallow a box of pills or powders in the papers and eat forbidden fruit. The deaconesses go out into the villages near Jaffa. Men and women gather about them and ask to hear something from the Book. They conduct mothers' meetings, a school for Moslem girls, and night schools, and a Bible-class for young men. Thousands of Moslems hear the Gospel every year. The light and love and life seen in this hospital must tell on the surrounding darkness. Miss Mangan, on one Christmas eve, made a feast for beggars. The blind, lame, diseased, people without hands or feet, cancerous, epileptic, in rags and dirt and loathsomeness unspeakable, assembled around her Christmas tree to hear the truth and to be warmed and filled. Years ago this saintly woman went to her reward. Miss Newton succeeded her as superintendent of the work.

In the afternoon I took the train for Jerusalem. Some think this was what Isaiah had in mind when he spoke of " a highway and a way " over which the ransomed of the Lord shall return and come to Zion with songs and everlasting joy upon their heads. This can hardly be so, for the prophet said, "*The unclean shall not pass over it.*" The train took us through the fertile plain of Sharon. In one field I saw a reaper at work; in all the others the harvesters used the sickle. The first stop was at Lydda. It was here that Æneas had been sick of the palsy for eight years. To him Peter said, "Æneas, Jesus Christ maketh thee whole; arise, and make thy bed." This miracle led all that dwelt at Lydda and Sharon to turn to the Lord. From this place Peter went to Joppa at the urgent call of the disciples, when Dorcas died. Our next stop was at Ramleh. Tradition says this was the Arimathea of the Gospels. The guide pointed out the valley of Ajalon and said that it was over it Joshua commanded the moon to stand still. Far up the mountain he called attention to a place which is said to be Beth-horon. We passed through Samson's country, and saw the place where he caught the three hundred foxes whose tails he tied together with firebrands between them before sending them into the standing corn of the Philistines. We passed near Beth-Shemesh. It was in Ekron that the Philistines laid the ark on a new cart drawn by two milch kine whose calves were kept at home. The kine followed the highway till they came to the border of Beth-Shemesh. We saw the ancient Bether. It was here that the Jewish nation, as such, ceased to exist. After a war with the Romans, lasting three years and a half, under Bar-Cochba, a false Messiah, eight hundred thousand Jews were put to death. Our train reached the Jerusalem station before sunset.

Once Jerusalem was beautiful for situation, the joy of the whole earth. "Glorious things are spoken of thee, Zion, city of our God." The Psalmist said, "Walk about Zion, and go round about her; tell the towers thereof, mark ye well her bulwarks, consider her palaces." In Solomon's time silver was as plentiful as stones. It is not now. The streets are narrow and crooked and filthy. They are badly paved, and are neither lighted nor sewered. The water brought in from Solomon's Pools has been cut off. The people are extremely poor. Beggars are everywhere. I saw no palace and no home that looked as if it was occupied by a family possessed of wealth and culture. I was told that out of the forty thousand Jews in the city not more than four are rich. The government is the worst on the globe. There is no incentive to industry and economy. If a man is successful he deems it prudent to hide his wealth. Nevertheless, Jerusalem is a place to which foreigners from all parts of the world come. It is sacred to the Christian, to the Jew and to the Moslem. Here the most stupendous events in the history of our race took place. Six miles away the Son of the Highest was born. In this city he preached and wrought miracles. Here he was tried and condemned. Without its walls he was crucified and buried. He rose and brought life and immortality to light, and charged his disciples to go into all the world and preach the Gospel to the whole creation. Near by he ascended to the Father. Here the apostles tarried till the Spirit was poured out, and here on the day of Pentecost the first Gospel sermon was preached, and three thousand souls were added. To the Jews Jerusalem was the city of the great King. To it the tribes went up to give thanks to the name of the Lord. Jerusalem was the center of all their hopes and joys and aspirations. "Out of Zion, the perfection of beauty, God hath shined." To the Moslems the city is second to Mecca only.

There is no lack of religious institutions. The Greeks have seventeen monasteries, and convents, and churches; the Latins have fifteen, while the Copts, Armenians, Syrians, and Abyssinians have buildings of their own. In the Church of the Holy Sepulchre there are between thirty and forty chapels and places of devotion. All the Eastern bodies have places of their own. These sects hate each other with a perfect hatred, and are so ready to fly at each other's throats that Turkish soldiers are kept on guard all the time to keep the peace. Bishops and priests and monks and nuns swarm on the streets. I was informed that while they are ready to compass sea and land to make proselytes, they do nothing whatever for the conversion of Jews and Moslems. If a Jew went near the Church of the Holy Sepulchre, he would be roughly handled, if not torn to pieces. Missions in Jerusalem are carried on by three societies and by some independent workers. Fisk and Parsons, agents of the American Board, were the first missionaries in modern times. The American Board, after some years, abandoned the field.

Dr. Barclay spent three and a half years here. His great book is still regarded as one of the best on Jerusalem. The London Jews' Society has a church, schools for boys and girls, a house for inquirers, in which they are taught trades, a book depot, and a hospital. I went through all the buildings and saw all the work. Dr. Wheeler and his associates are busy early and late. The in-patients in one year number 900; the prescriptions 45,575; and the patients visited in their own homes, 5,676. I went with him part of one day. It is impossible to describe the destitution and misery of these poor Jews. At the same time they are as proud as Lucifer, and are insolent, unmanageable, and unthankful. Because of God's oath to Abraham they are going to be saved in any event; the coming of Christ is a mere detail. The Church Missionary Society works among the Moslems and among the decayed churches of the East. This Society has agents in Jerusalem, Jaffa, Nazareth, Salt, Nablous, Ramalleh, Gaza, Haifa, Acca, Ramleh, Kefer Yasif, and Bir Zeit. It has eleven clerical, four lay, twenty-five female, and ten native workers. It has forty-five schools, with 1,873 pupils; 544 communicants; 232 in-patients, and 37,263 out-patients. Its policy is to have a church, a hospital, and a school at each station. The workers are expected to go into the towns and villages in the neighborhood, and publish the good tidings. I met most of the workers in the city. In Miss Welch's school there are 135 girls and twelve preparing to teach. I visited the famous school on Mt. Zion, founded by Bishop Gobat. There are fifty-four boys in the collegiate department and seventeen in the theological. When this school was started it was the only school in Palestine. Now there are a dozen of such schools conducted by the Latins and Greeks. Not only so, but the Turks have opened schools in every central town and in every village, and have prohibited Moslem children from attending Christian schools. The school on Mt. Zion has more applicants than it can take.

The Germans are doing a good work. Pastor Schneller has an orphanage with one hundred and fifty boys and twenty girls. He is enlarging the premises, and hopes to have a thousand in a year or two. The orphans are fed, clothed, educated, and taught trades. The cheerful old man took me through the establishment and showed me budding carpenters, blacksmiths, potters, turners, shoemakers, tailors, printers, binders, and teachers and evangelists. He has been in this delightful work thirty-six years. From the orphanage I went to the Talitha Kumi. This is a school for girls under the control of the Kaiserwerth Deaconesses. There are one hundred and seventeen boarders, and some day pupils. The girls are taught the common branches and housekeeping, and some other things. This school has been in operation for fifty years. Across the way is a large hospital under the same management. On the way home I called at the Moravian Leper Asylum. The buildings are spacious and attractive. Scriptural texts cover the walls. Some of the inmates have no hands or eyes. The building will hold fifty. It is not more than half full. The superintendent told me that lepers prefer to marry and beg rather than submit to the discipline of the asylum. The Germans have a church in the city.

Mr. Ben-Oliel and family are independent workers. He was born in Tangier of Jewish parents. He claims to be of the tribe of Judah and of David's line. The family motto is, "Arise, shine!" He was led to Christ in his youth, was educated for the ministry, and has spent forty years in the service. He has labored in Spain, in Rome, in North Africa, in Asia Minor, and in Palestine. He speaks eight or ten different languages. In his own hired house he meets Jews and Greeks and Moslems, and preaches the kingdom of God and teaches those things that pertain to the Lord Jesus. In the touring season he conducts services in an upper room. Mrs. Ben-Oliel has a class for mothers; Miss Evangeline has a girls' school, Miss Voltz has an industrial class. Two sons are in school in England, one is in Canada, Miss Florence is at work in the United States in the interest of the mission. I visited this family three or four times. Mr. Ben-Oliel took me to the top of the house and showed me the city and its surroundings. He pointed out Gordon's Calvary, the Mosque of Omar, the Tower of David, the Mount of Olives, the mountains of Moab beyond the Valley of the Jordan and the Dead Sea, and the new part of Jerusalem without the walls. He went with me to several places of interest and explained, as only an intelligent enthusiast can, many things that were obscure to me. This family showed me no little kindness.

Missionary work in Palestine is carried on in the face of many difficulties. The government is openly and actively hostile. Since England's recent humiliation it is more so than ever. There are decrees that accord religious liberty to all Turkish subjects. Professedly, all are equal before the law. But practically it is not so. If a Moslem should confess his faith in Christ, he would be drafted into the army, and in a few days he would die from poison or the sword. Confession means death. Among the Jews a convert is met with the scorn, contempt, and hatred of his people. He must renounce all hope of help which otherwise he would receive. Most of the people are entirely dependent on outside support. Their extreme poverty holds them back from avowing the truth. The priests warned their people not to attend the school conducted by Miss Ben-Oliel. The warning run thus: "If sons are born to those who disobey, there will be no one to circumcise them; if any get married, there will be no one to give them the nuptial blessings; if any die, they will not be buried with the Jews." In the Eastern churches a convert is denounced and persecuted. Bishop Gobat hoped to reform these churches from within, but he found it impossible to do this. Those who called for reforms were driven out. When one was found reading the Bible he was required to kiss a picture or kneel before it, or invoke the Virgin or some other saint, or else promise not to read the Bible any more. In spite of all these hindrances the missionaries' work goes on. They are assured that God reigns, and that no power will be able to prevail against him. They are permeating society with Gospel truths and with new ideas; they are making the people restive under despotism and eager for a change; they are preparing them to come out and confess Christ when the day of freedom comes. They are driving the government to do what it never dreamed of doing before. Thus in Nazareth it has a girls' school with 700 enrolled; in Jerusalem it has another with 200 pupils and a strong staff. Inquirers come to the missionaries and then go back to the priests for answer. They do this again and again, and compel their former teachers to meet their arguments or confess that they cannot. So the truth spreads and the kingdom is advanced.

I visited the churches, convents and hospitals. I saw formalism, ritualism, ceremonialism, but few signs of spiritual life and power. The worshipers kiss, bow and pray, and go away as they came. Candles are burning everywhere, but the people walk in darkness, though the true light is shining. In the company of a soldier, a messenger from the Consulate, and a sheikh, I visited the Mosque of Omar and the other mosque on the temple area. It was on this mount that Abraham offered Isaac. Here was the threshing floor of Ornan, the Jebusite, where the plague was stayed. Here Solomon and Nehemiah and Herod each built a temple. The mosque is a handsome building. Its dome is the most conspicuous object in Jerusalem. The other mosque was built by Justinian as a church. One cannot help being thrilled while standing on ground trod by prophets and kings and apostles and by the Son of God. Leaving the sacred inclosure, we came to the Jews' Place of Wailing. Men and women were kissing the stones that formed part of the wall around the temple, and weeping. They say in their sorrow, "The holy cities are a wilderness. Zion is a wilderness, Jerusalem a desolation. Our holy and beautiful house, where our fathers praised thee, is burned up with fire; and all our pleasant things are laid waste." From the Psalms and Prophecies and Talmud they select appropriate passages to express their grief.

I found a community known as "The Americans," though most of them are from other nations. They number about one hundred. I tried to learn their principles and practices. I found them more ready to argue than to explain. They do not believe in preaching, and hold no public services. They quote, "The *life* was the light of men." They have no schools, save one in which their own children are taught. Some of them teach in three Jewish schools. They teach German, French, music and drawing. If any one is sick they offer their services as nurses. If any come to them in need, they do what they can to afford relief. I asked one of the leading men what they were doing. He said: "We are waiting on God. He said, 'Thou shalt love the Lord thy God with all thine heart, and with all thy mind, and with all thy soul, and with all thy strength, and thy neighbor as thyself.' Is that not enough?" He went on to tell me that Christ waited for thirty years before he began his ministry. So they are waiting. They hear a voice behind them saying, "This is the way; walk ye in it." They are waiting for further guidance. They require wives and husbands to separate, and to be sisters and brothers. The leader has the seven eyes of God, and can discern thoughts and motives. Some of them have been here fifteen years. Some are growing old. For them the night is coming, and if they are going to do anything, it is high time they were setting about it. There is nothing in the Prophecies they do not understand. One woman began to talk about the tower of Hananeel and what the prophet had said about it, and many other things, till I was bewildered. I attended one of the services they hold for themselves. Each one took part just as he pleased. The comments were crude, and the repetitions a weariness to the flesh. The leader told me they were all poor; that they had no friends upon whom they could rely for support; that they published no reports; that, while they had seen very hard times, they were now out of debt; and that more had left all, as they had done, and were on their way to join them. I thought of the Frenchman's criticism of the charge of the Light Brigade: "This is magnificent; but it is not war." Thirty years ago, one hundred and fifty-five Americans came to Palestine to introduce the arts of civilization. They understood that the Jews were about to return, and the Millennium was about to begin. Two are left. They still hold fast to their interpretation of the Prophecies, but are engaged in pursuits other than those contemplated when leaving America.

I went several times to see the place that is now supposed by many to be Golgotha. It is outside the walls, not far from the Damascus Gate. Mr. Ben-Oliel pointed out the spot where he thinks the crosses stood. We went together to the garden of Gethsemane. There are olive trees of a great age, but it is not certain that they were there the night of the betrayal, or that the walls now standing inclose the real garden. But somewhere on that hillside the Savior prayed that the cup might pass without his drinking it. The valley of the Kedron lies between the garden and the city. Farther up the Mount of Olives he wept over Jerusalem. Over the ridge is Bethany. There he went for sympathy and rest at the close of busy days in the temple. The site of Bethphage was pointed out. From this village the young colt came on which he made his triumphal entry into the city. Somewhere near Bethany he said to the apostles: "But you shall receive power, after that the Holy Spirit is come upon you; and you shall be my witnesses both in Jerusalem, and in all Judæa and Samaria, and unto the uttermost part of the earth." Here he ascended and sat down with the Father on his throne. As we were walking about the city we came to the tents of Dr. Bliss. He is now in charge of the Palestine Exploration Fund work. He showed us what discoveries have been made and what they signify. Evidently the walls at one time inclosed a much larger area than they do now. He has discovered sections of a former wall and a gate on the edge of the valley of Jehoshaphat. It must be borne in mind that the walls have been broken down several times. The Romans plowed Zion like a field and sowed it with salt.

ST. SOPHIA, CONSTANTINOPLE.

ARMENIAN SCHOOL IN CONSTANTINOPLE.

The debris in places inside the walls is not less than fifty feet deep. We passed the Pool of Siloam and some monuments of considerable antiquity, and followed the valley of the Kedron till we struck the road leading to our hotel. I could not help thinking of the strange fortunes of this city. David took it from the Jebusites. In after years it was taken by the Egyptian, the Babylonian, the Macedonian, the Asmonean, the Roman, the Persian, the Arabian, the Frank, and the Turk. The names of Peter the Hermit, of St. Bernard, of Godfrey, of the Baldwins, of Richard Cœur de Lion, of Saladin, of Philip Augustus, and others are inseparably connected with this city.

In company with a friend I went down to the Jordan and the Dead Sea. On the way we passed through Bethany. There are some forty buildings, mostly in ruins. They show where the home of Mary and Martha stood, the grave of Lazarus, and the site of the house of Simon. Miss Crawford has built a mission house at the edge of the village. The government has scared away her girls, but they will return in a few weeks. The Dead Sea is a beautiful sheet of water. It is so salt that nothing can live in it. Six million tons of fresh water fall into it every day, but it is not sweetened. The Jordan is about thirty yards wide. It is a swift and muddy stream. We spent one night in Jericho. The village that bears this name is said to be built on the site of Gilgal. We were shown the ruins of ancient Jericho, the spring that Elisha healed, the scene of our Lord's temptation, the place where the Israelites crossed the Jordan, and Nebo and Pisgah beyond. On the way we rested for an hour at the Khan of the Good Samaritan. For some distance our road was in sight of the brook Cherith. It was here that Elijah was fed by the ravens. We made a second excursion to Hebron. We passed the tomb of Rachel, the place where Elijah slept one night and left the print of his body in the rock, the Pools of Solomon and the sealed fountain that supplied them. An English woman offered $100,000 to repair the pools and the pipes, but the government would not consent to have the work done except on conditions to which she could not accede. Hebron is in the Valley of Eshcol. It was here that the spies got the cluster of grapes which they carried back as a sample of the fruits of the land. It was in Mamre that Abraham dwelt. There God appeared to him and told him of his purpose to destroy Sodom. In the cave of Machpelah Abraham and Sarah, Isaac and Rebekah and Jacob and Leah are buried. The Mohammedans have built a mosque over the cave. The Prince of Wales and several other persons have been permitted to enter the cave, but all others are rigidly excluded. Here David reigned for seven years. Hebron is one of the strongholds of Mohammedanism. The people are intensely fanatical. Mr. and Mrs. Murray, agents of the Missionary Alliance, have been conducting a school here for girls. They had seventy pupils. Four times has it been broken up. For three months no one has dared to come. Parents have been threatened with a ruinous fine and imprisonment in case they sent their children. Mr. Murray is lame, Mrs. Murray is blind, but they see the Invisible, and walk in his ways. They feel that they are doing the Lord's work, and they have entered into his joy. The Mildway Mission has four agents here and a large dispensary. Dr. Patterson is a cheery Scotchman; his helpers are as brave and as hopeful as he is. The authorities say, "We like your medicine, but not your preaching." They have tried to break down the work. A decree said that if any woman went to this place she would lose her veil, and her husband would be driven through the streets with this veil about his neck. The people are scared away for a time, and then return. The day I was there the patients numbered seventy-two. Some days there are as many as one hundred and twenty. The workers in Hebron are, in my opinion, "friends of God" as truly as was Abraham. On the way home we visited Bethlehem, and saw the place where it is said Jesus was born of the Virgin, and where the manger in which he was cradled stood, and the field where the shepherds kept their flocks when the angels sang the first Christmas carol. This was the home of Ruth and Boaz, of Jesse and David. The women and children are cleaner and better looking than any others that I have seen in Palestine. There are churches without number in this place. The Germans have schools for boys and girls. At the close of a busy week in and about the Holy City, I took the train and returned to Jaffa.

LIII.

THINGS PALESTINIAN.

In Palestine the Monks and Moslems have located the scene of every important event. In most cases they have built a convent or chapel or mosque over it. The religious feeling and the desire for revenue are at the bottom of this. The place from which the dust was taken to make man, the grave in which Adam was buried, the dunghill on which Job sat and scraped his boils with a potsherd, the olive tree in which Abraham found the ram caught by his horns, the cistern into which Joseph was thrown, the spot on which Elijah slept on the way to Horeb, the stones that would have cried out if the children would hold their peace, the place where the cock crew when Peter denied his Lord, the ground on which the tree from which the cross was made grew, the way our Savior was led from Pilate's judgment hall to be crucified, the place where he spoke to his mother, the point where Simon was compelled to bear the cross, the hole in which the cross stood, the rock that was rent during the earthquake, the stone on which he was anointed, the tomb in which he slept, the exact spot from which he ascended to the Father—these and many other places have been identified. Pilgrims follow the traditional route and stoop down and kiss the stones and wash them with their tears. They do not stop to think that the streets our Lord walked are fifty feet below those over which they walk.

The claims of the Monks and Moslems are nearly all disputed. As accurate surveys are made it becomes clear that most of the places shown as the scenes of great events cannot be the true places. There is no event connected with our Lord's passion and death and triumph of which we can say with assurance that it took place on this precise spot. The Latins and Greeks have built the Church of the Holy Sepulchre over the alleged site of the crucifixion and burial, but competent judges hold that they were mistaken, and give such cogent reasons for their convictions that, to say the least, it is an open question. On the Mount of Olives the Mohammedans have a stone with a footprint in it, and they say that here our Lord stood just before he ascended. But the place does not fit the narrative.

Luke says that he led them out until they were over against Bethany; and he lifted up his hands, and blessed them. While he blessed them, he parted from them, and was carried up into heaven. But the stone of the Moslems is about two miles from Bethany. Speaking with Dr. Bliss about the uncertainty of the different places connected with interesting events, he said, "What does it matter? It is best so." Instead of thinking about places and worshiping them, we should rather think of the Christ and worship him. There is no room for doubt as to the site of Jerusalem and the temple, of the Valley of the Kedron and the Mount of Olives, of Bethlehem and Bethany, of the Jordan and the Dead Sea and the Sea of Galilee. We can be certain as to the main features of the land, but not of the very places where great deeds were done or where great events took place.

Most of the people in Jerusalem are supported by Baron Rothschild and other rich Jews. Sir Moses Montefiore, in his day, did much for his countrymen. I once heard Dr. Jessup make a remark to the effect that the early churches did a thing of doubtful propriety when they took up collections for the poor saints in Jerusalem, for they have been expecting collections ever since. There are no manufacturing concerns in or near Jerusalem aside from the industrial schools connected with the different missions. The country round about is a desert. The city is kept up by tourists and pilgrims and the gifts of people everywhere. It would be far better if such gifts were cut off and the people thrown on their own resources. The present system pauperizes them and robs them of their manhood.

"Backsheesh" is the commonest word in Palestine and in the whole East. It is the first word you hear on your arrival and the last on your departure. It signifies a gift. Rich people give simply because people ask. Americans are sinners above all others in this respect. Begging is a profession. It is as natural for these people to hold out their hands to a stranger as to breathe. Children are taught to do this as soon as they are born. I have heard little things that could scarcely walk or speak lisp "'sheesh." Here, as elsewhere, money is power. Give a Customs official some backsheesh and you can go through without a word. There is no door that will not open to the liberal hand. If you want attention at table or in your rooms or on the road, you can have it if you will pay the price. Churches, forts, mosques demand backsheesh in some form. The Consul's servant brings you a letter and insists on backsheesh. The donkey boy at the close of the day does the same.

No matter how much you give, the recipient is not satisfied. Some millionaire gave more. Precedent is equivalent to a statute. One does it; hence all must do it. This is an ancient custom. Solomon gave Hiram some cities in return for help afforded him in building the temple. He was not satisfied, and sneered at the gift as if it was beneath his dignity to receive. A donkey boy uses the same language to-day. The whole business of giving gifts, whether we call them backsheesh or tips, is a nuisance. For every service there should be a fixed price. When that is paid the obligation should be discharged. In Palestine and in Pullman palace cars and in hotels, the demand for gifts in any shape is provoking. The system is un-American, and should be abolished.

People are more demonstrative than at home. When they get on or off a boat there is the greatest possible noise, and the least possible system or speed. Pandemonium is a Sunday-school in comparison. Passengers and boatmen engage in fierce altercations. A stranger expects to see blood flow in torrents, and wonders what disposition will be made of the dead. He is surprised to find that no blows are struck and no blood shed. After the storm there is a great calm, and all depart in peace and harmony. At weddings the mirth is boisterous. At funerals hired mourners tear their hair and scratch their faces and scream as if their sorrow was boundless. Men kiss each other and women kiss each other on all occasions. When one lovely woman kisses another lovely woman the performance is stale, flat and unprofitable. The game is not worth the candle. When one big-bearded man kisses another big-bearded man on both cheeks and on the mouth, the performance is little less than scandalous. Not that kissing is to be always and everywhere and by all tabooed. The true view would seem to be expressed in the words, "A kiss in season, how good it is!"

Many races and languages are represented in Palestine. In Jerusalem there are between twenty and thirty languages spoken. On the day of Pentecost there were seventeen nations represented; there are more than that number now. One sees all kinds of dresses and people of all colors. A curious thing is this. The blacks do not envy the whites or feel any sense of social inferiority. Color counts for nothing. The blackest Soudanese and the brownest Bedouin feels as contented with his complexion as the whitest tourist from the North. The Moslem is catholic in his tastes. He takes black and brown and white beauties into his harem. The children are all equal.

Women are the inferior sex. Few can read. Little concern is

felt for their education. Marriage is the great goal of every girl's life. She is married at ten or twelve. Dr. Post tells of a grandmother aged twenty. Mothers' meetings are often made up of mere children in age, and babes in intelligence. Early marriage is an obstacle in the way of a thorough training. In Palestine Moslem women cover the whole face. In Egypt the eyes are visible. Divorce is easy and common. A Moslem says of his divorced wife, "She was my slipper, but I kicked her off." The marriage bond is as slight as that between the slipper and the foot. Owing to her degradation, she is not expected to have anything to do with religion. Thomson says, "Women never join in the prayers in the mosque." There is a place where they can hear, but that is separated from the auditorium by a screen. Spanish Jewesses are expected to go to the synagogue only once a year. Woman occupies a higher place in China than in Moslem lands.

In Palestine one sees the effects of bad government. In Solomon's time the population must have been 5,000,000; now it is about 650,000. In a trip to the Dead Sea we saw very few people. We met some Bedouins from Ramoth-gilead and the Jordan valley going to market. Every man had a long musket on his back and a sword or a knife in his belt. Their goods were on camels or asses. Tourists are required to take a military escort. If England or America was in Palestine there would be peace and safety. We saw some black tents occupied by nomads, but very few houses. The country is rocky and sterile. It is difficult to see how such a land could support a teeming and prosperous population. Palestine was called a land of wheat and barley, a land of fountains and depths, a land whose stones were iron, and out of whose hills the people could dig brass. It is not so now. One sees no vine-clad hills and no fertile valleys. Bad government causes the land not to yield her fruit. Trees are cut down to escape ruinous taxation. Flocks and herds are slaughtered for the same reason. There is no legal limit to the taxes imposed: If a farmer has one-tenth left for himself he is fortunate. If he refuses to pay the amount asked, it is doubled, and soldiers are quartered in his house. Before they will leave the last farthing must be paid, and every soldier must have a gift. With a good government the valleys would be covered with corn and the hills would bear grapes and figs and olives and pomegranates. Instead of the parched ground there would be a pool and grass with reeds and rushes. Gladstone has said that the function of government is to make it easy to do right and hard to do wrong. That is not the Turkish conception, but to tax the people. The Turkish power is not a government in any true sense of the word, but an instrument of oppression. The people are poor; under Turkish misrule they can never be rich. The worst elements of human nature are brought to the surface. Under an absolutism the subject races are compelled to resort to lying and subterfuge. Truth would result in spoliation and death. The government is opposed to Christian education. It fears schools more than any thing else.

I was in Palestine in June. The tourists were all gone. On this account the expenses were not more than half as much as in the season. The sun was not oppressively hot. In Jerusalem I slept under warm covers every night. The fleas and mosquitoes did not trouble me. I had heard much of these pests, and expected to be devoured by them. I thought of pennyroyal and insecticide and nets and screens. But I did not suffer. If there were any of these noxious creatures about they left me alone. It is said that the king of the fleas holds his court in Tiberias. It may be that his subjects were there in attendance upon his majesty. In any event I was thankful to be relieved of their presence and attention.

What of the future of this land hallowed for all time by the life and death and resurrection of the Son of God? Some are looking for the return of the Jews precedent to the coming of the Christ in power to carry on to completion the redemption of the world. Meanwhile other nations covet Palestine. Russia wants it. She has large buildings in Jerusalem and elsewhere. She has erected high towers for military purposes. From these one can look over the whole land. France wants it and Syria as well. The government could not be worse; it would be better under any other power. Palestine is still the Holy Land. To it pilgrims come from all parts of the earth and read the Divine Book on the ground where it was written with such sidelights as they can get from the geography and climate.

LIV.

FROM JAFFA TO CONSTANTINOPLE.

Leaving Jaffa, the first place of importance passed was Cæsarea. This was the home of Cornelius. Here Peter preached and opened the door of faith to the Gentiles. Here Philip the evangelist and his four daughters that prophesied lived. Before the fall of Jerusalem Cæsarea was the chief political city in Palestine. It was the residence of the Roman procurators. Here Paul was kept in prison for two years. Here he reasoned with Felix of righteousness, temperance and the judgment to come. Here he spoke before Festus and Agrippa and Bernice. Cæsarea is now in ruins. Our first call was made at Haifa, at the base of Carmel. Leaving Haifa, we proceeded to Beirut, and spent part of the day there. Between these points are Acre and Tyre and Sidon. Before Acre three hundred thousand Crusaders perished. Tyre was mistress of the sea. This was once the crowning city, whose merchants were princes, whose traffickers were the honorable of the earth. Tyre said of herself, "I am a God, and sit in the seat of God, in the midst of the seas; I am of perfect beauty." By her wisdom and understanding she got riches, and because of her riches she lifted up her heart and forgot God. We are told that from Arabia and Abyssinia on the south to Armenia and Georgia on the north, and from the frontiers of India to the utmost isles of Greece, and far beyond, caravans by land and ships by sea carried a commerce rarely excelled in extent or variety by any city of any age or country. To this proud and voluptuous city God said, "I will make thee like the top of a rock; thou shalt be a place to spread nets upon." Tyre was destroyed by Nebuchadnezzar, by Alexander and by the Saracens.

"Dim is her glory, gone her fame,
Her boasted wealth has fled;
On her proud rock, alas! her shame,
The fisher's net is spread.

"The Tyrian harp has slumbered long,
And Tyria's mirth is low;
The timbrel, dulcimer and song
Are hushed, or wake to woe."

At one time great nations were found around the Mediterranean. From all these the glory has departed. This is true of Syria, Phœ-

ARMENIAN PATRIARCH.

LEO XIII.

nicia, Palestine, Philistia, Egypt, Carthage, Rome, and Greece. The commercial supremacy enjoyed by Tyre, Alexandria, and Venice has passed to London and Liverpool, to New York, Chicago, and San Francisco. Only the sea remains as it was. "Time writes no wrinkles on thy azure brow; such as creation's dawn beheld, thou rollest now." Its beauty remains, but its relative importance is much less now than it was two thousand years ago.

From Beirut we went on to Tripoli and spent several hours there, taking on and putting off cargo and passengers. From there we steamed on to Latakia and Alexandretta. This last place is the port of Aleppo. On the way we passed Selucia and Antioch without calling. At one time Antioch was the third city on the globe. It was "The Eye of the East." In the history of the church it is second only to Jerusalem. Some men from Cyprus and Cyrene preached in this city to the Greeks. The hand of the Lord was with them, and a great number that believed turned to the Lord. Barnabas was sent to Antioch by the mother church. He found the work so great that he needed an associate, and went to Tarsus and brought Saul back with him. They labored here a whole year. In Antioch the disciples were first called Christians. Here the Holy Spirit said, "Separate me Barnabas and Saul for the work whereunto I have called them." From this point they started on their first missionary tour. From Selucia they sailed to Cyprus. As we crossed their course I read the account given in the Acts. Though Antioch has fallen, and though Mohammedanism has displaced Christianity as the dominant faith, it is pleasant to know that a little group of Disciples of Christ meet there week by week to break bread and to exhort one another to cleave to the Lord with purpose of heart. Our next stop was at Mersina, the port of Tarsus in Cilicia, the birthplace of Paul, the grandest man of the ages. Mersina is a flourishing place. The Reformed Presbyterians are at work here. We left in the evening. The next morning we were in Larnaka, Cyprus. I went ashore and called at the Presbyterian mission. The man in charge can speak a little English. He explained that an American was coming to take charge of the work. Paul and Barnabas and John landed at Salamis, and went through the whole island to Paphos. There they met Elymas, the sorcerer, and Sergius Paulus, the proconsul. Because of his opposition the sorcerer was smitten with blindness. The proconsul, seeing what was done, believed, being astonished at the teaching of the Lord. Cyprus is now a British colony, and is increasing in wealth and in population. Missionaries are free to enter and preach and teach Christ. From

Cyprus we proceeded to Rhodes. After a few hours we continued our voyage. We saw land all day. The isles of Greece were on the left and Asia Minor on the right. One of the seamen pointed out Patmos, the scene of John's splendid visions. Our last call before reaching Smyrna was at Chios, the birthplace of Homer.

Every Turkish village and city has its mosques. From the minaret the muezzin calls the people to prayer five times a day. Once all Asia Minor was Christian soil. Paul reasoned and persuaded as to the things concerning the kingdom of God. "And this continued for a space of two years; so that all they who dwelt in Asia heard the word of the Lord, both Jews and Greeks." The apostasy foretold took place. The people became engrossed in the discussions about dogmas and pictures, and the enemy came in like a flood and swept them all away.

On going ashore at Smyrna I got a guide and started to find the Isaac Errett Memorial Chapel. On the way we met one of the brethren. He could speak a few words of English. The building is in a good part of the city, and is well suited to the purpose. For five years there has been no pastoral oversight. As a result, some have gone back to the world. Those that remain are anxious that some one should be sent to aid them. Smyrna is a thriving city. The population numbers two hundred and fifty thousand. The American Board has a large work here. Besides preaching, it has a number of schools. In those schools English, Arabic, Turkish and Armenian are taught. All these languages are needed in this city. Mr. McLachlan, formerly of Toronto, explained to me the nature and extent of the work. The German Baptists have one man here. He was born in the East, and speaks many tongues. He came from America a year or two ago. I was told that there are no Turks in business in Smyrna. The Turks cannot compete with Greeks, Syrians and Armenians. In every case they go to the wall. This is one reason why the Turks hate the Christians. Their daily prayer is that the lives and possessions of the "infidels" should be given to the "faithful." Col. Madden, of Danville, Ill., is the American Consul in Smyrna. He is proud of the fact that he is an American, and is pleased to see Americans. In the touring season he goes out in a boat with the American flag flying to meet his countrymen, and to render them any assistance in his power. The Customs officer searched my pockets and felt me all over from head to foot. I asked him if that was right. He got his hat and cane and went with me to the Customs house. He spoke to the official in a way that alarmed him. He confessed his fault, apologized, and pledged himself not to do so again. This was not the first time that an American citizen had been subjected to this indignity, but the Consul is determined that it shall be the last. Praise God for such consuls as T. R. Gibson, of Beirut, and Col. Madden, of Smyrna. The Turks have not dined and wined and flattered their Americanism out of them. They are Americans first and last and always, and they take delight in assisting and protecting Americans whenever they can do so. Smyrna was the seat of one of the seven churches of Asia. The others were in Ephesus, Pergamos, Thyatira, Sardis, Philadelphia, and Laodicea. None of the seven now exists. When the Turks took possession of Asia Minor their only conception of land was that it could be only profitably used as pasture. Cities were destroyed that their sites might be used to raise grass to feed flocks and herds. Smyrna was the home of Polycarp. When he was called upon to deny his Lord he said: "Eighty-six years have I served him, and he has done me good and not evil; how then can I deny him?" He did not renounce his Lord.

Our first call after leaving Smyrna was made at Mitylene. After a little we rounded the cape of the Troad and caught our first glimpse of Europe. We saw the plain where the long duel between the Greeks and the Trojans was fought. Homer has immortalized the place and the contestants. We know Achilles and Agamemnon and Ajax and Diomede and Ulysses and Nestor and Hector and Paris and Priam as well as we know the heroes of the Revolution. We saw Mt. Ida and the Scamander. Here it was that Paul "saw in a vision a man of Macedonia," and heard him say, "Come over into Macedonia and help us." In answer to that call he carried the Gospel to Europe. We were obliged to stop at the Dardanelles and show our papers. Here are strong forts armed with Krupp guns. A little further on we came to the place where Xerxes built his bridges. The sea swept away his work. In anger he scourged the sea and threw fetters into it. Here the Ottoman Turks crossed and set up their standard in Europe. Here Leander and Byron swam across the stream. Further on still is Gallipoli, the first European town taken by the Turks. This is at the entrance to the Sea of Marmora. The Hellespont is thirty-three miles long; the Marmora is one hundred and ten miles. We fell asleep soon after entering the Marmora. The next morning we dropped anchor in the Golden Horn.

LV.

CONSTANTINOPLE, GIOL DAGH AND BARDEZAG.

We had scarcely dropped anchor when G. N. Shishmanian and his son John came to the boat to help me through the Customs Office and to take me to their own home. Entering a civilized country is a simple matter; but Turkey is not that. Turkey is the only country that required me to show my passport before allowing me to land. The guide books say that if one will give the official a franc, one's baggage will be examined at once and very slightly. I was in favor of doing this, but Mr. Shishmanian is opposed on principle to bribing officials. He has lost thousands of pounds because he would not bribe Turkish officers to do their duty. For this reason the bulk of his patrimony has been tied up in the courts for years, and is likely to remain there for all time. I could not but admire his conscience, though it cost me four times as much in the end as if I had followed the guide books. Because I did not hand the official a franc, my baggage was detained, that my books and papers might be scrutinized. Only one objectionable paper was found. The Turks are very careful as to the books and papers they admit. An Englishman had his copy of Milton seized. The reason assigned was that Milton had spoken disrespectfully of Adam. They consider Adam a distant relative, and they will brook no reflections upon him. Leaving the baggage in the Customs Office we went to the Mission House. The whole family united in giving me a genuine Kentucky welcome. I was at home in the twinkling of an eye.

The Mission home is in the Armenian quarter. The services are held in a part of the house. I spoke twice through Mr. Shishmanian. These were seasons of refreshing from the presence of the Lord. The day school has eighty-five pupils; it could have three hundred if there was room. For five years Mr. Shishmanian has been trying to get a permit to carry on this work. He has submitted the text-books used and the certificates of the teachers and the programme of the school. He has been promised a permit, but has not received it. When we called at the Legation the interpreter said that the Minister of Education told him the permit was ready, and to ask Mr. Shishmanian to call and get it. We called that very day. The Minister was delighted to see us, and treated us to cigarettes, and asked what he could do for us. The business was explained in a few words. He said that the clerk that had the matter in hand was not in, but he would attend to it and let him know when he could call and get it. He will hear no more until it is necessary to harass him again. As the case stands, the police can close the school at any time. When the property was damaged with the earthquake he asked for a permit to make repairs. He was put off from time to time with plausible excuses. Then he employed men and put them to work. The police called and forbade him to proceed. He locked the doors and went on. The police called to the workers through the key-hole to stop, but they were as deaf as adders, and kept right on till the work was done.

The second morning after my arrival we started to visit the brethren at Giol Dagh and Bardezag. We left home before day and reached the railway terminus in the evening. The next day we took horses, and, after a ride of six hours, reached Giol Dagh. There are no roads most of the way. Our guide had never been to the place, and we got lost. After wandering about like babes in the woods, we found the trail and soon reached the village. The people poured out to see us, and made every provision for our comfort. They gave us the best rooms, and killed and cooked their tenderest chickens. We had two public services. In the evening they filled the house, and we had singing, Scripture reading and prayer. One woman was pointed out to me. Her husband used to threaten to kill her if she did not cease coming to these meetings. She manifested the wisdom of the serpent and the harmlessness of the dove and the amiable obstinacy of her delightful sex, and gained her husband. Now he is as devoted as she is. One man threatened to kill Mr. Shishmanian. Now he is one of the most active men in the place. There are thirty-five believers in all. Eleven of these have been added recently. They need a house which they can use as a school and a chapel. They have a lot and the timber and the stones; they need $125 to pay the carpenters and masons for their work. The people are very poor. They live in the simplest style. Their raiment and homes are of the most primitive character. They are far from markets and are heavily taxed. They are afraid to raise fruits for themselves. If they did the Turks would rob them. They are so situated that they cannot prosper. Children are as plentiful as blackberries. If the saying, "Happy is the man whose quiver is full of them," applies here, these people must be unspeakably happy. The village is surrounded with Turks. In the past winter men were on guard every night. One night was fixed upon for an attack. That evening the Turks heard that the Armenians were rising, and that it behooved them to be on their guard. Because of this rumor there was no massacre. Giol Dagh is high up on the mountain side. The believers meet to sing and pray and to celebrate the Lord's death and to exhort one another to hold fast the beginning of their confidence steadfast unto the end.

Leaving Giol Dagh and coming down into the valley, we took a train for Nicomedia. At this point we left the railway, crossed the bay, and took a carriage for Bardezag. We found the people busy with their silk worms. Most of the men were away at work in the mountains. Those that were at home were pleased to see us, and gathered in the evening for a service. Their joy and gratitude were very touching. Here, as everywhere, the people are extremely poor. One family connected with the church is in fairly good circumstances, but they are preparing to migrate to America. There are about thirty disciples in Bardezag. They need a teacher and preacher and a house of their own. We returned to Nicomedia the next day, and saw the brethren there. There are only three in all. We comforted and exhorted them and departed. Nicomedia was once the capital of the Roman Empire. Here Diocletian had his palace and throne. Here he originated and superintended one of the "ten persecutions," and at its close wrote on the coins of the Empire, "The Christian religion has been destroyed." Here, after his abdication, he cultivated cabbages and turnips. Nicomedia is now a place of no consequence. That afternoon we took a train and returned to Constantinople.

One is not in Turkey long before one gets some practical knowledge of Turkish officials and Turkish misrule. When we came to the end of our journey we asked the Chief of Police to register our passports. He said that was not necessary, and handed them back. No sooner had we reached Nicomedia than the police asked to see our passports. They said that they had not been registered as they should have been at the end of the journey, and that we must pay a fine of twenty-five piasters each. Mr. Shishmanian told him what the Chief of Police had said, but no explanation would avail; we must pay the fine. There was no alternative. On our way down from Giol Dagh our guide led us up to the front of the station, instead of making a long circuit and coming up from the rear. The ticket agent would not sell any tickets till we paid a fine of two hundred piasters. We had no choice. We could not ride on the train without tickets, and we could not get the tickets without paying the fine.

Mr. Shishmanian's history and work are full of interest. He was born in Asia Minor, and took a course in Dr. Hamlin's Academy on the Bosporus. He spent some time in Egypt as an interpreter, and then went to America. At that time he hated the Disciples with a perfect hatred. He made the acquaintance of John Tomline Walsh, but when he heard that he was a Disciple he would neither visit nor eat with him. In Dallas, Texas, a quiet business man asked him to go to church with him, without saying anything to him about the church. Kirk Baxter was the preacher. He presented some truths in a new light. The hearer was interested and went again. It was not long till he was baptized. Soon after he was in Lexington preparing himself for the work of the ministry. God led him back to Turkey, and has protected and guided him ever since. He can eat anything and sleep anywhere. He sings and talks all day. He enters into all the trials and sorrows of his flock. They come to him for counsel and assistance. He is a father to the poor. His house is a castle. American flags hang on the wall. The people feel secure under his roof. I was reminded constantly of the words, "The name of the Lord is a strong tower; the righteous run into it and are safe." No wonder the people love him and confide in him. No wonder there are faces that watch for his coming, and look brighter when he comes. Mrs. Shishmanian was born in Lexington. She has the pluck of her race. Should the Sultan order a massacre in Constantinople, she will give a good account of herself. Of her it can be said that she has labored much in the Lord, and "has been a succorer of many, and of mine own self." John is a young man nearly grown. He is a fine lad, and will make his mark. He is a student in Robert College. His mind inclines to architecture. I feel sure he will yet find his way into the ministry. He and his sister, Orienta, aid in the music and in many other ways. They sing and play well. Lucy is the youngest, and is the pride and joy of the family. May the blessings of the Most High God be upon her and all dear to her. One cannot be in that family very long without feeling, "Surely the Lord is in this place; this is none other than a house of God and a gate of heaven."

LVI.

MISSIONS IN TURKEY.

Mr. and Mrs. Shishmanian reached Constantinople and began work in 1879. The Gospel was preached publicly and from house to house. Schools were opened and children taught. Tracts were published. These were carried far and near. The converts were scattered throughout the Empire. Dr. Kevorkian joined the mission later. He made Marsivan the center of his operations. Besides preaching and teaching he carries on a medical work. Hohannes Karagiozian was employed for a time in Marash. Other helpers have been raised up from time to time. As a result of this diversified activity, many heard, believed, and were baptized. The converts from the first, so far as they are known, number about one thousand.

Owing to sickness, the missionary family moved to Bardezag and lived there for a season. Mrs. Shishmanian gave me a graphic account of the first baptism. The house was full, and hundreds were without. They were eager to see and hear. They crowded about the door and tried to force an entrance. The wife of the owner of the building seized a club and stood at the door and said, "I am not a Baptist, but if any man comes in here he will get his head smashed." One lad hid himself in the ladies' robing room and watched the proceedings and listened to the preaching through a hole in the floor. The women discovered him and squealed as usual, and called for help. Mr. Shishmanian came to the rescue, and led the lad out by the ear. About midnight many left and the others became so quiet that the baptisms could proceed. Seventeen were buried with Christ on a confession of their faith in him. The woman that stood guard at the door was baptized subsequently, and is one of the most faithful of the flock.

Those who read the tracts sent out by Mr. Shishmanian wanted fuller information concerning the matters treated in the tracts. They sent him urgent invitations to visit them. He has visited Smyrna, Adàna, Biridjik on the Euphrates, Zarah, Sevas, Erzeroum, Bitlis on the Lake of Van, and many other places. When he was in Adana, Cilicia, a young man named Leon Filian came from Tar-

SCHOOL IN CONSTANTINOPLE.

sus, bringing a letter from Moses Filian, his father, asking him to visit Tarsus, if possible, on his way to Marsivan. He had read some of the tracts, and desired an interview. Two days later he visited Tarsus. They talked till midnight, and spent all the following day discussing and searching the Scriptures. Late in the evening father and son were fully convinced of the truth, and expressed a desire to be baptized. The next morning they were baptized in the River Cydnus. The father returned to Antioch and preached the Gospel there. There is now a church of thirty souls in that place. In June last, Mr. Shishmanian received a letter from a man who said: "Six years ago one of your tracts came into my hands and became the means of the salvation of my soul." He did not know the writer or the place of his abode. The letter went on to say that when he made known his convictions, the church of which he was a member thrust him out. He remained aloof from them for two years. When he heard of Azariah Paul he sent for him and was baptized. Since then he has preached to the best of his ability, and has baptized quite a number. At his preaching there are sometimes twenty-five, and sometimes more, present. Malkhas Melconian, a blind beggar, preached in Russia. He knew the Bible by heart. On his travels he fell in with one of the brethren and was baptized. He preached in Nachtiven and Shushee, and baptized seventeen. The Russian authorities arrested him and kept him in prison for three months, and took away his blind books. After he was let go he preached in Russia and in Turkey. Dr. Kevorkian lives in Marsivan, but he has opened a number of stations in that part of the country.

The work is carried on in the face of many difficulties and discouragements. Nothing can be done among the Moslems. They will not permit any book or paper attacking Mohammedanism to be published. No new school can be opened without the consent of the Sultan. That means that it cannot be opened at all. No permit to erect a school or a church can be obtained. Old laws are stringently enforced, and new laws, more severe than the old, are enacted. Officials are suspicious, and scent mischief where no mischief exists. Mr. Shishmanian took me to see a brother who had been in exile for seven years. He had been a school teacher in Sevas, and was respected by all who knew him. One day a brother asked him to write some words for him in Armenian and Turkish. These words were stuck on a board and carried through the streets. The words ran thus: "O men and brethren, perhaps this is our last day, and who knows whether we shall be alive to-morrow! There-

22

fore let us repent and leave off all our sins, and pray to God that he may teach us the way of truth, for the fearful day of judgment is at hand." This man preached some, and wanted to get an audience. For this act they were arrested and sent to Africa. After reaching the coast they were supplied with a camel and some bread, and given to some Arabs to escort them to Fezzan. The Arabs would not let them ride the camel or eat the bread. With some money they bought a kid. The Arabs used to say, "Pigs, become Mohammedans, or we will cut your throats." They drew their swords across their necks to give emphasis to their threats. They took them by force and circumcised them. They were allowed three loaves a day, and nothing else. They sold one and got some fuel to warm their drinking water or to get some vegetables. One died soon after reaching Fezzan, the other is in Constantinople, but he is afraid to go to church lest he should be arrested on the way. Last winter some fifteen or twenty of the brethren were massacred. Among the number was the blind beggar who had preached in Russia. He was asked to become a Mohammedan. He refused, and was murdered.

The Armenians are living in such dread that they do not dare to attend the services. Not only so, but they are afraid to sleep at night. In the morning they say, "Would God it were evening;" and in the evening they say, "Would God it were morning." There are rumors of all kinds in the air; it is impossible to verify them. If the Sultan orders a massacre, all who can are to make a bee-line for the mission premises. As many as can get in will be safe. There they will be under the protection of the American flag. But what of the thousands that cannot get in? They will fare as Armenians fared elsewhere. We know what their fate was. In one place the eyes of four hundred men were gouged out and strung like beads on a string. Three hundred girls and women were stripped and made to parade the streets. A hundred choice Armenian youths were bound like sheep for the slaughter. Sheikhs, reciting verses from the Koran, went along and cut their throats. In one place the people took refuge in the cathedral, expecting to find it a sanctuary. Soldiers went into the pulpit, and after the doors were locked began to shoot. This process being too slow they used the sword. Their arms growing weary, they saturated the building and people with coal oil and applied the torch. Mrs. Shishmanian told me how the son of her washerwoman was treated. He was arrested and asked what he knew about some secret society. He was a simple lad, and carried the clothes his mother washed backward and forward. He knew nothing and could tell nothing. They tortured him by rolling him in hot ashes, and then asked him to tell what he knew. He could tell nothing. Then they poured alcohol on the back of his hands and set the alcohol on fire and burned off the cords. The poor boy is a cripple for life. Old women were stripped to the waist, and boiling water poured over them to extort confessions. We hear of the meekness of Moses and the patience of Job, but these ancient worthies lived in better times and among civilized people. The Pharaohs were very decent fellows compared with the Sultan and his underlings. And as for dear old Job sitting on a dung-hill and scraping his boils with a potsherd, that was positive recreation compared with what missionaries in Turkey undergo every day. In the midst of it all our missionaries never forget that they are Christian gentlemen, and never cease to exhibit the gentleness and patience of Christ. Talk of heroism! This is the genuine article in a concrete form and of the purest and highest type. In no part of the world, not in Africa or China, is mission work so perilous and discouraging as in Turkey.

We called on the workers of the American Board. This Board has been in Turkey for many years, and has done a great work. It has twenty-six central stations and over three hundred out-stations. In these are one hundred and seventy-six American missionaries. The Board has property worth $650,000. The work has five departments, namely, the Publication, the Educational, the Evangelistic, the Medical, and the Relief. In times of famine, pestilence, or persecution, the last is the most important. There are fifty-one colleges and high schools, and four theological seminaries, and many common schools. The whole number of schools is 20,496; the whole number of native teachers, 564. Medical work is carried on in Aintab, Cæsarea, Mardin and Van. The evangelistic work is considered of supreme importance. The present number of churches is 125; of members, 12,787. The places for stated preaching are 327; average congregations, 34,370; ordained native preachers, 100; unordained preachers, 128.

In the recent massacres the American Board suffered greatly. The property destroyed is estimated at $125,000. Twenty preachers and teachers were murdered. One teacher was sent to prison for ten years. His offense was this: A copy of the London *Times* containing Lord Salisbury's speech was found in his house. The prisons are full of people. They are not brought to trial; no charge is made against them; their crime is this: *They are Chris-*

tians. The missionaries have acted a noble part, they have stood by their flocks and rendered such assistance as they could. There is no doubt that their presence awed the Turks and kept them from doing many things that they had it in their hearts to do. In Harpoot the American missionaries and three hundred Christians were in one building. A committee of Mollahs came and called Dr. Barnum out and said, "Your only hope is in becoming Mohammedans." Dr. Barnum said that that was impossible. The Mollahs went back to the others. The people within sang a hymn, prayed and pledged each other to die rather than deny the faith. The building was set on fire, but the Mollahs did not wish to kill so many Americans and drew off. Some boys went down and put out the fire. At one point the friends of the missionaries used their rifles and saved the girls' school from outrages worse than death. The Board was able to forward thousands of dollars, and to successfully intervene when all other help failed. Hundreds of thousands of destitute persons were fed and clothed, and, while overwhelmed by unexampled and immeasurable calamity, were pointed to the consolations of the Gospel. The work done by the agents of the Board during the past year is deserving of world-wide recognition and honor. They shall have their recompense at the resurrection of the just.

Those who know most about the condition of the country urged me not to go to Marsivan to see Dr. Kevorkian. Brigands of all kinds abound. Recently two women connected with the legations were seized and carried off to the mountains. The government paid $50,000 for their release. I reluctantly gave up all thought of going to Marsivan. Dr. Kevorkian is there alone. In the time of the massacres his school was closed for a little while. The wife of the Governor was very sick. He was called in, and by the blessing of God healed her. The Governor said to him, "You are a good man; go on with your school; no one shall molest you." This promise has been kept. Last year, when he was in Constantinople, his papers were seized and he was detained there for months. The American Minister said to him, "You are a fool to go back. The Turks will surely kill you." He said, "Get my papers, and I will go back at once; they can kill me if they wish."

Lew Wallace said: "I have often been asked, 'What of the missionaries of the East? Are they true, and do they serve their Master?' And I have always been a swift witness to say, and I say it solemnly and emphatically, that if anywhere on the face of the earth there exists a band of devout Christian men and women, it is

1. Greek Patriarch. 2. Armenian Catholicos. 3. Armenian Patriarch.

EASTERN PATRIARCHS.

these. They live and die in their work; their work is of that kind which will be productive of the greatest good." This evidence is all the stronger when it is remembered that its author is a Turkophile. Lord Shaftsbury spoke of the American missionaries as a happy combination of piety and common sense. And we know that this testimony is true.

LVII.

CONSTANTINOPLE AND THE TURKS.

CONSTANTINOPLE is situated at the junction of the Bosporus and the Sea of Marmora. It consists of three divisions: Stambul and Pera-Galata in Europe, and Scutari in Asia. The European divisions are separated by an arm of the sea called the Golden Horn. It was so named because it resembled a stag's horn and because it supplied the people with an inexhaustible quantity of fish. The Golden Horn is about a thousand yards wide at its mouth and about four miles long. There is room in it for twelve hundred ships. Its waters are so deep that the largest war ships can moor close to the shore. More than six hundred years before Christ a colony of Greeks settled on what is now called Stambul. They called their city Byzantium. Constantine took this city, doubled its size, built a wall around it, made it the capital of the world, and called it Constantinople. He invited ancient and wealthy families from Rome to make it their home. Artists, and scholars, and merchants were drawn thither by the hope of gain.

A glance at the map of the Roman Empire will show that Constantinople occupies an unrivaled position. It is in Europe, but within easy reach of Asia. It lies between the Black Sea and the Mediterranean. All ships going and coming paid her tribute. The provinces adjacent were populous and opulent. Under Constantine and his successors the New Rome became the center and source of good government and the teacher of law and civilization. Gibbon tells us that whatever was manufactured by the skill of Europe or Asia, the commerce of Egypt, and the gems and spices of farthest India, were brought to her for many ages. There was a prospect of security for life and property and increase in wealth.

Constantinople has a great history. The part she has played entitles her to be regarded with feelings akin to those we cherish towards Jerusalem, Athens, and Rome. In the year 668 the Arabs made their first attack. They were beaten back, but they were not dismayed. Mohammedanism never gave up the hope of ultimate conquest. One writer says that there is nothing in the history of the West to compare with the tenacity and continuity of the struggle in the East. In the West two or three great battles were fought. Charles Martel at Tours, and John Sobieski under the walls of Vienna, broke and beat back the armies of the Prophet of Arabia; but in the East there were ceaseless struggles for centuries. Constantinople was assailed by the Huns and other savages from the north of the Black Sea, and by the Arabs and Turks from the south. Army after army was annihilated, but others took their place, and the work had to be done over again. Constantinople spent her strength fighting the battle of Europe against Asia, of Christianity against Mohammedanism. And though she fell at last, time was gained in which the West grew strong enough to drive back the invader in 1683, and to say, "Here shall thy proud waves be stayed." Constantinople was the citadel against which the hitherto irresistible wave of Moslem invasion had beaten and had been broken. Had it not been for the perfidy and ambition of Venice it is very probable that this great city would never have fallen into the hands of the Turk. Venice prevailed on the leaders of the Fourth Crusade to turn aside from the mission in which they were engaged to conquer and punish their great commercial rival. The city was taken and sacked. It is a sad and shameful story. Never, we are told, was there a more barbarous sack of a city than that perpetrated by those soldiers of Christ, sworn to chastity, pledged before God not to shed innocent blood, and having on them the emblems of the Prince of Peace. The lust of the army spared neither the maiden nor the virgin dedicated to God. Violence and debauchery were everywhere. Pillage was unrestrained, lust unbridled. Soldiers acted as if they had been trained to commit every crime. They made the chief church in the city the scene of their profanity. A prostitute was seated in the Patriarchal chair, who danced and sang ribald songs for the amusement of the spectators. Because of this the Balkan Peninsula has been in the hands of barbarians for four centuries and a half, and all attempts to expel the Turks from Asia Minor have failed.

One historian says: "Under the Emperors of the East, Constantinople preserved the treasures of ancient thought and learning, whilst the rest of Europe was plunged in barbarism, and became the greatest commercial city in the world. She sent missionaries who gave to the Sclavs their alphabets, and imparted to them some rudiments of civilization, and most of the Greek manuscripts we possess were at one time stored in her libraries. The capture by the Turks scattered Greek learning among the Latin and Teutonic races; and Greek manuscripts of the Bible conveyed to Western

Europe were one of the principal causes of the revival of learning." Out of the revival of learning came the German Reformation. In this city Justinian's legal reforms were made. The Code, the Institutes and Pandects were prepared by his agents.

Mohammed II. took Constantinople in 1453. Since that time it has been the seat of Turkish Government, religious and secular. Saint Sophia has been changed into a mosque. This great church was built by Justinian. Columns were taken from the temple of Diana in Ephesus, from Aurelian's temple of the Sun, and from Egypt. When the building was completed, the Emperor said: "Glory to God, who hath thought me worthy to accomplish so great a work! I have vanquished thee, O Solomon!" A good judge pronounces it the fairest and noblest church in the world. The Greeks said to the Russian envoys: "What! do you not know that the angels come down from heaven to mingle in our services?" This noble structure was defaced and defiled. Minarets were erected and other additions made to adapt it to Mohammedan worship. But Saint Sophia was a church, and, please God, it shall be a church again. Mosques have been built in all parts of the city. They are by far the most conspicuous objects in the whole landscape. There can be no doubt as to the dominant faith in Constantinople. The city of Constantine and Theodosius and Justinian and Chrysostom is the most thoroughly Mohammedan city in Europe or Asia, with the exception of Mecca. The Sultan is not only an absolute monarch, but Khaliff as well. The whole Mohammedan world, with the single exception of Persia, look to him as their spiritual guide. Not only so, but the Greek and Armenian Patriarchs and the chief Rabbi of the Jews live there.

While I was in Constantinople, I could not but deplore that the feuds of Christian people enabled the Turk to enter Europe. For the Turk in Europe is as much out of place as a pig in a parlor. The Turks were converted to Islam while they were savages. Islam arrests development; consequently the Turks are where they were a thousand years ago. They have a thin veneer of civilization, and by courtesy they are called civilized, but they are not. In policy and in practice the Turk is a savage. He is not a builder; he is a destroyer. Asia Minor has been desolated. Ephesus is a ruin. Nicea is a village. Hundreds of towns and cities have disappeared; mines have been deserted. People do not raise more than enough to support life. The nerve of endeavor has been cut. All incentives to enterprise and economy have been done away. The countries under Turkish control are capable of supporting ten

Mrs. Shishmanian. G. N. Shishmanian. Dr. Garabed Kevorkian.

MISSIONARIES IN TURKEY.

times their present population. Mesopotamia is naturally one of the most fertile countries on the globe; Mesopotamia is occupied by nomads. Turkey ought to be as prosperous as the United States or England. There is there the natural basis of a populous and wealthy empire. But the people are indescribably poor. There are almost no roads. Agriculture is in a very backward state. Labor-saving machinery is all but unknown. The women spin and weave as their ancestors did three thousand years ago.

I was told by several that the Turkish government is not a government in any true sense of the word. It is a machine to tax and oppress and exterminate the people These are words of truth and soberness. The first duty of a government is to maintain peace, and to protect the lives and property of the people, and to foster industry. A great statesman has said: "What we wish is that where there has been despondency there shall be hope; where there has been mistrust there shall be confidence; where there has been alienation and hate there shall be woven the ties of a strong attachment between man and man." Nothing could be more foreign to the Turkish mind. There is no sense of security. The safeguards that Christian nations place around the individual, so that he can not be deprived of life, or liberty, or property, except for cause and by due process of law, are unknown in this empire. In former times the Armenians were the bankers of Constantinople. It is so no longer. They were accused, imprisoned, and their property confiscated. There are only a few left; soon there will be none. If the Turks covet the lands or homes of the subject races, nothing is easier than to get possession. The owner is arrested and tortured till he is willing to assign all his rights to his accuser. The streets swarm with police and soldiers. They parade the streets mounted and afoot. Spies are abroad in all sorts of disguises. Innocent men are sent to prison, or into exile, or to the gallows. They have no trial in which reliable witnesses are called to testify. The courts afford the accused no protection and no redress. Justice is bought and sold like any other commodity. If the Palace demands a man's condemnation he may as well abandon hope. I heard a court official tell of a man who was brought to trial. His innocence was demonstrated. One judge refused to condemn him. Another was called in, and the man was sentenced to fifteen years of hard labor. The Palace demanded that he be condemned. Men are hung on the streets, not because they have done any wrong, but to warn others.

Improvements are prohibited or discouraged. The telephone

and the electric light are forbidden. There is no local post in Constantinople. There is no such thing as rapid transit. These things might enable the people to concoct a revolution. An officer is in every newspaper office to see that no obnoxious words or sentiments appear. He reads the articles before they are printed. No criticism of any officer or of any action is allowed. Whatever is done must be praised. If any additional proof was needed that the Turk is a savage, the recent massacres supply it. Every intelligent man in Turkey believes that the Sultan planned and superintended these atrocities. The people did not rise of their own accord and kill and ravish; they acted under orders. The Sultan is responsible for the massacres and their attendant outrages. One proof is this: *No foreigner was killed.* Mobs do not discriminate so carefully. Not less than eighty thousand Armenians perished, and thousands of others were subjected to unspeakable outrages. This massacre was a blunder as well as a crime. The Turk does not work; he is a leech on the body politic; he expects to fill an office or serve in the army. The people put to death were among the most industrious in the nation. They created the wealth and paid the taxes. They supported the Turks. To kill them was to kill the goose that laid the golden egg. What is the result? The nation is on the verge of bankruptcy. No business is done. The custom house does not take in enough to pay the officials. Money has to be sent to the Asiatic provinces to support the Government. Police and soldiers and other officers are unpaid. The army is ready to mutiny. The interest on the public debt can not be paid. The Armenians have been decimated, bankers and traders have been plundered—but to what purpose? The savage has overreached himself. There is nothing in history to be compared with the Armenian massacres. Herod, and Nero, and Domitian, and Jack the Ripper were mere tyros in butchery when their deeds are placed beside those of the present Sultan. The Turk would not allow the name of Armenia to appear on the maps or to occur in any school book or to be published in any paper. He would blot the name from the records and minds of men. Meanwhile the world was ringing with "Armenia" and "Armenian atrocities." And if the Sultan shall find any place in history it will be as the destroyer of the Armenians.

Speaking to Mr. Shishmanian about those who had turned Mohammedans through fear, he said, "I wonder they do not all go over in a body. If a man says, 'I am a Mohammedan,' all persecution ceases. He is protected, provided for, and promoted to honor." But tens of thousands preferred death to apostasy.

We paid a visit to Robert College. Dr. Hamlin founded an academy; that grew into the present institution. Its property is worth $450,000. The pupils for the current year number two hundred and twenty-two. There are eight professors and fifteen other instructors. The pupils are from the Greeks, Armenians, Bulgarians, Protestants, Maronites and Nestorians. Robert College is built on one of the most beautiful spots in the world, and one of the most interesting in Turkey. It overlooks the Bosporus. From its tower one can see the Black Sea and Constantinople and the Marmora. It stands near the fortress built by the Turks before taking Constantinople. On the same place Darius crossed on his way to fight the Scythians. The Turks hate this school, and would be glad to buy and close it. They do all they can to hinder its progress. It took three years to get a permit to build a house for the President. They have difficulty in getting books and maps through the customs. Turkish boys are taken away from the school. Robert College helped to make Bulgaria. It trained its Prime Minister and other leading men. It has profoundly influenced Turkish politics. One Professor spoke hopefully of the future. He has seen the Turkish dominion curtailed. Persia, Hungary, Georgia, Greece, Algeria, Tunis, Cyprus, Egypt, Thessaly, Roumania, Servia, Montenegro, Bulgaria, Eastern Rumelia, Bosnia and Herzegovinia, and the strip of Eastern Anatolia containing Batoum and Kars: all these are either wholly or partly free from Turkish control. Because God reigns and his purposes can not be defeated, the day of Turkey's dissolution can not be very far distant. The Turk entered Europe because Christians did not keep the unity of the Spirit; the Turk is in Europe because of international jealousies. If these could be adjusted, he would leave Europe, bag and baggage, never to return. May God hasten his departure!

Mr. Shishmanian took me to see the Great Church and the Hippodrome. The Green and Blue factions used to contend there for the mastery. The seats have been used in building mosques. Half the site has been occupied by a mosque, the remainder is used as a parade ground. We went to see the old walls and the Seven Towers and the Golden Gate. Through this Belisarius and other successful generals marched in triumph. John took me to the top of one of the fire towers. The city has no fire engines or adequate fire department. There are two fire towers, and watchmen are there day and night. If a fire is seen, runners are sent to warn the people. Some firemen carry a machine on their shoulders and save the buildings of such as pay them for their services. Sometimes as many as two thousand buildings perish in a few hours. Mr. Shishmanian and John came with me to the ship. I had to show my passport to leave the country. A detective told the boatman that took us out to the ship that he took out two men without passports and he would hold him responsible for their return. I felt safer and breathed more freely after our ship got outside of Turkish waters. Turkey was the only country in my trip in which I felt any concern about safety. The first thing I did when I awoke in the morning was to feel whether my head was on or off. Then I looked around to see if the building had been burned during the night. Then I looked under the bed and searched the closets to see if any detectives were concealed there. I left with the highest admiration of those who remain and carry on the Lord's work in the face of manifold discouragements and dangers.

LVIII.

FROM CONSTANTINOPLE TO COPENHAGEN.

We left Constantinople as the sun was setting. As our ship steamed out of the Golden Horn and entered the Sea of Marmora we got our last view of this illustrious and picturesque city. The next morning we passed out through the Hellespont into the Ægean. During the day we saw the coast of Asia and Europe and many of the isles of Greece. We crossed Paul's course as he went from Troas to Samothrace, Neapolis and Philippi, bearing the Gospel to Europe. The second morning we dropped anchor in the Piræus. Going ashore, we took a carriage and drove to Athens. We felt at once that we were in a different atmosphere. Greece is as unlike Turkey as the sweet air of heaven is unlike a dungeon. Before one is through the custom house he feels that he is in a civilized land again.

After breakfast I went out to see the city. The center of interest to me was Mars' Hill. Standing where the High Court of Athens used to sit, I read Paul's address. Rejected at Philippi, he came to Thessalonica and Berea, and thence to Athens. In the synagogue he reasoned with the Jews and devout persons, and in the market-place every day with them that met him. Certain of the Epicurean and Stoic philosophers encountered him. They took him to the Areopagus, saying, "May we know what this new teaching is?" Athens then was the chief seat of Greek learning and civilization. She was, what Milton called her, "the eye of Greece, mother of arts and eloquence." No other city on the globe has produced so many great men. On all sides of Paul were masterpieces of genius. On the Acropolis were the Parthenon and the Temple of Victory. Over the most perfect building in the world stood the colossal statue of Minerva. Her shield and spear glittering in the sun, were seen by the sailors far out at sea, and served to guide them into port. The Agora was the center of a glorious public life. Here orators, poets, statesmen, philosophers, and artists found incentives of their noblest enthusiasms. Here the populace came together to hear or tell of some new thing. The place was adorned with temples, altars and other sacred buildings.

It is very different now. Athens is a modern city; there is little of the city of Pericles and Paul left. The Apostle's soul was provoked when he saw the whole city given to idolatry. It was easier to find a god than a man. They worshiped all the gods they knew and erected an altar to the unknown God. It is not so at the present time. These temples and altars have for the most part disappeared. The Temple of Theseus has escaped the hand of the vandal. Some columns of the great temple of Jupiter still stand. The Parthenon has been a church and a mosque; it is now a ruin. The Turks used it as a powder magazine. The Venetians bombarded it and fired the magazine and destroyed the building. Lord Elgin carried away most of the treasures that remained and gave them to the British Museum. The theater of Dionysos, the cradle of dramatic art in Greece, the place where the masterpieces of Æschylus, Sophocles, Euripides, and Aristophanes first excited admiration and delight, are silent and tenantless. The Pnyx was the place where the political assemblies were held. Here Demosthenes and others almost as eloquent were heard. This hill is deserted by all save tourists. The Athens of to-day has street cars, electric light, sewers, a palace for the king, schools, a university and a museum. It is now a crime to carry away any antiquities. I ran a race through the museum. Hurried as my visit was, it was sufficient to give a conception of its treasures. A month could be profitably spent within its walls. Some public-spirited men are endeavoring to reproduce as much of the old life and spirit as possible. The Olympic games are revived. A magnificent amphitheater of white marble is being erected. A new day has dawned on Greece.

One afternoon we drove out to Marathon. It was a long drive. The plain where the battle was fought is bounded by the sea and by a chain of high hills. Here ten thousand Greeks under Miltiades vanquished a Persian army twelve times as numerous. The Persians thought they were mad to attempt such an impossible enterprise. While they were musing the Greeks swept down upon them with incredible velocity and power and swept them into the sea. A large mound was built over the fallen Athenians; there is no other monument. As one stands on this plain he feels that "'tis haunted, holy ground." At Thermopylae, Leonidas and his three hundred held the whole Persian army in check till he was betrayed and his force annihilated. Soon after, at Salamis and Platea, the Persians were crushed and driven back from Greece forever.

As I walked through the streets of Athens, and as I met the people, I could not but ask: "What of the future? Is the golden age of this beautiful land in the past? Shall the race that gave to the world such men as Pericles, Themistocles, Socrates, Plato, Aristotle, Zeno, Phidias, Apelles, Praxiteles, not give many more of equal or greater ability? It should be so. In any case the past is secure. The whole world is thinking Greek thoughts and using Greek methods. The great names of Greece can never die.

> "Their spirits wrap the dusky mountain,
> Their memory sparkles o'er the fountain;
> The meanest rill, the mightiest river,
> Goes murmuring with their fame forever."

We crossed Greece from Athens to Patras by train. On the way we passed through many places; the most important of these is Corinth. In the New Testament time this city was noted for its wealth, its luxury and its profligacy. Aphrodite was its patron. In her temple a thousand priestesses ministered. In this city Paul came, after his apparent failure in Athens. Here he lived and worked with Aquila and Priscilla. Every Sabbath he reasoned in the synagogue and persuaded Jews and Greeks. When the Jews opposed and blasphemed he shook out his raiment and said, "I am clean; from henceforth I will go unto the Gentiles." He went into the house of Titus Justus. Crispus, the ruler of the synagogue, believed, and many Corinthians hearing, believed, and were baptized. The Lord appeared to him in a vision and said, "Be not afraid, but speak, and hold not thy peace; for I am with thee, and no man shall set on thee to harm thee; for I have much people in this city." Here he spent a year and six months. Here he reaped "the largest and noblest harvest ever given to ministerial toil." Corinth now is a small place. Most of the houses I saw are of mud, and are occupied by poor people. I met no missionary and heard of none. In Athens the American Minister told me that the Christians of the West evidently think the Greeks as good as themselves. Perhaps this remark applies to Corinth as well.

At Patras we boarded the ship which we left at Athens, and started towards Brindisi. Our course was through the Ionian and Adriatic Seas. We touched at Corfu and another small place. A ride of fourteen hours took us from Brindisi to Rome. The country is level much of the way. The fields are covered with vines and grain. The houses are small and poor. The people are meanly clad. The grain is cut and threshed in the most primitive way. Women work in the fields with the men. There are no signs of enterprise or prosperity. Towards evening we reached and crossed the Apennines. There are villages on the tops or far up the sides.

They were built there for defense. The peasants are grouped in villages, and seldom live on their farms. Long before reaching the city we saw the arches on which aqueducts rested for ages. Far against the sky we saw the mighty dome of St. Peter's.

Most of the buildings in Rome are modern. At the same time there are more buildings and ruins belonging to antiquity than in any city I visited. I saw the ruins of the palace of Caligula, the wall built by Romulus, the house of Germanicus, the church which Michael Angelo made out of the baths of Diocletian, the Coliseum, the church of St. John Lateran, the church of the Chains, the Forum, the Baths of Caracalla, the Pantheon, St. Peter's, the Forum and Pillar of Trajan, the Catacombs, the Vatican Museum and Gallery, the Tiber, the Cloaca Maxima, and St. Paul's Outside the Walls. The Coliseum is the most impressive ruin in the world. It held one hundred thousand spectators. On the arena gladiators fought, and Christians fought with wild beasts. The sports of that time were bloody and barbarous. The walls are standing; the seats and fixtures are gone or are broken down. The church of St. John Lateran claims to be the mother of all the churches in the city and in the world. It is the Pope's church. He lived in the palace adjoining before removing to the Vatican. St. Peter's cost fifty millions, and is the largest church in existence. It is built on the site of Nero's circus. Here Christians were clad in coats of pitch and burned like candles, while the Emperor acted as a charioteer. In the Vatican I saw the Laocoon, the Apollo Belvidere, the torso Michael Angelo so much admired, and all the other great works in that marvelous collection. In the Sistine Chapel I saw the celebrated frescoes representing the Creation and the Judgment. In Raphael's room I saw the Transfiguration and his other famous paintings. The earliest pictures of Christ made him as ugly as possible. The prophet had said, "His visage was so marred more than any man." Raphael and the latest painters represent him as the perfection of beauty. St. Paul's Outside the Walls has portraits of all the Popes, beginning with Peter and coming down to Leo XIII. This building claims to have the body of Paul under its altar. The Pantheon is the most perfect of all the buildings of antiquity. It is now a church. In it Raphael and Victor Immanuel are buried.

I called on the Methodist missionaries in their fine building. They gave me an account of their work in Rome and Italy. They have twenty-seven churches, property worth $160,000, twenty-four ministers, 1,083 members, 583 scholars in their Sun-

THE PARTHENON.

THE COLISEUM.

day-schools, ten boys in their Theological Seminary, while their publishing house sends out a million pages a year. The Waldenses, the Baptists, and several other bodies are operating in this field. In all, about 250 missionaries, pastors and evangelists are at work. The Congregation for the Propagation of the Faith has its home here. Its aim is to propagate the religion of Rome in all parts of the world. Its funds are adequate to the most expensive and magnificent undertakings. By it a vast number of missionaries are sent to the remotest corners of the globe, books of various kinds are published to facilitate the study of foreign and barbarous languages, houses are erected for the instruction and support of youths from pagan lands who are being prepared to return and work among their own people. It maintains charitable institutions for the relief of those who have suffered banishment or other calamities on account of their faith. Its revenues are vast, and its exploits incredible. Near by is the Seminary for the Propagation of the Faith. This institution is set apart for the education of those designed for the foreign field. Here they are brought up with the greatest care, in the knowledge of the languages and sciences that are necessary to prepare them for the most effective service. I called at the American Catholic College. The rector told me that sixty young men are there under instruction. The course is as high as that of the Catholic University in Washington. Rome is full of churches; the buildings are vast, and costly, and superb. At the same time they are of little value. The people are ignorant, and superstitious, and poor. It is with a sad heart one contemplates all this material grandeur and the condition of the bulk of the population.

Leaving Rome I passed through Pisa, Milan, Zurich, Schaffhausen, Heidelberg, and in due time came to Hamburg. In Switzerland I saw the Alps and several lakes, the St. Gothard Tunnel, and the Falls of the Rhine. North of the mountains the country appears more prosperous. Most of the workers in the field are women; the men are in the army keeping the peace. From Hamburg I went to Kiel. There we took a ship and crossed an arm of the Baltic to Korsor. From Korsor I went to Copenhagen by rail.

LIX.

IN SCANDINAVIA.

On reaching Copenhagen I found O. C. Mikkelsen and Julius Cramer waiting for me at the station. They took me to the pleasant home of Dr. Holck. I was surprised to learn that Mrs. Holck is an American. She was born and reared and married near Pittsburg. She has a good cook and a soft bed. The stranger within her gates feels thankful that he is alive to partake of such hospitality. Winsome little Maggie and John make the joy of the family complete. An American flag flies from a tall pole in front of the house. While I was their guest I slept under the shining folds of this banner of glory and of beauty.

It was on Saturday evening that I arrived. The next day I spoke twice to the church. Dr. Holck interpreted for me. The house was full. The people could not have been more cordial. They shook my hand till my arm was lame. The congregations were made up of intelligent and neatly dressed people. They are all poor; no member is worth as much as one thousand dollars. In view of their limited incomes they are very liberal. Persons earning four crowns a week give half a crown to the church. The building is the best Dissenting house in the city. It is well located and well arranged. It cost $22,000, and is worth more to-day than it cost. The work here began in 1876. Dr. Holck, the pioneer, was born and educated in Jutland. He came to America and practiced medicine. After uniting with the Central Church in Cincinnati, he was asked to go to Denmark as a missionary. He gave up a growing and lucrative practice and went. He has built a good church in Copenhagen, and has done a fine work in Norway. He has had to face much bitter and persistent opposition. Denmark has a state church. Dissenters have some difficulties relating to marriage, funerals, and baptisms. The people regard rebaptism as the sin against the Holy Spirit. For this sin there is no forgiveness, either in the present or coming age. If children are not christened, they are heathen; in case they die, they are damned. His own mother said to Dr. Holck: "If you had a child I would steal it and have it christened. I could not sleep till this was done." According to their views, people are regenerated in baptism, and are kept in a saved state by the sacraments. Dr. Holck was taken before the courts for baptizing a minor. Some rough fellows threatened to throw him out of the window. The court decided in his favor. Some years ago his health began to fail. Knowing that he would not be able to preach much longer, he began to publish a paper for children. This venture has succeeded far beyond his most sanguine expectations. For ten years he has had no salary from the Society. Not only so, but he has given a thousand dollars a year to carry on the work. His presence in any church is a joy and an inspiration. He has preached in Denmark and in Norway, and wishes to enter Sweden. He regards Sweden as the most fruitful field of the three. With ten thousand dollars a year, he could take the whole of Scandinavia. This is less than the annual grant of the Methodist Episcopal Society for thirty years. In addition to his other good works, Dr. Holck supports a young man in college who is preparing to enter the ministry.

O. C. Mikkelsen and Julius Cramer are at work in Copenhagen. They are directed and assisted by Dr. Holck as Timothy and Titus were by Paul. One preaches at the church, the other preaches at the mission. Besides preaching they conduct a little church paper. Mr. Mikkelsen is a Dane. He was led to Christ by his sister and baptized by his brother. In 1878 he removed to Copenhagen. Here he met Dr. Holck and united with the Disciples. Two years later he came to America. He attended Oskaloosa College for two terms and the College of the Bible for two years, returned to Denmark in 1885, and has aided in the mission ever since. He has a wife and three children. Mr. Cramer was born in Schleswig, went through the schools of Denmark, learned photography, and worked on a newspaper for three years. At the age of twenty-one he became a Christian and soon began to preach. In 1891 he came to America and attended Drake University. He was graduated from the English Bible Course, and returned to Copenhagen to preach the Gospel to his kindred and countrymen. They are both good and faithful servants.

On Monday morning Dr. Holck and I left to visit the churches in Norway. Before taking the train we drove around Copenhagen, and saw the principal buildings and places of general interest. We saw the royal palace, the museum of Thorwaldsen, many schools and churches, factories and stores, the docks and shipping. After an hour's ride on the train we crossed over on a boat to Sweden. On the way we saw the castle in which Hamlet lived, and near which he was buried. In Sweden we took a train for Fredericks-hald. All day we saw signs that the people are religious. The churches are numerous. Lutheranism is the predominant faith, but the Catholics, Methodists, Baptists and Presbyterians are also represented. The country most of the way is poor. We were in sight of the sea all the time. We spent a night at Gothenburg. This city has given its name to one method of dealing with the liquor traffic. In the evening we went out into the park to hear the music and to see the people. We saw much drinking, but the people were quiet and orderly. Men had their wives and children with them. They drank deliberately. We saw no drunkenness and no rowdyism. In England and Scotland, so travelers say, there is far more drunkenness than in Norway. The public houses are closed on Sunday. The topers get gloriously drunk on Saturday. They take enough to last them till Monday. The next afternoon we reached Frederickshald. That evening we had a service in the church. The building seats four hundred. Though they had short notice they had a fine audience. Dr. Holck gave them an address on his own account and then interpreted my thoughts. Frederickshald has a population of ten thousand. The church has two hundred and twenty members. A. Johnson is the preacher. He spent some time in Drake University, and will be remembered by many in America. The next day I went to Christiana, the capital of Norway. Niels Devold and Harald Wester went with me. A good beginning has been made in Christiana. The people propose to buy a building and repair it. They propose to rent the lower floors, and use the top story as a place of meeting. The service lasted two hours. No one was weary or in a hurry to get home. All seemed pleased. The "Amens" were frequent and fervent. The Norwegians are peerless listeners. I was told that if six men would speak in succession, each speaking an hour, the people would be as fresh at the end as at the beginning. Here an address an hour long is a weariness to the flesh; there an hour's address is only an appetizer. There are twenty of our churches in Norway. They are at the following places: Frederickshald, Christiana, Frederickstad, Horten, Moss, Holmsbo, Sande, Berger, Svelvig Naersnaes, Eidsvold, Risor, Kragero, Gjeithus, Naesodden, Onso, Thorsnaes, Sarpsburg, Skibtvedt, Aremark, Lillestrom, Vaaler, Holmestrand, Bogen. Ten of these churches have houses of worship. These houses are not large nor splendid, but they are sufficient for all purposes. The names of the preachers are as follows: Edvard Neilsen, Niels Devold, Harald Wester, A. Johnson, Henrik Nevland. The people are lib-

1. H. N. Wester. 2. Niels Devold.
4. K. Larsen. 3. Edw. Nilsen. 5. A. Johnson.

WORKERS IN SCANDINAVIA.

eral. Most of them do not earn over four or five dollars a week. When they give a thousand crowns for Christian work it means considerable self-sacrifice. The membership is intelligent. They support three papers. One is called *The Bible Friend*, one *Things New and Old*, and one *The Sword and Trowel*.

The Norwegians are very much like the Scotch, as Norway and Scotland are very much alike. Both are mountainous. The lakes of the one correspond to the fiords of the other. The Norwegians are serious and deeply religious. The Danes live in a level country, and are a light-hearted people. Norway is a much more hopeful field than Denmark. The Danes are addicted to pleasure. With them Sunday is a day of recreation. The Gospel is making its way in Norway. Every Christian carries his New Testament in his pocket, and is ready to give a reason for his hope and faith. There is no opposition from the State church. At the first baptism thousands came out to see. They got boats, and climbed upon every "coigne of vantage." They sang hallelujahs and praised God. The Norwegians are a polite people. They salute men whether they are acquainted or not. Men take off their hats to each other on the street. I was told that in Germany men take off their hats to men, but not to women.

The Norwegians are an amphibious race now as their fathers were. They live as much on sea as on land. They catch cod, mackerel, salmon and flounders. They fish in winter as well as in summer. They are true descendants of the old Vikings. These men issued from their bays and creeks and pillaged every part of Europe. They were found as far east as the Black Sea and as far west as Labrador and Rhode Island. Charlemagne shortly before his death saw their strange boats and burst into passionate tears. His courtiers said, "These ships must be from the coast of Africa, or Jewish merchantmen, or British traders." The great king said, "No; these are not the ships of commerce; I know by their lightness of movement, they are the galleys of the Norsemen; and though I know such miserable pirates can do me no harm, I cannot help weeping when I think of the miseries they will inflict on my descendants and the lands they shall rule." They became the scourge of every land and the terror of every sea.

After speaking in Christiana we took the train for Gothenburg and Copenhagen. Mrs. Holck and the children, Mr. and Mrs. S. Von Leimback, Messrs. Mikkelsen and Cramer and several others met us at the train. We had supper in the station. Then I took the train for Hamburg and Paris and London. Before leaving, Dr.

and Mrs. Holck supplied me with such things as I needed on the journey, and some things that will serve me well for years to come. On our trip to Norway Dr. Holck insisted on paying all bills. He did far more for me than I wished. He is a princely soul, and I had no choice but to submit. After such delightful comradeship, my ride that night was inexpressibly dreary, and made me realize anew that it is not good for man to be alone.

LX.

FROM COPENHAGEN TO LONDON.

We left Copenhagen in the evening and reached Hamburg the next morning. This city on the Elbe is interesting to the student of missions, for it was from here that the Gospel was carried into Scandinavia. Charlemagne undertook to Christianize all the tribes about the Baltic, and failed. Louis the Pious founded a bishopric at Hamburg and secured the appointment of Anskar as bishop and apostolic vicar over all the North. Anskar built a cathedral and monastery; he bought Danish boys and trained them for the priesthood, and sent many laborers into Sweden. When Louis died the Danish king apostatized, the Swedish missionaries were driven out, the Norse swept down on Hamburg and utterly destroyed the city and church and monastery and library. Anskar was reduced to the verge of starvation. Coveting the martyr's crown, he would not give up the task to which he felt called of God. In course of time Hamburg was rebuilt and elevated into a metropolitan see, and Anskar was made archbishop. He sent out new men into Sweden, and the work proceeded without further hindrance. Canute the Great and Olaf the Saint materially assisted the evangelization of Denmark. Norway was won to the faith by workers from Normandy and England. In the tenth century Hamburg was an outpost of civilization and was surrounded by savage tribes. Hamburg is now a great seaport. From this city ships go to all parts of the world.

At this point I took a train for Cologne. The principal object of interest in this city on the Rhine is the cathedral. This great building was seven hundred years in course of erection. As we had to spend three hours in Cologne, I walked about the cathedral and studied it from every side. I attended a vesper service. There were thousands present. Incense filled the house. The priests and acolytes went through their parts with precision, but I went away as hungry as I came. Better five words in a known tongue than ten thousand in an unknown. The rumbling echoes kept me from understanding a word that was said or sung. The priests were as barbarians to me, and I was as a barbarian to them. It was in

Cologne that Coleridge said he "counted two and seventy stenches, all well defined, and several stinks." Since that time this city has been cleansed, and now is as free from bad odors as any other place in Europe.

The next stop was made in Paris. As my stay was necessarily brief every hour was precious. Securing a guide, I went to the Eiffel Tower, the Luxembourg Palace, the Hotel des Invalides and Tomb of Napoleon, the Gardens of the Tuileries, the Pantheon, the Arch of Triumph, the Place of Concord, the Column Vendome, the Champs Elysees, the site of the Bastile, Notre Dame Cathedral, the Madeline Church, and the Louvre. Paris has in the Louvre the most extensive and valuable art collection on the Continent. There are works of such masters as Leonardo da Vinci, Correggio, Raphael, Holbein, Fra Bartolommeo, Titian, Murillo, Durer, Rembrandt, Van Dyck, Rubens, and Teniers, not to mention many others almost equally renowned. The most famous piece of statuary is the Venus of Milo. Paris is the gayest and most beautiful city in the Old World. The French people have taste and genius, and they have spared neither money nor labor in making their capital attractive.

While in Paris I called at the Bible House and at the headquarters of the McAll Mission. There are one hundred and thirty-six halls in which services are held. There are one hundred and eighty-two meetings a year in each hall. The Gospel is preached about twenty-two thousand times a year. In all the large cities of France there are agents of this mission at work. A map of the mission is a map of France. The Gospel has been carried into Corsica, Algiers and Tunis. Mr. McAll was past middle life when he went to Paris. The passions of the people, excited by the German Siege and the Commune, had not subsided. People regarded each other with distrust. The church was identified with an oppressive social order. Clericalism was the foe of the Republic. Priests had been murdered. Dr. McAll came from without. He belonged to no party. He came to preach a religion of freedom and reality. The French pastors assisted him in every way possible. Dr. McAll was peculiarly qualified for such a work. He had private means. He did not ask for anything for himself. He fancied that he was the happiest man on earth. His was a wonderful wealth of joy. He found that complete consecration of every energy to do what the Master requires is the secret of a quiet, unmingled and perennial joy of heart. He had that priceless gift, a sense of humor. The owner of a shop went to him and told him her terms. She had heard of the

DR. HOLCK AND FAMILY, COPENHAGEN, DENMARK.

meetings and inquired about them. Being told that they were not Jewish nor Catholic, she seemed puzzled. Then light dawned on her, and she told him that he was like herself, "a person of no religion whatever." As the staff of workers increased the municipal authorities reduced the police force. The government honored itself in making him a Chevalier of the Legion of Honor. The illustrious founder of the mission is dead, but God carries on his own work.

I left Paris for London by way of Rouen and Dieppe. I had heard so much about the Channel that I expected to be sick, but I was disappointed. I fell asleep before the boat started, and did not know that we were on the way till we reached England. I was glad to be among people who speak the English language. From there on I had no need of guides or interpreters. England is the chief missionary country on the globe. Her people give more money to evangelize the non-Christian nations than all other peoples combined. England is the great world power. Her colonies and ships are everywhere. Her colonial expansion has fostered the missionary spirit. The English people not only give liberally, but they go out to preach Christ to those who never heard the joyful sound. Many go at their own charges or are supported by their family. Some have gone from castle and palace and hall to take part in this the greatest of all enterprises. England is unquestionably the greatest country of the Old World. The average Englishman is a higher type of man than the average man of any other European nation. Well did her great bard speak of England as

"This royal throne of kings, this sceptered isle,
This earth of majesty, this seat of Mars,
This other Eden, demi-paradise;
This fortress built by nature for herself,
Against infection, and the hand of war;
This happy breed of men, this little world,
This precious stone set in a silver sea,
This blessed plot, this earth, this realm, this England."

Reaching London, I drove to the home of Dr. J. A. Brooks. The Doctor and Mrs. Brooks received me gladly. I was expected, and announced to preach at the Tabernacle. From this church missionaries have gone out to China, India and Jamaica. The people were deeply interested in all that I had to say. There is a debt of ten thousand dollars on the property. The congregation is far from wealthy. They are doing well, but they cannot meet their expenses and carry on all departments of the work without aid. In time the debt will be paid. Then the Tabernacle will be self-supporting.

This church has been served by Henry Varley, W. T. Moore and G. T. Walden. At the home of Dr. Brooks I met W. J. Hunnex, of China. He has spent seventeen years in that field and knows our men there. He took me to Hornsey Chapel. This is where William Durban preaches. The house was packed with eager and magnetic listeners. Mr. Durban was born in London and brought up in the Church of England. He studied in King's College, and was graduated from the London University. While reading Spurgeon's sermons his views of baptism were revolutionized. He taught in Hereford and in Spurgeon's College. Afterwards he preached on the Isle of Wight and in Chester. In Chester he met M. D. Todd and accepted the principles of the Disciples of Christ. After returning to London and serving as Secretary of the Monthly Tract Society, he was engaged by the Foreign Christian Missionary Society. He has preached at Tasso and at Hornsey. Meanwhile he has helped to edit the *Christian Commonwealth*. I am under many obligations to him and Mrs. Durban for hospitality and for many other kindnesses. On the way to the *Commonwealth* office he took me to see the grave of John Wesley. We went into the church and stood in Wesley's pulpit. Across the street is the Bunhill graveyard. Here Susanna Wesley, the mother of Methodism, John Bunyan, Daniel Defoe, and many other worthies, sleep.

In the *Commonwealth* office we found Paul Moore, R. G. Porter and C. C. Hetherington. Paul Moore is the managing editor. He is a worthy son of his parents. Though possessed of unusual literary ability, he rarely refers to himself. He puts his life into the paper, and allows that to speak for him. Dr. Porter has been helping in the office all summer. With him this has been a labor of love. Mr. Hetherington is the business manager of the *Commonwealth*. He has been with the paper from the beginning, and is a trusted friend and adviser of the proprietors. The *Commonwealth* was founded sixteen years ago by W. T. Moore and Timothy Coop. It is one of the few really able papers published in London. It is read by Baptists, Episcopalians, Congregationalists, and by believers of all names and creeds. It has exerted, and is exerting, a mighty influence. Many of the strongest and best men in England are among its contributors.

Jesse Stockford is in charge of the work at Fulham. He was born among the Primitive Methodists. When he came to years of discretion he was associated with Henry Varley at the West London Tabernacle. He served as deacon and elder for twenty and as the pastor for two years. Then he was called to succeed Mr. Durban.

In four years, between seventy and eighty have been brought into the Church. In addition to those already mentioned, I met in London George Rapkin and L. H. Gow. Mr. Rapkin was born a Roman Catholic. While yet a youth he united with the Baptists, and entered the Salvation Army. He traveled all over the British Islands and in seventeen other countries. He was on the staff. General Booth told him that if he was baptized he would have to get out. He fell in with G. T. Walden and was baptized, and left the army. Thirteen months ago he opened a work in Margate. For two seasons he preached every night on the beach. He baptized twenty-one and received six others. Mr. Gow labored in Jamaica for some time. After his return he took charge of the work in Southampton. This is the church that H. S. Earl organized. Mr. Gow reports good audiences and frequent additions. The church is preparing to erect a building for the Sunday-school. On a previous visit, I saw Parliament Buildings, Westminster Abbey, St. Paul's, the British Museum, and Spurgeon's Tabernacle.

LXI.

FROM LONDON TO CINCINNATI.

From London I went to Gloucester. E. H. Spring, the minister in charge, met me at the station. The people were excited. Gloucester had an epidemic of smallpox. Vaccination was on trial. Out of fifty-two that had been vaccinated twice, fifty died. A new method was tried and success reported. The physicians were said to be determined to maintain their creed and practice at any cost. Mr. Spring was the foremost champion of the new treatment. He and the church did what they could to aid the poor. He was fined ten pounds for some technical violation of the law. The citizens felt that he was persecuted and paid the fine. Mr. Spring is a most energetic man. He has gotten himself and his work before the public as never before, and expects to reap a great harvest. We had a service in the Tabernacle, at which I spoke. I spent the evening with Mr. and Mrs. Arthur Mitchell. He is a telegraph operator and a preacher of the Gospel.

T. H. Bates came down from Cheltenham to the meeting. He gave a good account of the work at that point. Mr. Bates is an Australian, and is known to many in America. He was educated in Lexington, being graduated in 1872, in the same class as C. P. Williamson and J. Z. Tyler. He has preached in Australia and New Zealand. When the panic struck Melbourne he walked four hundred miles to Coolgardie and spent four months there in the gold mines. Then he sailed for England. Some time after his arrival he took the work at Cheltenham. He reports frequent additions. The church needs a building of its own.

Gloucester has quite a history. Here Robert Raikes opened the first Sunday-school in a small building still standing. Here the eloquent George Whitfield was a bell-boy in a tavern. Dr. Jenner lived in this county and his statue is in the cathedral. Here Bishop Hooper was burned. John Long, a blind solicitor, and a remarkably intelligent man, took me in his carriage to see the places of renown. He is a charming conversationalist. It is a delight to listen to his glowing descriptions of things that interest him. He is a genuine Disciple, and is acquainted with our history and work.

1. Jesse Stockford, London. 2. H. L. Gow, Southampton.
3. J. A. Brooks, London. 4. T. H. Bates, Cheltenham. 5. E. M. Todd, Chester.
7. George Rapkin, Margate. 6. H. M. Black, Liverpool.

AN ENGLISH GROUP.

He is collecting all the versions of the Bible that he can find. He has some rare and valuable works, and some curious ones on his shelves. In one version a familiar passage runs thus: "Peter said to them, repent with unfeigned contrition, and let every one of you be baptized into the profession that Jesus is the true Messiah. If you do this your former sins will be expunged, and you also will be favored with the gifts of the Holy Spirit. For this supernatural donation which you now see conferred upon us is also to extend to you and yours, and to all persons in the remotest parts of the world who shall comply with this divine invitation." What a mercy that the Bible was not always translated in this stilted style! Mr. Long gave me a copy of Erasmus' Greek New Testament, and an armful of other books to read on the voyage.

From Gloucester I went by way of Birmingham, Wolverhampton, Crewe and Liverpool to Southport. Here the sainted Timothy Coop lived for many years, and here his two sons, Joe and Frank, have their homes. Timothy Coop was the first man among the Disciples of Christ to give on a large scale. His sons follow in his steps. They give as much time to the work of the church as to their own business. Joe is Treasurer of the English Committee. Since Geo. T. Walden left for Australia, Frank has been serving as Secretary. Their wives are as deeply interested and as active in church and missionary work as their husbands. Here I met W. T. Moore. He was rejoicing over the success of the Bible College in Columbia. J. H. Versey and E. M. Todd happened to be in Southport at that time. They came to attend a meeting of the Committee. The church here has been enlarged and refurnished. Alfred Johnson is the preacher in charge. The evening I spoke the house was comfortably filled.

After a day spent in Southport I ran down to Birkenhead. Eli Brearley and wife are in charge of the work here. Mr. Brearley has spent some time in India as a missionary. Since he came to Birkenhead the church has taken on new life. The audiences are large and conversions are frequent. We had a fine service in this church. Mrs. Brearley preaches, and preaches as well as her husband, and is most active and efficient in all departments of the work. Mr. Versey accompanied me to Birkenhead. He preaches in Lancaster and Ingleton. The work at these points is not without its difficulties and perplexities, but he works right on in the assurance that his labor is not in vain in the Lord. He spent some time in Jamaica, and told me some amusing incidents illustrating the way the humble people there get the Scriptures confused in their minds. One prayed for the pastor in charge, and added, "He is young in years, but old in sin, and desperately wicked." Another prayed for "our pastor, as he walks to and fro in the earth seeking whom he may devour." Another still referred "to Moses in the whale's belly, crying out, 'Almost thou persuadest me to be a Christian.'"

My next appointment was with the church at Chester. This is one of the oldest cities in England, and one of the most picturesque. Here Julius Cæsar had his camp before Christ was born. The many friends of Earl M. Todd will be glad to know that he is doing a good work here. He believes that wise, patient, and persistent effort will win the day. He is studious, prudent, and consecrated. He is a man of God, and his influence is telling on Chester. He is held in as high esteem as was his sainted father in his day. Mrs. M. D. Todd is editor of the *Gleaner;* she is a valuable helper in the work. Flora is the sunshine of the home, and gives promise of a life of great usefulness and nobleness. England is nothing if not conservative. Caste obtains here as in India. The lines are not so clearly drawn, but they are clear enough. The upper classes have their church connections, and will not listen to any new thing. Dissent is odious and vulgar. Even among the Dissenters there are strong prejudices. Earl Todd was not admitted to the Ministerial Fraternal. There is some talk now of admitting him. As long as there was any chance of his failing, he was heterodox; now that success is assured, he is becoming orthodox. A preacher must live in a certain way to be respected. If his wife should wash her own windows or scrub her own floors or answer the door-bell, she and her husband would exert no influence. Snobbery is still a power in the land, whatever may be said about the nobility of service.

My last visit in England was made with H. M. Black. He was in charge of the church in Liverpool. He preached in Australia and in Kansas before taking this work in England. His father and brothers are all preachers. Mr. Black has spoken to the Y. M. C. A. on the missionary work of the Disciples of Christ. On the streets he has spoken on the sin of sectism, the need of union, and kindred topics. He is a chemist, and goes back to his profession. He expects to preach nearly as much as ever. I met his brother Arthur. He is a successful dentist and an effective preacher.

Having seen the brethren in England, I left Liverpool on one of the largest and fastest ships afloat. We had a quick and safe trip across the Atlantic. Had it not been for a dense fog the last night we would have broken all records. Among the passengers were two ferocious Americans of Celtic birth. A concert was given for the benefit of the sailors' orphans. One of the two paid six pence for a ticket. When he saw on the programme that the last number was "God Save the Queen," he went and demanded his six pence back. The other was a woman. When the audience rose to sing the national anthem, she kept her seat as if she had been glued to it. She would not rise in honor of any "furrin queen." Such oddities add to the enjoyment of an ocean voyage. They supply something to smile at. Anyone who causes two persons to laugh where only one laughed before is a public benefactor. The great ship is elegant in all its appointments, but eighty-six stewards sleep in one room. When they get up in the morning they sometimes faint. Some bleed at the lungs, and others suffer from blood poisoning. It is the duty of the Board of Trade to prevent this abuse. When the inspector comes on board he is invited to a royal feast, and supplied with champagne, and forgets the business on which he came. Once in a while one steward will sacrifice himself in the interest of the others. He is dismissed, and in a few days things go on as usual.

One is not on American soil ten seconds before he feels that he is in a new world. The atmosphere is different: there is more ozone in it; the people are different: there is more life and push in them. New York is the greatest city I saw on my trip. London is larger, but London is an agglomeration of villages. London does not have an electric or cable car within her borders. The omnibus moves along at the rate of four or five miles an hour. No one in London is in a hurry. The waiters in the restaurants are delightfully deliberate; one course is eaten and digested before the next appears. You leave about as hungry as you entered. In New York every one is alive and active; steam and electricity are the principal moving causes. The train brought me to Cincinnati in twenty-four hours. On the platform were F. M. Rains, C. W. Paris, J. M. Hoffner, A. L. Chapman, S. M. Cooper, N. P. Runyan, John and Edward Dorman, and the preachers in and about Cincinnati in a body. It was pleasant to see their friendly faces and to grasp their friendly hands. That evening I went to Mt. Healthy and slept in my own room. In my absence, the good woman who cared for me so many years entered into rest. She and several other members of the congregation which I served were not at the reception held in honor of my return. They have joined the choir invisible whose music is the gladness of the world.

So ended my circuit of the globe. I was gone a year and two weeks, and traveled about forty thousand miles. In all that time I met no accident and missed no connection or appointment. The prayers of many thousands went up to God in my behalf, and he brought me back home in health and safety.

E. E. Faris. Dr. H. N. Biddle.

MISSIONARIES TO AFRICA.

LXII.

SOME IMPRESSIONS—CONCLUSION.

A TOUR of the world increases one's respect for the peoples of all lands. God has made of one blood every nation of men. The most backward people have all the elements possessed by the most advanced. Let them have the Gospel for a reasonable time, and we will not be ashamed to call them brethren.

> "Children, we are all
> Of one great Father, in whatever clime
> His providence hath cast the seed of life;
> All tongues, all colors."

All nations need the Gospel. Many think of non-Christian people as objects of pity, and feel that they should be evangelized on that account. These peoples are not conscious of need; they are not calling for help; it should be borne in mind that they need the Gospel apart from all considerations of poverty and misery. They would need it if they were clothed in purple and fine linen and fared sumptuously every day. The Brahman and Mandarin need the Gospel as much as the pariah and leper. The old faiths are not sufficient. God made the soul for himself, and it can find no rest till it rests in him. All peoples are capable of receiving the Gospel. I have seen Hawaiians, Japanese, Chinese, Malays, Tamils, Hindus, Singhalese, Eurasians and Arabs whose faces were made bright and beautiful by the truth and by the Spirit of God.

The Gospel has taken a firm hold of the non-Christian nations. In the nature of the case it could hardly be otherwise. The workers have opened chapels, schools, hospitals and orphanages. Every day in the year the truth is pressed home to the hearts and consciences of the people. In times of famine and pestilence the afflicted are relieved. The Scriptures have been translated, and Christian literature has been scattered far and near. The great inventions that are the glory of our civilization have been introduced. If the continual dropping of water wears the rock, the perpetual and varied efforts of the missionaries must accomplish much. If all the foreigners were driven out the native Christians would take up and carry on the work to completion.

The work of missions is now more widespread than most people know. It is not confined, as is sometimes said, to treaty ports and foreign concessions and well-known lines of travel. In all the Provinces of China, save one, there are missionaries at work. Not only so, they are in Mongolia and Manchuria, and are waiting for the doors of Thibet to open. They are in all parts of Japan. In India they are as far south as Ceylon and as far north as the Himalayas. If one would visit every mission station he would have to visit every part of the globe. True, the fields are not fully occupied. Every mission is terribly undermanned. Now, as of old, the harvest is plenteous, and the laborers are few. But in every land and in most of the large centers of population there are some witnesses for Christ. It may be a single family in a great province or a solitary man or woman in a great city, but there is some one there preaching the Gospel of salvation.

The results are great, even greater than we have a right to expect. In view of the facts that the fields have been open for so short a time, that the churches have sent out such a small number of workers and afforded them such a half-hearted support, and that the non-Christian nations are proverbially conceited and conservative, the marvel is, not that there are so few converts, but that there are so many. A century ago India had no Christian community, now the adherents number 600,000. Fifty years ago there were six Christians in all China, now the number is about 85,000. In 1872 the first church was organized in Japan; now the communicants exceed 40,000, and the churches number 364. Most of the converts walk worthily of that holy Name by which they have been called. Doubtless some are in the churches for the loaves and fishes. This need surprise no one. Of the majority it can be said that they have been born of God and know God.

As a class the missionaries are possessed of ability, culture and consecration. The same men and women at home would fill high positions and would command much larger salaries than they now receive. They are diligent and earnest. If any lead easy-going lives, they are careful to conceal the fact. The tendency is to work beyond their strength. Heber was not the only one that died of overwork. With so many things to do and so small a staff, they could not avoid this even if they were so inclined. They live much as at home. One sees comfort, but no luxury. They need good food and comfortable homes and suitable clothing. They live in a hostile climate. The demands on their physical nature and on their sympathies are far greater than at home. By taking proper care of themselves they live longer and do more than if they stinted and starved themselves. It is claimed by some that missionaries get closer to the people when they eat the same food and dress in the same way and live in their houses. It may be that some Americans could do this and have good health and long life, but it is plain that most could not. ,Missionaries must live in comfort if they are to do their best work. It is poor economy to send out a man and starve him, and so reduce his usefulness one-half. The poorest use a Society can make of a man is to allow him to die, when with a good home and wholesome food he might be in his glorious prime. If a living dog is better than a dead lion, much more is a living missionary better than a dead one.

One missionary said to me, "We live very much as we do at home; our trials do not pertain to food and clothing." They are of another sort. What are some of these? They are exiles, and so are deprived of the sunshine and strength they would find in the companionship of kindred spirits. I attended a farewell reception in Peking. The veteran in whose honor it was given said that it was *a thousand days* since his wife and daughter left for America. Isolation depresses the soul. Speaking to one man about the beauty of his surroundings he said: "There is no salubrity of climate, or beauty of scenery, or historical associations that can compensate in any degree for the loss of the intellectual and social and religious privileges one enjoys at home." He and others are where they are because God needs them there. The people are degraded. Lying and pilfering are almost universal. Cruelty abounds. Our workers found a living child in a coffin. Men die on the streets, and no one lays it to heart. China is unmistakably filthy. Stenches are omnipresent. Before you are out of one you are into two more. One sees beggars and lepers everywhere. Thousands are brutalized so that the Gospel makes no impression upon them. The work is opposed by the priests, and the converts are persecuted. The perplexities and annoyances are a thousandfold greater there than here. These all tell on the nerves and on the spirits. After a hard day's work it is right that the worker should have a comfortable chair and bed. Cut off as he is from friends at home, he should have the best books and periodicals. As a representative of Christendom, it is right that he should have a pleasant home. This is an object lesson to the natives. They see that the Gospel gives those who receive it something better than a mud hut paved with dirt and frescoed with cow dung.

On the way out and in the hotels and in newspapers and magazines one can hear or read of the failure of missions; that there are no genuine converts; and that the missionaries live in ease and affluence and accomplish nothing. Travelers visit the clubs and take up the gossip current in these places. If they were to visit the missions and see the work that is being done and know the spirit and service of the workers, they would tell a very different tale. The men that compose the clubs, for the most part, are men of unclean lives. The Gospel condemns them, and they resent its condemnation and revile its advocates. Men live in Shanghai and Tokio and Calcutta all their lives and know nothing at all about what the Lord is doing through his servants in these cities. The truth is, the lives of these men constitute the most serious obstacle to the spread and triumph of the Gospel. They drink, they curse, they have wives on the European plan, they abuse the natives and treat them like dogs, that they may know their place. A steamboat was going up the Yangtsze. A junk loaded with brick was crossing the river, and came in front of the steamboat. The pilot said to the captain, "Shall we turn aside?" He said, "No." The junk was cut in twain, and all on board perished. No effort was made to save the crew. Opium was forced on the Chinese. When the Emperor protested, he was urged to tax it and make it a source of revenue. He said he would not use as a means of revenue that which brought suffering and misery upon his people. There are notable exceptions. I met a missionary in Singapore: he left the Royal Engineers to engage in the work. I met another who had been a surgeon in the Army. Some of the most devout men in the East belong to the Military or Civil Service. The opposition of the others is complimentary to the missionaries. Whatever may be said to the contrary, the Gospel is making progress. There are converts, and many of them are of a high standard. It should be borne in mind that spiritual results, like spiritual truths, are spiritually discerned. To the natural man they are foolishness, and he cannot know them. The missionaries are living lives of usefulness and nobleness and self-sacrifice. They represent the heroic element in modern Christianity. Praise God, from whom all blessings flow, for their lives and labors! One could sail over the earth in a balloon and tell at once whether he was over a Christian or a non-Christian land by the sights and sounds and smells. He could tell in the same way whether he was over a Protestant or a Roman Catholic country. And one could go through China or India or Japan and pick out the Christians by their bright and joyous faces.

The evangelization of the world is a tremendous enterprise. It is the most colossal task ever undertaken by men. More workers should be sent out and thoroughly furnished for the work. All the energies of the church should be devoted to it. Hundreds should go at their own charges. Nearly one-half the workers connected with the China Inland Mission are self-supporting. Some should undertake to support one or more workers. The task is great, but not impossible. God has sworn by himself that the whole earth shall be filled with his glory. Every plant which he has not planted shall be rooted up. All the signs of the times point to the fulfillment of these promises. The Gospel is running and being glorified. People are forsaking dumb idols and evil practices and are serving the living God and are walking in his ways. Temples and shrines and altars are being deserted. The number of the saved is being increased daily. Those that have been longest on the field and know most of the power and methods of the forces arrayed against the faith of Christ, are most confident of the final victory. All that they have seen strengthens their confidence. They have no thought of leaving the field. They praise God that to them was this grace given, that they are permitted to preach among the nations the unsearchable riches of Christ. The non-Christian faiths feel that they are doomed. On every field they are making a last desperate stand. The effort is in vain; the Gospel will triumph and fill the earth as the waters fill the sea.

Missions are drawing Christian people closer together. In Shanghai, Nankin, Peking and Tientsin the workers have union services every week. They feel the need of combining that they may present a solid front to the foe. They are closer to one another than at home, for their preaching is more scriptural and more simple. Baptism is seen in its true relations on the mission field. People may believe anything and do anything, provided they are not baptized. That one act severs every tie that binds one to the old faith. It was so in the early church.

One rejoices to see that the English language is so widely spread. In Japan English is taught in the public schools. The youth of China and India are anxious to speak and read English. This is a hopeful sign. The English language is full of great ideas respecting the worth of man as man, the dignity of woman, the sanctity of marriage, of liberty and progress. Wherever the English language goes these ideas go and bear fruit. One rejoices, too, to find the English power so widespread. This is no accident. Why is it that Portugal, or Spain, or France, or Holland, is not the world-power? Because English civilization is of a higher type, and because it is

God's purpose that the fittest should survive. These other nations were in the field first, but they were all driven out. Wherever England goes there the Bible goes. There, too, you find roads and bridges and free schools and just laws and equal advantages for all. There you find peace and prosperity.

The Gospel gives woman her rightful place in society. Heathenism degrades her with an infinite degradation. This is characteristic of all the non-Christian faiths. In all pagan and Moslem lands polygamy and concubinage obtain. In India a woman is taught that her husband, however worthless, must be worshiped as a god. Her chief business is to minister to his comfort. The Japanese think ignorant woman more easily managed. A Chinese poet expressed the feeling of the nation—

"The serpent's mouth in the green bamboo,
The yellow hornet's caudal dart,
Little the injury they can do;
More venomous far is a woman's heart."

One thinks more of America after seeing other nations. A friend said, "If you would foster your patriotism, make a trip abroad." The average American is better fed and clothed and housed and taught than the average man of any other nation. I am persuaded that the typical American is a broader and a better man than the typical man of any other country. This is Immanuel's land in a very peculiar sense. Let it not be forgotten that where much has been given, there much shall be required. On a foreign tour one sees America from the standpoint of foreigners. This keeps him from being exalted above measure. One Oriental spent some years within our borders and wrote his experience. His idea of Christian America was lofty, religious, and Puritanic. He dreamed of its templed hills, and rocks that rang with hymns and praises. Hebraisms, he thought, to be the prevailing speech of the people, and cherub and cherubim, hallelujahs and amens, the common language of the streets. He heard some Hebraisms, but they were more suggestive of the imprecatory Psalms than of the Beatitudes. His pocket was picked and his umbrella stolen. He saw burglar-proof safes and cemented cellars, stone-cut vaults, watched by bulldogs and battalions of police. Every housewife had a bundle of keys at her girdle. At home the houses are open; things dropped in the street are safe. He thought Christendom a beastly land! We have the worst and the best. Christendom alone produces such people as John Howard, Lord Shaftesbury, Abraham Lincoln, Chinese Gordon, David Livingstone, Florence Nightingale,

Grace Darling, Frances E. Willard, and Clara Barton. Christendom needs to be Christianized.

One word of testimony I must bear. On board ship and in hotels men urged me not to drink water, but to drink champagne, wine, beer, or brandy and soda. I did not like to abandon my principles and determined I would not. I drank water everywhere, and refused to taste brandy and soda, beer, wine, or champagne, and came home in perfect health. Water is the most wholesome of beverages. The idea that in Europe or Asia and Africa we must drink some alcoholic beverage is a delusion and a snare. One Scotchman said to another: "Whiskey is a bad thing." His friend cautiously replied: "Yes, *bad* whiskey is." It's all bad, and always bad.

It would be a good thing if some representatives were sent out every two or three years. They would do the workers good. They would cheer and bless the native helpers and converts. They would widen their own vision and stimulate the work at home. Many are able to go at their own charges. Yokohama is only two weeks from San Francisco. Bombay is only four weeks from New York. In a month or two one could visit all the stations. This would not cost any more than a summer in Europe, if so much. Europe is modern. One can see as good cities at home as there. In Asia one sees different races, religions, civilizations. He is in a different world. J. W. Foster says: "I advise a larger visitation of the missions and closer personal supervision. There should be one Secretary on the field every year." Dr. Blodgett, a veteran missionary, indorses this view.

I was sent out partly to rest and partly to see the work. I saw the work; I trust I shall get the rest in the sweet by and by. Several men talked of going with me, but all decided to remain at home. The decision was a wise one for themselves. Seeing missions is exhaustive work. Editing a paper, managing a loan agency, conducting a large medical practice, presiding over a college: all these are a picnic in comparison. If the men who talked of going had gone the visit would have been immeasurably more dignified and impressive. The people would have come out and worshiped us. They would have said: "The gods are come down in the likeness of men." But when they saw one foreign devil wearing a Chinese petticoat they smiled and went back to their business.

To those who made this trip possible and actual, and followed me all the way, I extend my heartfelt thanks. First and foremost among these is my associate, F. M. Rains. In my absence he did double duty. The clerks in the office caught his spirit and went without their vacation that the work might not suffer. He and they had the supreme joy of being able to report a year of unprecedented prosperity. Above all are thanks and praise due to Him who put it into their hearts and power to do this, and who watched over me every step of the way and brought me back in peace and safety. "Blessed be the Lord God, the God of Israel, who only doeth wondrous things. And blessed be his glorious name for ever: and let the whole earth be filled with his glory."

INDEX.